# Birding to Change the World

**ALSO BY TRISH O'KANE**

*Guatemala in Focus:*
*A Guide to the People, Politics and Culture*

*The Right to Remain Silent:*
*An Anthology of Class Writings*
*from Julia Tutwiler Prison for Women* (coeditor)

# Birding to Change the World

A MEMOIR

Trish O'Kane

ecco
*An Imprint of* HarperCollins*Publishers*

Thanks to those who gave permission to have their words included in the book, specifically: Wendell Berry, J. Drew Lanham, and the students from the University of Vermont and the University of Wisconsin–Madison.

This is a work of nonfiction. The events and experiences detailed herein are all true and have been faithfully rendered as I have remembered them, to the best of my ability. Some names, identities, and circumstances have been changed in order to protect the integrity and/or privacy of the various individuals involved, in particular the students I have taught.



FIRST EDITION

*Designed by Alison Bloomer*
*Interior illustrations by Valerie Downes*

Library of Congress Cataloging-in-Publication Data

Names: O'Kane, Trish, author.
Title: Birding to change the world: a memoir / Trish O'Kane.
Description: First edition. | New York: Ecco, [2024] | Includes bibliographical references.
Identifiers: LCCN 2023031179 | ISBN 9780063223141 (hardcover) | ISBN 9780063223165 (trade paperback) | ISBN 9780063223189 (ebook)
Subjects: LCSH: O'Kane, Trish. | Bird watchers—United States—Biography. | Environmentalists—United States—Biography. | Bird watching—United States—Anecdotes.
Classification: LCC QL677.5 .O53 2024 | DDC 598.072/34 [B]—dc23/eng/20230713
LC record available at https://lccn.loc.gov/2023031179

23 24 25 26 27 LBC 5 4 3 2 1

For my parents, Felix O'Kane and Bridget Fleming O'Kane,
who crossed an ocean.

# CONTENTS

# Prologue

*Be joyful*
*though you have considered all the facts.*
WENDELL BERRY, "MANIFESTO: THE MAD FARMER LIBERATION FRONT"

I AM SPEEDING DOWN A DARK VERMONT ROAD, HURTLING THROUGH A STAR-STUDDED October night on an urgent quest: to witness the banding of the smallest owl in the Northeast, the northern saw-whet. Five of my most bird-crazed college students are stuffed into my Toyota Matrix, one girl curled shrimplike in the hatchback. One student works at a birding gear store. Another knew nothing about birds until he discovered a large barred owl in the campus forest during his first semester. He started following Barry the Barred Owl for hours, every day, filling my inbox with photos of Barry hunting, Barry musing, Barry ripping apart a cedar waxwing.* As I drive, we shout out species' names to a birdcall CD in our game Name That Bird. A shy freshman squeezed into a corner watches silently, eyes as round as a young owl's.

It is a big night because this will be our first saw-whet. One of the most common owls in the northern United States, it is also one of the most mysterious, confounding scientists and avid birdwatchers.

* This was not Barry, the famous Central Park owl.

Robin-sized, it lives in the woods all around us, yet we rarely see it. The owl can be six feet above you and still invisible. With feathers the shade of tree bark, it simply blends into the trunk, like a small woody knot.

Scientists barely understand the basics about saw-whets: where and when most of them migrate; how many there are (David Brinker of Project Owlnet estimates the global population at 2 to 5 million based on banding records); how old they are when they start to breed; how many owlets they'll raise in a lifetime; or even how long that lifetime lasts (the oldest captive lived to be sixteen). But we do know some pretty weird random stuff. A graduate student in Appalachia watched owls storing their food on branches—mostly mice, but also bats, squirrels, and birds—while other scientists observed owls defrosting that prey in winter by sitting on top of it like a feathered microwave.[1] And in 1903 an Ohio fishing boat captain watched a flock of tiny saw-whets land on the steamship *Helena* while it was crossing Lake Huron.[2]

The weirdest of all is John James Audubon's story. In his famous 1838 book, *Birds of America,* he wrote: "This species evinces a strong and curious propensity to visit the interior of our cities. I have known some caught alive in the Philadelphia Museum, as well as in that of Baltimore, and, whilst at Cincinnati, I had one brought to me which had been taken from the edge of a cradle, in which a child lay asleep, to the no small astonishment of the mother."[3]

**MY STUDENTS AND I ARE ARRIVING AT THE BANDING STATION DURING PEAK FALL MIGRA**tion. The temperature is in the mid-50s. The sky is clear. And the wind is blowing eight miles per hour from the north, ideal for owls flying south at night, and for owl banders, bundled up all over the Northeast. The banders hide in bushes near invisible spider-web nets forty feet long and six feet tall. Ears perked, they sip hot chocolate and wait for the sudden whooshing of wings, an owl lured in by the saw-whet's call—an eerie, high, monotonous toot—playing on hidden recorders.

We park in a muddy field and a series of handmade signs reading

"OWLS" leads us to a shadowy shrub-lined clearing surrounding an old red barn. The banding station is a card table illuminated by floodlights. There is a s'mores station at an adjoining table, with Hershey bars, graham crackers, and bags of large marshmallows. Across the clearing, wizened birders sit in lawn chairs around a fire, roasting marshmallows and swapping stories.

I expect a grizzled veteran bander behind the banding table, a taciturn tall, bearded natural resource agency type sporting a khaki vest with many pockets. Instead, a strawberry-haired girl of thirteen holds court. She draws herself tall to address the crowd and explains that "owl extractors" are checking the spider-web nets nearby, every fifteen minutes. They should catch an owl soon and will bring it to this table so she can do a health check before banding the bird and releasing it.

Three hours later, the girl bander asks my students if they'd like to help release a captive, a furious female saw-whet who has been clicking and clacking her black beak while being weighed, measured, and banded. The bander tells my students to kneel on the ground in a tight circle around a low stool. She has them extend one hand, palm up, fingertips pointed toward the center of the stool. As they each lay a hand down, side by side, the circle of young hands mushed together forms a large fleshy launching pad. Then, using leather gloves, she tips an eight-inch owl the shade of coppery leaves on her back, laying the bird right on their fingertips at the center of that launch pad. *Be very still,* she says. The owl lies on her back, huge black pupils staring straight up at a starry sky, feathered talons clutched into her chest. We hold our breath. The owl lies there for an impossible ten, fifteen seconds. Then suddenly she realizes she is free, sits up, rises straight in the air like a tiny helicopter, wings parting the sky over my students, and disappears into the frosty autumn night.[4]

**ALL BUT ONE OF THE YOUNG OWL-SEEKERS ARE STUDENTS ENROLLED IN "BIRDING TO CHANGE** the World," a class I teach at the University of Vermont. In this course I pair college students as birding mentors with children. Every Monday, students meet in a college class to learn about birds, education, and

social justice. Every Wednesday, we drive five miles to a Burlington elementary school, where my students walk, learn, and play with their fourth- or fifth-grade "co-explorer" for three hours in a neighborhood wetland and woods. Each of my students is paired with the same child all semester. I walk just behind the boisterous human flock and am always deeply touched to see a child reaching for the hand of their college mentor, the pair walking the mile back to school, chattering away like finches.

On the second day of this program in 2016, a fourth-grader named Jean Baptiste found a bald eagle along Lake Champlain. The kids and college students stood in a huddle fifteen feet away and stared reverently. The eagle was perched high in a tree, peering out over the lake, but every few minutes it swiveled its huge head and stared at us, as the smallest kids ducked behind their college mentors.

On another memorable day, I was trailing behind the group on that same lakeshore path when the kids up ahead suddenly began pulling on the binocular straps around their mentors' necks, trying frantically to wrench the binoculars away. I was mystified. The kids hated carrying the binoculars. *There must be an incredible bird,* I thought, and started running. When I finally caught up, every single kid was carefully focusing those binoculars on a glistening, hairy naked man emerging from the waters of Lake Champlain.

My students fall in love with the birds as much as the children. After years of teaching I can read the early warning signs of bird obsession—the inability to sit still, the head twitching when something feathered flies by the classroom window, and the emails like this one:

> TRISH!!! I just heard birds outside and ran to get my binoculars! Then something CRAZY happened!! On my porch I have a window box and a chickadee swooped in and grabbed a bug off the mint plant, right in front of me! AND THEN a hummingbird swooped in to check out the flowers LITERALLY 3 FEET from my face!!! AND THEN!!! The hummingbird flew to a tree and perched. THEN THE CHICKADEE CAME AND CHASED THE HUMMINGBIRD FROM BRANCH TO BRANCH ALL AROUND THE TREE!!!! WHY?!? I just had to tell you, I got so excited!!![5]

And then there are the student "rescuers" with "bird emergencies" (I sometimes regret giving students my home number). One winter I got a call from a frantic freshman named Oliver who had found a blinded house finch still alive, deep in the snow on a campus athletic field.

"Oliver, sounds like house finch conjunctivitis. Grab the bird and put it in a container. I'll call you back when I find a finch doctor."

Thirty minutes later, Oliver the new finch ambulance driver meets Ellen, a member of the quiet bird-helper army that exists everywhere. Ellen takes the tiny patient home, starts him on a ten-day course of tetracycline, and a few hours later sends Oliver a video of that house finch with his eyes open, flying around his new cage.

**IN THE LAST FIFTEEN YEARS, I'VE SPENT APPROXIMATELY 1,960 HOURS OUTSIDE WATCHING** birds, filled thirty-three field notebooks with scribblings on their doings and dramas, helped raise baby chickadees, bluebirds, wrens, and swallows in tiny birdhouses, volunteered in a baby bird nursery at a wildlife rehabilitation hospital, and taught hundreds of college students and children about them at two major universities. Scientists criticize anthropomorphizing—the application of human attributes to animals. But during those 1,960 hours outside with birds, I've begun to turn anthropomorphizing on its head and think about which avian attributes, talents, and skills our species urgently needs. I've been particularly struck by the strategies birds use to fiercely defend their home territories. What if humans employed some of these same strategies to protect the places we love?

My favorite such strategy is called a murmuration, when silver-speckled black birds funnel across the sky by the hundreds, thousands, even millions. As if to the beat of a giant invisible baton, the black birds all tilt in the same direction, diving and pirouetting, arcing and falling in a massive choreography of beating wings.

The choreographer and performer is the European starling. Despised in the United States because it is not native, the starling is often called a "sky rat" because there are so many. And yet it's their very numbers that make the aerial dance so spectacular.

Scientists are not exactly sure how the birds coordinate their movements. In a project called STARFLAG, a team of Italian theoretical physicists spent nearly eighteen years on the rooftop of the Palazzo Massimo—the Museum of Roman Art—in the center of Rome, photographing starlings at dusk.* They discovered that when one black bird abruptly tilts its wings and changes course, seven neighboring birds follow suit, and then these seven birds each activate seven

* I interviewed lead STARFLAG researcher Andrea Cavagna on Zoom on October 20, 2022. Cavagna explained that researchers used three cameras to do a 3-D reconstruction of murmurations to detect starling interactions and discovered that while flying, the birds are continuously reacting to their closest neighbors' movements. Cavagna cautioned against romanticizing murmurations because our species already *has* made sudden turns and changed course, often with disastrous results, alluding to fascism.

more, and so on, in a feathered law of seven to create that choreography.[6] Researchers observed that that first bird often tilts its wings because a hawk is approaching, a predator and threat to the entire flock. The murmuration helps the flock escape.

When I read this study, I began to think about social change and what our species can learn from starlings. Could we change course like that, too? In other words, what if we were as smart as birds—or at least smart enough to learn from them?

**AVIANS HAVE PROBABLY BEEN TEACHING OUR SPECIES FOR THE ESTIMATED HALF A MILLION** years we've been on the planet. The earliest human art shows that they were among our very first teachers. We may have learned to build our own nests, weave, sing, and group together to drive away a predator all from our feathered friends.

And we are still learning from them. Avians are part of the inspiration for a discipline-spanning movement in engineering and sustainability science called biomimicry, biomimetics, and bioinspiration for sustainable design. For scientists in this movement, nature is their teacher. They believe the answers to some of our most urgent questions can be found in creatures ranging from microbes to whales—structures, systems, and survival mechanisms based on millions of years of evolution that are marvels of efficiency compared to the way we design things.[7]

One of the most famous examples is how birds taught us to take to the skies (granted, while spewing poisons into the air, making a hellish racket, and lacking their grace, beauty, and agility). In the fifteenth century while he was studying birds, Leonardo da Vinci drew many designs for flying machines. Intrepid experimenters tried to fly his contraptions three centuries later (mostly crashing), but one helped the Wright Brothers make aviation history in 1903.[8] Since Leonardo, aviation engineers have continued to study birds, basing improvements to planes on avian bones, which are hollow and feature an internal structure that makes them strong and lightweight. Future planes with an avian design would be not only stronger but also much more fuel efficient.[9]

Birds are upending the worlds of engineering, architecture, aviation, medicine, transport, robot technology, and water conservation. One of Japan's prettiest and most beloved birds, the common kingfisher—anything but common-looking, with a glittery turquoise back, an orange chest, and bright red legs—taught train engineers how to build a better speedy bullet train. The bird is not only gorgeous but can dive in and out of water almost silently, with hardly a splash. So engineers modeled the Shinkansen train on the kingfisher's anatomy, giving the Shinkansen a long beak-shaped nose and creating a train that is 10 percent faster, uses 15 percent less energy, and, most important, does not make a huge sonic boom when it exits tunnels, a source of noise pollution and public complaints.[10]

Woodpeckers are teaching scientists how to better protect space shuttles from space debris and football players' heads from brain injury as they study the bird's skull and beak structure. And emus and ostriches, who can run 45 miles per hour, have inspired scientists in Germany to create the BirdBot, a robot that runs 300 percent more efficiently on avian-inspired legs than a robot on human-based legs. Hummingbirds have inspired helicopter design. And sandgrouse in Africa are teaching water conservation experts how they gather water droplets in their feathers at watering holes, miles from their breeding grounds, and carry life-giving water to their waiting flightless babies. The structure of their feathers allows them to do this, just as those structures create the beautiful colors birds grace our daily lives with. Feathers and other structural miracles of nature such as the scales on butterfly wings and peacock spiders may even help our species shift to renewable energy. Scientists and engineers are currently increasing the ability of solar panels to absorb light by emulating these structures.

Though I greatly admire the work of these scientists, I was never smart enough or humble enough to think that a bird or any other nonhuman could teach me anything. I am an accidental birder. My students stare at me in disbelief when I tell them that until I was forty-five years old, I never cared about birds. "*Birds?*" That summed up my attitude. For most of my life I'd been a peace activist trying to change US foreign policy. Right out of college I moved to Nicaragua to join the Sandinista revolution (that didn't work out so well if you've kept up on the brutal dictatorship of Daniel Ortega), and then I became an investigative human rights journalist. For ten years in Central America I studied *Homo sapiens* and the terrible things we do to one another. I researched massacres committed by the United States–backed regime of Guatemalan general Efraín Ríos Montt. And I was deeply inspired by Central American human rights defenders who organized to change their countries. This is why when foreign biologists descended from the Global North to do research in jungle areas, I thought they were insensitive and just plain weird—well-fed, binoculared foreigners running around in jeeps counting birds and monkeys in countries where people were still trying to count their dead. I was *never* going to be one of *those* people.

After I left Central America, I got a job at a civil rights center in Montgomery, Alabama, as a hate crimes researcher. How to stop war, how to end economic injustice, how to fight racism and white supremacy—these global problems were the focus of my life and work. I never paid any attention to environmental issues. I simply did not see the connections. But then life took a sudden wild turn. Everything fell apart in a single day—a matter of hours. There was a life before that day and a life after. In that life after, I found the birds.

CHAPTER 1

# Strange Teachers

*Scientists say we are made of atoms.*
*A little bird told me we are made of stories.*

EDUARDO GALEANO

I AM BOTH AN ACCIDENTAL BIRDER AND AN ACCIDENTAL TEACHER. I BECAME A teacher because of a visit to one of the worst prisons in the United States.

While I was working as a hate crimes researcher for the Southern Poverty Law Center in Montgomery, Alabama, a friend asked me to volunteer in a women's prison. She ran a literacy project to connect imprisoned mothers to their children through reading. I showed up at the forbidding metal gates of Julia Tutwiler Prison for Women on a gray Saturday morning in March, mostly out of morbid curiosity. As a journalist, I'd visited prisons in Central America to interview soldiers who had committed massacres. But I'd never been in a prison in my own country.

About fifty excited women in white prison uniforms were waiting. We trooped into the chapel carrying tape recorders, mailing supplies, donuts and coffee, and boxes of children's books. The chapel was abuzz with women's laughter as volunteers and prisoners who had known one another for years hugged and shared news. We set up a donut station. Then we laid the books in rows on long tables. The prisoners milled around, fingering new books about dinosaurs and lost puppies, trying to pick one for their children. Our job as volunteers was to record them reading the book aloud, and then to mail the book and the tape to their family.

The first prisoner to approach me for help was a shy, petite blonde who looked twenty-one, maybe. She'd picked a dinosaur book for her five-year-old boy. She wanted to practice reading aloud.

She was sailing right along until she hit the word "Triceratops." I scooted closer to her, tracing the word with my right index finger and breaking it into syllables. We said it together a few times: "Tri-cer-a-tops." After the practice run, I held the recorder close to her face as she reread the story, more confident now, but then she looked up, panicked, when she hit that word again. I smiled and nodded. She nailed it. I pictured her five-year-old, sitting on an aunt's or a grandmother's knee, slowly turning the pages of this book, hearing his mother's voice. After she finished, she asked if there was time on the tape to sing to her son. It was a lullaby, something about light falling through the oak leaves. As she sang, tears rolling down her cheeks, all around us women stumbled over words and sang songs like this one to their children.

The last prisoner I sat with was an exuberant ball of energy with a huge smile. As she pumped my hand forcefully, she talked about her three children in foster care, a disrupted college education (she wanted to be a psychologist), and the drug addiction that had gotten her into this place. Then she asked two questions that changed my life.

"What do you do for a living?" she said.

"I'm a writer."

"Would you come in here and teach us to write? We need a writing teacher."

I didn't have the heart to tell her that I really, really did not want to be a teacher. I'd been told ever since I was about six years old that I was going to be a teacher. In fact, my mother told me that I was going to become a piano teacher. A piano teacher was even better than a schoolteacher, she reasoned, because you could work from home and spend more time with your three or four children. You would have the three or four children, of course, after you married Mr. Right, the Irish Catholic doctor who somehow has a lot of money even though he comes from the same working-class background as you.

My parents emigrated from Ireland to the United States to work on an orange ranch—my father the manager, and my mother the cook and maid. Even though they settled in liberal Southern California, I was born into an ultraconservative Irish Roman Catholic immigrant clan that felt like the familial equivalent of a tiny police state. In my extended clan there were just three approved roles for women: mother, nurse, or teacher. "Wife" was not a role—it was destiny.

If you threw the last pope, not Francis the Groovy but Benedict the Inquisitor, and the Ayatollah Khomeini into a blender, you'd get my family's culture of Catholicism. My mother marched around our home (tiny holy water fonts on walls, gloomy virgin statues in alcoves with flickering candles) preaching "Rome is always right" and "Bad things happen to girls if you don't keep your legs crossed." In my family, every terrible thing that ever happened to humanity happened because some wild woman somewhere, starting with Eve, grabbed the wrong apple, didn't keep her legs crossed, or wore a short skirt. My mother always claimed that "the Virgin Mary cries when a girl whistles." So I became a dedicated whistler. I thought the Virgin Mary was so lame. Why couldn't she raise her fist once in a while and scream?

I escaped the family police state and become a journalist in a war zone, instead. But there was no escaping this prisoner in Wetumpka, Alabama. She asked for my address. Within a week, letters from her and other prisoners arrived, begging me to teach them. There were poems in these letters about broken pianos and grandmothers chewing snuff and first training bras and a sexy guy named Filet Mignon. And the letters kept coming until Aid to Inmate Mothers hired me as a writing teacher.*

Three years after that first visit, my prison students, another writing teacher, and I copublished a book called *The Right to Remain Silent*.[1] I'll never forget the first time my students held that shiny new book in their hands, fingers tracing over the small miracle of their own byline. The way some of them suddenly sat up straighter. They weren't just prisoners anymore; they were published writers.

Up until this moment, my job as a journalist had been to take people's stories away. I was a story excavator, a miner of dreams, fears, pain, and mostly gritty, often horrific, detail. Now I suddenly realized that everything I had ever read and loved was a gift to share. Instead of extracting stories, I was bringing stories into the glorified prison storage unit that was our classroom, to give to my students. Every class became Christmas.

I brought in the work of my favorite poet, Pablo Neruda, and they wrote Neruda-style odes extolling the virtues of onions, wine, salt—the stuff of daily life. Thanks to Neruda, the broken-down computer perched on a file cabinet became, in a student's ode, "an octopus with

---

* Julia Tutwiler Prison became infamous for sexual assaults by guards and for discrimination against prisoners who were either HIV positive or had AIDS; these prisoners were not allowed to mix with the general prison population. My students were all HIV positive and lived in a special segregation unit that prevented them from participating in work release or educational activities to work off their sentences faster. This segregation unit was also next to the prison hospital. Prisoners called my students' unit "Death Row," because the women with the weakest immune systems were forced to live in the part of the prison where they were most likely to get sick.

ninety-eight eyes" that brings "fire to the brain" and "sits exiled on a rugged mountain-top waiting for someone to arouse him."

My students were also hungry to know what was going on "outside." In every class they asked about the news, about my work, and about my former life in Central America. I brought in Frida Kahlo prints and in their writing they related to her pain and how she turned that pain into beauty. I shared Rigoberta Menchú's memoir with them, *My Name Is Rigoberta Menchú*, about the young Mayan maid in Guatemala City who later won the Nobel Peace Prize for her indigenous rights work.

When I wasn't teaching, I was thinking about it—reading, brainstorming, wondering how my students would react to new stories. My students mailed me their homework, which turned the daily jaunt to my mailbox into a thrilling event. I loved those letters addressed to "Trish, the Butterfly on the Outside." My students called themselves "The Butterflies on the Inside."

I loved teaching at the prison so much that I began teaching journalism at Auburn University. There I taught students how to interview old civil rights warriors and everyday heroes. At Auburn, I realized that teaching was a lot like journalism because I was always learning something new and stretching myself emotionally and intellectually. And like some of the stories I'd covered, teaching gave me hope as I watched young people grow into their better selves. But all these years later, what I still love most about teaching is what hooked me that first day at Julia Tutwiler Prison: I get to share so many things I love with my students. And I can honor my parents and mentors by passing their gifts forward. Today, that gift is birds. But it didn't come easy.

**A FEW YEARS AFTER I BEGAN TEACHING, I WAS OFFERED A POSITION AS A JOURNALISM** instructor at Loyola University, a Jesuit college in New Orleans. I'd ended up working in Sandinista Nicaragua right out of college because a revolutionary Jesuit priest had offered me a job at his research institute in Managua (in my family, you didn't say no to a priest). So progressive Jesuit Loyola seemed like the perfect fit and a return to my political roots. New Orleans had the same steamy tropical weather as Managua, pelvis-pulsing vibrant music, and plenty of eccentric people. I also wanted to continue teaching in prisons. I planned to take my Loyola students into Louisiana's prisons as writing tutors. It would be Emma Goldman's revolution of bread and roses. Only better—beignets and roses.

My fiancé, Jim Carrier, and I drove toward New Orleans on July 30, 2005. We moved into a small house in a neighborhood of pink and purple crepe myrtle bushes and magnolia trees with white flowers the size of a child's hand. Old-fashioned gas lamps flickered from doorways. Statues of modest blue-caped virgins graced the lawns. From our new house you could walk to an Italian grocery store with fresh crab and a local coffee shop with croissants baked in-house. Within a five-minute bike ride, I could kayak, get a haircut and pedicure, flail around in a yoga class, and buy a pretty dress.

Our neighborhood, called Lakeview, was within walking distance of Louisiana's largest lake, Lake Pontchartrain. We were also sandwiched between two major levees. I'd always thought of levees as ugly concrete structures (I'm a native Southern Californian who grew up in a desert). But the levees near our house were part of a citywide network of gorgeous green trails with grass-covered banks canting down to murky waters. I began walking my two dogs on the nearest levee every morning. They'd drag me on their leashes past what I now know were egrets delicately tiptoeing in the muck, past sparrows and thrushes diving into bushes as we noisily approached, past the eight-foot alligator my neighbors said snoozed in the tall grasses, and maybe even past a wild boar. Past the fish leaping out of the water in a frenzied attempt to escape from something chasing them from the depths, and the manatees that had returned to the lake and its levee canals because of the hard work of local environmental organizations. Past the poor people fishing for protein underneath the levee bridge next to the sign warning them not to eat the fish because of their high levels of mercury.

The levee ended at the lake, where my dogs and I jumped in every morning. Lake Pontchartrain was named after a count in the court of Louis XIV; the Choctaw called it Okwata, meaning "wide water." A 630-square-mile rough oval averaging 12 to 14 feet deep, it is surrounded by oil and gas industries that have polluted its waters and destroyed its wetland filters.*

If you happened to be a gull flying over, you'd see that this levee was a dividing line between the suburbs and wild New Orleans. On one side, our neighborhood stretched for miles in a neat grid of homes and shops on streets named after Confederate generals. Cross the levee to the other side and you were in City Park, a gorgeous, 1,300-acre expanse of fields, marshes, cypress swamps, and woods of sycamore, maple, and live oaks, some trees so massive that it took several people to hug their wide girth. Well-maintained trails wound around fishing ponds, horse stables, and botanical gardens. Swans and ducks swam placidly in eleven miles of serpentine lagoons. Signs warned: "Do not feed the alligators."

When Jim and I decided to move to New Orleans, I was dreaming of Friday-afternoon art gallery hops, fabulous dinners at trendy restaurants, Sazerac cocktail parties, Jazz Fest. For years I'd been driving from Alabama to the city for Mardi Gras parades. I loved the Big Easy's sassy wackiness. But the New Orleans I was now discovering was wild in a way nothing like Bourbon Street. It was a flock of urban parrots squawking and streaking over the neighborhood, emerald flashes with lapis-lazuli-tipped wings diving into palm trees that lined the main drag, which was named after General Robert E. Lee.[2] It was the swamp on our doorstep, the tiny green lizard I found one morning hiding in the dish rack.

One night when I took the two dogs for a walk down our street, neighbors had roped off the intersection just a block away, forcing cars to turn around. I crossed under the rope and into a scene right out of Fellini. There in the middle of our street, neighbors were tucking into

---

* According to the Southeast Louisiana Flood Protection Authority, oil and gas companies dredged more than 10,000 canals in southern Louisiana, which caused the destruction of 2,000 square miles of wetlands that served as a hurricane buffer. See Bob Marshall, "Science to Be Key Factor in Lawsuit Against Oil and Gas Companies for Coastal Loss," *The Lens*, July 23, 2013, https://thelensnola.org/2013/07/23/science-to-be-key-factor-in-lawsuit-against-oil-and-gas-companies-for-coastal-loss/.

an elegant supper. No paper plates here. I stared at the long dining table covered with a white tablecloth, candlesticks, gleaming silverware, and steaming food heaped on platters. It was nine o'clock on a weeknight and they were all sitting around laughing, wine goblets clinking as they toasted.

That night I congratulated myself for moving to the wackiest and most beautiful place in the United States. Never mind the daily headlines that August about young Black men murdered in drug-turf wars or the dead zone in the Gulf of Mexico the size of New Jersey.[3] A massive fertilizer-fueled algal bloom was consuming the oxygen in the water, creating that dead zone, which killed creatures who couldn't swim or crawl away fast enough. The city warned us not to drink the dead zone greenish water pouring from our taps. We'll just drink Abita beer instead, Jim and I joked.

**THERE ARE A FEW OTHER MOMENTS FROM THOSE FIRST THIRTY DAYS I REMEMBER CLEARLY.** There was the afternoon I decided to mow our new lawn. I was determined to be more environmentally friendly, so I'd bought an old push mower. It was a steaming August afternoon, and after a few pushes I was drenched. In less than an hour, three male neighbors offered their power mowers. They must have thought the new neighbors were crazy. I politely refused and pushed on. Suddenly a frog the size of a thumbnail leapt ahead of the revolving steel blades. I picked him up, marveling at his Lilliputian perfection. He seemed out of place on this side of the levee, among the clipped lawns and poodle hedges. There was nothing marshy here except the levee canal a block away and wild City Park on the other side of it. I set the frog under a bush, hoping he'd stay off my lawn. After that I mowed more carefully, to give advance warning to him and his relatives.

Then there was the morning I picked up *The Times-Picayune* and read a long, stern article advising everyone to update their household hurricane evacuation plan. It was unusually hot that August. Sea surface temperatures in the Gulf of Mexico were the warmest ever recorded. Warm water fuels hurricanes—the hotter the water, the stronger the storm. So this will be a rough season, *The Times-Picayune* warned. Gather all important documents. Put them in a crate or suitcase. Decide where to evacuate to. Map out your route to avoid traffic jams. Buy bottled water, candles, batteries, flashlights, and canned food. Make a plan for your pets.

*You've got to be kidding,* I thought. We'd just hung our paintings and had our first dinner party with homemade crab cakes. I'd spent hours arranging hundreds of books and an entire day organizing paints, yarn, ribbons, buttons, and recycled Mardi Gras beads by color in my new art corner. I'd just bought towels, bed linens, and rugs. Half a dozen pretty new dresses for my job were hanging in a line in the closet, a rainbow of linen, silk, and combed cotton. I'd be teaching in a week. I needed to revamp my syllabus, not come up with an evacuation plan. I tossed the newspaper onto the recycling pile.

**ON THE AFTERNOON OF FRIDAY, AUGUST 26, 2005, I FINISHED SETTING UP MY LOYOLA OFFICE.** It was a sunny second-floor space with a wall of glass facing the quad. A large statue of the school's patron saint, St. Ignatius (Iggy, the students called him), stood in the center of that quad, arms outstretched, one hand holding an open book.

After unpacking all my crates, arranging my files, and figuring out where to put the plants, I gave the syllabus one last go-over. Then I made twenty-five copies to pass out to my new students. I was nervous but ready for my first "Communications Writing" class at 11:30 a.m. that following Monday.

As I left Loyola around 5:00 p.m., excited about meeting my students in three days' time, the sun was still blazing. I cruised slowly down St. Charles, a main drag, window open, hand hanging out. The air was heavy and thick. Cars were already lining up at New Orleans Original Daiquiris—the drive-through drinking joint just blocks from Loyola and Tulane. Drive-through daiquiris near two major colleges. I shook my head and laughed.

At Carrollton, another main artery, I turned right and headed home. The Friday-afternoon traffic got heavier as I headed out of the center toward our suburb on the lake's edge. At a major intersection, I got stuck, engine idling along with dozens of cars backed up. The heat rose in undulating waves from the asphalt. I could smell the tar. Then my left eye recorded a flash of sunlight on steel, a sudden movement in the median. There was a row of low, wide palms in that median, their huge fronds touching the grass, creating large impenetrable umbrellas. The blinding glint had come from underneath the palm closest to my car. A frond stirred. The steely flash became the rim of a wheelchair. There was a man in it, an amputee shielding himself from traffic, tar, and heat. My eyes picked up pieces of rumpled clothing under the palm, a bedroll. This must be his house. What is he doing here, a disabled man, living under a palm tree in the middle of a median?[4]

The light turned green. I hit the gas pedal. Jim and I were going to celebrate the end of my first workweek with champagne and shrimp, so I stopped at the Italian grocery store. Inside people were grabbing bottled water and canned food off the shelves. As I stood in line clutching a bottle of dry Spanish brut, surrounded by people discussing evacuation plans, I began to get nervous.

It was only then that I realized that maybe I shouldn't be totally ignoring warnings of a powerful hurricane called Katrina that had been beating Florida. We had been watching the news, but forecasters thought it was going to hit Mississippi, not us. And I'd been in faculty cocktail orientations and swanky mimosa-with-shrimp-and-grits jazz brunches all week long. Loyola felt like a Jesuit cruise ship—I already loved it. Nobody there had said one word about a hurricane. I was supposed to be going on an eco-tour for new faculty the next morning and then attend a faculty luncheon at a seafood restaurant on a pier stretching out over the lake. People were preparing to evacuate? What was the university going to do? Today was move-in day. Our new freshmen had just arrived from all over, escorted by clucking parents. School started in three days. Hours earlier, I'd met some of these parents. I'd shaken their hands, even hugged them and promised to take care of their kids. What in the hell was going on?

In the parking lot, a man who had parked next to me was climbing out of his car. Tall and authoritative looking, he wore a long white lab coat and a large ID that read: "Charity Hospital, Emergency Personnel."

*He must know something about this hurricane,* I thought. So I asked him. He scrutinized me, intensely, as I stood there clutching the champagne.

"Get out," he said. "This is the big one."

He'd just come from a several-day meeting with medical and security personnel. We're preparing for a worst-case scenario, he said. The levees could collapse. At my hospital we've been warned that we could be stranded and without power for ten days.

Get out now, he repeated, before it gets too crazy.

I drove home, stunned. When I told Jim, he scoffed. A journalist who'd covered hurricanes for *The New York Times*, he'd sailed across the Atlantic in a small aging sailboat. (I vomited my way across the Gulf of Mexico, then said, *Find yourself some other crew.*) He'd written a book about the impact of Hurricane Mitch. He'd been watching the track of this hurricane all week.

"That guy sounds like a blowhard. I don't believe him," Jim said. "The eyewall's going to hit Mississippi, not us."

**THE NEXT MORNING, SATURDAY, AUGUST 27, I WENT TO GET GAS BEFORE HEADING TO THE** new faculty eco-tour and lunch. When I saw the long lines at the gas station and the panic in people's faces, I filled the tank and drove straight home. Screw the eco-tour and faculty luncheon on the end of a pier.* That doctor was no blowhard and I wasn't going to be stuck in a low-lying ranch house between Louisiana's largest lake and the Gulf of Mexico with two big dogs, a crazy man in denial, and just a small yellow kayak to escape in.

Jim and I shouted at each other for an hour, thundering back and forth while our dogs cowered behind the plants. Jim wanted to stay to cover "the big story." I wanted to evacuate to friends in Alabama. I

* That welcome-new-faculty luncheon was the last meal ever served. The restaurant was swept away.

stormed out of the house with the dogs to walk on the levee and think about it.

It was around noon. I remember being struck by the gorgeous weather that day—the sun blazing in a piercingly blue sky, bright white wispy cirrus clouds fanning out. The hurricane was still hundreds of miles away, over the gulf. There were no signs of it I could see or feel—no wind, no rain. It was one of the most beautiful walks I'd ever taken on that levee. The approaching menace felt totally unreal.

In retrospect, I've realized that one thing was different that day. The birds. They were so loud. Birds are usually quieter at noon. But that day, there was a cacophony, especially of gulls, whirling and shrieking. It sounded like a bird convention on the levee and all along the canal to the lake. Of course I knew nothing about birds then. This was the first time I began to think of them as more than pretty flying objects and instead as creatures with their own agendas. As I stood on that levee and listened, I asked myself: Are they doing the same thing Jim and I are doing? Arguing about whether or not to evacuate? But they can't watch CNN, so how could they possibly know that a massive hurricane is going to hit us in less than forty-eight hours?

Seventeen years after I stood on that levee, scientists know that there are certain signals that fire up an avian news network (ANN), particularly changes in barometric pressure. According to the National Hurricane Center, while I was walking on that levee, barometric pressure was plunging out on the ocean as the hurricane gathered force.

"The birds you were observing and listening to were undoubtedly responding to the huge and rapid drop in air pressure," Erick Greene, an avian communications expert, told me. "Birds have a breathtaking level of sensitivity to barometric pressure on par with the most sensitive pressure gauges in our planes. I would expect that birds have special calls to relay this type of information. They have calls for just about everything else important in their lives, so this would make sense."[5]

Greene would know. He published a groundbreaking study in the journal *Science* reporting that black-capped chickadees, with their signature *dee-dee-dee* call, were actually activating an avian rapid-relay

information system, warning as many as fifty different bird species that a hawk or owl was nearby.[6] Greene and his research team used life-size robo-raptors, feathered robotic owls and hawks, to provoke chickadees into sounding the predator alarm. After ten years of recording and analyzing chickadee calls, Greene discovered that the larger the predator, the more *dee-dee-dee*s a chickadee makes, as many as twelve for an owl. Greene—who loves chickadees so much that he composed a symphony inspired by them—clocked the chickadee's alarm signal "traveling up to 100 miles per hour for the length of two football fields, much faster than a hawk can fly."*

If a chickadee, a land bird that normally doesn't migrate, can transmit a predator alarm call at 100 miles per hour, then maybe those shrieking gulls I was hearing that day, some of them heading inland, were transmitting their own hurricane warning over hundreds of miles, bird by bird from ocean to shore.[7]

---

* Greene placed microphones every 50 meters and recorded alarm calls relaying between several bird species. He also discovered that squirrels and chipmunks understand the chickadee's alarm, and that birds respond to squirrel and chipmunk alarms.

Infrasound is another signal that triggers an avian news network—low-frequency ground-transmitted waves produced by volcanoes, earthquakes, waterfalls, storm systems, and tsunamis. Many birds can hear it. We cannot.

In 2014, a bird weighing just 9 grams—the equivalent of nine small birthday candles—became an ornithology rock star when scientists discovered that the golden-winged warbler can hear infrasound produced by storms hundreds of miles away.[8] That spring, a small group of golden-winged warblers had just left their wintering grounds in eastern Colombia and flown 3,000 miles north to their breeding grounds in Tennessee's Cumberland Mountains. While the birds were traveling, a wall of supercell thunderstorms developed into one of the most damaging weather systems in US history. On April 26, 2014, twenty-four hours before the storm hit neighboring Arkansas, these warblers that had just arrived from Colombia immediately evacuated from Tennessee. Researchers discovered that they flapped their golden wings an extra 900 miles to Florida and Cuba and escaped a storm system that dropped 4.5-inch hail, spawned 84 tornadoes, ravaged seventeen states for 61 hours and killed 35 people, while causing at least $1 billion in damage.

"At the same time that meteorologists on the Weather Channel were telling us this storm was headed in our direction, the birds were apparently already packing their bags," ecologist Henry Streby told *ScienceDaily*. "They then came right back home after the storm passed."[9]

Birds have evolved to migrate during severe weather over millions of years. Long-distance migratory birds have been flying from Latin America to the north and back for 13,000 to 15,000 years, since the glaciers melted.[10] They arrive from Latin America in the spring and return in the fall, many crossing the Gulf of Mexico or the Atlantic during the peak of hurricane season. If they didn't know more about these storms than we do, they would have long since disappeared.

Like our species, avians have developed a variety of severe-weather survival strategies: get the hell out of Dodge, fly into the storm's calmer eye and ride it out, or hunker down. The choice depends on a bird's resources such as food, physical energy reserves, skills, and knowledge of flight paths and refueling stations. Some seabirds outfly a storm, staying just ahead or skirting around it. Scientists followed one such bird, Machi the whimbrel, as she escaped Tropical Storm Irene. (Whimbrels are large shorebirds with nearly four-inch beaks that curve downward, allowing them to pluck crabs out of mud flats.) Via satellite tracking, scientists discovered that Machi had flown over 27,000 miles in two years, and that on her last migration from the Hudson Bay to the Caribbean, she'd veered hundreds of miles off her normal route to avoid Irene. Unfortunately, just hours after Machi landed on the island of Guadeloupe, a hunter shot her.[11] Another satellite-tagged whimbrel named Hope flew straight into Tropical Storm Gert in 2011, off Nova Scotia. This appropriately named bird flew into the storm at a leisurely 7 miles an hour and shot out, unscathed, at nearly 90 miles an hour.[12]

Other, smaller songbirds migrating over water may get sucked into a hurricane's outer winds. Known as hurricane birds or storm birds, these birds fly downwind until they reach the calm in the eye of the hurricane, which is usually 20 to 40 miles in diameter but can be a space of blue sky and warmer temperatures stretching 2 to 200 miles. The calm circular eye is surrounded by the hurricane's strongest winds in the eyewall, which create a giant swirling birdcage of sorts. Hurricane birds must stay inside that swirling eyewall cage until the storm reaches land. They fly hard until the storm peters out or until they drop from exhaustion. This is why birders rush to coastal areas after hurricanes to see the "fallout," thousands of migratory birds blown back to shore or birds that had been trapped in the storm's eye.

Meteorologist Matthew Van Den Broeke analyzed radar data from thirty-three Atlantic hurricanes between 2011 and 2020 and found radar evidence of bioscatter—insects or birds trapped in the eye of every single one, mostly birds.[13] The more severe the hurricane, the harder it is to leave the safety of that calm eye, Van Den Broeke told me. Trapped birds might fly thousands of extra miles and spend days in the air before they could refuel.[14] Thousands of birds have died this way, including a huge flock of migrating chimney swifts trapped in Hurricane Wilma, which clobbered Florida in 2005, just two months after Katrina. Some lucky survivors landed in the Azores, the Canary Islands, and on the Irish, French, and English coasts, thrilling birders who had never seen this American bird. But most of them met a terrible end; at least 727 of their tiny bodies were found later. It's very hard to find dead birds. Millions are never recovered, so scientists count their absence instead. This particular Quebec swift population plummeted an average of 62 percent the year after Hurricane Wilma. Many swifts found alive after this storm were severely emaciated, in an "advanced state of exhaustion," and had lost 30 to 35 percent of their average body weight, according to Canadian researchers.[15]

Then there are the stay-putters, birds that live in our cities and towns year-round and do not migrate. You see them every day, what ornithologists call resident birds, like cardinals, house sparrows, and chickadees. Some may move elsewhere; scientists don't know for sure. But this would be a last-ditch strategy: since these birds are not migrators, they don't know the best flight routes or where to find emergency avian gas stations.

Some songbirds can take shelter in a tree and hang on by clamping onto a good branch and activating an avian toe-lock mechanism. This is how they sleep upright without falling over. Their toe lock can help them survive as long as their chosen tree doesn't come down. Another strategy is to find a thicket to hide in or a porch or shed to dive under. Urban backyard birds know their urban territories and possible hiding places. A woodpecker can hide in the roost hole where it sleeps at night, protected from high winds (as long as that tree withstands the storm). But birds that have just blown in, outracing a storm, especially marsh birds and seabirds unused to urban areas, cannot easily find places to hide. That's how Ralph the brown pelican from North Carolina ended up on the roof of Ralph's Place, a strip club in Halifax, Nova Scotia, during Hurricane Earl in 2010. Ralph was lucky. After the bird spent six months in a Canadian rehab hospital, a volunteer drove three days to return her to the Carolinas (Ralph turned out to be female). But many pelicans stranded on bridges over water during storms are hit by cars.[16]

When birds get very stressed by storms, they take advantage of any available shelter. William Bruso, a forty-five-year-old taxi driver in Houston, was out shopping for last-minute supplies just before Hurricane Harvey in 2017 when he noticed a small hawk at the side of the road. He hopped out to take a picture and a cat ran by, spooking the hawk. The bird dove into his open passenger window and refused to leave his taxi.

"He looks like he's scared. He doesn't know what's going on . . . He just kind of hopped on in and doesn't want to leave," Bruso said in one of ten viral videos he made of Harvey the Cooper's hawk.[17] Harvey (who also turned out to be female) spent two nights in Bruso's apartment next to his liquor cabinet eating raw chicken hearts. Then a wildlife rehabber saw the Harvey videos and took the hawk to a refuge. Harvey wasn't injured, just "extremely stressed." Rehabbers later released her in a wooded area.

**THERE IS YET ANOTHER STRATEGY SOME BIRDS MAY USE TO OUTWIT HURRICANES—PREDICT** the weather months in advance. I believe it's more like a superpower.

The veery is a shy, drab little thrush slightly smaller than a robin. An elusive bird that summers in our northern woods, it's hard to see, but its whistly, ethereal song sounds like a tiny fairy playing the flute. Veery expert Christopher Heckscher has been studying the same Delaware group of veeries for nearly twenty-five years.[18] Veeries leave the Brazilian Amazon every spring to raise their families in the moist woods of the northern United States and Canada, returning to Brazil in the fall, right in the middle of hurricane season. But after analyzing nearly two decades of data, Heckscher realized that during severe hurricane seasons, veeries nested earlier, had fewer young, and molted earlier, which allowed them to migrate earlier and avoid the worst storms. An early molt is a strategy that many migratory birds employ before they travel because it takes too much energy to replace their feathers and fly thousands of miles at the same time. Veeries, who sometimes raise two broods, also lay more eggs in the first nest during bad hurricane years, as if they know they will not have time to have another family.

Hurricane season has not even started when the birds begin to nest in May. Yet somehow veeries alter their breeding schedules three to four months in advance of the worst storm systems so they can avoid them.

Heckscher suspects that while the birds are still on their Amazonian wintering grounds, they can read different weather patterns such as the El Niño and La Niña cycles that influence rainfall, drought, and hurricanes. He theorizes that the birds have learned that during a La Niña year, there are generally more hurricanes in the Atlantic than during an El Niño year.

"Whatever it is, they [veeries] know by mid-May . . . It sounds out-there, but then again if you think about it, it makes sense these birds would take advantage of anything they could across their evolutionary history to avoid hurricanes," Heckscher told *Audubon Magazine*.[19]

If only New Orleanians had had that veery superpower in 2005.

**WHEN I RETURNED HOME AFTER WALKING THE DOGS ON THE LEVEE, SOME NEIGHBORS WERE** already boarding up their homes and leaving. Others had decided to stay, particularly our elderly neighbors. This happens every year, they told us wearily. The weathermen always say the big one's coming. It never does. The levees have always held. We're sick of evacuating two to three times a year. It's expensive. It's a hassle. We feel safer in our home.

Jim and I were in the street, asking for evacuation tips, when a young man drove up and parked. He was coming to help a relative leave. He was close to tears.

"We're in the bowl," he said, distraught. "I've been hearing this my whole life and now it could happen. The lake could spill over that bowl."

I hadn't paid any attention to sea level when the real estate agent showed us our lovely little house because it was one of the only ones we could afford. But Lakeview was at least six feet below sea level, parts of it much lower, parts of it higher if you lived on a ridge, where property was more expensive. That's what the young man meant by "the bowl."

As we put our dogs in the back seat and drove away that night, I noticed that our neighbors across the street had left their red tabby behind. She sat on the front porch, staring at our car.

That horrible evacuation day, Jim and I knew our migratory route well: a five-hour drive on the interstate to Montgomery, Alabama. We had a car that worked. We had friends to stay with. And we had financial resources: credit cards and money for gas and food. In 2005, over 25 percent of New Orleanians lived below the poverty line, many paycheck to paycheck without credit cards or savings. Katrina hit on August 29, two days before payday. It takes tremendous resources to evacuate, whether you are avian or human, and it is very stressful. Many New Orleanians simply didn't have these resources.

ON THE MORNING OF MONDAY, AUGUST 29, THE HURRICANE HIT NEW ORLEANS AROUND seven o'clock. By late morning, the storm had blown through. At our friend's home in Montgomery, we cheered when we heard President Bush's announcement that the levees had held.

The streets always flood in New Orleans when it rains, so after the hurricane blew through, our neighbors who stayed behind didn't think the water on their doorsteps was strange. But around 11:30 a.m., right when I should have been giving my first lecture at Loyola, our New Orleanian neighbors noticed that the water was rising, not falling. It continued to rise slowly, one brick every twenty minutes. The levee a block away had held, but as one brick became two, then four, then six, and the neighbors began retreating up the attic stairs, they wondered about the massive 17th Street Canal Levee, half a mile away.

For the rest of the day, the water steadily climbed, until 12 feet of it filled the bowl that our little house sat in and filled our house with 11.5 feet of water. Later that night, the neighborhood lay silent, engulfed in darkness, water gently lapping the eaves. Suddenly the air exploded with a deafening chorus of thousands of frogs. Our suburb had been built in the 1960s on top of a filled-in marsh. That night the frogs reclaimed it. When I read this news online in Montgomery, five hours away, I remembered the tiny frog I'd found that steamy Saturday, leaping just ahead of the mower blades.

**ONCE IN A WHILE SOMEONE STILL ASKS, "WHAT DID IT FEEL LIKE?"**

A few days after Katrina hit, when we knew our house was underwater, we realized the obvious: we needed a place to stay. Our friend in Montgomery begged us to stay with him. So, reluctantly, I went to the nearest hardware store to make copies of his house key. I really didn't want to do this. It meant admitting that we couldn't go home, and that somehow the incomprehensible scenes we were watching on TV were real. I remember sitting in our friend's living room watching it all and thinking, *Yeah, but that's not our little house. Our little house is still there and it's okay. I just know it is.*

The hardware store in Montgomery was tiny. Quite a few customers were shopping for paint and other supplies. I made the key and got in line. When I got to the cashier, she was focused intently on the register's screen. She punched in the sale, and out of the corner of her mouth she drawled, "What's your address, ma'am?"

Address? I stood there thinking really hard.

Well, my address is 7038 General Haig Street, New Orleans, Louisiana, 70124, I thought. But that address is underwater. And that means that all the crepe myrtle trees and the virgin statues and the flickering gas lamps that look so pretty and old-fashioned are underwater, too. Are the virgin statues floating around? And the little Italian grocery store—it's underwater. And the tiny hardware store next to it, just like this one I'm standing in right now in Montgomery with cans of paint stacked nearly to the ceiling—underwater, too. What happens to all that paint underwater? I wondered. Do the cans open up? Does the paint turn the floodwaters different colors? And the coffee shop where they make their own croissants. Underwater. The tiny post office. Underwater. All underwater. Which means they can't deliver the mail. And what about the horrible news story saying that New Orleans has been poisoned by industrial toxins and buried superfund sites and that the city might be uninhabitable for decades . . .

"Ma'am? Uh, ma'am? Are you all right, ma'am?"

The cashier was staring at me, eyes widening. The people in line behind me shifted hip to hip, impatient.

"New Orleans," I mumbled, realizing my cheeks were wet.

"Oh, New Orleans," she said gently. "That's okay, ma'am. I'm really sorry, ma'am."

For a long time after the Storm I felt like this. I was sitting at the bottom of a well, hugging my knees to my chest. The water was cold and clear. I'd look up and see people like that cashier staring down at me from the surface. I could see their mouths opening and closing. They were trying to tell me something. But I couldn't hear them. And every time I tried to speak, all that came out was a stream of bubbles.

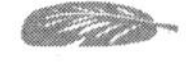

BECAUSE THE NATIONAL GUARD HAD TO SEARCH EVERY HOUSE FOR BODIES AND BECAUSE A lot of people had drowned in our neighborhood, ours was the second to last to reopen. After forty days we were allowed to return for one day just to look. The EPA had warned all returning New Orleanians to protect ourselves from toxins in our homes. I was scared because I'm allergic to mold. So we bought heavy-duty respirator masks, rubber gloves, rubber boots.

I was determined to go back as a reporter, not as a resident. I was going to take control of this situation. I wasn't a victim; I was a journalist. This wasn't a disaster; it was a really big story. No matter how out of control things were (and they were pretty out of control—we didn't know if I had a job, we didn't know where we were going to live), I could still pick up a pen and notebook and make sense of it all. I'd been writing stuff down since I was seven years old. I was a reporting machine, a vacuum cleaner of details. Recording colors, smells, textures, weather, the exact time, a precise phrase, calmed me down. So in addition to the shovels, picks, crowbars, ladder, hammer, and other implements we needed to dig through our house, I brought my tiny tape recorder. I could talk faster than I could write. I would record every detail.

We left Montgomery at 2:37 a.m. on Thursday, October 6. It was raining hard. I was hoping that it wasn't raining hard in New Orleans because the last thing we needed down there was more water.

The five-hour drive from Montgomery to New Orleans was a blur of abandoned boats along the highways, rotting mattresses in trees, dead animals everywhere—even a dead bear—and a McDonald's with half a golden arch in Mississippi. Katrina's eyewall had sheared the top half off most of the pines. There were so many signs leading to nowhere on the I-10: Pass Christian, Waveland, Chalmette, St. Bernard Parish—places hit with a twenty- to forty-foot wall of water. For over a hundred miles, the windows or broken panes of dark empty houses and apartments stared out like hollow, sad eyes. The highway was thick with government workers and FEMA personnel, all men driving huge trucks, all streaming toward New Orleans. It reminded me of the refugee resettlement zones I'd worked in in Guatemala—the uniforms, the packaged supplies, the testosterone, the sense of urgency.

We entered the city through a neighborhood that hadn't flooded, on the good side of the levee. It was 8:30 a.m. and there was actually morning traffic as people like us flowed back in to take a look. On this side of the levee, colorful street signs in front of car dealerships, hair salons, and restaurants said, "We're back" and "We're open." Our favorite donut shop was open. A line of customers sat at the 1950s-style counter drinking coffee, joking around. My heart rate began to slow. It looked so normal. Maybe it wasn't as bad as they said. Maybe the reporters were exaggerating. Maybe those horrific images on TV and the internet were just plain wrong.

WE CROSSED THE BRIDGE OVER TO OUR SIDE, WHERE THE LEVEE BROKE. I TURNED ON THE tape recorder and picked up my notebook. I was in war zone mode. A switch in the heart flipped off and a switch in the brain flipped on. Adrenaline surged through my veins. My heart pounded. My eyes scanned the horizon, hawklike, seeking details. On this side of the levee, several small abandoned boats lay on the road's shoulder. Their owners must have made it to this bridge, I told the recorder. They got out. Survivors.

A line of signs said, "Got Mold?" "What's your home worth?" "Demolition Services," and then there was an improbable "For Rent" sign in front of a destroyed home. There was no traffic, just a line of bulldozers, each one story tall, pushing a mountain of dead trees on top of a mountain of garbage in the space that was our park. Faceless city workers in white masks with bodies covered completely in hazmat suits manned the bulldozers.

Clouds of khaki-gray dust swirled around, coating everything. On the other side of the levee there was color: people sitting at counters eating powdered sugar donuts with raspberry jam oozing out of them, shiny new cars in car lots—red, black, teal, maroon. On this side, we were driving into a yellowing black-and-white photograph. The only sounds were the beeping of the bulldozers and our truck tires crunching on broken glass, bits of wire, wood, branches, children's plastic toys. Jim slowed to a crawl. I rolled up the window. And then I turned off the tape recorder and set it down on the dashboard, along with my notebook and pen.

**JIM AND I SPENT A FEW HOURS EXPLORING OUR HOME, TAKING BREAKS TO BREATHE OUT**side. Inside, I felt like a forensic anthropologist excavating the grave of my own life, rooting things up, scrutinizing mysterious objects that were once familiar. In the front room, several inches of oozing muck sucked on our rubber boots—a viscous stew of thousands of books and paper files from two print journalists' lives, the ceiling that had collapsed, paint from the walls, the fluffy pink insulation that had fallen down with the ceiling, toxic stuff from all our electronics and household chemicals, plus oil, sewage, the waters of Lake Pontchartrain, and whatever oozed out of over 250,000 drowned television sets, 134,000+ refrigerators, and at least a quarter of a million cars that had sat in the water for days and weeks, including my old pickup truck. In the rest of the house, we crept tentatively over the new carpet of broken windows, mirrors, champagne goblets, cocktail glasses, mason jars, flower vases, picture frames, and Central American sculptures crunching under our feet. In the living room, the hundred-year-old

player piano that Jim's grandmother had bequeathed him was lying on its back, disintegrating, its paper rolls of World War I– and II–era love songs like George Gershwin's *Rhapsody in Blue* scattered all over. Most of the ivory keys had come off and were clinging like fingers to unrecognizable items.

Other slivers of our former lives waited untouched, intact, like the purple negligees hanging on the back of the bedroom door. The six-inch blue-and-white gloomy wooden virgin that I'd left to protect the house still stood in her tiny alcove, muddy and sorrowful. A lime-green flip-flop lay next to her, upside down.

My eyes paused on a turquoise-and-silver thread peeking out from under the remains of the couch. I began to pull, excited. It was a Guatemalan tapestry from Atitlán, stinky, slimy, threads still glittering, but intact, a piece of my past, and for me, maybe the most important piece. As I pulled on it, I remembered the day I bought it and the women scrubbing brilliantly colored blouses and skirts against large rocks on the shores of Lake Atitlán, reddened hands moving the cloth up and down against rough stone, the suds of lard soap floating lazily on the lake water. They were Mayan women from the Tz'utujil ethnic group, a group that survived centuries of colonial occupation and three decades of terror waged by soldiers in the military base down the road from their village. The entire village had finally revolted and forced the military out, the first Mayan community in Guatemala to liberate itself. I reported on that liberation. A tapestry made by these women would survive anything.

At some point, maybe the same moment as at an Irish wake when people have enough whiskey in them to joke about the dearly departed, we began taking photographs of the unimaginable. On top of a goop mound in the living room sat the book *Alabama Canoe Rides.* I had to go outside and take off my respirator mask to laugh because this was absolutely fucking hilarious.

But the greatest cosmic joke of all was lying on an old trunk that we'd used as a coffee table. My parents brought this trunk from Ireland when they emigrated on the *Queen Mary* in 1958. They gave it to me when I went to college. I plastered it with anti-nuke bumper stickers when I discovered my first political cause. On top of that rotting trunk, next to the bumper sticker "One Nuclear Bomb Can Ruin Your Whole Day," someone had placed a white flyer, weighing it down with a rock. The flyer read: "ATTENTION: Residents of New Orleans: The Mayor of New Orleans has authorized house to house secondary searches in the areas affected by flood waters from Hurricane Katrina . . . Law enforcement conducted a search of your house to look for hurricane survivors and victims. We have made every attempt not to disturb your personal items."

**JIM TOOK A PILE OF PHOTOS THAT DAY TO PROVE TO THE INSURANCE COMPANY THAT OUR** home had filled with water for three weeks. There was one photo that I still show today to students whenever I have to give a scary "Climate Change and Katrina" lecture. My students stare at it in disbelief, their gaze shifting back and forth between that person from seventeen years ago in the photo and the person standing behind the lectern in a Vermont classroom.

In that photo I was standing just inside what was left of our front door after the National Guard had kicked it in to search the house for bodies. My right foot was planted on the back of a collapsed rotting bookcase. My left foot was deep in several inches of that oozing muck. In my right hand, I was gripping an old blue bottle with a candlestick in it, not a particularly useful item. I rescued it because it had survived. I was wearing an old Krispy Kreme baseball cap and a large respirator mask in the photo. The mask covered most of my face so that just my eyes peeked out. I looked like a giant stick insect. I was headed decisively out the front door, clutching that candlestick, knee bent, foot pushing down to propel myself up and over that disintegrating bookcase, into the light, into the fresh air.

"Trish," Jim the photographer yelled.

The shutter clicked. My eyes, flat and empty, stared straight at the lens.

**TODAY I TELL MY STUDENTS THAT AS HORRIFIC AS THIS PHOTO LOOKS, IT WAS THE FIRST** time that I was truly standing on the earth. I realized that day that as a journalist, I'd lived in so many places, but I was "covering" stories, just passing through. I wasn't really connected to the soil, the waters, or any of the creatures that lived in those places, besides the humans. That day I had to protect myself with rubber gloves and a mask from the poisons I'd left in my own home, poisons I'd purchased. I'd left a vehicle in my yard that had created its own small oil spill. I suddenly wondered how many creatures had died simply because of the way I'd lived. And I realized that it was I who was out of place in this low-lying neighborhood, not the tiny frog I'd found hopping on my lawn the month before the hurricane or the diminutive green lizard hiding in my dish rack.

I was enraged with myself. I'd worked for the United Nations. I'd published two books. I had two master's degrees. But I didn't understand what a wetland was or what sea level really meant, even though I'd moved to a neighborhood built on a filled-in swamp. I'd spent hundreds of hours as a journalist interviewing humans, trying to understand *Homo sapiens* and why we do the terrible things that we do to one another. Now I just wanted to interview the worms.

I also felt deeply ashamed, a shame I still feel whenever I give a Katrina talk in a lecture hall full of eighteen-year-olds studying the environment, kids who were just two or three years old when Katrina hit. I tell them that I'm from Madonna's "Material Girl" generation—the roaring Reagan eighties—a rejection of the environmentally conscious 1960s and '70s. Many of my students have been recycling since they were toddlers. They are strict vegans or vegetarians. They are zero-waste practitioners who try to fit all their trash from their freshman year into a single mason jar. Many don't have driver's licenses or own cars. Some don't even believe in driving. When I grew up in Southern California, to get a car at sixteen was your birthright if you were middle or upper class. At my alma mater, USC, the University of Spoiled Children, there were kids driving around in Mercedes-Benzes. We thought the planet was a credit card. We maxed it out driving and flying around.

I tell my students that since Katrina I've replaced my drowned truck with a pink cruiser bike (today I own four bikes and use studded tires to ride in Vermont winters). I stopped using chemicals. I grow organic vegetables. I composted my lawn and replaced it with a wildflower meadow and I have a worm composting bin in the basement. But I probably have the carbon footprint of an entire town in a poor country because I practically tossed a whole house into the waters of Lake Pontchartrain. And I believe that if I'm not working to change government policies, my individual actions since Katrina to atone for my environmental sins are just a form of green "feel-goodism."

I can never forget what we left in our house and how those toxins eventually flowed into Lake Pontchartrain and the Gulf of Mexico. I still think about it when I watch robins or doves in Vermont bathing in puddles or I see the great blue heron standing in the water at the river's edge. What's in that murky water? What are we doing to our animal neighbors?

I realized that before Katrina I'd never thought about water as a living entity with power and its own agenda. I'd grown up in an irrigated California desert. We were surrounded by cactus but had a glittering turquoise swimming pool and acres of orange groves. It was magical realism as water policy. In California, water magically appears, after being stolen from Mexico via the Colorado River. In Louisiana, it magically disappears behind those green levee walls.

Just after Katrina, a friend in Alabama who was getting a PhD in limnology—the study of inland waters—tried to console me when I told her what I had done to the waters of Lake Pontchartrain and the gulf.

"The answer to pollution is dilution," she told me gently, reciting the mantra her professors had taught her. I stared at her, seeing those TVs and desktop computers bobbing in the Gulf, the sunlight hitting their screens and lighting them up like giant eyeballs, electric cords twisting eellike in the tide. I wondered what the manatees and the oil-coated egrets would say.

"I think that's spelled D-E-L-U-S-I-O-N," I yelled.

**WHEN WE FINISHED SEARCHING THE HOUSE, I LEFT A BOUQUET OF FLOWERS ON OUR DOOR**step. Then I scattered birdseed and dog and cat food to feed the animals left behind. After this ritual, Jim and I stood silently in front of the little house for a few minutes. We said goodbye to it. I knew we would never live there again. Then before we got into our truck to leave, we stripped down to our underwear, put our contaminated clothes and shoes in trash bags, and changed into the clean clothes we'd brought.

We still had one more stop to make, one more bouquet to deliver. We drove to Lake Pontchartrain, just a few blocks away. I sat on the shore for a while and cried. I apologized to the lake. As I tossed the flowers into the water, one by one, I swore to that water, to all the creatures who lived in it, and to all the waters of the earth that I was never again going to live in a way that poisoned the water. I had no idea how I was going to do it, but I pledged to learn how to live on this earth without destroying it.

**WHEN JIM AND I DROVE AWAY FROM THE LITTLE HOUSE THAT AFTERNOON AND WERE WITHIN** cellphone range, I checked my new phone. This was before everyone had a cellphone. I'd never had one before. But when we fled the city and knew we were going to be away from our landlines indefinitely, suddenly I needed one. Katrina hit on a Monday, and from Montgomery I'd called our landline, that heavy old black rotary phone in our house, for the next three days. As I sat there in our friend's house in Alabama, receiver to my ear, listening to it ring and ring and ring in New Orleans, I wondered if you could hear that ringing under the

11.5 feet of water in the house. At least that sound was a connection to the house—it was like checking someone's pulse even though you know they're already dead. I didn't know it then, but New Orleanians scattered all over the country were doing the same thing, sitting in a motel or some relative's or friend's home, receiver to their ears, listening, hoping. On the fourth day, the Thursday after Katrina, instead of the ringing, there was a disembodied computer recording. The landlines in the flood zone had finally died.

That strange afternoon, just after we drove away from our ruined home, there were three messages on my new cellphone all from the same number, my parents' house in California. My parents never, ever called me or even returned my calls. They didn't even call me after Katrina to see if I was alive. They'd stopped speaking to me three years earlier because I was "living in sin" with Jim, the ultimate betrayal for an Irish Catholic daughter. Unfortunately, Jim wasn't Catholic, wasn't rich, and wasn't a doctor; he was eighteen years older than me; and worst of all, he was divorced. When I brought him to California to meet my parents, the visit was so traumatic that I wrote a fifty-two-page play about it called *The Troubles,* which is probably truly awful but was way more fun than going to another therapist. My father had told me that I was "dead" to him and that he'd rather that I be "a drug addict or a criminal" than living with a boyfriend. That drama three years earlier was the last time I had seen or spoken to my parents.

So when I saw their home number on my cell as we drove away from New Orleans, I laughed.

"It's my mother," I said to Jim. "Someone must be dead or dying."

I was right. My father had a tumor in his stomach the size of a grapefruit and was starving to death. He had stomach cancer. A surgeon was removing his stomach in five days. He wanted to see all his children before the surgery. Could I get on a plane?

I'd just spent eight hours in my destroyed house. We had no home—we were crashing temporarily with kind and infinitely patient friends in Alabama. And now I was being asked to immediately return to the place where I was born, the place that should feel like home, where you go to lick your wounds, where you know you will be loved unconditionally. But for me, Orange County, California, golden land of citrus and surfers, was a war zone, a microcosm of the one my parents had come from in Northern Ireland.

I listened to my mother's frantic messages, over and over again, as we drove away from the ruins of New Orleans. And I thought about the other side of my father, the man who picked my brothers and me up from school every day, helped us with our homework, supervised our chores, taught us to garden, and ferried us to hundreds of hours of piano, trumpet, and Spanish lessons, surfing sessions, and Laguna Beach every Monday afternoon on his day off. I remembered as a child the sound of his work boots hitting the pavement as he ran toward my brothers and me whenever we fell down and scraped our knees, the strong arms scooping us up and carrying us into the kitchen, where he'd set us on the counter. Then the magic would begin. With a bottle of bright red-orange mercurochrome, he'd paint elaborate hairy spiders all over our wounded limbs. I remember not wanting to bathe for days so my spiders wouldn't wash away.

As soon as we reached Montgomery, I bought a plane ticket to California.

CHAPTER 2

# C'est Levee

*What bird wilt thou employ*
*to bring me word of thee?*

HENRY DAVID THOREAU, MAY 23, 1843

CANCER IS A STRANGE AND BITTER GIFT IN THE SENSE THAT IT'S HARD TO BE ANGRY with someone who is dying, no matter how much of an asshole they've been. You're so aware of how little time is left. I think it must have been the same for my father. On that very first visit after three years of estrangement, he greeted me with a huge hug, only pulling away to joke about "the return of the Prodigal Daughter." Then he proudly showed me the latest house renovation. He'd installed a bay window in the family room looking over the yard and the wild-sage-and-prickly-pear-studded hill that towered over their home. My father had barely graduated from high school; no one in his Irish village went to college "except the Protestants" because "they were rich." He'd never studied biology, but he'd grown up on a farm and loved animals.

That night he didn't mention the impending gnarly surgery to remove most of his stomach or the twenty pounds he'd just dropped. Instead, he talked about all the wild animals passing through his yard as if it were an expressway. The coyote who sauntered around my parents' tiled portico, sniffing their cars. The huge hawk who came down with a great whooshing of wings, talons extended, grabbed a rat, and sailed off into the air with the rat still wriggling. The mountain lion stalking up the cement driveway, peering through the window at my father, and then turning tail and slinking under the wrought-iron gate.

The animals of my childhood were still there because my father was part of a group of neighbors who'd organized to stop developers from building condos and McMansions on that hill right behind us. I was a feral teenager when this happened, too boy-crazy to pay attention. But my father testified before county commissioners about all the "wee animals" that lived on the hill. Some people complained about the coyotes, wanting them exterminated because they regularly descended from the hill to snack on pets. The coyotes were here first, my father told the commissioners. That red hill was their home. It took months of meetings, but together my father and the other coyote/rabbit/mountain lion/skunk/raccoon defenders prevailed. Our beloved hill became a permanent greenbelt and a bird refuge treasured today by birders. I thought it was poetic justice during that last year of his life that the animals my father had defended now showed up in his yard to look in the window at him.

One morning during that California visit, I walked up that hill. I just sat there and marveled at all the life hidden amid the cactus and sage. There were so many different kinds of birds I'd grown up with but never learned the names of. Now I know that they were California quail, towhees, thrashers, roadrunners, mockingbirds, and hummingbirds, small clouds of them buzzing and dipping into the desert flowers, sipping their delicate nectar.

A flock of wild parrots caroused above it all, making a tremendous racket, just like the parrots in Lakeview, New Orleans. As I sat there, I was suddenly flooded with the feeling I had as a child whenever I was at the edge of the hill, on the border between our manicured yard and the mysterious wild. We were always warned: don't go up on that hill or the coyotes and rattlesnakes will get you. I loved it and I feared it. That morning I could feel dozens of pairs of eyes watching me quietly. Coyote eyes, deer eyes, snake eyes, lizard eyes, quail eyes, ancient desert tortoise eyes, mountain lion eyes, raccoon eyes, skunk eyes, opossum eyes, rat eyes, bobcat eyes, and desert cottontail eyes, their wet noses twitching. When I was a child, they were my silent ominous babysitters.

At night, other animals reminded me of my childhood. I woke around midnight to hear the call of a great horned owl, a species that had been nesting on my parents' property for decades. That repetitive hooting was one of the very first animal sounds I became aware of, probably when I was just four or five years old. I'd wake up to hear that owl high in the eucalyptus windbreak that protected the citrus groves. I slept with the window open so I could hear my "friend." I thought it was talking just to me. It made me feel special, like we shared a secret. That owl taught me that there were many types of friendships.

I spent a week with my parents. I knew from sneaking a look at my father's medical records that he'd be lucky to last a year. But he told us that he didn't want anyone, including his three children, to hang around watching him die. We all had our own lives. He wanted to live his life the way he always had, outside tending his beloved plants. Come and go, visit when you can, he said, but "let me have my peace."

I still didn't know what was happening in New Orleans. But I'd decided that once Loyola reopened, I would return to teach and help rebuild. I told my father I'd visit several times in the coming months, but that I had to return to New Orleans as soon as I could.

"Sure, you're a plucky wee lass," he said.

**AFTER THAT FIRST TRIP TO SEE MY FATHER, I TRAVELED BACK TO MONTGOMERY. IT WOULD** be months before Loyola reopened. We rented a fully furnished apartment on a crumbling Montgomery estate that had belonged to a widow who had died two years earlier. Miss Mabel's empty white-columned home sat at the front of the property on what had once been a majestic lawn rolling out to the street. Two massive cast-iron lions stood guard at the steps to the main house.

Our new refuge had been the caretaker's quarters, a cozy nest above the garage behind the main house. It looked out over an abandoned garden of rosebushes, persimmon, fig, and peach trees, and honeysuckle vines. Broken elves and crumbling angel statues peeked out from beneath overgrown grape arbors. Inside the screened back porch of the main house, a dusty ceiling fan still revolved, creaking slightly, as if Miss Mabel had forgotten to turn it off two years before.

On the very first morning, I sat on the ground in Miss Mabel's garden and wrote in my journal:

> First came the birds this morning, from six to seven. Then at seven, a great cacophony of laughter, shrieking, squealing, jumping and dodging. It is the children arriving to the middle school across the street. In their white shirts and dark pants and skirts, they cluster in small swarms like excited bees. My dogs sit watching them in astonishment . . . So much life across the street for that joyous hour with groups of kids walking to school along Miss Mabel's back fence. So much life compared to so much

> death in New Orleans . . . At eight the bells of the beautiful brick United Church of Christ across the street begin to toll. And like a great flock of boisterous, exuberant crows, the children fly to the school door. A deafening silence descends on the neighborhood. As if the tide has gone out. How can all that life be contained in those brick buildings? I expect them to explode any minute . . . Thirty minutes later, at 8:30 a.m., the church bells are tolling "Amazing Grace."

I began every morning this way for the next few months, sitting in Miss Mabel's yard and scribbling in my journal. My moods varied wildly. Some days I was writing about seeds spinning down from the trees, tiny paperlike husks lying on the ground like me, waiting for spring so they could open and grow. Other mornings I riffed in my journal on the word "evacuated." We were called Katrina "evacuees," which my dog-eared Merriam-Webster defines as "a person removed from a dangerous place." And the verb "evacuate, -ed/-ing," defined as "empty," "to discharge wastes from the body," and "to remove or withdraw from."

That first term defined me: "empty." I couldn't focus on anything. Thoughts flitted through my head like frenetic minnows. I felt like someone had vacuumed out my brain and heart. I withdrew from the world to listen to the whistling of the pines, in the company of my dogs and Miss Mabel's broken elves.

During this post-Katrina time, my plans changed as quickly as my moods. One morning I'd know with certainty that I was going to get a PhD, become an environmental scientist, and somehow stop global warming (even though I was a math dunce). And so I began filling out applications for graduate ecology programs, albeit halfheartedly, since it was a long shot and I'd be piling student loans on top of Katrina debt. A week later, I'd decided to become a professional baker and started fooling around with the bread books I was accumulating. But then I'd sit in Miss Mabel's yard, staring at the children across the street in the school playground, and realize that my new true path was to turn this yard into a community garden for those children. If that didn't work, I'd become an artist and build giant papier-mâché virgins raising their fists in the air to make people think about what we were doing to Mother Earth. And the days passed with me lurching from one scheme to another.

My friends were patient. They gave me bath salts, self-help books, and free massages, and repeated teeth-grinding mantras like "Just be quiet and the path will open" and "Listen to your inner voices."

I didn't want to listen to my inner voices; they were scary. I was too depressed to sit inside behind a computer screen. And what for? Loyola had closed for the semester; we didn't know when or even if the college would reopen. During the day, the only thing that lifted my spirits was to sit outside on solid ground. That was home for now.

I discovered entirely by accident that I felt better if I was using my hands. There is an ancient wisdom in our hands, far more wisdom than in our brains. It started one morning when I found a garbage bag stuffed with yarn outside next to Miss Mabel's trash can. Suddenly I heard my Irish granny's voice: "Not too loose and not too tight."

I WAS SEVEN YEARS OLD THE YEAR MY PARENTS PULLED ME OUT OF SECOND GRADE FOR MY first trip to Ireland. It was April of 1970, the height of the Troubles. Belfast was on fire with widespread rioting, curfews, and house searches by the British army in my aunties' neighborhood. I remember the young British soldiers, the strange armored cars, the barbed-wire barricades. This place my parents called "home" felt sharp, metallic, and thorny to a golden California child, everything a shade of gray or black. I remember holding my auntie Ann's hand as we stepped carefully down a street littered with window glass and tear gas canisters the morning after a riot, my seven-year-old eyes scanning the ground and spotting a strange long, hard object. It was a six-inch rubber bullet; I took it back to California for second-grade show-and-tell. But most of all I remember the hypnotic comforting clicking of my granny's needles as she sat by her turf fire, stitching a little dress for my doll. Then she bought a pair of tiny red plastic needles and tried to teach me.

She lived in a rural village in County Derry where my father had grown up. It was a postcard vista of stone bridges, moss-covered churches, and frolicking lambs, except for the truckloads of British soldiers rumbling by her house and special forces troops swinging big guns around in her backyard, pointing them at her windows and inspecting under the cars. Where my father was raised, it was totally normal for my grandparents to be in the kitchen, my grandfather sitting at the table buried in the *Irish News* and my granny standing at the counter making bread, when a young man running from those soldiers would suddenly tap on the front door, open it without waiting for an answer, and jog silently through the house with a quick nod to my grandfather, a "Hullo, Mary," to my grandmother, and sprint out the back door, disappearing into the fields.

Thirty-five years later, as I stood beside Miss Mabel's trash can in Alabama, I realized I hadn't touched knitting needles since my granny held my tiny hands in hers. At seven, I thought knitting was boring. But the post-Katrina me suddenly understood how she raised nine children in a war zone, grew all their food, made all their clothes, and tended fifty chickens. She couldn't go to yoga or get massages. She knitted her way through it all, warm socks and Aran sweaters dropping from those needles. "Not too loose, not too tight" seemed like great life advice in my present circumstances.

I grabbed the yarn, marched into the local knit shop, bought needles and a five-dollar book called *How to Knit,* and sat night after night in our rented nest, needles furiously clicking away. During the day, I sat outside on the ground at Miss Mabel's for months after Katrina, knitting and watching the clouds change shape and bumblebees loading their back legs with pollen and the yard birds going about their business. As my nervous system calmed down, I began to ask different life questions. Before Katrina, my question had always been, *How can I make the world a better place? What can I* do*?* But when I returned to New Orleans for that one day and stood inside the ruins of our house, I realized how much harm I had done just by the way I lived, how I'd poisoned the water and soil. I'd always believed in the edict "Do no harm." But I had done so much harm even while I thought I was making the world a better place through activism, teaching, and writing.

During those months of sitting and knitting, I could feel my question changing from *What should I do?* to *How should I be?* As I sat there outside pondering this very new question, a woodpecker was knocking on the side of the house or mourning doves were splashing in the birdbath or a robin was pulling a worm out of the ground six feet away from me. I was surrounded by teachers and just didn't know it.

Years later, I stumbled on a newspaper article about the final sale of Miss Mabel's house in Montgomery. I had thought it very odd at the time that Miss Mabel's daughter never allowed anyone inside the big house. I'd skulked around, trying to peek in, but the windows were shuttered, not a snippet uncovered. I suspected that there were some valuable antiques inside. According to the article, Mabel's husband had died thirty years earlier, but he had been a collector of large stone German bird sculptures, some worth thousands of dollars. As I read, I realized that during all those months of ellipsis that I had been sitting in her garden, agonizing about the future and surrounded by the birds in her yard, just a few feet away, behind the shutters of that house, those stone birds sat in the dark in their own ghostly ellipsis, waiting to be sold on eBay.

WHEN I FOUND OUT LOYOLA WOULD REOPEN IN JANUARY, I FLEW TO CALIFORNIA TO SEE MY father before I returned to teach. He was withering away. Two months had passed since I'd last seen him. He'd been through heavy chemotherapy and had lost at least forty more pounds. One month he was out pruning his rosebushes. Two months later he was sitting at the window watching the gardener he'd hired prune them. He was a thin man to begin with, and I could feel his bony back when I hugged him.

My father couldn't tell a Mugimaki flycatcher from a Hudsonian godwit. But watching the birds was one thing he could still easily do and would be able to do until he died. Hummingbirds were his favorite. He had turned the yard into a hummingbird haven with bougainvillea covering the fences and stone walls. There were scores of trees, bushes, cacti, and other places for the hummers to weave their thimble-sized nests out of spider silk, lichen, feathers, vines, and moss. The eggs

are pea-sized, and the mothers build nests that stretch as the babies grow—imagine a crib that would grow with your baby up until it was a teenager. The female usually raises the young on her own and tolerates the male only briefly to mate.

Between the feeders and the nesting habitat he'd created, my father had attracted at least five hummingbird species. A rainbow of brilliant red-orange, glimmering green, violet, and dark pink birds zipped in and out of the flowering vines, even flying backward. They were noisy, too, making zinging and buzzing sounds as they jostled over their territories to defend the 1,500 flowers a day they needed to survive.

One day as we sat at his bay window, a hummingbird hovered right in front of us, looking in.

"You see," my father said, "it's come to tell me that the feeder is empty."

I rolled my eyes and thought, *Right, Dad.* Then he told me about a mockingbird that followed him around as he watered the plants. He said this bird started following him after our golden retriever Tara died. He believed this bird was the reincarnation of our dog, so he called the mockingbird Tara.

I thought my father was starting to lose his marbles, just a wee bit. But then I remembered that his mother—my grandmother the knitter—believed in the "wee people." She told her children that the hawthorn tree in a corner of a field was a "fairy tree," and that the muddy rings around it they saw in the morning were where the fairies held a dance the night before. The fairies were knee-height and wore funny hats, she told them. My father and his siblings scoffed at her stories, but as he grew near death, I could see that he was grappling with where he was headed and pondering the existence of unseen realms. He told me he was reading about angels. He was wondering how he was going to take care of us all, even after he died.

FIVE MONTHS AFTER KATRINA, IN JANUARY OF 2006, LOYOLA FINALLY REOPENED AND I returned to teach. Jim stayed in Montgomery with the dogs because half the housing in New Orleans had been destroyed or badly damaged. Rents had doubled. A friend offered a cheap room in her house on the "island"—what New Orleanians now called the areas of highest elevation that did not flood.

The island was an oasis of marzipan-filled almond croissants, double-shot cappuccinos, and shiny new laptops in cafés that had reopened. The universities were there. Bars were packed. The flooded part of the city, now called the Dead Zone, was about ten minutes east of us. A dark stinky stain that stretched for miles, it covered block after block of abandoned homes fronted by huge mounds of debris—rotting furniture, appliances, clothing, toys. Whole neighborhoods had become open caskets. Feral dogs darted between the houses and trash piles, furtive shadows. Every time I drove out to visit our bulldozed home I half expected mutants to jump out of the ruins.

In the new post-Katrina lexicon, the city had been divided into an island and a Dead Zone, and time had been divided into B.K. and A.K.—"before Katrina" and "after Katrina." My first A.K. morning in New Orleans that January, I woke early to a strange sound in a city—silence. I lay in bed in my friend's house and listened for several minutes, thinking about what that silence meant: all the people who hadn't returned, who might never return; the over 1,400 people who had drowned, including some of my neighbors.

Then cardinals began to click in my friend's yard.

That A.K. morning I didn't know that they may mate for life, that they can live fourteen years, and that they stay in the same territory, which meant that this yard was the cardinals' yard—not my friend's. And that cardinals "mate feed," the male bringing the choicest sunflower seeds from a feeder to the female waiting on a branch, where he feeds them to her, beak to beak.

But I did know this: the cardinal's metallic clicking meant that there was something beautiful, something wild, something *alive* in the hurricane-trashed yard. And suddenly that bird seemed like the most precious being on earth, like the first animal descending the plank from Noah's ark. I wanted to run outside and hug it.

The new human neighbors were inspiring, too. Early every morning, one neighbor slipped out the front door in a polka-dotted clown suit with a big red rubber nose. Another sat on his porch beating on bongos and singing an odd song to the trees for the pure joy of it. One night I leaned against our doorway and listened for an hour.

The houses were shotguns, long, skinny rectangles like railroad cars, just twelve feet wide and stretching into deep yards. A popular building design since the Civil War, they were painted bright purple, yellow, orange, sea-green, and tourmaline-blue with white trim, many with newly planted "We Believe" signs in their yards. One house was festooned with so many Christmas decorations you could barely see the building. A string of yellow happy-face lights wearing tiny Christmas hats covered the black wrought-iron fence. Huge blow-up Santas, reindeer, and cartoon dolls swayed in the breeze. It looked like the set for a Christmas porn flick. I loved walking by it.

The shotguns were so close together that you could hear neighbors on their porches. To the west of us, two women yelled "GIRL!" and "Amen!" morning and night. But often it was couples fighting over money, which I could relate to, since I had looming credit card bills for a new house full of stuff that had drowned and no idea how long I'd have my job.

That January I expected most people to be totally preoccupied with gutting their homes and rebuilding their lives. And they were. What I did not expect was that people were also already putting up Mardi Gras decorations and covering the houses that didn't flood with gold and purple streamers. At night, some were beginning the month of balls and parties and practice parades that starts right after New Year's. But Mardi Gras was the last thing I was interested in. To me it epitomized everything that was wrong with New Orleans. It had just been five months since Katrina, and half the city was inhabited exclusively by mold colonies and resembled a Hollywood set for a horror movie. The mail service didn't work. Most of the streetlights didn't work. Mountains of trash sat rotting everywhere. So now we were all going to get drunk for two weeks and throw tons of shiny beads made in China at each other?

Even though my new roommate's yard was still trashed and her roof needed fixing and she had a demanding new job in hurricane relief, she started talking about Mardi Gras right after I moved in. *What are we going to wear? Trish, we have to get our costumes ready,* she said, as if Mardi Gras were some kind of urgent mission. I was rifling through thrift-store racks to find clothes for teaching. Costumes weren't on my shopping list. I thought she was nuts. But I couldn't write her off as a party bubblehead; she didn't fit any of my rich white southern belle stereotypes. Her house was in a marginal neighborhood that had barely escaped the flood. There were drug dealers across the street that she was always calling the police about; she wasn't afraid of them (I was). She was fixing the damage to her home on her own and was as handy with a hammer as she was with glitter and beads and a sewing needle. She started bringing thrift-store ball gowns home, ignoring my eye rolling. I had to admire her spirit.

I began to understand this visceral attachment to New Orleans's unique culture one night when another New Orleanian friend invited me to a "goodbye party" for her flooded home. She'd spent seven years painstakingly redoing this old house, panel by panel; it was her pearl. Then it flooded. She decided to clean it up, sell it, and move to higher ground. I expected some wild voodoo ceremony with tearful speeches by her friends. But when we piled inside the dark, empty shell, they raised their glasses in a toast, said quietly, "Goodbye, House," and returned to her ruined yard of lemon trees.

We gathered around a rough wooden construction table, on which the hostess had placed two smelly cheeses and bottles of red wine. As we grazed, she plunked a large gray bowl on the ground, filled it with dog chow, and said to her dog, "The Last Supper." We drank as the sky turned the color of the Cabernet—the sunsets were spectacular because there was no electricity. Then, instead of reminiscing about the flooded house, all everyone talked about was how to scrounge up a costume for the upcoming parades. The chief organizer for one of the most famous parades was at this party. He placed a stack of newsletters titled *Le Monde de Merde* next to the smelly cheese. It read:

> We've learned a lot this past year . . . new meanings for "open house" and "waterfront property." We've learned that there are nine different types of mold and they all smell worse than a congressional appropriations committee . . . We've learned that FEMA's just another word for nothing left to lose. And all because the Army Corps of Engineers doesn't know the London Avenue Dike from a Bourbon Street Dyke . . . "C'est Levee," Life's a breach . . . so pop a cold one . . . and pretend that convoy of National Guard Hummers rolling by is just another parade.

His parade's theme was Ejaculation Routes, a critique of the city's lack of hurricane evacuation planning. "Come dressed as giant condoms," he told us.

Everybody started brainstorming how to create a condom suit. And suddenly Mardi Gras made so much sense to me.

**IN STAFF MEETINGS AT LOYOLA THE WEEK BEFORE THE SEMESTER STARTED, EVERYONE** looked shrunken, older. Over 60 percent of the faculty's and staff's homes had been damaged. People were crashing with relatives or living in motels or trailers. After our first department meeting, I commiserated with two professors who had lost their homes.

One professor had lost her childhood home in Gulfport, Mississippi. Her parents lived there next to an elderly disabled couple. The disabled couple didn't evacuate, so they drowned—one was in a wheelchair and the other was paralyzed. They had stayed in the house with their caretaker. They tried to convince the caretaker to save himself, but he wouldn't leave. He stayed until the water swept him away. He survived by clinging to a corner of the house, watching huge trailers turned into torpedoes by the flood slam into the professor's parents' home next door, destroying it. The professor was trying to take care of her distraught parents; they lived with her now. She was drinking a lot, she said.

The other professor had lived in my neighborhood for twenty years and raised a family there. We should never have been living there to begin with, he told me. I admired his brutal honesty. He said that the thing that depressed him the most was that humans just keep making the same mistakes over and over again.

"I wish all the politicians had drowned," he said.

I thought that because I'd lost a home, too, I had something in common with these new colleagues. But I quickly realized I had absolutely no clue what native New Orleanians were going through. Their friends had evacuated to Houston or Atlanta or Dallas; some were never coming back. My colleagues had not only lost homes, they'd lost their social support networks. One professor told me she'd raised a family in four different homes in New Orleans, all in one of the worst flood zones. Every house was gone; every store, church, and school.

The administration warned faculty to prepare to deal with distressed students. Many students were from New Orleans or the Gulf Coast. Most had spent that canceled fall semester temporarily enrolled in other colleges across the country, far from friends and family.

*I can handle this,* I thought. I've taught in one of the worst prisons in the country. I worked in a war zone for ten years. I'll get all my writing students out into the streets, into that Dead Zone. Reality will be our teacher, and our homework, to change that reality.

That first Monday morning, I arrived early. I wanted to make sure my office was bright and welcoming. I'd bought an electric teapot and stocked herbal teas, chocolates, and cookies. On the wall to the right of my desk, I taped Loyola's instructions for dealing with mental distress. There was a counseling hotline for students. I highlighted that number.

Then I watched through the glass wall in my second-story office as young people clad in bright colors and sporty new backpacks began to stream in from all directions like tropical birds. They gathered in the quad in little clumps under the outstretched arms of the statue of St. Iggy, hugging, squealing, crying, filling the quad with joy.

There was a soft knock on my door. A thin, dark-haired, nervous-looking young man stood there, clutching his class schedule as if it were a compass. He'd found his classroom, he told me, but there was no one there. Look, it's right across the hall from you, he said. He pointed up at the room number and then down at his schedule.

I examined the schedule. He'd found the right room, all right, but he was an hour early. I'm used to college students being late; I'd never had one who was an hour early for class. I invited him in.

"Where are you from?" I asked.

He was a freshman, from Mississippi, from Pass Christian.

I remembered a ghostly exit sign on the highway on that first horrific drive back to New Orleans, a sign now pointing to nowhere. Pass Christian had been flattened; it was one of the worst-hit areas on the Gulf Coast.

Oh my god, why did I ask this fucking question?

I forced myself to breathe. Then I glanced quickly at the highlighted hotline number taped to my wall, dreading his answer to the next question I had to ask.

"Is your family okay?"

"Yes, ma'am."

A 39-foot wall of water had slammed his childhood home. All that was left was a concrete slab. This was his first semester of college. He was going to be a music major. We both played the piano. I told him I'd lost my home, too. I praised him for being early to class.

He said that he had been very forgetful since the storm. I told him that we were all forgetful because we were trying to comprehend something really big and terrible. Our brains were like overloaded hard drives. We needed to delete some stuff in order to heal. So what if you couldn't remember when your classes were or your new address or your new cell number? Just write everything down, I told him. I carried a small notebook everywhere. He nodded.

Then we joked about the difference between his 39 feet of water and my 11.5 feet. We shared a few tears. After that, we just sat there. We didn't need to say much. I knew that everything he wore—the clean jeans, the T-shirt, the sneakers, the book bag—was brand-new, perhaps gifts from a stranger or church group. That he'd lost his music collection, every book he ever had, maybe a pet, even a neighbor. That after several months of losing control over everything, he and I were walking around in a daze, clinging to class schedules and grateful for a room with a number on it and a time when everyone would be sitting in neat little rows, snickering or surfing the internet instead of listening to a writing instructor warn about run-on sentences or the perils of participles.

At the end of that first crazy day, students and faculty gathered on the lawn around the statue of St. Iggy to watch a PowerPoint photo presentation on Katrina projected onto a building wall. Everyone was crying. Then I noticed the line of more than a thousand candles on the balcony to honor the dead. I'd discovered how many had drowned near us only when I stumbled on a map of our neighborhood in *The New York Times* months after Katrina. Every dot on the map was a neighbor who had drowned in their home. I sat down on the lawn at Loyola and cried, too.

I left the campus and walked past Loyola's gorgeous Canterbury-inspired cathedral as the sky was turning dark pink. Large flocks of black birds, an acrobatic swirl of black and purple, were crossing St. Charles Avenue, leaving the huge park across the street, funneling into their roost at the top of the cathedral. They were European starlings, those silver-speckled black birds that create murmurations.

My favorite writer on birds, Lyanda Haupt, calls a murmuration a "flock-prayer."[1] And as I left the university that first day, that huge swirling flock did seem like a prayer. *We are alive!* the starlings seemed to be saying, just like the cardinal in my new yard.

On the second day of school, another student cried in my office. A gorgeous green-eyed model, she had recently survived cardiac arrest brought on by bulimia. As she talked, I noticed her receding hairline and the gray hair in her dark mane. She was twenty-one.

She was in my creative writing class and really wanted to write. After years working as a model, she was tired of being objectified. She wanted to change the way women were portrayed in the media. I sent her to the library to check out *Reviving Ophelia* by Mary Pipher—book as medicine. I prescribed many books during that strange semester. Read it, I told her, and get back in here. We're going to get you published.

Then there was the nineteen-year-old freshman determined to be a science fiction writer; he'd been writing stories since he was a kid. He marched into my office, plunked a stack of papers on my desk, and announced: "My writing portfolio." I sent him straight to the college newspaper. A New Orleanian sports fanatic, he was assistant sports editor within two months. Within a year, he'd become an editor, and the newspaper had won a national award.

And so they came, one after another, with their stories, their truths. After class some days there would be two or three sitting on the floor in the carpeted hallway, waiting. I began individualizing assignments to help students write through their fears and rage. I didn't know what I was doing as a teacher, but I did know the power of writing things down.

From the moment I looked into my new students' faces, I felt so much joy. For the first time since the hurricane, I felt like I belonged somewhere, that I had a purpose. There was sadness, weariness, and fear in those very young eyes. Parents had lost jobs. Families who had lost their homes were in Houston or Atlanta. Some students were working over thirty hours a week in restaurants to cover tuition. But I also saw hope in their eyes, and I wanted to channel that hope. I'd returned to New Orleans full of we-can-do-it spirit, imagining that it was going to be like Managua in the 1980s, a roll-up-your-sleeves partying revolution. We can write our way out of this, I kept telling my students. If you're pissed off, sad, scared—write it down. Let's take a Category 5 lemon and turn it into a swimming pool full of lemonade. And if you want to be published, get into my office.

The fact that I had lost my own home now seemed like a tremendous teaching advantage. If my students could see me every day, standing in front of them smiling, crying, swearing, laughing, and just plowing ahead, it would help them. They needed an example of a strong adult who could lose it for a minute and then get right back to work. I needed them to need that example. I was determined to be that example.

But I also needed help. Fast.

Before Katrina, as a journalist and news junkie, for twenty years I had always started my day with the newspapers or NPR. But after Katrina, I couldn't do that—the news was too dire. There were stories about asbestos clouds floating in the air from demolitions minutes away. There were reports from scientists measuring carcinogenic benzene in the soil from oil spills during the flooding. And climatologists were already discussing the next monster hurricane season fueled by global warming. If I started the day with all this, I'd just go back to bed. I desperately needed another news source.

I thought about my father sitting at his bay window in California, watching his hummingbirds and talking to Tara, his mockingbird. I talked to him almost every day now, and instead of discussing his next big date with the chemo chair or his three anti-nausea medications, he talked about his birds or his plants. Even though he was getting sicker, by filling his feeders he was still able to care for something. He was determined to focus on whatever joy he could squeeze out of every day he had left.

I'd rejected many life lessons my father had tried to teach me because I was so angry at how I'd been treated compared to my brothers, just because I was female. But he didn't need to tell me to go out and buy feeders or watch birds. I just heard in his voice how much joy those ten-dollar feeders brought him, even as his life was ebbing away.

Now I think about this as a teacher—about how much we teach just by being and doing, not by lecturing and preaching. Sometimes I feel my students' eyes on me, especially when it seems like the world is falling apart. They watch the way I move through this world, how I face reality, how I find daily joy. And I realize that during that final year of his life, my father was preparing the most important lesson plan of all for his children: how to live while you know you are dying.

Maybe there was something to this birdwatching business.

I walked into a hardware store, bought a bag of seed and two bird feeders, and hung them on the back fence of the hurricane-trashed yard of my temporary New Orleans home. The next morning, I began a ritual that became a lifestyle: sitting on the back stoop with a cup of coffee and starting the day with "The Sparrow Show," live and in color. As I watched those feeders, instead of thinking about where I was going to live and work, about what was going to happen to Louisiana, to the Gulf Coast, to the planet with global warming, I started wondering why one sparrow was lording it over all the others and hogging the seed. I started thinking about the sparrows' resilience, their pluckiness, their focus on their most immediate needs. If my feeders were empty, they went somewhere else. If they lost a nest, they built another. The sparrows didn't have the time or energy to sit around grieving. They clung to the chain-link fence in raggedy lines waiting for the feeders, heckling one another like drunken Mardi Gras revelers on Bourbon Street. Their sparring over seeds made me laugh. And I've been laughing ever since.

CHAPTER 3

# Song of the House Sparrow

*There is only one question:*
*how to love this world.*

MARY OLIVER

For every birdwatcher, there is a portal bird, one that opens your eyes to a world governed by curiosity, daily surprises, and sudden intimate glimpses into feathered lives. Some birders love to brag about rare birds they've seen on birding junkets, exotic additions to their "life lists." But for most birders, including me, that portal bird is the most common of creatures, the house sparrow, a scrappy little brown-and-black bird. The males sport black bibs on their throats. The females are a dusky brown. Invariably they are the first bird my new birding students tell me about breathlessly—the "adorable little puffballs" that they find chirping inside campus hedges during their first solo birding expedition on a 20-degree January morning.

Truly global citizens, house sparrows live everywhere but Antarctica. In the United States, you'll find them 280 feet below sea level in Death Valley and 10,000 feet above sea level in the Rocky Mountains. Go to the beaches of the Dead Sea and there are house sparrows chirping at 1,400 feet below sea level. Climb the Himalayas and you'll find them at 14,763 feet.[1] And they live in every elevation in between, even inside buildings. Whole flocks thrive inside warehouses, supermarkets, and garden centers (just follow the chirps at your nearest Lowe's or Home Depot). If I were creating a future colony on another planet, the house sparrow would be the first avian astronaut.

As I hung out with them before work in New Orleans, I had absolutely no idea that my new little friends were also among the most hated bird species on earth, rivaling pigeons and European starlings, all despised because of their numbers. "Sparrow Clubs" killed hundreds of millions of sparrows during extermination campaigns in England from the 1700s to the 1930s. Google "house sparrows," and one of the first questions that appears is "Are house sparrows bad?" Like European starlings, they are one of the few bird species not protected by federal law; it is legal to trap and kill them. And dozens of online resources will show you how: gas them; sever their spinal cord; put them in a bag and shoot them in the head; stuff them in a drawstring bag and then smash them against a wall, tree trunk, or flat rock; squeeze them to death (chest-thoracic compression); chop off their heads; drown them; or stick them in ziplock bags and freeze them.

Their history as international outlaws has not helped them. In 1960, a house sparrow allegedly carried a burning cigarette butt to the thatched roof of a cottage in Suffolk, England, and set it on fire.[2] And in 2005, in Leeuwarden, the Netherlands, after volunteers from a hundred countries spent a month setting up 4,321,000 dominoes in preparation to set a new Guinness World Record, a house sparrow flew in through a window, hit a domino, and knocked down 23,000 before the rest of the setup could be saved. That bird was executed on the spot. Its execution caused a furor in Holland, and this avian criminal became a Dutch martyr, known as the Domino Sparrow. It was later stuffed and displayed in a museum exhibit.[3]

I understand the strong emotions. If you're asking a bluebird house manager like me about house sparrows in Vermont, and one of these feathered raiders just got into your bluebird's house and murdered the entire family, leaving the grisly evidence behind, then you can imagine why for just a second I would love to catch that black-bibbed assassin in my hands and squeeze him until his eyeballs pop out. But I would never do it. If these little birds hadn't caught my attention and lifted my spirits all those years ago in New Orleans, I probably wouldn't even know what a bluebird was, much less be managing their houses.

Today these unpaid teaching assistants help me teach students to be critical thinkers as they analyze debates raging over what constitutes an invasive species, what "natural" even means, and how we should relate to other beings. House sparrows do compete with some native species for nesting sites, especially bluebirds, and will kill nesting birds and nestlings to take over those nests.[4] They could be seen as invaders, conquerors, and imperialists continually expanding their feathered empires. But I believe we hate house sparrows simply because they are so much like us.

World house sparrow expert J. Denis Summers-Smith, a Scottish physicist who studied these birds from 1947 until he died at ninety-nine in 2020, theorized that the sparrow's march across the globe began at the end of the last Ice Age, some 12,000 years ago, when humans began cultivating crops. As our ancestors shifted from harvesting wild grass seeds to deliberately planting the seeds, *Passer domesticus*, or "the sparrow of the house," took note. Wherever farmers appeared, this little bird followed the trail of spilled grains and seeds. Summers-Smith believed the earliest sparrows were African and that the bird followed humans out of Africa and into the Middle East and Southern Europe. The shelters humans built provided the nooks and crannies the house sparrow needed to weave its soft soccer-ball-sized nest. Later, as our species built cities, this bird followed us again, finding a bonanza of food scraps everywhere.[5]

Roman invaders took the bird with them to Britain as food for troops, which is why it is known worldwide as the English sparrow. (Songbirds are still a delicacy in some parts of the Mediterranean.)[6]

In 1850, the Brooklyn Institute in New York had eight pairs brought over—not to eat, like the Romans, but because European immigrants simply missed the birds.[7]

This species is not migratory and typically stays within a mile of the nest from which it hatched. But within a few decades of those first eight pairs docking in New York, house sparrows had chirped their way from sea to shining sea, to thirty-five US states and five Canadian territories. They spread across the United States mostly by their own devices. According to British naturalist Mark Cocker, author of my go-to book for global avian history—the encyclopedic *Birds & People*—this bird hitched rides on trains, ships, even planes. In Brazil, Helmut Sick, an expert on Brazil's birds, watched house sparrows sailing on ships down South America's fourth-largest river, the São Francisco. They established themselves on the Falkland Islands by stowing away on a Uruguayan whaling vessel. Cocker writes that the "most remarkable stowaways" boarded a ship in Bremerhaven, Germany, staying onboard until they reached Australia, where the bird is now as common as the kangaroo.[8]

Just two decades after the house sparrow landed in the United States, the state of Pennsylvania declared war on it; other states followed suit. In 1883, the *Pennsylvania Messenger* editorialized: "The little sparrow has been declared an outlaw by legislative enactment and they can be killed at any time. They were imported into this country . . . as a destroyer of insects, but it has been found they are not insectivorous. Besides they drive away all our native songbirds . . . Let them all be killed."[9]

Late-nineteenth-century bird lovers believed that house sparrows thrived by pushing at least seventy native birds out of their nesting areas. But Summers-Smith pointed out that during that same period in the United States, Americans radically transformed the landscape, converting fields and wetlands to cities and suburbs. The United States lost almost half its wetlands by the beginning of the twentieth century.[10] Most native birds could not survive in the new concrete urban habitat, Summers-Smith argued. So the house sparrow simply did what it's always done—took advantage of the new ecological niche we created for it.* Another reason the bird spread so fast is that not everyone hated it. In 1877, Colonel William Rhodes, the commissioner of agriculture and colonisation for Quebec, who is also credited with personally bringing house sparrows to Portland, Maine, wrote:

> I imagine no live Yankee would wish now to be without the life and animation of the house sparrow in his great cities . . . I admit the bird is a little blackguard—fond of low society and full of fight, stealing, and love-making—but he is death on insects, fond of citizen life, and in every way suitable to be an inhabitant of the New World.[11]

My favorite house sparrow story is not of this little bird sailing down mighty Brazilian rivers or disrupting international domino tournaments. It is the story of how three tiny sparrow nestlings tamed one of the most notorious criminals in prison history, Robert Franklin Stroud, known as the Birdman of Alcatraz.

Stroud spent more time in solitary confinement than almost any prisoner in US history, forty-two of his fifty-four years in prison in an isolation cell smaller than my chicken coop.† He became famous when Burt Lancaster played him in the 1962 film *Birdman of Alcatraz*. The grandson of a judge and the son of an abusive alcoholic father, according to the movie and a biography, Stroud ran away from home at thirteen, traveled with hoboes, and then worked in Alaska at the age of eighteen building railway lines and ports (he may have been a pimp on the side). It was there in Juneau that he fought and killed a man because of a conflict over his girlfriend or a prostitute, depending on the version of events you believe—it's a murky story. In prison, Stroud stabbed another prisoner, and then stabbed and killed an allegedly

---

* In some places, that niche is disappearing. London lost 70 percent of its house sparrows between 1994 and 2001. And Europe has lost some 247 million house sparrows since 1980—one in six birds, according to the Royal Society for the Protection of Birds (RSPB). In 2002, the RSPB added the house sparrow to its Red List, signaling that it is a species of global conservation concern.

† According to Amnesty International, Albert Woodfox spent forty-three years in solitary confinement in Louisiana.

abusive guard. A judge sentenced him to hang, but Stroud's mother petitioned President Woodrow Wilson for mercy. In 1920, Stroud's sentence was commuted to life in solitary. He was sent to Leavenworth Penitentiary in Kansas.

According to the incredible story told by Stroud's biographer, Thomas E. Gaddis, in *Birdman of Alcatraz,* Stroud's path to birds began with a thunderstorm. One day during his exercise time in the prison yard, a violent storm hit. Gaddis wrote that Stroud noticed a fluttering in the corner of the yard where branches had tumbled over a wall. There he found a busted nest with four tiny nestlings in it, one dead, the other three alive. He scooped them up and hid them in a handkerchief.

In his cell, Stroud heated a sock over a light bulb and set the babies in the heated sock-nest. One had a broken leg, which Stroud splinted with a match and thread. For days he shared his meager rations with them, bread crumbs dipped in cold vegetable soup. As the nestlings begged for food, opening their beaks all day long, Stroud realized they needed protein. He stalked cockroaches and beetles in his cell, catching them in a rag and smashing them, and then making an insect/bread crumb paste. His exercise time in the prison yard became insect-hunting expeditions as he gathered grasshoppers, crickets, and butterflies for his babies, now named Percy and Runt (he gave his third nestling to another inmate).

Stroud had big plans for Percy and Runt. He couldn't escape the prison, but these two little birds were going to liberate him even inside those walls. He'd learned from a sympathetic guard that the deputy warden was a bird lover who raised canaries. So he began training his sparrows, rigorously, using beetles as a reward system. When Percy and Runt were ready, Stroud asked the guard to tell the warden that he wanted to see him.

As the warden entered his cell, Stroud snapped his fingers. Percy and Runt came flying out of nowhere and landed on his palm, startling and delighting the warden. Then Stroud whistled and turned his head to the side. The sparrows dove into his shirt pocket to retrieve their beetle treats. But this was the master trick that changed Stroud's life and avian history: he snapped his fingers on both hands twice, and the sparrows flew to his bed, lay down on their backs, and raised their feet in the air, playing dead.

The warden howled. He told Stroud he wanted to teach the same trick to his canaries. And he agreed to let Stroud purchase birdseed to feed his talented wards. This was the beginning of a distinguished ornithological career in which Stroud raised hundreds of canaries, conducted experiments to find a cure for hemorrhagic septicemia in birds, published two scientific books on bird diseases, and corresponded by mail with hundreds of bird breeders and enthusiasts who requested his advice. Stroud entered prison with a third-grade education, but because of university extension courses, he learned to use a microscope, taught himself to read scientific journal articles in Spanish and German, and died in prison as an internationally respected ornithologist.[12] In one of his books he wrote:

> The lives of literally thousands of birds, the heartbreaks of blasted hopes have gone into these typed pages . . . For every truth I have blundered through a hundred errors. I have killed birds when it was almost as hard as killing one's own children . . . I have dedicated my book to the proposition that fewer birds shall suffer because their diseases are not understood.[13]

*Stroud's Digest on the Diseases of Birds,* a 483-page tome illustrated by the author and published in 1964, still gets five-star reviews on Amazon today.

Stroud's mother and followers failed to get Stroud out of solitary despite years of petitioning. But this is something that they probably could not understand: as long as he was allowed to keep his birds, Robert F. Stroud was never alone.* Gaddis wrote: "Birds once stood upon his gallows; later they stood upon his shoulders and tangled

---

* In 1942 Stroud was transferred from Leavenworth Prison to Alcatraz. He was forced to leave his birds and lab equipment behind. He never touched a bird again. He spent his final years researching the history of the federal prison system and published the 522-page book, *Looking Outward: A History of the U.S. Prison System from Colonial Times to the Formation of the Bureau of Prisons.*

their feet in his hair. Barred from people for all of his life, he found his greatest love elsewhere."[14]

And sitting on my back stoop in New Orleans, forty-three years after Robert Stroud died in prison, I started to fall in love with birds, too.

**AFTER THE HOUSE SPARROWS, I BEGAN TO NOTICE OTHER BIRDS. ONE MORNING I STEPPED** out of my favorite coffee shop near Loyola, and a flash of brilliant green streaked over me—a flock of wild parrots just like the ones in Lakeview and my parents' canyon. They settled on the top of a palm tree in the median, squawking. Eyes skyward, focused on those gorgeous, exuberant birds, I charged right into several lanes of traffic and almost got hit by a taxi.

Every day on my way to work, I scanned the sky for those parrots. Don't google "urban parrots" unless you are looking for a major hobby. I learned that there are flocks of wild urban parrots all over the United States. The New Orleanian birds were called monk parakeets—parakeets are smaller members of the parrot family. They had been living in the city for over fifty years, and local ornithologists believed they were probably escaped pets mainly from Argentina. Out of over 350 parrot species, the monk parakeet is the only one that builds a nest, often on top of palm trees, on stadium lights, and on power stations. The ultimate urbanites, these birds build condo-type nests, creating 20 to 200 separate nesting chambers in one parakeet condo that can be as big as a refrigerator and weigh up to a ton.[15] According to the Cornell Lab of Ornithology, the snug condo nests are probably the reason these birds can survive winters in Chicago and New York.

I went down a parrot hole and read Mark Bittner's *The Wild Parrots of Telegraph Hill,* his deeply philosophical memoir about how a failed rock guitarist who was homeless in San Francisco for fourteen years became a parrot expert. Bittner had a Zen Buddhist approach to life. I was struck by how he spent fourteen years waiting for whatever it was he was supposed to do to just appear. And it did one day when he stood for hours, St. Francis like, arms extended and hands full of birdseed.

I showed the documentary based on Bittner's book in my classes and then sent a copy to my father in California. I thought it might take his mind off the cancer. And it did for a few weeks. My parents loved it so much that they decided to try Bittner's feeding approach. They covered the glass tables on their deck with seed and waited. And the parrots came. And they came and they came until they covered the glass tables and the deck chairs and ate all the seed and left piles of poop everywhere. And they kept coming like a plague of screeching locusts until my parents realized that they were not Saint Francis or Mark Bittner. They loved the birds, but not their poop or their infernal squawking in the morning.

The parakeets and sparrows helped me slow down and savor tiny moments of joy; they were teaching me how to be. I thought maybe they could help my fifty-five stressed-out writing students, too. So I created a new homework assignment, instructing my students to pick a living creature, anything—a bug, bird, squirrel, rabbit—to watch that creature for fifteen minutes a day, and then to journal about it. I wanted my students to see the new life hatching and molting around them, despite the devastation.

Loyola is right across the street from Audubon Park, a 300-acre marshy bird sanctuary full of century-old live oaks dripping with Spanish moss. It was named after John James Audubon, the continent's most famous bird artist, who lived in New Orleans in the 1820s; he painted some of his best portraits there. The large glass wall in my classroom looked out over that park, and I found myself staring longingly through it as I lectured my students on journalistic skills and ethics. Outside, joggers wound their way around serpentine paths that graced the former French sugar plantation. Ducks perched in the trees and splashed in the water. Young lovers and musers sat on the benches or lay on blankets contemplating the clouds.

I started going into the park between classes, to eat lunch and hold office hours. The young assistant sports editor often joined me to discuss writing and our favorite books. The beautiful young woman struggling with bulimia, who had just published her first column, also came. We sat on the bench facing Bird Island, an important nesting area for birds in the city. As we ate lunch, egrets, herons, and ducks went about their avian business.

Whenever I felt overwhelmed, Audubon Park was an instant dose of peace, a big green chill pill one minute away. Out the door of the university I went like a zombie, pulled across the street by the soft breeze rippling the water, the huge elephant ears twisting slowly on the muddy banks, and those placid ducks vacuuming up the duckweed, the world's smallest flowering plant. I particularly loved to watch the turtles, large and small, basking on logs in the water. While they sunned themselves, they stuck their four legs out of their shells, as if they were flying. It looked as if they felt so much joy out there in the sun. I suppose I related to them, too, because they carried their homes on their back.

I started to love and need that park so much that I wanted to know more about it and more about the birds. I didn't even know what a mallard duck was at that time. So I asked Bob Thomas, a conservation biologist at Loyola, to take my students and me on a bird walk.

He told us that at least 15 percent of the US population calls themselves birdwatchers.* I was fascinated by how he described a taxonomy of birdwatchers, not just the birds. There were the extreme listers, who raced around from one species to another, building their life lists. And there were birders who could sit and watch just one bird for an hour. Some birdwatchers listed only the birds they'd seen on television. Some listed only dead birds. Some listed birds they saw in their yard. There were also different field guides. He recommended a funny one to identify bird poop on your windshield called *What Bird Did That?*

He showed us how to identify birds by watching the way they flew, their colors in the light, the distance they flew, where they flew from, and where they landed.

"It's like detective work," he said.

The phrase "detective work" is what hooked me. So birdwatching is like investigative journalism, I thought. You observe. You listen. You take good notes. You piece together clues. I loved doing all these things as a journalist. I wasn't ready to call myself a birder yet—I didn't

* This figure varies depending on the source and how "birder" or "birdwatcher" is defined.

even own binoculars. I just enjoyed watching the sparrows and the parakeets. But birding and birders suddenly didn't seem so weird.

I began taking all my writing classes into the park. We'd sit on the grass, spread all over the place, observe, scribble, observe, scribble. Some students liked it so much that they started going on their own and writing about it. My star student, the assistant sports editor, fell in love with ducks. One day while sitting on a bench, distracted in a young writer's reverie, he looked down to find a mallard pair inspecting his suede sneakers. He began visiting this mallard pair every day, just before lunch. In a paper he wrote: "And so the days passed—watching them swim, closing my eyes but hearing their webbed stomps and chattering beaks nearby. I began to nab slices of bread my roommate bought to make salami sandwiches he never ate and fed it to the two of them."

He became curious about duck migration and the comings and goings of all the ducks in the park. In a paper he read to his classmates, he reported that some birds migrate mind-boggling distances: the Arctic tern logs 20,000 miles a year.

"That's 250 trips between New Orleans and Baton Rouge," he told his classmates. "It would take an LSU student who drove home every weekend his entire undergraduate education to cover that distance.

"These ducks face a difficult and dangerous journey every year," he said, pointing at the feathered residents of Bird Island. "And they come back here. They're like us—tough, like Katrina evacuees. We were scattered all over, but we made it back home."

**I FOUND MYSELF SPENDING MORE AND MORE TIME OUTSIDE, BY MYSELF AND WITH MY** classes. I immediately felt calmer, and so did my students. But I was teaching journalism and didn't want them to ignore the facts. I struggled to strike a balance in assignments: to teach them to see the clown slipping out of his house early in the morning, to see the tourists swaying to the brass band under purple parasols in the French Quarter, to see the cardinals and sparrows in the bushes, but also to see the people living under bridges and in rotting, abandoned buildings in the Dead Zone. So I sent them out to interview people, and I started bringing in speakers like Jesús, a Mexican worker who was gutting poisoned homes and cleaning out the flooded basements of hospitals without protective clothing or equipment, handling biohazards without even a decent mask. Part of a silent, underpaid invisible army, Jesús told my students how he'd been brought in on a giant ship by a local company along with hundreds of other workers. They were living on that ship docked at the city's edge, fifty workers per large room in bunk beds stacked to the ceiling.*

I brought in another guest speaker, a young man from the National Guard who had just returned from duty in Iraq. I'd met him in my favorite bar, where I often stopped to sip whiskey and gut my way through the scary stories in the newspapers before heading home. The Maple Leaf Bar, or the Leaf, as locals called it, had a speakeasy feel, with a perpetual smoky haze smudging bloodred walls and a bartender in a halter top and beaded headgear. It claimed to host "the longest-running poetry reading in North America." The ashes of the poet who started it were supposedly buried under the patio.

The first thing I noticed about the young guardsman, besides the fact that he was very attractive, with jet-black hair and large strong hands, was a certain coiled muscularity. It was familiar to me—that hyper-readiness to spring into action. We started chatting the way strangers do in bars in New Orleans. He was twenty-seven, from Mobile, Alabama. Stirred by President Bush's call to defend the nation, he'd signed up for military service immediately after the 9/11 attacks. He'd been in Iraq nearly a year when the military pulled his unit out and sent them straight to New Orleans right after the flood.

"This feels like Baghdad," he said, sucking the life out of a cigarette. His right knee was doing a little jig under the table.

I knew that he and the other very young guardsmen and -women

---

* The New Orleans cleanup is a very dirty story. In interviews with more than 1,000 immigrant workers lured there to rebuild, the Southern Poverty Law Center (SPLC) discovered that US contractors and subcontractors paid by FEMA were refusing to pay millions of dollars in wages while forcing workers to live and work in dangerous conditions. The SPLC filed three major lawsuits on the workers' behalves, winning millions in settlements for unpaid labor and abuses. See the SPLC report "Broken Levees, Broken Promises," SPLC's Immigrant Justice Project website (https://www.splcenter.org/issues/immigrant-justice), and the powerful book *The Great Escape: A True Story of Forced Labor and Immigrant Dreams in America* by Saket Soni.

roaming the streets in creepy camo-covered Humvees were the same young people who'd been ordered to kick in our swollen doors and search our homes for bodies. Many were from the flood zone themselves and had lost their own family homes. They were the ones who had found my drowned neighbors before we were allowed to return. I felt so grateful to them for doing the hardest of jobs. As I listened to him, I wondered if he'd been in my neighborhood, maybe even in my little house. I didn't ask.

Because of that gratitude, I found myself in a serious moral quandary. I'd been a die-hard peace activist since I was nineteen years old. I couldn't stand George Bush. I thought the Iraq War was a crime. I helped found a peace group in Montgomery to try to stop that war. For six months before the war started, every Monday at noon we stood on the marble steps of Alabama's state capitol building—a block from where Dr. Martin Luther King Jr. gave one of his most famous speeches—and we protested. Montgomery is home to the Air War College and a very pro-military town. People drove by at noon shouting at us and giving us the finger. We were not a popular group.

*I have to tell this young guardsman the truth,* I thought. I owe him that.

I waited for him to pause, let him sip his whiskey, and tried to keep my voice calm as I explained why I thought George W. Bush was a war criminal who should be behind bars.

My new buddy leaned forward and squinted at me. Then he slammed the table and laughed. He thought this was great. George Bush was at the top of his shit list, too. He was sick over what he'd seen in Iraq. So as the bar filled with regulars, we drank some more and yelled about George for a while. George had just given his 5,000-word State of the Union Address and dedicated a mere 161 words to the destroyed Gulf Coast. Then he toured New Orleans in a helicopter and told the press that it was "a heck of a place to bring your family."

I didn't want to ask my new friend too much about Iraq. I really hate it when people ask "So, how was Guatemala?" What do you say? Oh yeah, it was great. Lots of Mayan pyramids and bodies tossed on the roadside with their wrists bound with barbed wire.

But he told me anyway, a horrific detail here and there, in between swearing, silence, and cigarette sucks. His marriage fell apart when he returned. His wife couldn't understand what he was going through. He was always reaching for his gun.

I asked him to talk to my classes. Many of my students love George Bush, I told him. They think the invasion of Iraq was a good idea. You could change the path of a young life.

The guardsman was afraid he couldn't sit in a college classroom for an hour without a cigarette, and I didn't know how to disable Loyola's smoke alarm. But a week later he overcame his fear and strolled in in his jeans and T-shirt, looking like one of my students. The girls checked him out and I could see they approved. He sat down, took off his baseball cap, and held it in his two hands. Then he began moving the cap round and round in a slow circle.

He was twenty-four when he joined the National Guard because of "a sense of patriotism," and to pay off college loans. One month after the United States invaded Iraq, he was sent to the Middle East.

"Welcome to Iraq. Here's your gas mask," his workmates told him.

Suddenly he was living in 130-degree weather and dealing with giant camel spiders. There was trash everywhere and it stank. At first he thought M4 carbine assault rifles and missile launchers on trucks were "pretty cool." Then there were the bombs hidden in dead dogs at the roadside, and decapitated Iraqis that insurgents had made "examples" of.

"You have to partition your mind," he told my students, looking down at his rotating baseball cap.

What he could not partition was the growing sense that he'd been sent there under false pretenses. He no longer believed the United States had invaded Iraq just to oust Saddam Hussein; it was a "flawed effort to impose democracy" on a very complex culture. He no longer believed in his military superiors or the leadership in Washington; they just thought the troops were "expendable numbers."

"There are people in charge of large groups who shouldn't be in charge of a 7-Eleven. And it's lives they're playing with. Our major general wanted to die a badass. So he drove alone from base to base. They ambushed him, cut his throat, dragged him through the streets."

I was getting a little nervous for my buddy. He was swearing more and couldn't sit still. His right knee was doing its jiggle dance and his baseball cap was still making its slow rounds. He needed a cigarette break. I should teach him to knit, I thought—whiskey for the hands. He wouldn't make eye contact with my students and kept glancing at me furtively. It was the hunted look of an animal who wants to run and hide. I reassured him with my eyes, ESP-ing him, *Please breathe.*

"The media doesn't show the bodies, the coffins," he said. "That's reality." He "hated" the "slanted and idealized" televised war coverage, specifically Fox News.

A student asked what it was like for him in New Orleans with all the military presence, the camouflaged Humvees patrolling the city and the Black Hawks thundering over us.

When he drives around New Orleans, he can't help it, he said. He's still in that military convoy: "Every obstacle could be a life-or-death situation. Every traffic jam is a potential ambush. Every bystander could be the enemy."

Every day in New Orleans he had to fight the urge to ram people off the road as he'd done in Iraq: "You're used to dealing with things a certain way because it's your ass. You'd be surprised at the things you get used to."

Then a student asked, "What was the most interesting thing you saw in Iraq?"

He paused and stared out beyond that classroom.

"I saw a huge flock of black birds. I timed it. It took an hour for them to fly over me. It was my most peaceful moment. It was so nice to see something so beautiful in the middle of all this crap."

For all of us, sitting in that classroom in a city in ruins, the young guardsman's focus on beauty in the midst of ugliness was something we could relate to. My students were struck by the bird story. One young man wrote in a paper: "I learned that sometimes, even when it seems nothing can be salvaged, beauty comes in different shapes and forms and flies by like a flock of birds."

I imagined the young guardsman on patrol in the 130-degree desert, sweating, loaded down with heavy guns and gear, sucking on that cigarette, and suddenly looking up to see a feathered mass roiling toward him. He was witnessing a murmuration, much larger but similar to the ones I loved to watch at sunset as starlings swirled around Loyola. I could see him halting abruptly, glancing around quickly to make sure it was safe, and then sitting down, tipping his head back, and wondering as hundreds of thousands, maybe even millions of black birds poured over him for a solid hour. The sky filled with something other than the steely grays of war and instruments of death, birds dancing through the air instead of fighter jets.

Birds as respite. Birds as refuge.

**I WANTED TO TAKE MY STUDENTS ON A FIELD TRIP. SO I TOOK THEM TO MY RUINED HOME TO** teach them how to interview a disaster victim—me—thinking this would be uplifting, since I was obviously okay. We drove into the Dead Zone and over to my house, now a bulldozed pile of rubble. I'd been to the site a few times on archeological digs. Most recently, I'd gone there at night with a girlfriend and a bottle of champagne for my own goodbye ceremony. That night the whole area was dark and sour-smelling, no electricity, not a human for a mile. But a bright moon smiled upon us as we swigged champagne right out of the bottle. Then we picked up a concrete chunk of my bulldozed home and hurled it through the windshield of the flood-ruined Toyota truck I'd stupidly left behind. "Do it again!" my buddy shouted. We laughed like maniacs at the smashing sound. It was better than months of therapy.

After all that, I thought it would be easy to stand on the rubble and let my students interview me about what had happened. I was done with emotion. But grief is sneaky. I was as surprised as they were when I had a meltdown right in front of them, cursing and crying.

"WRITE!" I growled, pacing back and forth, waving my arms around. "Don't just stand there. Get those pens moving. Come on. Ask me a question. But you damn well better not ask me how I feel. NEVER ask a disaster victim how they feel. You know how they feel? Like SHIT. Got it?"

My students stood in a line, staring at me with big eyes, pens frozen mid-sentence. Then an older student from Spain, a woman studying psychology, began asking questions in a gentle, kind voice. She must have been the only one who'd read the assigned chapter about reporting on "Disasters, Weather, and Tragedies." She asked me to share a story of a special moment. She didn't interrogate me; she really wanted to know about the house and my aborted life there. This is exactly what I wanted the students to learn—that an interview is a conversation, not an interrogation.

My students knew I'd spent ten years in Central America. After I'd calmed down a bit, a student asked if my destroyed neighborhood was the worst thing I'd ever seen.

"No," I told him, seeing Guatemala in my mind. "It's one thing to see your house like this, in a pile, and it's another thing to see over two hundred dead people in a hole in the ground. That's the worst thing I've ever seen."[16]

I led the class away from my home, down the ruined block and to the grassy top of the levee where I used to walk the dogs. We sat up there above the city, able to see the devastation for miles, and silently ate our picnic lunches. I don't know how they felt, but I felt better. At least my bulldozed house was good for something.

It was gloom-and-doom teaching one day and *Saturday Night Live* the next. "Laugh" was instruction number six on the list Loyola handed out to deal with post-Katrina stress. So I used a *Saturday Night Live* comedian's book to teach basic writing skills. I brought in cake for students to eat during exams. And I typed these instructions on their midterms: "Please relax. No one is going to live or die based on your exam score. You are not going to fail. Please breathe during the exam. I have no training in mouth-to-mouth resuscitation."

I also wanted to empower my students by encouraging them to physically help with the city's massive cleanup. I started taking groups of them to pick up trash with a new organization called the Katrina Krewe (krewes are Mardi Gras groups that organize balls and parades). One woman started it after the storm by emailing thirty friends. And those emails became a murmuration. Her thirty friends emailed their buddies, who emailed their buddies, and within a few weeks, an army of hundreds of rubber-gloved people were combing and scouring street by street, picking up all the debris, every single grimy Mardi Gras bead, every lipsticked cigarette butt.

Block by block, neighborhood by neighborhood, we began to reclaim the Dead Zone and return it to life, spit-shining the city as if it were a beloved vintage car. It was a way of saying to the local government, *Okay, you don't have your shit together, but we do.* Some of my students showed up on Saturday mornings and loved it and then wrote about it. People in the neighborhoods thanked us and drivers honked and gave us a thumbs-up.

But the best medicine for me continued to be the birds. My days and even my nights had begun to fill with birds. I still didn't own binoculars or a field guide, but my alarm clock every morning was a bird singing, a woodpecker tap-tap-tapping, or a little bird scraping its beak on the ladder leaning against the house near my open bedroom window. I'd ride my bike to school as the parakeets screeched overhead. Later in the day I watched the ducks in Audubon Park, followed by the starlings at sunset. Then birds began appearing in my dreams. One night I dreamed that I was trying to feed birds by hand. Finally, a small bright green bird with a line of little rose thorns sticking out of its back landed on my palm. In my dream, it looked like a tiny dinosaur. I would never have thought that one of my life goals would be to learn how to hand-feed birds. It took ten years after Katrina for me to coax a chickadee to pluck a sunflower seed from my outstretched palm in Vermont. But I dreamed it in New Orleans, first.

**AS THE SEMESTER DREW TO A CLOSE, REALITY BEGAN TO OVERWHELM US. ONE MORNING I** stepped on campus to find TV news cameramen prowling around and students in the hallway talking in hushed voices to their parents on cellphones. A student had been found dead of meningitis in his dorm room. Rumors of an outbreak flew across campus. Most doctors had not returned to New Orleans, hospitals barely functioned, and the campus clinic had been overrun for weeks by students with "Katrina cough."

The student who had died was the best friend of one of my students.

He knocked on my door later that day. Earlier in the week, he'd been wearing a peacock headdress and dancing down the hallway in a conga line, handing out king cake to faculty. Today he had to write an obituary for a teenager. Could I help him?

One of my students was raped. Two were diagnosed with cancer. By April, professors commented that our students were dropping like flies. We strategized on how to help them just finish the semester. Then colleagues started getting sick. One day a work buddy came in limping with sciatica. Then some of my students started limping. Then I woke up limping.

I'd adopted Wendell Berry's dictum—"Be joyful though you have considered all the facts"—as a personal credo. But it wasn't possible to be joyful that last month of the semester, when journalism students were bursting into tears over stories that reported that a football field of Louisiana's wetlands were falling into the ocean every hour.[17] The daily newspaper was already advising us to update our evacuation plans for the next hurricane season, which started in less than sixty days. The girlfriend who'd swigged champagne at my ruined home with me, a highly organized administrator and activist now living in a second-floor condo in a higher area because her own home had flooded, told me that when she heard the words "evacuation plan," her brain got stuck.

I handed her a key to Miss Mabel's in Alabama, where I planned to return for the summer, and said: "This is your evacuation plan. Throw your most important shit in a box. Put that box and your dog in your car. And then you hit the gas for five hours until you reach Montgomery."

Two young women, freshmen, decided to do an extra-credit assignment. They asked a FEMA engineer to take them on a levee walk. On their walk, he told them that the levees would not be ready for the next hurricane season. I saw the fear and confusion in their young faces as they described that interview to the class. They were so distraught that they stayed afterward to talk with me. They didn't care about grades or extra credit. They were worried about their city. What is going to happen this summer? they asked.

As things started to get rough in those final weeks, I did what

I'd always done—dive into work to avoid any feelings. But the harder I worked, the more papers I assigned and graded, the more faculty meetings I attended, the more I just wanted to sit on my back stoop and watch the sparrows. I realized that I was teaching my students the wrong thing—that to be a professional adult was to be a crazed workaholic. Frenetic busyness is a drug, and as a journalist, I'd been addicted to it for a very long time. A few months sitting with sparrows couldn't cure that. I now understand that what we needed back then in New Orleans was to slow down and accept that after a disaster, you just can't do as much. Nor should you. You need time to think, to ponder. What have we learned? What have the waters of Katrina taught us? I knew I needed a great slowing down, but the only way I'd ever been able to do that was if I got very sick.

And then I woke up one morning and couldn't figure out what day it was or what time I was supposed to teach. Thanks to my roommate, I managed to get to school ten minutes late for class. Students stared at me, perplexed, when I walked in, shamefaced—I'm a stickler about tardiness. Car trouble, I told them, a bald-faced lie because my truck had drowned and I'd replaced it with a large pink bicycle. I knew every one of my fifty-five students' names, whose parents had lost their jobs, whose father had just developed testicular cancer and had to leave the city to get treatment in Houston, whose grandparents had died of heartbreak after Katrina, and who secretly wanted to become an artist-photographer. But how could I tell them that I couldn't remember what day it was? I didn't want them to think that I also could not remember their stories and heartbreaks and the small triumphs they'd shared during office hours.

Right after class that morning I got lost trying to find the cafeteria. Loyola is tiny, so I knew something was wrong with my brain. I decided to go home while I could still remember how to get there, then called in sick for the rest of the week. I later realized I had what New Orleanians were calling Katrina Brain. It was spreading fast. A famous psychologist from New York City had just given a public presentation on post-traumatic stress disorder. He'd listed over two dozen symptoms, and New Orleanians in the audience started elbowing one another, laughing, and couldn't stop. We all have these symptoms, they told him, still laughing. That's Katrina Brain.

I cured my Katrina Brain by sitting on the back porch for a few days plowing through Alexander McCall Smith's mystery series The No. 1 Ladies' Detective Agency, in which the worst thing that happens is that someone's cow gets stolen (doctors should prescribe these books). And of course I watched my sparrows. They weren't worried about the impending hurricane season. They were flying around with their beaks full of nesting materials. I ignored the news and spent hours watching them instead. They were better than drugs.

Just a few weeks before the semester ended, a student in a news reporting class asked a question that pierced my bird bubble.

She raised her hand: "If New Orleans is underwater by 2050, what will happen to our degrees?"

Every student stared at me, waiting. The air conditioner whirred loudly just above my head. I realized as I stood there that I had no answer. And that I needed to leave the city.

**LOOKING BACK, I REALIZE THAT THE THINGS THAT GIVE ME THE MOST DAILY JOY TODAY ARE** gifts from that Katrina year. That time is the reason I buy bicycles instead of cars. That time is why I knit my way through troubles, great and small. That time is where I learned as a teacher how important it is to balance ugly truths with daily joy. And most of all, New Orleans is where I first became acquainted with my new "little friends," as I called them in my journal, the house sparrows, my portal birds.

In my last journal entry in New Orleans, I wrote: "The birds are watching me. They don't know whether or not to trust me, yet. I hope that my roommate will love them the way I have."

I'd lost everything in New Orleans and I'd found everything I needed to build a new, saner life. I just didn't know it yet.

CHAPTER 4

# Our Lady of the Applesauce

*You must do the thing you think you cannot do.*

ELEANOR ROOSEVELT

As summer began, I left New Orleans and returned to Miss Mabel's in Montgomery to sit and knit and think because I had a difficult decision to make. It seemed improbable, but a prestigious environmental PhD program at the University of Wisconsin in Madison had accepted the application I'd halfheartedly filled out months earlier. And UW-Madison was offering me a research job to partly earn my way through a doctorate in natural resources. I'd still need student loans, but it was a hell of a deal. But I could barely remember my own zip code and I was swimming in Katrina debt with no savings. As I reacquainted myself with Miss Mabel's yard birds, I realized I wasn't ready to move in three months to begin a demanding graduate program and a research job. And Wisconsin might as well have been the Arctic; I'd spent most of my life in short sleeves or no sleeves. I also had a very vague notion of the Midwest, influenced by the movie *Fargo*. I know—that movie isn't even about Wisconsin, but when I got the acceptance letter I suddenly saw myself trudging through a blinding white landscape while serial killers tossed people into woodchippers.

I decided to defer school for a year and teach in Montgomery instead. Jim and I could stay at Miss Mabel's indefinitely, and I could visit my father. The chemo had stopped working, he had just months to live, and for the first time in my life, my father and I had come to an emotional truce. The birds and parrots in his yard had given us something new to talk about and had created a demilitarized zone in our relationship, a space where we could focus on these beautiful creatures and avoid the religious and political land mines between us.

I flew to California to see him. He was excited and proud that I'd been accepted into a PhD program—as far as we knew, no one in our entire clan had ever had those two magic letters, Dr., in front of their name. In fact, in his generation, no one had a college degree of any kind. As we sat at that table facing the bay window and his bird feeders, I explained that I was definitely going to do it, but that Wisconsin was too cold; I needed another year to apply to schools in warmer climes. I reminded him of the horror stories he'd told me about his childhood, tromping through the deep snows of Derry, holes in his shoes, frozen socks. I recounted how I'd flown from New Orleans to Madison in April for a weekend just to check it out. Yeah, I loved the campus. Yeah, it was beautiful, Dad. Yeah, there were great classes on animals, plants, and water, and ecology courses to tie it all together. The place was a gigantic science-candy store. But, Dad, it was 85 degrees when I flew out of Louisiana that April weekend, and so cold when I landed in Madison that I'd had to defrost my face with a blow dryer.

I'd be miserable, I told him. And I'd miss the sunny, gregarious cultures I'd lived in my whole life. "In a year I'll have more choices," I said.

My father just listened. He was a quiet man and he sat there thinking. I wonder now if he was remembering his own aborted education. Out of nine siblings who survived a Northern Irish childhood, he was one of the few to graduate from high school. (My mother dropped out of school at thirteen to care for her younger sisters when her mother died of tuberculosis, a childhood right out of *Angela's Ashes*.) My father loved school. His teachers had told him he should become a teacher. But there wasn't enough land to farm, there were younger siblings to feed and clothe, and so he'd headed to Belfast at seventeen to work as a rock smasher in a quarry. He was so grateful to even get this first job that before he died, he'd dictated a thank-you letter to that quarry owner in Northern Ireland, which I mailed. But I remembered that during my days as a kid in California he had turned a closet into a workshop, and he would disappear in there every night like a mysterious elf, taking apart televisions, putting them back together, and then teaching himself how computers worked. He pored through technical manuals on how to fix everything. He could have been an engineer. And he also loved every plant in his yard, nursed them like children, and gave me precise instructions before he died on how to care for each one. Given half a chance, my father would have been a botanist or an engineer, or both. A scientist.

As a child, I'd adored science, too, maybe because he did. My passion was the stars. My father bought me a telescope, and on summer nights, I'd drag it and one of my little brothers up to that hill behind the house. We'd sit there under the dry desert sky, drinking

7UP, eating saltines, and scanning the heavens. I was determined to see a UFO. This was the age of *2001: A Space Odyssey*. Instead of playing with Barbies, I built model spaceships and hung them from the ceiling. Star charts covered my walls. I had a brown rabbit named Andromeda. Arthur C. Clarke was my hero. I was going to be an astronomer.

Then math got in the way, along with a fifth-grade science teacher whom I vaguely remember as a gray granite block named Mr. Hollis. I amused myself and my classmates by pouring hydrochloric acid into the Kleenex box. This experiment turned the box into a smoking, churning, sizzling mess. Unfortunately, Mr. Hollis did not have a sense of humor. Instead of praising my spirit of scientific inquiry, the gray eminence sent me to the principal's office, where I became a regular.

My interest in science sputtered out like those flaming Kleenex boxes. Instead, I got hooked on the Nancy Drew detective series. Goodbye, Arthur C. Clarke—hello, Carolyn Keene. I owe my investigative journalism career to Nancy Drew. But if I'd had even just one female science mentor, I might have pursued that dream of studying the universe.

**THAT NIGHT IN THE FAMILY ROOM, MY FATHER TOLD ME HE WANTED TO WATCH A FUNNY** movie. He plugged in *Snow Dogs*, about a Miami playboy dentist living the balmy good life. Then the main character suddenly discovered that he was adopted and was really an Alaskan, not a Florida native. And his Alaskan mother had just died and left him a dog sled team. The main character didn't want to go claim his canine inheritance, but during his slapsticky journey from 85 degrees in Miami to 37 below in Alaska, as he falls repeatedly on the ice, he also falls in love with the dogs, the place, and a woman.

I don't know how many times my father had watched this film. I don't know why he'd bought it. But maybe when you're dying you laugh every chance you get. When it was over, he turned to me and said, "Don't be afraid to go to Wisconsin."

MY FATHER DIED PEACEFULLY, ONE YEAR AFTER KATRINA, IN THE FALL OF 2006. HE HAD what my mother called "a good death": in bed at home, surrounded by his family, just as he'd wanted. The parrots showed up outside his bedroom window the morning before he died. The small flock of green-and-red birds perched on the tall cypresses, their plumed weight making the tips sway back and forth as they screeched raucously and stripped the trees of their hard green berries. I opened the sliding glass door to my parents' bedroom. My father could no longer talk or get out of bed, but I told him that the parrots had arrived. His eyes were watching me as I spoke. I wanted him to know that the birds were there.

At three-thirty the next morning I gave my father his last dose of morphine. An hour later he slipped away from us.

My mother, brothers, and I spent that Sunday holding a wake around his bed. Finally out of pain, he lay there as we drank hot chocolate, prayed, watched mass on TV, ate breakfast, and told stories. My mother gave a short speech that she must have rehearsed with him before he died. She told my brothers and me that from now on, we didn't need to worry about anything. Our father would be around, watching over us. He would bring us good luck.

I'd made two promises to my father before he died. First, I'd promised that we would bury him in that small Derry cemetery, full of O'Kanes, next to the moss-covered centuries-old stone church he had attended as a "wee nipper." So a few months later, my mother and my brother, Michael, and I flew to Ireland with my dad's ashes in her purse. I'd knitted a small blanket in a dozen shades of green to wrap his tiny coffin in.

After a standing-room-only mass that was broadcast on the parish radio and after I'd shaken the rough hands of the long line of very old farmers waiting by the grave craggy-faced men who solemnly told me that they went to elementary school with Felix, I returned from Ireland to keep the second promise. I'd promised him that I would face my fear of serial killers and the Cold North. It was time to pack up in Montgomery and head to Madison, Wisconsin, to begin a PhD in natural resources at the University of Wisconsin–Madison in the fall of 2007.

That spring, as the magnolias bloomed in Miss Mabel's yard, Jim and I said goodbye to our Alabama comrades, piled our dogs into the car, and migrated 900 miles due north. As we drove away, one of our wild southern hounds, Amos Moses, howled all the way to Birmingham. Then he hid his head between the seats. I felt like he did, leaving the South and all our friends.

**WHEN WE ARRIVED IN MADISON, THE SNOW HAD JUST MELTED. A REAL ESTATE AGENT HAD** helped us find a one-story white ranch with an open floor plan and natural light, similar to our house in New Orleans. I walked in and glanced at the ceiling and walls, going down my mental checklist: hardwood floors, white walls, plenty of windows, a decent backyard, and 873 feet above sea level.

We took the dogs out for a long walk in the park right across the street, called Warner Park. A green path wound through two groves of what I now know are ash, walnut, hackberry, pine, and oak, rimmed by thickets of staghorn sumac and honeysuckle. The trail led us through meadows and down a gentle rise to a large lagoon—no dog-eating alligators lurking in there. There was a marsh island in the middle of the lagoon covered by cattails. Geese honked loudly from the island and fuzzy goslings were swimming and exploring along the shoreline.

Later that first night at dusk, Jim and I sat on the couch in a daze and stared out our new huge front picture window. We were facing a small clearing in Warner Park. Right in the middle of that clearing, a 25-foot blue spruce stood like a giant Christmas tree. It was a stoic tree, with neat lines, not like the gnarled live oaks I loved in New Orleans, dripping with Spanish moss. It looked so solid, so peaceful—a tree you could depend on.

We cautiously toasted our turn of luck with champagne, hoping fervently to make a new start.

"Look!" I shouted.

Across the street in the park, three large deer slowly walked past the spruce, white tails flashing.

Early the next morning, the doorbell rang. A gray-haired woman in a bathrobe stood at the front door holding a large pan wrapped in kitchen towels. She thrust the pan toward me.

"You have coffeepot?" she asked in a thick German accent.

As I clutched the pan, she drew back the kitchen towel—homemade apple coffee cake, still steaming. She'd made it with apples from that tree, she told me, pointing toward Warner Park. Every year she made over eighty jars of applesauce from that one tree. But our new neighbor didn't want to bother us. We must have a lot to unpack. She just wanted us to eat. Welcome, she said. She turned abruptly and shuffled back across the street as I stood in the doorway, holding the pan, mouth open.

She didn't know who we were. She had no idea where we'd just come from. She didn't even ask. So she had no way of knowing what this steaming apple coffee cake meant to two Katrina evacuees on the first morning in their new home above sea level. I soon learned that this is just what Hedwig, "Heddie," does for everyone. But I felt like the Virgin Mary had just appeared on my doorstep.

This is a very good place, I said to Jim.

All our new neighbors turned out to be friendly. Their cats were friendly, too. Across the street, Our Lady of the Applesauce had a stringy ancient red tabby named George who looked a hundred years old in human time. The Harley-Davidson mechanic next door had two cats as well; he was in the throes of a divorce and his kitties were his "babies." He'd noticed that we had two large, friendly dogs. "Maybe they'd like a playdate with my kitties?" he asked. I couldn't possibly tell this kind feline-loving neighbor the truth, so I just said, "Well, maybe after our dogs settle in."

**WHEN I WAS A CHILD, MY FIRST AND VERY BEST FRIENDS WERE TEN CATS WHO LIVED ON THE** sprawling orange ranch my parents managed. One of them, a jet-black battle-scarred warrior named Midnight, probably saved my life when

I was just three or four years old, when she scratched me and hissed to keep me from reaching out to grab a rattlesnake that had slithered into our garden. This is why four decades later, when I discovered that I had inadvertently rescued a wild Alabama pup who chased cats and sometimes killed them, I was horrified. But I'd fallen madly in love with mange-covered Amos Moses the minute I saw him tossing a banana peel in the air on a horse farm. Amos Moses grew into a strange-looking beast nearly the size of a dwarf pony, a weird mix of airedale, black lab, and god knows what galloping on four long legs after anything that moved. When people asked his breed, I told them "Irish mastodon," referring to the prehistoric elephant that went extinct at least ten thousand years ago.

"How interesting," they commented. "Where can I get one of those?"

I had to keep Amos on a tight leash, but I told myself I could control him and maybe he'd settle down. This never happened, of course, because I was a hopeless dog trainer (both Amos and I had failed a training course). And so I lived in mortal fear of his escaping because he was a canine Houdini who always seemed to be plotting his next great escapade.

Our beautiful new Madison yard had no fence, so Jim and I spent that first week frantically putting up a chain-link barrier as fast as we could. Meanwhile, Amos Moses stared out our front window observing the neighbors' cats as they conducted their daily routines. I imagined the wheels clicking in Amos's brain as he mapped ancient George's route, calculating distances and the number of seconds it would take the arthritic feline to get from the spruce where he was sunning himself to the safety of Heddie's back porch.

The morning the fence was ready, I walked around the yard kicking it hard. Jim strengthened several weak spots. Finally, I opened the back door and let the hounds go. And then I heard a terrifying sound.

"Meow. Meow."

Oh, my god. Oh my god. It couldn't be.

Amos Moses's long donkey ears shot skyward. The dogs ripped along the fence, thrashing through the bushes, sniffing. I ran ahead, panting wildly, eyes desperately seeking the beloved feline that had somehow gotten into our yard. We raced around the yard's perimeter, a tight pack of three, two deranged dogs and one panicked human. The meowing continued. It was getting louder, sounding angrier. It sounded like a baby crying, a wheel squeaking. Wait a minute, this can't be a cat. It can't be a baby.

It's . . .

A bird?

I stopped. Then I sat down on the ground and laughed and laughed and pounded the grass.

Safe at the top of a honeysuckle bush, a small gray bird had a black button eyeball fixed on me and my snarling dogs. He looked like a miniature train conductor in a neat gray suit and black cap. Every time he opened his black beak, a blast of squeaking, flutelike whistling, rasping, chattering, and chirping erupted, interspersed with that annoying me-yowl. I couldn't believe all this noise was coming from that tiny body.

I went inside and brought out the only bird book I owned and realized I was in a stare-down with a gray catbird. I'd never heard of this species, yet it nested in forty-six states and across southern Canada. The book said it was a close relative of the mockingbird, a southern bird I did know. Both birds belonged to the Mimidae family, or "mimics," and I'd watched mockingbirds at major intersections in the South perch on stoplights and parrot the beeping signal that tells people when it's safe to cross.

According to that book, we had just moved into this catbird's territory. He migrated for the winter to a southern refuge, but catbirds usually returned to the same midwestern nesting site—possibly the same bush—in April or May. I realized that this bird had probably just returned from the South, maybe even arriving the same day that we did. I thought about our arduous two-day drive from Montgomery to Madison. I imagined this little bird flying high above our car, flapping hard as we crossed 900 miles of mountains and valleys.

Catbirds live as long as seventeen years, so this one might have been in my yard for a long time. After raising a family here all summer, he had to leave in September or October because he ate fruit and insects—not much of either survived a Wisconsin winter. Migration maps showed him leaving Wisconsin to head due south. As my finger traced his potential routes, I was stunned to see that this little bird might have migrated through or lived in all the places I'd called home: Nicaragua, Guatemala, Mexico, Alabama, Louisiana, and now Wisconsin. We shared a life migration route.

I wasn't the only catbird fan in the neighborhood. Our mechanic neighbor, Greg, was also an amateur wildlife photographer. One spring morning he woke up and thought he heard a whole flock of parrots in his yard. He ran outside but couldn't find any—the entire racket was coming from a single little gray bird. Greg started reading about the bird and found out that since the bird is a mimic, when he arrives from Central America, he sounds just like a Central American bird. But by the end of summer, he's singing like a Wisconsin bird.

Our catbird sometimes sounded like a whole flock of parrots because he is a member of the songbird family, avians that can sing two entirely different songs at the same time or a duet by themselves. Humans produce sound through our larynx in our throats, which birds also have. But birds have a unique instrument that no other animal has: the syrinx, a bony structure buried deep in their chests.[1] The syrinx is a double-barreled box of cartilage, not even a third of an inch thick, surrounded by an air sac, a resonating chamber with elastic vibrating membranes. As a bird inhales and exhales, the air passing over the membrane folds in the syrinx produces sound, allowing songbirds, including the catbird, to sing continuously for several minutes without pause. The feathered virtuoso adjusts the sound by tightening his syrinx muscles to control volume and pitch. Because the syrinx is double-barreled and the two sides operate independently, a bird like my catbird can sing two different songs at once.[2] Like us, birds have lungs, but they are the only vertebrate with a respiratory system that includes seven to nine tiny air sacs all over their bodies that function like a bellows, allowing a one-way continuous airflow.[3] This more efficient and greater flow of oxygen allows them to fly long distances and sing.

Our species uses only 2 percent of the air passing through our larynx to produce sound, while many songbirds use almost 100 percent of the air flowing through their syrinx.[4] This is why our catbird is his own one-bird band and choir. Because songbirds can use air much more efficiently than we can, a bird as tiny as a winter wren—weighing the same as three-quarters of a tablespoon of sugar—can produce ten times the sound of a rooster, pound for pound, filling the eastern woods with its piccolo-like trill, an octave-leaping musical roller coaster.[5]

Birdwatchers and ornithologists have heard the catbird mimic at least forty-four different bird species, along with crying babies, chainsaws, car horns, car alarms, and tree frogs.[6] But he's not just a mimic. The catbird is also a vocal acrobat, inventing his own songs and mixing them with mimicry to produce musical outbursts as long as ten minutes described as "improvised babble" or "avian jazz."[7] He punctuates his vamping and riffing with a signature meowl, which the 1936 *Birds of America* called a "most unbird-like snarl."[8]

My favorite description of the catbird's song comes from Alexander V. Arlton's 1949 musical analysis of birdsong, *Songs and*

*Other Sounds of Birds*: "There is a certain lawless freedom to the song of the Catbird which invests it with a characteristic essentially wild."[9]

**MY NEIGHBOR HAD SPENT HOURS VIDEOTAPING OUR BIRD. HE HANDED ME A CD OF THE CAT**bird's singing.

"I really love this bird," he told me. "I look forward to his return every year. Some summers he nests in your yard. Some years he nests in mine."

Here I was, a stranger in a strange land, a Katrina evacuee—scared and confused, wondering how a tropical bird like me could ever adjust to the cold North and such a radically different culture. But this loud little bird was already helping me bond with neighbors, giving me courage, and making me laugh. He lived half the year in Wisconsin and the other half probably in Mexico or Central America and stopped in the Deep South along the way. He belonged to all these places. And wherever he went, he learned to sing new songs. As I watched him blasting away in my yard, I thought, *If he can do it, maybe I can, too.*

**AFTER I DISCOVERED OUR CATBIRD, I REALLY WANTED TO KNOW WHERE HE WENT EVERY** winter. So I decided to take a basic "Birding for Dummies" course to learn about him and the house sparrows and cardinals I'd noticed in New Orleans. This class was also a way to stay close to my father, although I wasn't conscious of that at the time. I was surprised then that there were so many small things I missed about him, particularly his voice on the phone. I suddenly realized that I'd never again be anybody's "wee girl," and that nobody would call me Duckie, his pet name for me.

But UW-Madison didn't have a "Birding for Dummies" course. So during my second semester, in the spring of 2008, I enrolled in Ornithology 521, a class for students headed to veterinary school with years of biology under their belts. My dogs had much more than a measly catbird to contend with. They were confused, running around the house searching for the herons, woodcocks, snipes, and loons whose songs blasted from the CD player, week after week, as I studied birdcalls.

The professor, Dr. Mark Berres, was an ornithological Jon Stewart, part mad scientist and part giant parrot. Three days a week at noon, the absolutely worst time for a lecture because most college students are about as alert as a cooked noodle at that hour, he captivated over a hundred slumping undergraduates. Back and forth he strode across the front of the large auditorium, waving his arms around when he got excited, which was about every three minutes.

"This professor is so enthusiastic that by the end of the semester, he's going to start flying around the auditorium," I scribbled in my lecture notes.

It probably helped that he talked a lot about bird sex. He told us that after decades of believing that birds were mostly monogamous and had 1950s-style marriages, scientists using DNA testing recently discovered that both male and female birds have "affairs."

"She's not just sitting on those eggs with her little apron on," he told us, wagging a finger. "When the male is out and about, she takes a coffee break and visits another male nearby. These avian affairs are called EPCs, or extra-pair copulations. College students call this 'hooking up,'" he said as a wave of snickering swept across the room.[10]

In class I sat next to a new study buddy named Stacy. We kept glancing at each other throughout the lectures, raising our eyebrows at the professor's antics. Stacy was in her forties like me, returning to school to escape reality. We were stunned when we realized that we'd been living in Guatemala at the same time, although we'd never met. She'd worked as a human rights attorney helping Guatemalan organizations that were trying to prosecute the generals responsible for some of the massacres I'd investigated. Now she was an immigration attorney trying to help Central Americans stay in the United States. Many of her clients were in detention centers and about to be deported. Like me, she was a bit fried mentally and had discovered birds after she left Central America. It relaxed her to watch them.

We began studying together. After the professional lives we'd had, we found the rules and rigors of ornithology comforting. There were no ambiguities; everything had to be exact. In a scientific context, a Yellow-bellied Sapsucker was just that—not blue-bellied, and the "Yellow" had to be capitalized and the "bellied" had to be lowercase. I made a set of flash cards and pasted bird photos on them. I carried the cards around like a security blanket, quizzing myself on the bus, in the library, and in cafés.

I knew absolutely nothing about ornithology, which was humbling and refreshing. I had to give up on the idea of expertise and cultivate what Buddhists call "beginner's mind." I had also never learned in a way that required all my senses, including a sense of wonder and love. I started hanging out every day in the tiny ornithology library, wishing I could inhale the shelves of books on birds from all over the world. I lingered in the stacks, fingering old leather volumes of Darwin's adventures, loving their dusty, rich smell. I carried piles of ancient books to my table and sat there for hours, leafing through drawings and photos of birds and letting weird new words roll off my tongue: marvelous terms like "zygodactyl," which meant birds like owls, parrots, and woodpeckers with two toes pointing forward and two backward, allowing them to climb trees and hang upside down; and "plumulaceous," such a fun word that sounded like the soft, downy feathers it described, which cover adorable bird babies and provide the insulation allowing avians to live on every continent; and my new favorite bird name, kookaburra, the carnivorous Australian bird with the crazy cackle used in 1930s Tarzan movies and *The Wizard of Oz* as a proxy for wild jungle sounds.

Stacy and I began to look forward to the noon lectures on Mondays, Wednesdays, and Fridays with the enthusiasm of cult followers. That spring I learned that my father was right—birds are smart, at least as smart as or even smarter than primates. And some can recognize individual humans.[11] So call someone a "birdbrain," and you are paying them the highest of compliments, Dr. Berres told us. Birds can sleep while they fly by closing one eye. And some scientists suspect they dream while they sleep and even practice singing in their dreams.[12]

"Birds are artists, musicians, inventors, navigators, tree doctors, tree planters, and acrobats," our professor shouted, pacing the room. Every word sounded as if there were three exclamation points after it, especially whenever he said "*BIRDS!!!*" *BIRDS* make tools. They learn and compose songs. They travel thousands of miles to their many homes with the sun and stars as their guides. And they build complex "green" nests out of recycled materials that can withstand 50 mph winds. I could hear those winds whooshing as he spoke. I could see those baby birds hunkered down in that strong nest.

"Crows are the smartest of all avians," Dr. Berres proclaimed. They can recognize the faces of individual humans. In Japan they've learned to use the stoplights to crush walnuts. While the light is red, they drop the walnut in the intersection. The light turns green, a driver runs over the walnut, and when the light turns red again, the crows swoop down to scoop up their shelled treat.[13]

Because of the professor's passion for crows, I started to watch them on campus. I discovered that they dragged pizzas out of dorm trash cans on Friday mornings. The crows seemed to have figured out that weekends in this college town started on Thursday nights.

But my favorite lecture was about migration. Dr. Berres clicked to a PowerPoint slide of a large Canada goose flapping hard with a ruby-throated hummingbird riding on its back.

"Raise your hands if you think this is how billions of birds leave the United States every fall and travel to Latin America!" he shouted.

Stacy and I smirked as a few undergraduates hesitantly raised their hands. I'd read enough about my catbird and the birds in New Orleans to know that this professor was having fun with us. He should have been a game-show host.

"WRONG!" he shouted. We all laughed.

But what he told us that day was no less fantastic or miraculous than the image on that doctored photo. Every year researchers use radar to watch 4.7 billion birds like my catbird on their journeys.[14] As the birds head north every spring, biologists sitting at huge computer monitors follow the flocks on the same radar used to track weather systems. The radar sends out beams of microwave energy that hit objects in the sky, such as raindrops, butterflies, and birds. When some of the beam bounces back, the screens of biologists and birders across the country, watching live on websites like Cornell's BirdCast, light up with small blobs that bloom and spread, covering whole swaths of land as huge flocks pass over New York City or the Great Lakes at night. The beamed-back data allows scientists to measure how big the flock is, how fast those birds are flying, and which direction they are headed. Meteorologists call the big blobs "birdbursts" and must learn to distinguish huge flocks from storm systems.

To prepare for their migratory journey, the professor told us, some birds double their body weight. They need that extra fat because they burn as much as 10 percent of their body mass in one night of flight. They also increase their flight muscles by as much as 35 percent to help carry the extra fat they burn up. And they can shrink their organs to make room for the extra muscle and fat.

Many species like my catbird migrate at night to avoid predators and because there is less wind, which allows them to save energy. But it is still a very dangerous journey; the mortality rate for long-distance migrating birds is 50 percent, he told us. Fifty percent, he repeated slowly. That meant that half the birds we saw in Madison in the summer might not make it back next year. Birds who fly across the Gulf of Mexico at night can get confused by the lights on the over 6,000 oil rigs, flying into rigs or circling them until they drop from exhaustion into the ocean (researchers have found tiger shark stomachs full of songbirds, including catbirds). If the birds make it to land, they can also get confused by the lights on cell towers. Biologists have found hundreds of dead catbirds at the base of towers during migration.

As I listened to the professor, I suddenly remembered a small yellow bird I'd seen years earlier while sailing across the Gulf of Mexico with Jim. We were living in Alabama at that time. A weathered mariner, Jim was preparing to sail his 35-foot fiberglass yawl across the Atlantic to Portugal. His boat was docked in Mobile, Alabama, and he needed to sail it to Florida to prepare it for the transatlantic journey. He invited me along for the Florida leg of the trip. I had zero sailing experience, so he also invited a seasoned first mate to join us, an Englishman named Darryl.

The lights of Mobile disappeared as we lurched into a darkening sky and washing-machine sea. For the five-day sail, I'd brought my purple yoga mat, recipe books, a cooler full of steaks, and fine wine. I soon realized that I should have brought Dramamine instead. I spent the next three days belowdecks squished into a coffin-like bunk, vomiting into plastic Piggly Wiggly grocery bags.

On the fourth day, I was finally able to surface. The sun had come out. I was sitting on the deck, dazed and dehydrated, clutching the wooden rail and trying not to notice the sharks occasionally circling the boat (studying me, I thought). I was contemplating my tenuous position on the food chain when suddenly Darryl and Jim began pointing at something and shouting.

Small brown and yellow birds whizzed by us, dipping and hitting the water. It was April, the height of bird migration from Latin America to the Gulf Coast. I realized that these were not seabirds; they were land birds, far from shore. They were running out of gas and in trouble.

"Come on! Come on!" the three of us started shouting, begging the birds to land on the boat.

A tiny yellow bird landed on the cabin roof, just a foot away from where Darryl was perched. The bird looked up at him. We all froze. We began to whisper. Should we give it water? Crackers?

We decided to do nothing. We sat there like three statues, watching the tiny yellow bird watch us. Twenty minutes ticked by. The bird just stood still, staring. Then suddenly it lifted off the cabin roof and shot across the water toward that distant Alabama shore, a yellow speck of hope.

"Good luck!" we shouted.

I loved Dr. Berres's lectures and his hilarious stories. But then I got a C on a major exam—the hardest and most science-loaded test I'd ever taken. The nineteen- and twenty-year-olds around me bragged about As and Bs, and my Guatemalan lawyer bird-buddy had done well, too. I began to panic. Ornithology 521 was a tough course geared toward pre-veterinary and zoology students—not for dabblers and wannabes like me. The professor was scribbling long mathematical formulas on the board so we could calculate the physics of flight. I'd never taken physics and I hadn't sat in a math class since Algebra II in high school, in which I got a D—even with a tutor (it didn't help that I smoked pot right before that class). Each week we also had to learn to identify 20 Wisconsin birds by sight and sound, as well as their Latin names (250 birds that semester). And each week there was a species quiz, with points subtracted for every misspelled letter in a Latin name.

I was now a forty-five-year-old PhD candidate living on student loans and paying off Katrina debt—I couldn't be getting Cs in undergraduate courses. I wondered if I should drop the class. There was no way I could catch up on science and math this late in life and compete with twenty-year-olds.

It wasn't just the math and physics in ornithology that scared the hell out of me. It was the weather. The class had a weekly bird identification lab in which a teaching assistant took us birding all over Madison. I was shocked the first day of bird lab in January when the TA gave a very stern talk about weekly attendance and grades, emphasizing: "This lab is NEVER canceled. Weather doesn't matter."

*Weather doesn't matter?* To a Southern Californian/Central American/New Orleanian transplant? Most of the students in the class were from the Midwest and had grown up in long underwear. But this was my first real winter ever, and it was turning into a record-breaker—Wisconsin's worst in a century. By April, 100 inches of snow had fallen—sticky snow; powdery snow; sugary snow; snowman-making snow; cave-in-your-roof snow; and heart attack snow, so heavy that the public health department warned people not to shovel too fast because two or three men died of heart attacks annually. I no longer thought those little plastic snow globes were cute. Wisconsin was beginning to look like one of those horrible, blindingly white *Fargo* scenes I'd dreaded.

On February 12, 2008, we had our first class field trip. At 7:00 a.m., it was 10 degrees outside. The instructor took pity on us and took us to Madison's zoo to gawk at the caged tropical birds inside the heated buildings. For the second field trip a week later, our lab instructor drove us to the still-frozen Yahara River to look for geese and ducks in areas where there was open water. It hit a high of 4 degrees at 8:30 a.m.

"Colder than shit," I scribbled in my field book.

That morning, standing huddled together on the ice with my classmates, wearing Frankenstein monster polar boots that weighed two pounds each and that were supposed to stay warm at –50 degrees, I began to question my sanity and the sanity of our instructor.

He asked us to study the difference between the Canada geese and the snow geese standing on the ice about fifty yards away. *Who cares?* I thought, wondering instead if the mucus was going to freeze in my nostrils.

I've been teaching basic field ornithology for thirteen years since those first frigid mornings. When I tell my new students in January in Vermont that "weather doesn't matter" and that we are going outside at 8:00 a.m. to tromp across a frozen marsh to find a single bird, I recognize that "Are you insane?" look on some of their faces. I give them the same advice a Minnesotan gave me when I first moved to the land of real winters: from November to March, expensive supersonic long underwear is your new best friend. And I tell my students to just stick with it. One morning something will suddenly shift, and your life will never be the same.

**IT HAPPENED TO ME LATER THAT WINTER WHEN I WENT TO DO MY BIRDING HOMEWORK BY** myself in Warner Park across the street from my house. At 7:45 a.m., it was 12 degrees Fahrenheit. The air was so razor-sharp cold it snapped at my skin. A deep heavy blanket of snow covered everything in the park, and crystal-covered branches glittered in the sun.

I heard three birds in an hour: the demented cackling of a white-breasted nuthatch, the high-pitched whinny of a downy woodpecker, and a red-bellied woodpecker's rolling chirr. The only bird I could see was a bright red male cardinal at the top of an ash tree.

I sat down on a snowbank and drank coffee out of a thermos and watched him. He faced the bright sun, thrust his chest forward, tilted his head back slightly, and threw his whole body into his song, throat feathers quivering. I no longer heard the dim roar of morning traffic or the harsh coughing of a cold engine as a driver tried to coax a vehicle to work. It was just me, the cardinal, and that cold, bright moment.

The male cardinal reminded me of an Irishman, standing up to leave his pub at midnight, head held high and chest inflated as he sang his traditional a cappella goodbye song. As I watched the brilliant red bird, I thought about what it means to sing or do anything with your whole heart and soul. And I realized that in fact I wanted to do everything—sing, speak, teach, garden, write, organize, love—with the full focus and joy with which this cardinal greeted the sun.

I realized that the reason I could focus on just him was because of the deep blanket of snow. A buffer of frozen ice crystals, it provided a silence and stillness deeper than anything I had ever experienced. This silence meant that I could truly hear this single bird. I was no longer thinking, *Holy shit, it's only 12 degrees. What the hell am I doing sitting out here on a snowbank?* I was thinking, *How lucky I am that the cold is keeping everyone inside so I get this bird, this silence, this place, this peace, all to myself.*

CHAPTER 5

# The Quiet Broken Ones

*We create wonderful places by giving them our attention.*

DAVID GEORGE HASKELL

I HAVE AN ADDICTIVE PERSONALITY—IT RUNS IN THE FAMILY—AND WHEN I FALL IN love with a person, place, or hobby, it can get a little extreme. When I was sixteen, I had a terrific crush on an Italian boy. A gorgeous body builder and a runner-up in the Mr. California contest, he was way out of my league; I hung out with a brainy crew viewed by the golden boys and girls of Orange County as a cerebral leper colony. But this did not deter me from driving to Mr. Almost California's house late one night, filling his mailbox with spaghetti and chocolate cake, and then decorating his front lawn with "borrowed" hideous golden Egyptian sphinx statues. My ardor did not persuade him (it probably scared the hell out of the guy), but my girlfriends and I laughed about it for years.

So when I picked up that very first pair of binoculars for my ornithology class, there should have been a red warning label on the box: "CAUTION: Addictive and obsessive individuals should NOT use these to look at birds. ESPECIALLY WHILE DRIVING."

The professor assigned us to go birding for an hour a week as homework. But after that cardinal showed me the magic of winter, instead of an hour a week, I was in Warner Park an hour a day, and then two to three hours a day, and then all day on weekends, and at night on owl walks.

I began each morning stepping out the door and crossing the street, drawn into Warner Park's green embrace, just as I'd been pulled like a zombie across the street from Loyola into Audubon Park in New Orleans. I walked past that stalwart blue spruce and Heddie's yard full of birds at her feeders into Warner's meadows. A green path through those meadows led me down to the wetland and to the park's border on the railroad tracks. Warner's waters funneled through an arch under the tracks. If I followed that water just a hundred paces beyond Warner Park's border, I found myself on the shore of Madison's largest and deepest lake, Lake Mendota, a gorgeous, peaceful gem of 9,781 liquid acres on which paddleboarders, kayakers, and ducks cruised in the summer, and in winter, the frozen surface became a playground for ice fishermen, snow kiters, ice hockey players, and winter ice festival

# WILD WARNER PARK

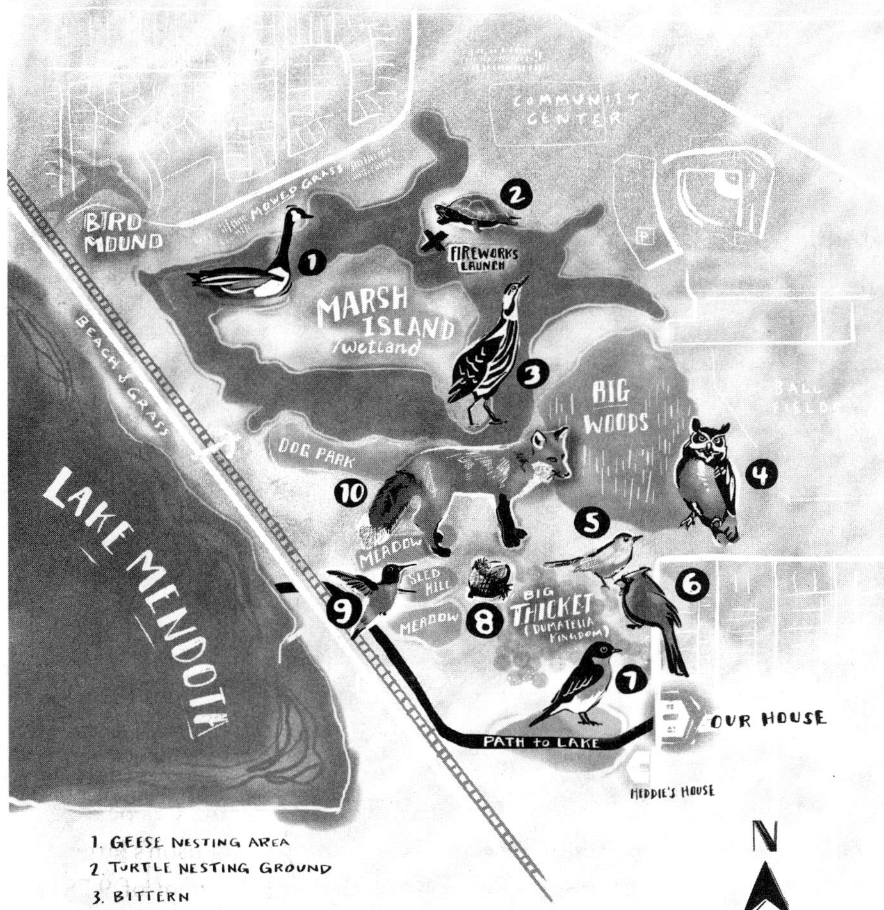


1. GEESE NESTING AREA
2. TURTLE NESTING GROUND
3. BITTERN
4. GREAT HORNED OWL
5. CATBIRD
6. FIRST WINTER CARDINAL
7. BLUEBIRD MEADOW
8. BUR OAK
9. HUMMINGBIRD PERCH
10. RED FOX

goers. We'd not only moved next to the city's second-largest park. We'd moved next to its greatest lake.

Lake Mendota was just one of Madison's five lakes. I'd always thought of the Midwest as a never-ending expanse of flat prairie. But I realized that like New Orleans, Madison seemed to be more a city of water than one of land. In New Orleans, all that water had meant danger. But in Madison, I was about to discover that the water meant *birds.*

When that very first harsh winter lifted and spring arrived, Warner's marsh began to look and sound like an avian Grand Central Station as birds returned from the South. Huge chevrons of geese zoomed in, flapping and honking loudly as they landed in the wetland. Protesting clouds of sparrows and blackbirds rose off the cattails to avoid the geese. Sandhill cranes delicately picked their way like dancers across the marsh island, booming a duet to each other. The geese honked at the cranes, upping the volume. Necks stretched out like snakes, male geese hissed loudly as they drove other geese from their nesting spots.

I scribbled furiously to record each new arrival—over fifty robins grazing in front of the dog park, grackles whistling from treetops, a pair of killdeer careening high in the air and shrieking overhead. The killdeer had just arrived maybe from as far south as Mexico. And the herons, too, probably from the Gulf Coast.

One morning there was a new song I couldn't place. The sweet lilting line was maddeningly familiar. I flipped through the bird guide trying to remember the birdcalls I had just learned in class.

"Song sparrow!" I shouted to the red-winged blackbirds staking out their cattail territories.

*Melospiza melodia.* The Latin name rose and fell like the bird's buzzy trill. Just three feet to my right, beside the bench, one faced me, chest thrust out, feet clinging to a scraggly bush. His tiny cream breast feathers vibrated in the sunshine. I could see the delicate baby-pink skin inside his beak as he loudly repeated the same phrase. He stared at me. The bench I was sitting on was in his new territory. He was letting me know it.

My binoculars became an extension of myself, another set of hands. I took them everywhere. I also kept an extra pair in the glove compartment. (By the way, this is a terrible idea—don't do it unless you want to end up in a ditch or in trouble with the police.) Whenever I drove to the bank, there was a large red-tailed hawk perched across the street in a huge oak in front of Walmart. After my banking business I'd spend five minutes ogling him or her from the parking lot. Large traffic-choked intersections, usually places where you sit and curse for several minutes, were the perfect venues to scan for hawks perched on the lights, waiting for roadkill.

The other new tool of the birding trade was my beloved bird field guide. On a visit to my mother in California, I'd found my father's old field guide right below his bay window. It was an out-of-date 2002 edition and some of the species names had already changed, but I didn't care. I began carrying it everywhere, thumbing through it, knowing that my father had done the same. (A few years later when I went to visit my brother in Oregon, that exact same field guide was lying on his coffee table. I said, "Harry, I have that same bird book. It belonged to Dad." And he said, "No it didn't. *This* is Dad's book." Then we realized that Dad had two copies of this book and we had each snagged one, thinking we had the prize.)

The birds changed how I viewed and moved through every single place. Even inside buildings, my eyeballs were constantly scanning the windows for feathered movement outside and my ears were listening for birdcalls beyond the walls. For the first time in my life I was viscerally connected to the nonhuman creatures around me. I learned a new language: territorial calls, harsh alarm calls, parents' soft whispering calls, "You big ugly human, get your hands off my nest!" calls, and contact calls that kept small flocks of migrating birds together, the soft clicks and *tchek*s that meant "I'm here in this backyard," or "Over here in the garden," or "She just filled up the feeders!"

One night at dusk, Jim and I were walking the dogs in the dog park near the shoreline. Suddenly I heard a chickadee call *Chicka-dee-dee-dee-dee-dee-dee-dee.*

I froze. That's too many *dee*s, I told my now-husband, who was getting sick of walking with someone who thought she was a mobile Bird Britannica. He'd been a good sport about it, especially given that he wasn't interested in birds, but we'd just gotten married and I think he resented the fact that I'd spent most of our Florida honeymoon ogling a great blue heron instead of him.

"STOP the bird lecture," he said, waving his arms. "PLEASE."

He went ahead with the dogs. I stayed behind. I knew there was a predator around. And the more *dee*s, the bigger the predator.

One minute later, a great horned owl swooped overhead, rounded wings flapping silently, casting a shadow as it flew over dogs, people, protesting chickadees. It perched in a large tree facing the dog park. In the distance, silhouetted against a darkening sky with its tufted ears standing up, it resembled a giant cat peering down on us all.

Birds have favorite perches, especially small birds on the lookout for predators. It's usually the branch of a dead tree where they have a clear view and can turn toward the sun in the morning, puffing out their little chests and soaking up the rays. It's a place where they can also see insects zooming by, breakfast on the wing. And from which they can observe a birder observing them.

I found my own favorite perch on Warner Park's Sled Hill. A flat expanse at the top of the highest vantage point, it was encircled by wildflower meadows and grassy banks. I started mornings there with coffee, a sugary bun from the nearest bakery, and my field guides spread out on the grass.

One morning I stared down into the meadow, watching a flock of robins grazing for worms, and noticed a very odd chicken at the edge of the robin flock, with reddish pantaloon legs blowing in the breeze. When I examined the pantalooned chicken through my binoculars, I realized it was a teenage red-tailed hawk, trying to fool the robins into thinking it was just another robin. The teenager edged ever closer to the robins before they all took off.

From my perch on Sled Hill, I quickly discovered that birds have their own routines and rhythms, like the great blue heron who zoomed in every morning around seven from the southwest. I watched him

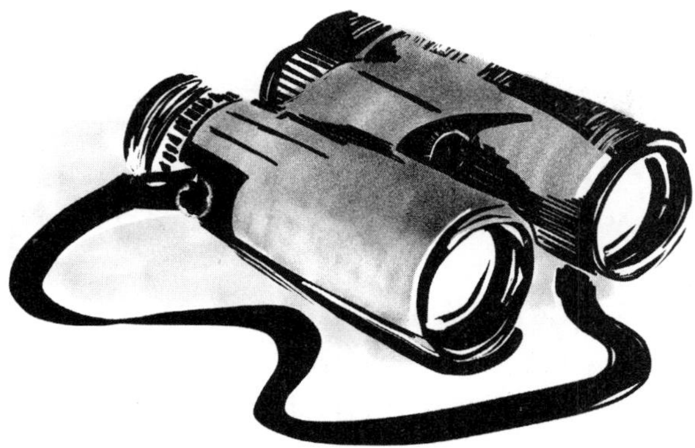

descending toward the marsh to fish for breakfast with that sword-like beak, noticing the giant bird's pterodactyl profile, the slow, steady flapping of its wings, which span six feet, and that signature squawk, which sounds like a dying monster. As the weather warmed up, squadrons of swallows pirouetted and divebombed above the grassy banks around me, plucking tiny gnats and moths flitting up from the tall grasses as the sun rose.

One bitter March morning in Warner Park, I stepped outside in deep snow and bone-chilling winds to find a new brown-headed bird making a frog-like *fee-bee* call from a bush next to the dog park bridge. I consulted my father's field guide and was thrilled to discover that the newcomer was an eastern phoebe, an insect-eating migratory bird I'd never expected to find with snow still on the ground.

The eastern phoebe belongs to the flycatcher family; several species are so similar that even experts have trouble identifying them. But I quickly realized that the phoebe was a beginning birder's best friend because it returned from the South at least two months earlier than other flycatchers, making it easy to recognize. It raised its families as far north as the Canadian Northwest Territories and south to Florida, and as far west as Colorado and all the way east to the Atlantic (the West has its own phoebes).[1]

Field guides are not kind to the phoebe: "dull-colored" is how this dark olive and sooty gray–backed bird is often described. Birders learn to identify avians by details like eyebrow stripes, crests, tufts, wing bars, spotted or stripey chests, and long or wide tails. The phoebe's most distinguishing physical characteristic is that it has none of these. Plainest of the plain, it is an avian wallflower. And yet this little bird changed ornithological history.

Approximately 205 years before I identified that eastern phoebe in Warner Park, a nineteen-year-old John James Audubon was cultivating a friendship with his own phoebe in Pennsylvania. A nature boy on steroids, young John James had a room full of birds' eggs, nests, snakeskins, fresh animal carcasses, and drawings he'd made of all of it. His favorite hideout was a cave near the house where phoebes nested. Audubon spent hours there, reading and drawing, and the birds became used to him. He noticed that this pair left every year in the fall, and in the spring a pair returned to the nest. The teenager wanted to know: Are the same birds returning every year? So when the parents left to forage for food, he tied silver threads to the baby phoebes' legs. The next year, he found adult phoebes with silver threads in the surrounding area. Young Audubon did not know it, but he had probably just banded the first birds in North America, paving the way for future avian research and conservation.[2]

Flycatchers are tiny fighter pilots that hunt by "sallying forth" or "hawking" in ornithological lingo, diving and careening as they race after dragonflies and moths, flying up to 33 miles an hour.[3] A satisfying metallic snap of their flattish beaks signals the end of that race. Then they zoom to the ground or a favored perch and beat their prey to death. Although most flycatchers are drab, this avian family includes some spectacularly named and striking birds, like the northern beardless tyrannulet, the great kiskadee—a blaze of yellow and rust with a black-and-white-striped helmet—and the vermilion flycatcher, which looks like its head is on fire.

Like the house sparrow, the phoebe is a bird that often uses human structures—sheds, barns, picnic shelters, and especially bridges—as nesting spots, along with rocky ravine ledges and cliffs. This bird has also nested in some very odd places: around the socket of an electric lamp, on a strip of wallpaper hanging from a ceiling, and seven feet underground in the air shaft of a coal mine.[4] Anyone who has grown up on a farm in the eastern United States or near a bridge probably knows a phoebe. Historically, many farmers viewed this bird as a free pest controller because it is a dogged hunter of cotton boll weevils, strawberry weevils, corn leaf beetles, ants, grasshoppers, locusts, moths, and caterpillars, as well as spiders and ticks.[5]

"We have come to look on it, not as a wild bird, but as a member of the happy community that makes up rural life—the pigs in their sty, the hens in their coops, the horses and cows in the barn, and the phoebe in the back shed. Busy all day catching insects, inobtrusive . . . it is popular with the farmers," wrote Smithsonian ornithologist Arthur C. Bent, the bird biographer bar none, famous for his twenty-one-volume series on avian life histories.[6]

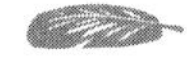

**WHEN I READ THAT PHOEBES OFTEN BUILT THEIR CUP NESTS OF MOSSES AND LICHENS ON** beams under bridges, I scrambled down onto the frozen marsh to look under the dog park bridge. I couldn't find a nest, yet there was the bird every morning, calling from its usual bush. When you live in a place where winter lasts until April, by March, you are dreaming in Technicolor because your eyeballs are so weary of white, gray, and black. Finding this single migratory bird in Warner Park lifted my spirits immediately, because right behind that phoebe, I knew that billions of birds in the South were stuffing their little beaks and preparing to take wing; six months of color deprivation was about to end. A universal avian herald of spring, the phoebe also meant I'd soon say goodbye to the down jacket, long underwear, and hideous Frankenstein polar boots, and hello to flip-flops, raggedy jeans, and soft T-shirts.

This nondescript little bird has taught me many lessons over the years, not least of all that I should never discriminate when birding by looking just for colorful, flashy birds. From the phoebe I've learned that the presence of our species doesn't have to hurt other species. We can share our buildings and transport structures, creating habitat instead of destroying it.

Before I began birding in Warner Park, I had a wall in my brain separating "nature" from anything human. But the phoebe started to bust down that wall by teaching me to value even the trashiest areas of Warner, places I never expected to find wildlife.

One late fall afternoon I followed the railroad tracks to a hidden part of Warner's wetland, the storm pipe that feeds into Lake Mendota. A sickly brown-gray pool of stagnant water lay between the Civilian Conservation Corps railroad arch and the storm drain emptying into the lake. A line of bright blue stained the stones and earth around the pool, as if someone had dumped paint into it. A red cotton shirt hung on the brush and two beer cans lay on the slopes beside a frozen custard cup. I didn't expect to find anything in the park's ugliest of spots. Then I saw a small dark-headed bird streaking after a white-winged moth. On the second dive, the phoebe snapped the moth in its beak, flitted to the nearest branch, and gobbled it down.

But what I will always be grateful to the phoebe for is that it led me to a seventy-six-year-old retired feed-mill worker named Jan Einfieldt, who knew more about Warner's animal residents than most biologists.

I was looking for the phoebe one morning, expecting to find it near the dog park bridge, but it was gone. Instead I saw a huge bear of a man with a ruddy bald head sitting under the tiny picnic shelter a few hundred yards away. He was staring at the marsh. And there was the phoebe flying all around him, flitting in and out of the picnic shelter, wagging that tail. The bird was so close to him that it looked as if it was going to land on his head. As I approached the shelter, I noticed that the man had a large metal cylinder on wheels next to him—an oxygen tank. A clear tube fed into one of his nostrils. I could hear his labored breathing from several feet away. The phoebe took off and perched in a tree, watching.

While I kept my eye on the bird, I sat down and introduced myself, and he told me his story. His name was Jan and he had chronic obstructive pulmonary disease (COPD), which meant his lungs were inflamed, the air passages narrowing, making it harder for air to flow through. A heavy smoker with fifty years of feed-mill dust in his lungs, he'd been ordered by his doctor to walk in the park. Jan lived in an apartment on the meadow's edge and spent every waking hour he could watching the animals. It reminded him of the dairy farm he'd grown up on, particularly the meadows and thickets.

"The one advantage of having a lung disease is I don't move fast. So I have more time to look at things. I have to stop and catch my breath, so I see more than you do if you're walking," he said.

This was how Jan learned that the foxes loved a certain acorn from a certain oak species. He watched two young foxes come and clean up the acorn carpet in the fall (I'd assumed it was the squirrels). He called the concrete canal running into the marsh "the hawk's dinner table," because a sharp-shinned hawk perched in the bushes and then dove and caught small songbirds as they came to the water's edge to drink. Then he discovered that in order to avoid the hawks, the songbirds had moved deeper into the thicket to drink from a large puddle.

Jan knew that the woodchuck family trotted down the dirt path through the thicket to get to the marsh to drink water—he'd seen four of them trooping in a line. He knew that the crows liked to eat hamburgers and French fries thrown out during baseball games. And he loved to watch the orb-weaving spiders that filled the meadow in early fall with dew-laden webs to trap the grasshoppers.

After his daily dose of park medicine, Jan researched everything he'd seen at home; the park had become his passion. But the animal he knew best was the phoebe.

She nested in this shelter, he told me, pointing at an old beam. There in a corner sat the small round grass nest I'd spent a month searching for. Jan wasn't exaggerating when he said that he "knew" this phoebe. While I was talking to him, the bird would not return to her nest. She skirted around the shelter's edge from tree to tree, twitching her tail, watching me, waiting. I began to feel bad—I was keeping her from doing her job. Don't take it personally, Jan told me. This bird did not trust humans she didn't know. He sat there for hours every day. She'd gotten used to him.

The phoebe is a loner bird that barely tolerates members of its own species except to mate—phoebes frequently chase their mates from the nest. Yet this female spent hours with Jan each day. Phoebes can live over ten years, so this bird probably really did know Jan.

I said goodbye, glancing over my shoulder as I walked away, watching the bird. Within seconds, Jan's phoebe left her tree perch, zoomed into the shelter, zipped over his red head, and headed for the beam directly above him. Jan leaned on his oxygen tank, breathing very slowly.*

Then I met Sandy, another animal lover who also found her body and soul medicine in Warner Park. Like Jan, she lived in an apartment a few doors from me. The building was very noisy, she said. People yelled at all hours. Someone overdosed on heroin in the apartment above her. Warner Park was her refuge. She spent an average of four hours a day walking with her rotund golden retriever Willie, and sometimes as long as eight hours in the park.

Sandy moved to Madison from Kansas after a series of devastating losses. First, her marriage fell apart. Then she got cancer in her jaw, and during chemo she lost her job and health insurance. Then she had to file for bankruptcy because of the hospital bills. She lost her beautiful home and huge yard as a result of the bankruptcy. In the middle of all this, she had two major surgeries. When all this was over, she was mentally confused and could barely walk. So she'd moved to Madison to live with her son, just down the street.

"You have to get that healing juice from somewhere," she told me, "or you don't make it. I was in very bad shape. The park revives you, in spirit as well as physically. I go sit in the park when I just can't stand it anymore, when I'm upset about life in general, when I'm kind of needy. I like it best at night when it is so still with the snow—very, very healing."

Like Jan with his oxygen tank, Sandy moved through the park at a snail's pace, one leg still recovering from surgery. She carried a folding chair with her and sometimes sat for hours even in the winter, reading and watching animals.

Sandy's face lit up as she described how she had listened to a

* Jan Einfieldt was a talented naturalist who became one of my most important park teachers over a four-year period. He died in his apartment next to Warner Park on January 1, 2014.

mother owl and her baby talking to each other late one morning, and how on summer nights she lay down on a picnic table, her dog Willie at her side, and stared at the stars or watched the park's little brown bats eating clouds of insects floating high above. And the night that she let Willie out to pee at 2:00 a.m., only to find a huge buck with antlers standing under a streetlight, staring at her.

"Have you heard the weird 'screamy' sounds the fox kits make when they're playing in the meadow?" she asked. And she told me about tiny yellow wood violets that appeared briefly in the spring in the dog park. Sandy identified them with a wildflower guide, one of several she carted around. Like Jan, she was another ecology gold mine.*

Soon I was talking to Sandy and Jan every day in the park. But there were other park lovers who sat silently in hidden corners as I walked by. Sometimes I was watching a bird through binoculars when the lens would catch a person tucked away in the vegetation, as still as the park's glacial boulders. When I first started going into the park and we spotted each other, we did not speak. We exchanged a slight nod, and then the person would shrink back into the shadows. They were quiet people, like the animals they watched. They wanted to notice, not be noticed. I understood, because that's exactly how I felt during those first post-Katrina years. But after seeing me walk around the park carrying binoculars, a field notebook, and a camera, they began to share their animal stories.

If I wanted to know what the red fox was up to, there was a man always in a baseball cap, always sitting on the bench in front of the huge bur oak with an update: fox at 7:00 a.m. running along the meadow path toward the chicken people's yard (the chicken people had a supersonic coop to guard five hens named after first ladies), fox napping on tennis courts in the woods, fox sitting on top of Sled Hill barking at the dogs in the dog park below. When he didn't see his favorite animal for days, the fox watcher got worried. Maybe the fox tried to cross the main avenues around the park and got hit by a car? Maybe someone called animal control?

* Sandy became another important teacher, comrade, and friend. Details in this section came from two interviews and conversations over a five-year period.

There was a young homeless woman who sat on another bench facing the meadow. She rolled a hard black suitcase through the fields and slept under a bush on Warner's beach. She loved to watch the animals, too. Chris was a young man with an anxiety disorder whom I met strolling down the path. He was on disability and walked in the park every day to calm himself. Like Jan and Sandy, he lived in an apartment without a yard. He enjoyed watching the geese, particularly when they paraded their new families around. In the dog park, I met a newspaper delivery man who was grieving the recent death of his wife. He worked very early in the mornings, and after he finished his shift, he headed to Warner Park, where he spent hours watching birds. He threw his arms out like wings and tilted his head backward as he told me about the park's vultures.

"They're the coolest birds. I love watching them float on the currents," he said with a huge smile. In treatment for severe depression, he called Warner Park "my sanctuary . . . I wouldn't leave the house otherwise."

And there was Golden Helmet Man, a string bean of a man who sat at a picnic table under an ash tree across from my house. It didn't matter whether it was 10 degrees or 85, he was always wearing a faded gold football helmet that fit like an acorn shell, so snug it looked like a child's helmet. He, too, lived in the apartments. His face was weathered and brown from sitting outside. He told neighbors that he was a prince.

My new park buddies moved slowly and sat still a lot because of their various illnesses. This was why they noticed things most of us never see—the tiny things that hold the planet together. I was learning about some of these relationships in my ecology and zoology courses, where we studied animal skeletons and skins. But in Warner Park I could see the red fox and follow her fresh tracks at 7:00 a.m. in the snow. Sometimes I ran headlong into her behind the chicken people's house. I was even beginning to recognize the musky scent of her urine, stronger than dog pee. What I was reading about in books and hearing in lecture halls, my new friends were teaching me in the park every day.

We were a silent tribe of quiet broken ones. We'd all had our various Katrinas. Warner Park was our medicine.

What my park buddies and I were learning in Warner Park—that being outside during those years was healing us—has since been confirmed by public health studies. These studies began with a boy and a pine tree. Roger Ulrich, today one of the world's foremost experts on hospital design and the healing effects of nature, began his long and distinguished career as a sick boy in bed in Michigan. Continually plagued by strep infections that led to kidney disease, he realized that he felt better not in sterile, windowless medical buildings, but at home, staring out the window at his "friend," a stalwart pine.[7]

In 1984, Ulrich published a pioneering hospital study showing that patients with even just a window view of a tree healed faster, required less medication, and suffered fewer complications.[8] Ulrich's initial study spawned more than a hundred studies on the potential links between nature and mental health.[9] Researchers have documented how trees and natural green spaces calm the parasympathetic nervous system, boost the immune system by reducing stress hormones, lower blood pressure, reduce glucose levels among diabetics, and relieve depression. Large medical studies controlled for income have documented that living near a green space like Warner Park can help people live longer and live healthier, with lower rates of obesity and diabetes.[10]

In 2019, Danish researchers published the largest epidemiological study to date—tracking more than 940,000 Danes—documenting a link between access to green space and improved mental health over time. By comparing personal information from Denmark's massive national tracking system (addresses, medical records, and socioeconomic data spanning decades) and high-resolution satellite imagery showing green space in neighborhoods throughout the country, scientists showed that Danish children who grew up in greener neighborhoods had far fewer mental health problems, even years later, regardless of income level. When researchers examined sixteen serious mental disorders, ranging from schizophrenia to depression to substance abuse, they discovered that a child born and raised in a neighborhood with fewer trees and parks was a whopping 55 percent more likely to develop these disorders than a child from a greener neighborhood, whether or not their family had a history of mental illness. The study also showed that the "prolonged presence of green space is important" in childhood, somehow preventing mental health illnesses into adulthood.

"Loss of human-nature interactions presents a health risk," researchers concluded. They recommended that urban planners consider the importance of green space to public health when designing urban environments, particularly school systems.[11]

When I read this study, years after leaving Warner Park, I thought about how after Katrina I knew I had to be outside as much as possible, how I was drawn to Audubon Park in New Orleans and then Warner Park in Madison. It's because I carried those childhood orange and avocado groves inside me, that tiny creek that ran through the ranch my parents worked on, the sharp astringent perfume of those eucalyptus windbreaks, the music of those creaking tall trees during a Santa Ana wind. Roger Ulrich had his pine tree. I had my favorite avocado tree, where I escaped from chores and my shouting mother by climbing up under the huge sheltering leaves with a Nancy Drew book and a bing cherry jam sandwich.

That wild hill behind our house was the first thing my eyes lifted to every morning, a deeply comforting and ancient presence. The groves, the creek, and the hill were all my personal safe places. I learned this as soon as I could walk, just as Jan Einfieldt carried his childhood farm inside him, and my Warner Park buddies from rural areas carried farms and creeks and lakes in their hearts. Even if we'd experienced financial, physical, and/or emotional ruin as adults, this knowledge was a hidden reserve of strength, a wisdom lodged deep inside us from when someone led us by the hand into that woods or meadow or onto that hill. We learned that the medicine our bodies and souls needed was all around us for the taking.

What Ulrich proved in his groundbreaking 1984 study—the healing power of nature, even through a window—a very determined girl in England learned nearly two hundred years ago. Florence Nightingale was the first person to turn her hunch that our environment impacts our health into public policy. I love her story in part because her family shares the name of the most lauded singer in the avian world, the cardinal-sized British African migratory thrush that sings in the darkness and has been a favorite of poets for millennia. Michael McCarthy, England's leading environmental reporter, describes the nightingale as a "bird-legend supreme . . . the small bird whose voice in the dark had moved people for as long as human feelings had been written down."[12] The daughter of a wealthy nineteenth-century English family, from the time she was sixteen, Nightingale used her voice and writing skills to reform health care during a century of ignorance and dangerously unsanitary conditions in hospitals. As I read her 1860 classic text, *Notes on Nursing: What It Is and What It Is Not,* I felt her passion and anger. I could hear her shouting: Throw open those windows! Give the patients fresh air, sunlight, color!

Nightingale preached, lectured, wrote, and implored until she died at ninety, bedridden for decades with various illnesses.* To minimize the spread of disease, she changed how hospitals were designed and lobbied hard for hospital gardens and floor-to-ceiling windows. She laid the foundation for future health reformers like Ulrich.[13]

I think most history is too anthropocentric. After years studying birds, I search for the feathered agents in human stories, like those baby sparrows that tamed the most notorious prisoner in the US. So when I read Nightingale's book, I was struck by how she repeatedly emphasized the importance of "colour and form [as a] means of recovery" and complained that the "effect in sickness of beautiful objects, and especially of brilliancy of colour is hardly at all appreciated . . . People say the effect is only on the mind. It is no such thing. The effect is on the body, too . . . They have an actual physical effect."[14]

These passages screamed "BIRDS!" to me. And it didn't take long to find an avian assistant in Nightingale's healing career.

In the summer of 1850, Nightingale traveled to Greece and Egypt on vacation. She was thirty years old. She was visiting the Acropolis when she came upon a group of children tormenting a tiny ball of

* There is a raging debate over Nightingale's legacy. For a century in biographies she has run the spectrum of saint to sinner. But even her worst detractors admit she saved many lives.

fluff. Nightingale was an ardent lover of birds who fed them out of her window at home: "There is nothing makes my heart thrill like the voice of birds, much more than the human voice. It is the angels calling us with their songs."[15]

She paid the children for the owlet, which had fallen from a nest, named it Athena, and returned home with it along with two tortoises and a pet cicada named Plato (alas, the owlet soon ate Plato).

Athena was a little owl (*Athene noctua*), a species just an inch or two bigger than the northern saw-whet profiled in this book's prologue. According to the delightfully strange book *Life and Death of Athena: An Owlet from the Parthenon,* penned by Nightingale's sister, the owlet became Nightingale's inseparable companion, riding on her shoulder or peeking out of a large dress pocket. Nightingale taught Athena to perch on her finger to accept treats and to "curtsy" in gratitude. Athena lived the good life of an English country manor owl for a few years; imagine *Downton Abbey* starring an owl as a family member in the nineteenth century, with birthday parties to celebrate her presumed hatch date and family excursions to the country.

The owl spent most of her day in the family's library perched among the tomes, where she hid fur cuffs and ladies' jewelry she'd stolen.[16] But then Nightingale discovered that Athena could help her heal people. At that time, Nightingale was attending a little girl who had been severely burned. Her sister wrote: "She [the owl] assisted greatly in the cure of a little burnt child, who suffered dreadfully when her wounds were dressed, but in the contemplation of Athena's bows and curtsies opposite her bed (brought for that especial purpose) forgot her woes and lay quite still while she was doctored daily."

Athena also helped Nightingale heal herself when she was sick, which was often. Nightingale's sister wrote: "When she [Nightingale] could bear no one else of larger size . . . she [Athena] sat on the bed and talked to her, she ran races all round the room after imaginary mice."

When Athena died at the age of four, Nightingale was so distraught that she had her feathered assistant stuffed and embalmed. (Athena now resides in the Florence Nightingale Museum in London.)

As she said goodbye to her embalmed pet, Nightingale declared: "Poor little beastie, it was odd how much I loved you."

Nearly 150 years later, researchers have documented how nature-based videos and music "significantly" reduce pain and anxiety in burn patients who watch or listen while their dressings are being changed, similar to the effect Athena had on that little girl.[17] But there are very few studies examining the healing power of birds because it is difficult for scientists to parse out precisely which elements of living near a green space are the most beneficial. In 2017, a research team at the University of Exeter surveyed 270 people from a wide demographic range in three cities and found that in neighborhoods with more vegetation and greater numbers of birds, residents had lower levels of depression, anxiety, and stress.[18] They concluded that people's mental health improved when watching "common" birds such as blackbirds, robins, and crows.

"Birds around the home, and nature in general, show great promise in preventative health care, making cities healthier, happier places to live," lead researcher Daniel Cox told the media.[19] This is why English hospitals and clinics now partner with the Royal Society for the Protection of Birds to offer bird walks to recovering patients.

If you still doubt the healing power of birds, consider the medical mystery of Phoebe Snetsinger, a frustrated 1960s housewife, mother of four, and avid birder. In 1981, a doctor diagnosed the fifty-year-old Snetsinger with terminal melanoma—she had one year to live. In *Life List: A Woman's Quest for the World's Most Amazing Birds,* biographer Olivia Gentile tells the story of how Snetsinger immediately decided that she would forgo treatment, and that when she got really sick, she would shoot herself. Without telling anyone, she bought a gun, wrote a suicide note, and hid both items away.[20] In the meantime, she decided to spend whatever time she had left traveling all over the world, seeing as many birds as possible.

Fourteen years later, Snetsinger became the world birding champion, the first person to see 8,000 species. Her cancer recurred every five years or so and then went into remission: birds were her only treatment.

"Birding has meant a variety of things to many different people, but for me it has been intricately intertwined with survival," Snetsinger wrote.[21]

The world birding champion died at sixty-eight, eighteen years after that terminal diagnosis, in a van accident chasing birds in Madagascar. She was hot on the trail of a small golden-yellow and green bird called Appert's tetraka.

CHAPTER 6

# A Category Five Plan

*The most common way people give up their power is by thinking they don't have any.*

ALICE WALKER

FOR MILLENNIA, OUR SPECIES HAS SEEN BIRDS AS SYMBOLS OF LIBERATION. Well, they were certainly liberating me. They'd liberated me from the worst depression of my life after Katrina, when I'd sunk into a hole of hopelessness. They'd liberated me from a journalism career that had gone stale after too many years focusing on the ugliest stories. They'd liberated me from the mental cage of a toxic decades-long relationship with my father, both of us stuck in old roles and victims of our respective cultures and generations—he the macho Irish patriarch from the Old World and I the rebellious "Wild Irish Rose" daughter from the New. And they'd liberated me from the tyranny of a life indoors staring at screens. Bird by bird, every chickadee, nuthatch, catbird, wren, and owl forged a new neural pathway in my brain, a joyful pathway. And then one bright birdy morning, I discovered that my feathered liberators were in big trouble.

It was the summer of 2009, just two years after I'd moved to Madison. I was sitting outside in Heddie's yard facing the park, my favorite stop after the morning bird tour. We were sipping coffee and eating her delicious apple pastries. It was one of those magical mornings when Heddie told me stories about the animals. She'd showed me a crack in the ground on the edge of her garden where Gertrude, the resident toad, had laid her eggs. Heddie's whole face had lit up as she told me about watching the tiny toads emerge. How she'd planted Swiss chard in her garden just for the deer and spent at least $300 every winter on birdseed. How she'd left water in pots and pans outside her open bedroom window so on summer nights she could listen to the animals lapping that water just beyond her bedroom wall. And then she would peek outside and watch the mother skunk that brought one little baby.

"The mom skunk is kind of ratty-looking. But the baby sat out there, the wind blowing in his tail. He was so pretty," she said.*

But that morning Heddie was worried. She'd come to Wisconsin from Germany after World War II, a teenage bride on the arm of an American GI. They'd moved to the edge of Warner Park in 1965,

* These stories come from conversations with Heddie over a five-year period and two interviews for my dissertation.

and she'd seen so much destruction, with the city building and mowing more and more, driving the animals away. Heddie was sad as she pointed to her fence, telling me that there was once a badger that walked on top of it. He'd disappeared by the 1970s. She once counted fifty pheasants in the meadow.* When the large mowers came and the pheasants were nesting, she'd rush out and invite the workers over. She'd set them up at this table with home-baked cookies and a pitcher of lemonade, then zip back to the meadow to shoo all the pheasant chicks into the thicket, out of harm's way, before the mowers finished their cookies. She did this for years, but the pheasants still disappeared, along with many other beautiful birds.

Now she'd heard that the city wanted to build a sidewalk leading from near her house into the meadow, paving a natural trail. The park already had a paved road running through it, and there was a sidewalk on my side of the street. So why pave through a meadow? She used to keep an eye on neighborhood politics, she told me, but she was over eighty and afraid of falling. It was hard to go to meetings at night.

That morning Heddie suspected that the sidewalk was just the beginning of something else. Why can't the city leave the meadows and woods alone? she asked. You're studying ecology. Will another sidewalk affect the animals? Could you go to a meeting and find out about this?

I didn't want to fight a stupid sidewalk. I'd come to Madison to hide in the ivory tower. And I had another goal—to find 100 bird species in Warner Park and become a "real" birder. I was stuck at species number 85 and needed to spend more time in the park. I'd been in school only two years and was just beginning to understand ecology; I had no time for activism. Besides, Madison was a progressive city that had already figured everything out. I didn't need to get involved.

And I'll admit it—I also had a rotten attitude about local politics. In Nicaragua and Guatemala, local politics were fascinating to me. But in the United States, the doings of city councils and school boards

* An Asian species brought to the United States in the 1800s, the ring-necked pheasant was introduced in Wisconsin for hunters.

seemed trivial. Years earlier I'd been an interpreter during secret meetings between US congressmen and Salvadoran guerrillas in swanky hotel rooms in Mexico City and Caracas. I'd interpreted for former president Jimmy Carter when he came to Nicaragua to meet with then president Violeta Chamorro. I'd schmoozed and strategized at urgent NGO conclaves in Panama City, San José, and Geneva. Yet I'd never once been to a neighborhood or city council meeting anywhere I'd lived except Managua during the revolution.

But this was Heddie asking me to do it. Heddie, our lady of the applesauce, who had also become our lady of the breaded pork chops, the homemade currant jelly, and the freshly baked green bean pie right from her garden. I just couldn't say no to her.

And that's how I ended up at my very first neighborhood association meeting in the country of my birth. Years later as I page through old journals, I realize that maybe this was the night I became a citizen of a place, not just of the world. My Irish parents had to attend night school for a year and pass a test to become citizens. I still have the tiny green book they used to study, *Twenty-Five Lessons in Citizenship*, published in 1943—"our bible," my mother called it. But in Madison, there was no test, no hoopla, no swearing in or singing of an anthem. I simply went to a drab little meeting in a drab little room, raised my hand, and asked a question.*

"Can you please tell me about that new sidewalk on Monterey Drive, on the park side? When is that going to be built? And why do we need another sidewalk?"

"Oh," a neighborhood leader said, "that won't happen for years. Don't worry about it. It's part of the new neighborhood plan. Half that stuff won't get done. It's just a plan. People in Madison like to make plans," he added with a laugh. "Most of them never go anywhere."[1]

My whole professional life as a journalist had been based on the power of the printed word. Gongs started clanging wildly in my head when he said "plan." I rushed home to google it. That same night,

---

* More than 30 percent of my neighbors were people of color, and the percentage was higher in the apartments on my street, so I was surprised that the dozen attendees were all white and over fifty years old. I didn't recognize anyone. The meeting focused on fear of crime.

165 pages later, I realized Heddie was right—this was not about a sidewalk. Our park was about to get a radical redo. In this plan, a field where deer grazed in the morning would become a parking lot—this field was also the front yard for a block of apartments housing dozens of families. The shallow wetland where herons and egrets fished and shy wood ducks raised their families would become a pontoon concession. And the swampy inaccessible marsh island where geese, marsh wrens, and sandhill cranes nested—a "ceremonial site" to rent out for weddings and other events. A small bridge would lead to it, meaning a stream of humans and dogs on that island. Goodbye, shy nesting birds. The plan also called for the installation of lights all over the park, the replacement of natural wooded trails with paved paths, the "clearing" of the catbirds' thicket on the meadow's edge—the same thicket where the foxes dug their den and from which the doe emerged every May with a fawn. And city planners thought that the wild meadow was a great spot for another lighted soccer field or a community garden.

Half the park's 213 acres was already covered by mowed grass, buildings, sports facilities, or parking lots. Warner Park was the second-largest municipal park in Madison and easily the busiest park in the entire state, with soccer fields, basketball courts, tennis courts, baseball fields, parking, playgrounds, a 31,655-square foot community center, woods, a wetland, a white-sand beach, a boat landing, an off-leash dog park, and a 6,750-seat baseball stadium. The parks department claimed that more than 750,000 people visited Warner Park every year. Many came to the park just for "the largest firework show in the Midwest," Madison's annual Rhythm and Booms, which Jim and I discovered was held right across the street in the wetland (our real estate agent had neglected to mention this). Just before every Fourth of July, F-16s hurtled over the crowds and skydivers jumped out of planes before pyrotechnicians launched thousands of mortars into the turtles' and beavers' marsh.

This park was so many things to hundreds of thousands of people, but what I loved most about it was that at the very same time, it was also a major urban wildlife refuge, a living example of how we—the furred, finned, feathered, and human—could share the planet. On my daily bird walks I'd discovered that the railroad tracks on the park's border were a wildlife highway where a mother fox taught four kits to hunt and a killdeer laid her eggs in a rock nest just inches from the rails. Snapping turtles measuring two feet in diameter crawled out of the wetland and lumbered up the railroad banks to dig nests all along the tracks, their tiny babies scrambling out of the gravel covering them in the spring. At dusk, the designated dog park was the hunting grounds of that great horned owl perched high in a cottonwood. Sandhill cranes had been nesting on the marsh island for decades. The cliff swallows built mud nests on the metal walls of the Warner Park picnic shelter.* Mink and beaver cruised the wetland along with hundreds of migrating ducks and geese. The red-tailed hawks both courted and hunted inside the baseball stadium, even during home games, when they occasionally thrilled fans, whizzing by with a freshly killed squirrel. And the red fox napped on the shaded tennis courts on summer afternoons.

The animals shared all these spaces with us, so why couldn't we continue to share it with them? The plan, which specifically targeted the last hundred wonderfully wild acres, home to so many nonhumans, was going to change all that.

I started digging into Madison's parks history to figure out what was going on. I discovered that the city had a dual recreation and conservation parks system, which protected some wetlands and not others. The conservation parks were where the "real" nature was supposed to be; buildings and sports facilities were discouraged or even prohibited. All animals and plants were protected with strict rules for public use. But Warner had been designated decades earlier as a recreation park, which was why it had all the sports facilities, buildings, and fireworks shows. It was where nature was not supposed to be. But somebody forgot to tell the birds that.

* As of spring 2014, there were sixty-five nests—an entire cliff swallow colony. The parks department removed all the nests. They told Wild Warner that there were complaints about bird poop. These nests had been there at least seven years. Cliff swallows are long-distance migrants who winter as far south as Argentina and Brazil, and then return to Warner Park.

By now I had a small stack of orange ornithology field books full of species lists from two years and 135 hours birding in the park. During those blissful hours, I'd found 85 species, at least 60 percent of them long-distance migrators like the catbird in my yard. In just that first year and a half of birding, I'd discovered two important facts about Warner Park: First, it was a major feeding station for migrating birds passing through, birds coming from much farther north heading south in the fall and passing through again in the spring. Second, like New Orleans's Audubon Park or New York's Central Park—a world hot spot for birding—my neighborhood park was also a bird paradise, a gigantic bird nursery where so many avians raised their families.

I was learning in my classes and from my blissful hours of reading in UW-Madison's gem of an ornithology library about the perils of migration and the field of stopover ecology. Scientists were studying how the Warner Parks of the world—urban green spaces in New York City, Washington, DC, Seattle, Chicago, New Orleans, San Francisco, Berlin, Madrid, and other cities worldwide—provided a vital network of feeding and resting stations for migrating birds facing an increasingly perilous journey.[2]

I'd spend a happy afternoon reading about all this and step outside the next morning in spring or fall to find five hermit thrushes hiding in the sumac just across the street on Warner Park's edge. They were quiet birds, hard to find because they were the color of fallen leaves. But their eerie fluting song was unmistakable. These hermit thrushes, on their way south, stayed in Warner at least a week. Other species of migratory birds stayed for a precious day and some for a week or more. They were feathered ambassadors on their way to the South or Latin America; I felt such a thrill every time I caught a fleeting glimpse of them or heard a scrap of a new song.

Yet another fall morning, a cacophony of weird roaring was coming from the dog park marsh. To my astonishment, I found hundreds of blackbirds rattling from the tops of the cattails—red-winged blackbirds mixed with grackles making their squeaky door call—a din that drowned out the barking dogs and migrating geese. I sat at the base of a cottonwood on the wetland's shore watching and listening for an hour before they zoomed off in a giant black rattling cloud, heading due south.

Small battalions of ducks also came through in all colors and shapes to rest, feed, regroup, and reconnect with their flocks before taking off. My favorite were the Arctic ducks—the buffleheads—that look like black-and-white rubber duckies. I probably would never see a bufflehead duckling—one of my secret birder ambitions—because they breed so far north. But I didn't need to go to the Arctic because the Arctic flew through Warner Park every spring and fall. Here were the adults cavorting in Warner's wetland during every migration.

Some bird species migrate as individuals, but most migrate in flocks. For some avians, migration is innate. For others, the adults have to teach teenage birds how to do it. Since many birds remember their migration routes and those gas stations, some of these birds may have been stopping in Warner Park for years.

Most birds migrate at night when it's cooler and there is less wind. Leaving at dusk, they flap hard until they reach a good stopover point to refuel for the next day. Birds usually migrate at altitudes ranging from 1,300 to 20,000 feet except on stormy or foggy nights when they can't see through the clouds and have to fly close to the ground.* They use the stars and earth's magnetic field to navigate.[3]

Long-distance migratory birds coming through Warner may have been making this epic journey from Latin America to the United States and Canada for at least 10,000 years. But in the last century, our species has turned their flight routes into death-defying obstacle courses. Ornithologists have known for decades that strong lights can confuse birds' navigation systems. The lights of buildings and cell

---

* A bird's migration altitude can vary enormously. Swedish researchers tracking birds migrating from Sweden to Africa discovered they may fly much higher than formerly believed: see Sissel Sjöberg, "Migratory Birds Found to Be Flying Much Higher Than Expected—New Research," The Conversation, September 13, 2021, https://theconversation.com/migratory-birds-found-to-be-flying-much-higher-than-expected-new-research-167582. However, birds on the eastern side of the United States tend to fly much lower, making the journey through skyscraper cities much more dangerous: see Gustave Axelson, "New BirdCast Analysis Shows How High Migrating Birds Fly," *All About Birds,* Cornell Lab of Ornithology, October 13, 2021, https://www.allaboutbirds.org/news/new-birdcast-analysis-shows-how-high-migrating-birds-fly/#.

towers lure them to their deaths either by collision or exhaustion, since some circle around the lights for hours until they drop. The worst known recorded bird kill caused by lights in the United States happened in October 1954—106,804 birds in four nights—when a storm forced birds migrating south during the fall to fly below 800 feet. At just one airport near Macon, Georgia, lighted towers and the airport ceilometer—the light beam used to measure the cloud ceiling—lured in more than 50,000 birds on one fatal night.

"An observer at Warner Robins Air Force Base noted birds flying straight downward in the beam and bouncing off a concrete runway! . . . The innumerable instances of hemorrhages and broken bones now provide undisputed evidence that death came as the result of collisions with solid objects . . . Dead birds were strewn by the hundreds over the runways, taxi strips, grassy plots, and tops of buildings . . . and had been shoveled up and raked together," wrote ornithologists David Johnston and T. P. Haines.[4]

This horrific die-off made ornithological history simply because it was so obvious. The fact is, this scenario is repeated every year in major cities across the United States and Canada where skyscrapers and buildings are lit up throughout the night. According to NYC Audubon, collisions with lighted buildings (especially with windows) kill at least 600 million birds a year in the United States, 230,000 in just New York City.* This is why in the mornings during migration, volunteers scour city streets searching the base of skyscrapers for dead or injured birds.

Anyone who lives in New York City can easily see how lights affect birds every September when the Tribute lights are turned on to commemorate the victims of September 11, 2001. The two columns rise four miles into the sky, right in the middle of fall migration, trapping thousands of birds in the light.[5] A seven-year study of the Tribute's effect on bird migration found that bird density increases up to 150 times in the area when the lights are turned on. Researchers estimated

* Audubon has a national Lights Out education program that has helped dim the lights during migration in many major cities. Anyone can easily petition elected officials and building managers to dim the lights to help the birds. Go to https://www.audubon.org/lights-out-program.

that the light columns affected the migration of 1.1 million birds during those seven years.[6] Scientists now working with Tribute employees count the birds trapped in the beams, and when the numbers hit over 1,000, the lights are turned off for at least twenty minutes, giving the feathered migrators time to move on.

These are some of the reasons that approximately half of all migrating birds do not survive the trip. But the birds that nested in Warner and survived migration probably came right back to the park. Loyal to their place—biologists call this "site fidelity"—every spring they returned to their marsh, their cattail island, their thicket. The park's eastern wood pewees that nested in the largest bur oak could fly as far as the Andes. Warner's hummingbirds probably crossed the Gulf of Mexico in one daunting eighteen-hour flight to return to their favored trees or bushes, where they built those tiny expandable nests. The sandhill crane pair disappeared every fall to head somewhere south. A sandhill crane could live twenty-five years. Warner Park was their home.

But their home was about to get trashed. I stared at the plan online and imagined all those birds, returning in the spring from Latin America, exhausted after flying thousands of miles. In my mind's eye I could see them hovering over Warner Park, staring down at an unrecognizable landscape, wondering where in the hell their bush, their tree, their cattail marsh had gone. I knew exactly what that felt like, remembering when I found that first horrific aerial photo online of my home underwater in New Orleans.

I could not sleep that night or many nights afterward. Now when I gazed out our living room window, instead of enjoying that spruce tree and the deer, I imagined bulldozers ripping out those black walnut trees that fed the squirrels and shaded the trail. I was going to wake up one morning and hear that bulldozer beeping, branches crashing, and giant roots being torn from the earth, reaching for the sky like gigantic dismembered fingers.

I showed the plan to Sandy and Jan. Sandy was very upset about the proposal to increase mowing of the meadows. She loved watching the clouds of dragonflies that hovered over the meadow in late summer, feeding on insects. With no grasses to hide the insects, what would the dragonflies eat? Jan was disturbed, too, and had already noticed an increase in mowing. People didn't understand the importance of hedgerows and thickets like we did on the farm, he told me.

I knew I owed that park and the birds my life. It was the same for Jim. Just the sight of all that green across the street—the spruce, the pines, the black walnut trees—calmed our nervous systems after Katrina. It was like Ulrich's 1984 study of the healing green view through a window.

**JIM AND I DECIDED WE HAD TO FIGHT FOR THE PARK AND ITS ANIMAL RESIDENTS, BUT I HAD** no idea how. I'd been involved in many movements—for human rights, for peace, anti-apartheid, civil rights, gay rights—but had never done any environmental activism. As I watched the birds and wondered how to help them, I started thinking about how they defended their own territories in and around the park. One morning I heard a group of crows angrily cawing. I followed the noise and found about thirty crows perched in a pine tree cluster, all vociferously scolding a huge great horned owl, who was trying to hide under a top branch. After ten minutes of crow hell, the owl gave up and flew away.

I had just witnessed what ornithologists call "mobbing," one of many strategies avians employ to defend their homes and drive away predators. I witnessed it again when I climbed into a bush to examine a gray catbird's nest in my yard; only this time, I was the predator. The mother catbird gave a loud alarm call, and I was suddenly surrounded by twelve species of diminutive birds—including nuthatches, house finches, chickadees, goldfinches, and a downy woodpecker—all giving me a piece of their avian minds. If you've ever wandered near a red-winged blackbird's nest in a marsh and had to shield your head and run from the tiny enraged feathered dive bomber, you know what it is to be humbled by a creature that weighs 2.8 ounces.

Birds can be violent; they are not feathered Bambis. A sibling can eat a smaller sibling. Males in some species physically fight over nesting territories. But in general, most bird species do not fight hard physically. They can't afford to. If they get injured, they can't fly. A grounded bird is a dead bird. Birds defend their places and families mostly by singing. Loudly.

But the very first thing birds do when they move into a new area is gather information. A bird's survival depends on its ability to find food, figure out where predators hang out, find fresh water, and detect potential roosting holes and crannies to stuff themselves into on bitter nights.

I thought about my knowledge of my new Madison territory. I was beginning to know the park well since this was where I spent most of my time. But I didn't know much about *Homo sapiens* in my neighborhood. The streets and houses were also part of my territory—not just the park.

I read and reread the Plan, chewing on it, scanning for clues. Although I was pretty horrified by the chapter overhauling the park, this was just one chapter of nine; the others were mostly about how to help lower-income neighborhoods around the park. The neighborhood plan was part of a city-led effort to spur economic development in our area, and we badly needed it. The plan stressed the need to beautify our region, known as Madison's Northside, which included Warner Park. According to planners, we needed "a brand."

When I studied a demographic map and census data for the Warner area, I realized that on the northeast side of the park, the minority population was 39 percent, the median income was $28,542, and 10 percent of the residents had a college degree. We lived right on the edge of that northeast area. Meanwhile, just a bike ride across the park, on the park's southwestern border in a tony neighborhood where the governor's mansion stood, the minority population was 2 percent, the median household income was $151,875, and 82 percent of the residents had a college degree. I realized that Warner Park was surrounded by some of Madison's starkest inequality, and Jim and I were living right in the middle of it. But we were also surrounded by cultural richness. Many of our neighbors were immigrants from Africa, Iraq, the Philippines, Central America, Mexico, and Cambodia, and white people of all backgrounds. Local schools resembled mini United Nations, with over a dozen languages spoken in the hallways.

My husband had begun volunteering as a cook at our neighborhood food pantry. The recession had just hit a year earlier in 2008, and the number of people coming for a free dinner and groceries had nearly doubled. Jim was stunned at the growing number of families coming with small children. Most "clients" had jobs, he told me late every Friday night when he came home exhausted after chopping piles of onions and potatoes. He was handing a plate to Madison's working poor, the people who lived outside the university's Oz-like bubble that dominated the city's center. Their jobs as janitors, nurse's aides, grocery clerks, construction laborers, fast-food servers, and cafeteria workers simply did not pay enough to keep up with rising rents, monthly bills, and the cost of food.

Even though I was studying for a PhD and employed by the university, our financial situation wasn't much better. Jim was an award-winning journalist and filmmaker who had published eleven books. But in the age of online free everything—music, writing, photography—to be a "writer" now meant to be perpetually unemployed. When Katrina hit us, we'd lost everything and had no savings. As well-established freelance journalists, we'd never had to look hard for good work. Then with the rise of the internet, the employment market changed dramatically, and journalism as we knew it collapsed like the New Orleanian levees. Suddenly, after decades of earning a living through research and writing, neither of us could earn a penny by wielding a pen.

You never expect the worst to happen. Until it does. We'd applied for a post-Katrina government loan to rebuild our lives and buy this little house. Now I'd added college loans. Like some of our neighbors, we were hanging on to the middle class by our fingernails.

But living next to this park made us feel rich. When we walked through the wildflower meadow every day, surrounded by bumblebees and monarchs, for that hour we forgot all else. Our daily walk reminded me of the words of Rose Schneiderman, a labor activist, feminist, and socialist in the early twentieth century: "What the woman who labors wants is the right to live, not simply exist—the right to life as the rich woman has the right to life, and the sun and music and art . . . The worker must have bread, but she must have roses, too."

The park and the birds had become our daily ration of roses.

One day I was gazing out our picture window, musing, when I saw two boys, one Black and one white, tossing a football back and forth in that green corridor on a summer afternoon. They were playing underneath that line of twenty-one black walnut trees in the planning bull's-eye—set to be chopped down if that proposed sidewalk got built. That green corridor and the sumac thicket that bordered the tiny playground was what Richard Louv, author of *Last Child in the Woods: Saving Our Children from Nature-Deficit Disorder,* calls an "unofficial playground." Children tumbled on the grass and ran between the trees. Someone had dragged an old rotting brocaded armchair into the sumac, a soft golden throne. On summer days I'd see kids clambering all over it and hiding behind it. They turned sumac branches into swords and held jousting matches. Later I'd find their abandoned sumac swords lying in the grassy path. What video game or fairy tale or movie scene had they been re-creating for themselves while northern cardinals clicked in the bushes and the yellow-bellied sapsuckers tapped away? A sidewalk would tame all this.

I decided to talk to those two little boys playing football. I walked over and asked if they thought there should be a sidewalk there.

"Why? It's stupid. We like to play here," one of the boys said.

"If we get in a tackle and fall, we could get hurt. This is a park," the other one said.

When I told them the city was definitely going to put in a sidewalk, they both started talking at once. They really loved the trees because the trees gave them shade in the summer. They didn't want anyone cutting the trees down. They also loved the deer that emerged from the thicket, sometimes standing in the playground.[7] The boys said they would go home and make signs to tell people about the trees.

Two hours later, there was one of them trooping back and forth in front of my house with a homemade sign that read: "Save the Trees!" I went outside and took a picture of him. I wondered if city planners ever consulted the children who lived and played in these places.

That fall, several city commissions were meeting to approve the final version of the neighborhood plan. It had become clear that our only chance to stop it was these public meetings. But the one thing I absolutely did not want to do was become the privileged white NIMBY enviro-homeowner defending the birds and the park in her front yard. I would not speak out at these meetings and oppose a plan that my neighbors supported, especially if they were neighbors living in the low-income apartments down the street.

I consulted a friend, a hardened and wizened politico involved in city and state politics. When I asked if it was hard to stop a neighborhood plan, he snorted. Forget about it, he said. People had worked hard for years on this plan and attended dozens of meetings. I would be an outsider dropping in at the last minute to oppose it. I hadn't helped. I hadn't attended any public meetings or participated. They'd take that very personally, he said. The people who put all their time and energy into these plans, especially elected officials, became deeply invested in them, he warned, even if some of these plans weren't very good. It became about their egos, their political legacy. Don't waste your time, he told me. Focus on your dissertation.

But that conversation with the two little boys had really made me wonder. What if a group of people from the neighborhood spoke out at the upcoming meetings? What if there were a lot more people like those kids and me and Heddie and Sandy and Jan? What if we organized our own avian-style mobbing?

I still had no idea what most neighbors really thought of the park. So I decided to explore the human side of my territory, by doing what the birds do—avian reconnaissance. Over the next month, on weekends, I knocked on doors.

One of the first neighbors I talked to was a young woman who lived in the apartments facing a field that would soon be a parking lot. She'd dropped out of college because she got pregnant, she told me. Now she had two children. She'd moved here two years ago because these were the only affordable apartments in Madison with green space.

"Everywhere else I'd have been looking into someone's bathroom."

Her kids loved to play in the park. She had six jars of snails in her kitchen that they'd been collecting.

"They're boys," she said ruefully.

She worked nights and described driving home early in the morning and seeing that field across the street covered with mist, deer feeding. That patch of beauty made life "bearable."

When I told her that that field was going to be a parking lot, she got upset. She'd never heard of the plan or the parking lot. She gave me her name and phone number. I told her about the upcoming meetings. She said she'd try to come, but it would be hard, since she worked at night.

I started hanging around the apartment parking lots on Saturday and Sunday afternoons when a lot of people were outside. I asked them how long they'd lived there and what they thought about the park across the street. Did they like it or not? I also asked what they thought about the neighborhood plan. In case they hadn't heard of the plan, I'd copied and pasted excerpts from it to hand out.

I expected to learn a lot about my neighborhood during this informal survey. What I did not expect was to learn even more about the birds of Warner Park. One weekend I was walking around with my clipboard on the park's perimeter and I started talking with a married couple, a Black man and a white woman. They were standing outside their apartment across from where the new parking lot was going to go. They told me that they "loved" the park, especially the deer they saw grazing in that field. They'd never heard of the neighborhood plan, either. They didn't know that this field was going to be another parking lot. They were very unhappy to hear this.

"What about the hoot owls?" the man asked. He specifically wanted to know how a new parking lot and lights and cutting down trees in those woods was going to affect the park's great horned owls.

I knew the owls he was talking about. I'd found one in the woods very near his apartment in the winter. One night I was sitting in our living room next to our woodstove around six o'clock when I heard an owl hooting. The sky was darkening fast, but I grabbed my binoculars and ran into the park. A small blond boy came tearing out of the apartments and stood next to me. His name was Aaron.

Aaron and I peered deep into the woods together with our best owl-eyes, trying to discern a large shape in the shadows. And then we saw it—a strange brown cylinder shape two feet tall, high in a pine about fifty feet away. The owl stared straight at us with those huge yellow-orange eyes—the largest in the owl world—its tufted horns blowing in the fall winds. The bird looked half the size of the little boy standing next to me.

"WOW," Aaron said, "is that an owl?"

"It sure is."

Aaron's face left the owl for a millisecond and turned up, looking at me.

"That's the first time I've ever seen an owl," he said solemnly.

For several minutes we stood in silence, side by side, two strangers watching one owl. Then the boy heard another call. His mother was yelling for him to come inside.

"Goodbye," he said, and scampered off into the dark.

**I DON'T KNOW HOW THE PLAN WILL AFFECT THE OWLS, I TOLD MY NEIGHBOR, SOMEWHAT** chagrined. I told him and his wife that I knew the owls nested around here somewhere, but I didn't know where. After Aaron and I saw the owl, I'd spent several January nights tromping through two feet of snow in Warner's woods like an idiot with my bird buddy Stacy, both of us yelling "Hoo, hoo, hoo,roooooo, hoooo," trying to find the nest. I'd felt so frustrated. How could two ornithology students possibly miss such a big nest in the woods?

My neighbor set me straight. The owls didn't nest in the woods or in the park, he told me. He led me over to a tall evergreen just a few feet from his apartment. He pointed skyward. High up in a large fork sat a messy stick nest 1.5 feet wide. A telltale whitewash of bird feces was running down the tree trunk. The nest was right in front of his second-story window.

"Better than TV," my neighbor said. He and his wife and kids sat at their window and watched "The Owl Show" all winter. They were thrilled when the parents flew in with food for the babies. They heard them hooting all the time. They loved the owls.[8]

That "Owl Show" would have been better than any Netflix series. Most great horned owls avoid the hassle of nest-building and find a decently built hawk's or crow's nest that has been abandoned, like the one in my neighbor's tree. Wisconsin owls start nesting as early as late January, so my neighbors may have seen the owls bringing bark and leaves to spruce up the old nest, but most likely the female simply plucked a few of her own breast feathers to make the nest soft and warm. She might have used rabbit fur or feathers of birds she'd killed to line the nest before laying two to four eggs.[9]

Since great horned owls have one of the longest incubation periods of any avian, my neighbors would have seen her sitting on that nest for at least a month. Meanwhile her mate came back and forth, carrying squirrels and rodents. Most male and female owls work as a team, so some days he might have sat on the eggs, when she needed a break. Of course he would fly in to defend her if crows tried to mob her on the nest, and given the number of crows in our neighborhood, that probably happened.[10] But mostly they would have seen her sitting there, day and night, even during blizzards, completely covered in snow, protecting her eggs. The miracle technology of feathers allowed her to stay on that nest in temperatures as low as 40 below zero. Her layers of feathers meshed like Velcro, keeping heat in and allowing her to survive. Like the females of many avian species, she also had a "brood patch," her own built-in heating pad to incubate the eggs. All she had to do was keep that patch of bare skin right on top of them.

If my neighbors had been watching on Hatch Day, they would really have gotten a thrill. A few hours before owlets hatch, they whimper from inside their white eggshells; the mother would have heard those cries. She would have stood up, stared at the eggs, maybe bent over to listen more closely or examined the eggshells for cracks. She might have conferred with her mate. Then the tiny white fluffballs would have come crashing out, chipping their way into the world with a special egg tooth.

Now the Warner owl parents' work really began. When they hatched, each owlet weighed approximately 35 grams, or as much as two medium-sized chocolate chip cookies.[11] The owlets would have gained that same amount in weight every day for five to six weeks until they reached 75 percent of an adult's weight. Feeding is a major operation when babies first hatch. This mother had to keep the owlets underneath her chest and belly, using her huge feathered feet and talons as a kind of cage to corral the squirming, bobbing, chirping owlets between her legs. Then she would have bent over, poked, and got a dead squirrel into position with one of her feet, still rocking her big fluffy body side to side to keep the owlets underneath her while she tore at the squirrel and stuffed the bloody squirrel bits into the tiny beaks. Meanwhile the babies were either clacking their beaks contentedly or begging with a grating rasp of a call. And for days and nights she just kept bending, tearing, twisting, pulling, rocking, and stuffing in an ancient rhythm of mothering, a numbing repetition of a series of motions whether you're a breastfeeding mammal or a carnivorous avian.

I suppose for a human the mothering most analogous to feeding two owlets would be nursing twins together. Except that the human mother doesn't have to worry about one adorable baby gnawing on and then eating their little brother or sister because they didn't get enough milk.

By day 15, my neighbors' owlets would already have known about "stranger danger," and hissed and swayed side to side, raising their emerging wings and furiously snapping or "clapping" their tiny beaks in warning if a human had tried to approach their nest. And woe to the human or scientist who tries to do this. The great horned owl is one of the fiercest birds on the planet, as some ornithologists have discovered too late when they've climbed trees to examine nests and almost gotten scalped.[12] Great horned owls can beat up an eagle—a larger bird over four times an owl's weight—and they can take over an eagle's nest. A three-to-four-pound owl can catch and carry off a house cat or little dog up to four times its weight. The females are at least 20 percent larger than the male owls, which is true for all raptors—hawks, owls, and eagles—with some females up to 50 percent larger. Some scientists believe this is because females on the nest need to be able to fight off predators.

By day 21, my neighbors might have seen the owlets trying to use their tiny agile toes to grab squirrel snacks in the nest to nibble on, just like a toddler picking a cookie off the floor. By the end of week 4, they were scooting their little butts up to the very edge of the nest and shooting their feces out over the edge, as that telltale whitewash on the trunk indicated (meditating under a great horned owl's nest is not recommended).

My neighbors might have witnessed moments of owl tenderness when the mother returned to the nest from a break and covered the babies with her feathers, quietly uttering, *Hut, hut, hut.*[13] And they probably glimpsed some very comical scenes—what might appear as owl yoga, with owlets and their mother extending one leg at a time in stretches or raising both wings over their heads. But owl parenting is mostly gory, with the mother crushing rabbit skulls and other prey and tearing the unlucky meals apart, limb by limb. Some owls use their nests as a pantry as well as nursery, so there could even have been a few dead animals in that nest. Owl researchers studying nests in the Yukon found a dozen snowshoe hares stored in one nest, along with fifteen northern pocket gophers.[14]

The Warner owlets would have stayed in that nest until around day 40—Fledging Day—a universally harrowing and exhausting time for parents of many species, including ours. The owlets still cannot fly for a few more days, so this is the most dangerous time for them. They climb out and venture onto nearby branches, but there's always the risk they'll plunge to the ground. These owlets were lucky. With my neighbors there, they probably would have been saved.*

Like the phoebe, the great horned owls in front of the apartments also helped erode that wall in my brain separating humans from nature. The nest was across the street from the ball fields, just twenty feet from a streetlight and twelve feet from my neighbors' window. It was a noisy, busy spot, where police cars often parked—absolutely the last place I'd expected to find an owl's nest, which showed what an ornithological dunce I was and revealed some of my biases. I'd assumed that wildlife and "nature" should be in the woods, not in front of public housing. But Warner Park provided just the right combination of what these owls needed to raise a family.

Although the city's plan for Warner Park had been developed with the best of intentions—to help economically struggling neighborhoods like mine—city planners apparently shared some of my wrongheaded assumptions and biases. The plan's message was that my neighbors living in public housing on the park's perimeter needed "development," and a new "brand," and "beautification," whatever that meant. They

* After the initial fledging period is over and the owlets can fly, they may follow their parents for months. Sibling owlets may sleep together at night for several weeks while parents sleep elsewhere (some ornithologists speculate it is to get away from the insistent begging for food). Biologists have observed fledglings as old as five months still begging.

did not need or value an owl family in their front yard or the sight of deer grazing in the morning mist or an empty field across the street.

**WILDLIFE AND CONSERVATION ORGANIZATIONS USE PHOTOS OF LARGE "CHARISMATIC" ANI-** mals like tigers, lions, elephants, polar bears—animals that stare back at us with those humanlike eyes—to solicit donations. After meeting my owl-fan neighbors, I realized that these owls could be Warner Park's conservation icons, our flying tigers, and maybe they could help rally neighbors to stop the plan. I found an arresting photo of a great horned owl, horns raised, with huge midnight-black pupils and glowing yellow irises, and stuck it at the top of a clunky one-page flyer headlined: "LET'S PROTECT THE WILD SIDE OF WARNER PARK." Then I cut and pasted in the plan's most egregious excerpts and listed every forthcoming public meeting.

The owl flyer was my version of an avian alarm call. I purposefully did not put my name on it because I was trying to muster up a "we." If you want to build a flock, first you have to imagine one.

Whistling away, I plastered that owl's mug on every windshield and every apartment and park bulletin board. I followed residents through locked lobby doors and then ran up and down each floor corridor, knocking, handing out the flyer and asking for phone numbers so I could remind people about meetings (landlords called the city councilor to complain about the owl flyer). Then I tacked the owl flyer to the trees along Warner's winding path, where walkers, cyclists, and joggers would see it. I targeted Warner's heavily trafficked dog park, popping into the informal morning canine-lovers' coffee hour at a picnic table.

By the end of that month of surveying and flyering, I'd talked to at least thirty people about the park and the plan. A few, like the owl lovers, were passionate about the park. But most were more neutral, saying, "It's fine the way it is." "It's nice." "It's okay," or "I don't know." In academic terms, my informal unscientific survey was a failure. I really couldn't say what most neighbors thought about the park or if they even thought about it at all.

This was particularly true for my neighbors of color. Some

conversations with Black neighbors felt like the forced casual chats I'd tried to have with rural Guatemalans in war zones when they'd stare back at me—a white foreigner with a tape recorder and a notebook—as if I were a dentist about to extract a large molar. But I'd been recruited to work in Guatemala by Mayan refugee organizations and was also working very closely with the Catholic Church's human rights office, so all I had to do was drop a name or two and the door would open; people had to know who you were and where you stood. It was the same when I was conducting hate crimes research in the Deep South. As soon as I mentioned that I was with the Southern Poverty Law Center and a member of the NAACP, hate crime victims would share their stories because they knew who I was and that I was part of a movement for change.

Jim and I had quickly sensed from our Madison white neighbors' coded language about "people from Chicago" that racial dynamics in the Midwest could be as bad as in the Deep South. At least in the South, people (those we knew) talked about racism, instead of pretending that everything was fine and midwestern "nice." In Madison we could see micro-segregation, block by block. Our neighborhood was divided between white homeowners and apartment residents, many of color. There were rarely any neighbors of color at neighborhood association meetings. And the university was overwhelmingly white. There wasn't a single Black student or professor in any of my courses.

And I was not working with civil rights organizations in Madison. I'd chosen to exercise my white privilege and focus entirely on environmental issues; I'd become "the bird lady." I made this choice after Katrina because I suddenly viewed birds, frogs, and the Earth itself as part of the "underdog" community that I'd always identified with and tried to show solidarity with through journalism and activism. But "bird lady" wasn't going to bust through my neighbors' distrust, and I was learning that "graduate student" was just as bad. Because my university, like too many research institutions, mostly worked in the "community" when researchers needed people of color and other "marginalized" groups to "study" and for public relations to raise money for grants.

"Social scientists and journalists in America generally operate under an ideology-laden code of professional conduct that requires objectivity. Only if you have no commitment to the people studied, it is argued, can you tell the truth about who they are and what they are doing. But this objectivity is in effect a commitment to the ruling class . . . In no way can modern social science come to understand the American Black man . . . from the posture of disengagement," wrote sociologist William W. Ellis in his 1969 book, *White Ethics and Black Power: The Emergence of the West Side Organization.*[15]

So given my "posture of disengagement," it should have been no surprise that neighbors of color weren't interested in answering my survey questions about the park. But there was one thing that every single person did tell me: they had never heard of the city's 165-page neighborhood plan.

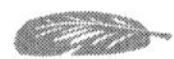

**IN ONE MONTH, THE FIRST PUBLIC MEETING TO APPROVE THE PLAN WOULD BE HELD AT THE** parks commission. Jim and I decided to host a strategizing session to prepare for it. I contacted every passionate park lover I knew and invited them over on a Sunday. And then I did the second most important thing when it comes to neighborhood organizing: I baked two apple pies.

Sunday came, and just eight neighbors walked in the door. I was very disappointed. Jan didn't show and neither did the owl-watching family. Even Sandy didn't come, telling me later, "I'm not a meeting person." But Heddie was there, with her husband and park-loving daughter, a fireball named Marie. Marie grew up playing in Warner Park and was just as passionate about the place as her mother. She was also a successful, get-shit-done businesswoman who ran a florist shop and managed rental properties.

Another attendee was a social worker I ran into nearly every morning on Sled Hill, where he walked his little dogs. Warner Park was Andy's emotional fuel for the day, "a blessing" that helped him help his clients, some of whom lived in the park-facing apartments. Andy was particularly incensed at the city's proposal to put a new parking lot in the only green space some of our neighbors had access to. Our neighborhood had a drug-dealing problem, he told us—that's why there were often police cars. And drug dealers loved to meet in parking lots where they could drive in and out quickly—not in fields or woods.

"Create more drug dealer habitat and they will come," Andy said.

Just like Heddie and her family, Andy had lived through several cyclical pushes to pave the park. He told us about an elderly neighbor named Earl, who years earlier had stood in front of the mowers, defending the wildflowers. Earl protected that meadow, one brown-eyed susan at a time. Earl was in a group of elderly neighbors who called themselves the Wild Ones, all of whom had either died or moved away.[16] Another neighbor walked into the meadow one day to discover parks employees digging it all up and laying out boundaries for a soccer field. He told them he was going home to call the parks department and begged them to stop because they would just have to undo it. Then he rallied two dozen neighbors to attend the next parks commission meeting. The commission reversed the soccer field plan and ordered parks to reseed that meadow.[17] As I listened to these stories in our dining room, I thought, *If the Wild Ones could do it, so can we.*

The neighbor whose voice made the critical difference that afternoon was Paul Rusk, our county supervisor, whose backyard faced the park. During his day job he ran Madison's Alzheimer's and Dementia Alliance; he was one of the city's most passionate advocates for the elderly; Paul served as county supervisor in his "free time." He told us that his evening park walks on which he often saw the animals fed his soul.

But Paul was not at all optimistic about changing the plan. Like my other politico buddy, Paul warned that people had spent two years working on it, bonding during dozens of meeting hours. By the time these plans got to the approval stage, it was usually too late. We would be walking into the parks commission meeting as total unknowns with just three minutes each to speak. Eleven city commissions were ready to approve this plan. Paul thought we had a chance if we directly challenged only the most egregious proposals—the pontoons in a shallow wetland, the parking lot in a green space, the ceremonial site on a marsh island. Stop the worst stuff and stall the rest, Paul advised, by asking city planners to insert "study the need for" into every paragraph where we want changes. (If you're a budding environmental activist, this four-word phrase is an extremely useful tool in your rabble-rouser toolbox.)

One of the most important strategies we agreed on was to use the W word—wetland—to describe Warner Park, because it was a federal designation with legal clout.* In city documents, Warner's wetland area was called a lagoon, a marsh, or a swamp, squishy terms with no legal protection. The wetland's history seemed to have been lost. The plan's proposal to create more impermeable surface would hurt water quality, which contradicted the city's sustainability goals. These proposals also showed that this wetland was not valued by city officials, particularly the wetland's importance as a filter to protect neighboring Lake Mendota. Somehow, like the animals, Warner's waters had become invisible.

We didn't know it that afternoon, but this Apple Pie Power meeting was the birth of Wild Warner, a neighborhood-based group to defend Warner Park. It would take us another year to formalize the group, but it began the way most organizations and movements begin—in a kitchen or living room with a handful of people, fueled by love and outrage and pie. It's an old story: you show up, listen, say your piece, eat your pie, and meeting by meeting, fight by fight, you become part of a mighty, messy, squawking flock.

* In 1956, the US Fish and Wildlife Service published its first national wetland inventory, *Wetlands of the United States,* a taxonomy of twenty wetland types. The survey covered nearly 75 million acres and surveyors rated over 22 million of these acres as important to waterfowl. The report signaled a major shift in national views toward wetlands because it used science to assign a value to these areas. This is the era when the word "wetland" began to be used. https://www.fws.gov/wetlands/documents/Wetlands-of-the-United-States-Their-Extent-and-Their-Value-to-Waterfowl-and-Other-Wildlife.jpg

CHAPTER 7

# Hail to the Thunder-Pumper

*To speak a true word is to transform the world.*

PAULO FREIRE

OUR COUNTY SUPERVISOR'S WARNING THAT WE WERE OUTSIDERS WALKING INTO parks commission meetings to face hostile audiences gave me great pause. I realized that it wasn't enough for my neighbors and me to speak. We needed a heavy hitter. I picked up the phone and called the Madison Audubon Society.

Several hours later, I was squeezed on a couch between bird warriors in the tiny cabin-like home of Dorothy, the elderly leader of Audubon's education and outreach committee. Paintings and drawings of birds covered the walls. I was surrounded by bird pot holders, bird mobiles, bird place mats, clay birds, and crystal birds. Dozens of pairs of beady glass eyes stared at me from the heads of stuffed birds perched wherever there was room.

This group of badassy gray-haired women fired away with a battle plan: Do an immediate bird survey to show people what is in Warner Park before the plan destroys it. (I'd brought my list.) Stress environmental education for local kids because Warner Park is the nature they don't have to be bused to. And they offered to lobby Audubon to put a nature center in Warner Park's community center. Most important, they were going to post an "Action Alert" in their next *CAWS* bulletin, calling for Audubon members to attend the upcoming parks commission meeting, our first chance to stop the plan.

I spent the next few weeks in reporter-warrior mode, my adrenaline pumping. Early in the mornings I tried to find more birds in the park to boost our species list. In the afternoons I pounded on my laptop and called people on the phone. Then I drafted an op-ed for the major state newspaper describing how the plan would hurt migratory birds. The editor placed it in the Sunday edition, just four days before the parks commission meeting. This was a stroke of luck.

By the day of the meeting, I was exhausted. Early that morning, I went birding in Warner Park just to clear my head. I was done looking for new species. I was going for solace; I needed help from the birds. I felt anxious and depressed, afraid that my neighbors and I were going to lose. It felt as if we were trying to stop a train going 100 miles an hour. I sat down in the marsh, and instead of seeing and hearing the birds, I was seeing those proposed pontoon boats cruising through the tiny wetland and hearing their motors.

I had no idea how city commissions worked, let alone how to stop a city plan or defend animals. I'd been studying environmental issues for only two years. Now I was about to stand up on behalf of the birds and criticize environmental policies in a city that thought of itself as a green mecca, full of ecology PhDs.

For days I'd been trying to write the 390 words that I could comfortably deliver in the three minutes allotted to each speaker at the meeting. I'd sat at my desk, stacks of bird studies, park histories, maps, demographic charts, the 165-page plan, and news clippings about the neighborhood rising in paper towers around me. I was swimming in facts and statistics. In twelve hours I would be speaking in front of the commission, and I still had no idea what to focus on.

I was sitting on the edge of the dog park bridge that September morning, staring into the marsh, my mind as muddled as the waters. A light wind was blowing from the north and the temperature was in the high 50s, the slightest hint of fall chill in the air. The sky was a pale eggshell blue, clear and tinged with light pink on the horizons.

At exactly 7:15 a.m., I saw the bird.

About twenty-five feet away on the marsh island, hidden in the cattails, stood a medium-sized heron I had never seen before, taller than the green herons but shorter than the great blue heron. As I watched, the bird raised its head, lifted its long, saber-like beak to the sky, stretched out its elegant buffy neck with vertical brown stripes on it, and began to sway in the breeze along with the reeds. It was the classic defense stance of an American bittern—an avian master of camouflage—which my ornithology professor had described with great gusto.

Holy shit. Bird number 86.

I was so excited that I dragged over a man walking toward the dog park and made him look through my binoculars. I wanted a witness to see this bittern so people didn't think I was crazy.

I didn't know much about bitterns, but I knew that it was rare to see one and even more rare in a city park. And people value what is rare. I also knew from an environmental history class that we'd erased at least 50 percent of our wetlands in the past century, and the bittern along with them. Lose a wetland, lose this bird. And here it was standing right in front of me in Warner Park. Maybe we had a fighting chance.

**TWELVE HOURS LATER, STILL A BUNDLE OF NERVES, I WAS SITTING ON ONE OF ABOUT A** hundred folding chairs set up for the meeting, in a large imposing conference room. Seven parks commissioners were seated at a long table at the front behind microphones: two white women, a Black man, and four older white men. A cranky-looking secretary sat next to them ready to pound out the minutes on a laptop. Beside them, a glass wall looking out onto the marsh where I'd found the bittern that very morning rose to the ceiling of the Warner Park Community Center. There was a podium with a microphone for speakers. The commissioners addressed the chair as "Mr. President" or "Mr. Chair." I could see why some people might find it intimidating to speak. It almost felt like a courtroom.

The room was filling fast. I saw a few neighbors who had been at our house meeting and others I recognized because they were daily park walkers. But I didn't know most of the people. Were they here to speak for or against the plan?

I kept glancing at the door, crossing my fingers. I was waiting for one extremely important person to arrive. The night before, I'd called the president of Audubon's Madison chapter and begged him to come. I'd never met him, but over the phone I'd tried to convince him of the importance of ordinary urban birds, not just endangered species.

The meeting was about to start when a reedy yet muscular white-haired man at least six feet tall strolled in. He had a beaky nose. He stood in the back, shoulders wide, head held high, regally scanning the crowd, like an eagle from a high perch. That must be him, I told myself.

The meeting began with the stiff-looking secretary spouting fifteen minutes of bureaucratese: "Under the informational item, the first one was the amended substitute ordinance amending names of committees, codifying the creation of committees, deleting obsolete committees, and renumbering sections of chapters 3 and 33 in accordance with . . ."

I'd learned at our Apple Pie Power meeting that the parks commissioners were citizen volunteers, appointed by the mayor. This commission was the first city commission of eleven that had to approve the plan. City planners had drawn it up at the request of the city councilor, so several city staffers were also involved, along with parks employees. I had no idea what the relationship was between citizen commissions and city staff, but to me they all looked pretty chummy sitting up there.

Some of the commissioners looked like they might doze off, but finally the three city planners who had worked on the neighborhood plan stood up. In a showy PowerPoint with impressive maps and graphs, they laid out the plan and insisted commissioners should adopt it that very night. They described the eighteen-month public input process that had produced this plan. The mayor had appointed a twenty-three-member steering committee of residents and local business owners to lead the planning process and represent the area's twelve neighborhoods. That committee had met thirty-seven times in the past two years and had hosted four large-scale open houses, all well attended, they explained. They'd held two public input coffee hours and conducted twenty interviews with community organizations and "stakeholders."

At this point, I started sinking in my chair. It's over, I said to Jim. Most of the people in the audience must be members of that committee. They're going to be piping mad at us.

The city had spent $107,000 on this planning process, they continued. Local media covered the process, thoroughly, so that every household in the area would understand this plan. It had been a public process with "very good participation throughout," they emphasized. This plan was a "big win" for the community.

"It was pointed out by people who actually read this document that there are some things that have caused the neighborhood to be concerned," one planner said. The planners wanted to mention "real quickly" that they knew there were "errors" in the document. Like the item about a soccer field in a meadow, well, that was a mistake. And "we weren't suggesting pontoon boats, but we were suggesting a few paddle boats, kayaks, canoes." And the proposals for a new parking lot—"just ideas."

The commissioners asked the planners a few questions. One commissioner admitted he hadn't read the entire plan and congratulated the public for reading it, thoroughly. Another commissioner said he was worried about the environment because the city was becoming more urban. We should be saving the green spaces for our kids in the future, he said. They opened discussion for public comment. Mr. President warned us all to stick to the three-minute limit, pointing at his timer.

Jim, my husband, was up first. This was lucky because he was a master crafter of words. (Our courtship began because of one killer quote in a newspaper.) An award-winning journalist who had written for *National Geographic* and *The New York Times* and whose work had been featured in the *Best American Science and Nature Writing*, Jim began by establishing his environmental credentials; he'd written a book on Yellowstone and covered national parks. He passed out aerial photos of Warner Park to the commissioners, showing parking lots in red and mowed areas in yellow: yellow and red already covered over half the park. It was a stark visual very different from the planners' PowerPoint and showed just how little wild green space was left. As the commissioners studied Jim's photos, he explained that in addition to the hundreds of thousands of humans who used the park, it was also used by "thousands of birds, fish and animals who raise families in the trees, waters, wetlands, and grasslands . . . They are pushed into what is not mowed or paved."

Jim emphasized that no one spoke for the wildlife in the neighborhood plan: "Thus we have a plan that wounds this fragile park with a dozen cuts—a parking lot here, a sidewalk there, and dredging to make room for boats."

He'd written city officials to request that the city's ecologist, the Department of Natural Resources, and the city's committee on the environment all review the plan. Those requests had been denied. Why? He did not accept the planners' assertion that the plan was "just a set of ideas."

"Words have power," he warned. "This is a pro-development plan."

Jim asked the commissioners to conduct an environmental impact study and reminded them that a standard option in such a study is to do nothing.

"And maybe that's what we should do in Warner Park," he finished.

The president of the commission called the next speaker to the podium: "Peter Cannon, the president of Madison Audubon."

"*Audubon?*" one of the commissioners muttered, incredulous.

Eagle-Man stood tall and did his job, telling commissioners that the Madison Audubon Society had adopted a resolution just the night before supporting a plan for Warner Park that would "sustain a healthy wildlife population in the park and especially the existing natural areas." He sharply criticized the plan for having just one sentence about natural plantings—the rest was about parking lots and playing fields. The amount of mowed grass in the park should be reduced, he said. These urban areas provide food and shelter for birds. He thought that Audubon and the city should do more to protect habitat in neighborhoods where people lived, not just in wildlife refuges and conservation parks that people had to drive to.

I was up next. After all that morning bittern glory, I'd spent the whole day frantically crafting a speech that was still a hundred words too long. But I went behind the podium, clutching my speech with sweaty hands, took a deep breath and looked down the line, making eye contact with every single commissioner. I told them I was an ornithology student who'd clocked 135 hours in the park and found 86 species. The "ornithology student" was a stretch, because UW-Madison had only one ornithology class and I'd taken it two years earlier. But I was inspired by that bittern, who had taught me an important life lesson early that morning: if you want people to think you're a cattail reed, act like a cattail reed. So I was going to act like an ornithologist.

I told them that just twelve hours earlier, I'd been watching a row of wood ducks next to a heron and two sandhill cranes. And then I'd found Warner's newest bird species, number 86, hiding in the marsh—an American bittern.

Mr. Commission President leaned forward in his seat and gave me a laser-like stare.

Then I did exactly what I tell my college students not to do today when I train them to speak before city councils—I threw everything and the kitchen sink into those three minutes: how our park was a gigantic bird nursery, how a third of our nation's bird species were in trouble with dropping populations, how that summer our cedar waxwing flock had grown from seventeen to over forty, and how two pairs of eastern wood pewees nested in the park—birds that migrate as far as the Andes—and the great horned owls, and, and, and. Yet here in Madison, in the green capital of the Midwest, land of Aldo Leopold, Wisconsin's nature champion who invented wildlife ecology, we were mowing and paving and manicuring birds' homes to death, even though the United States had signed the Migratory Bird Treaty Act in 1918, granting federal protection to 800 species of migratory birds . . .

I sputtered out, just over the three-minute limit, and gathered my papers to return to my seat. I didn't get very far because the president of the century-old Madison parks commission could no longer contain himself.

"You got to see *an American bittern* in Warner Park?" he exclaimed. "That's a great bird, really shy, very hard to see. Anybody want to hear its call? I've got that bird's call on my cellphone!"

There were a few titters as the president whipped out his phone to play the call for an astonished audience who had no idea what a bittern was or what the hell was going on.

But I knew exactly what was going on. The president of the august Madison parks commission was a feathered brother, and I could tell from the wild gleam in his eye that the bittern was his bird.

**I SUSPECT A LOT OF BIRDERS ARE LIKE WAR ZONE JOURNALISTS—ADRENALINE JUNKIES.** Tell a birder that a bird is "elusive," "cryptic," "shy," "stealthy," "solitary," "timorous," "a shady character," and "a denizen of desolate places"—all terms used to describe the American bittern—and you've just offered them the equivalent of birder cocaine.[1]

Birders rarely see this bird because it lives in wetlands and is so well camouflaged. So although it has been around at least two million years, even the most basic facts about this bird's life are unknown.[2] As beautiful as it is mysterious, the bittern is subtly colored in soft gold, russet, rust, and cream, the tawny shades of drying cattails and tall marsh grasses. It has what British birders call a "moustachial stripe,"

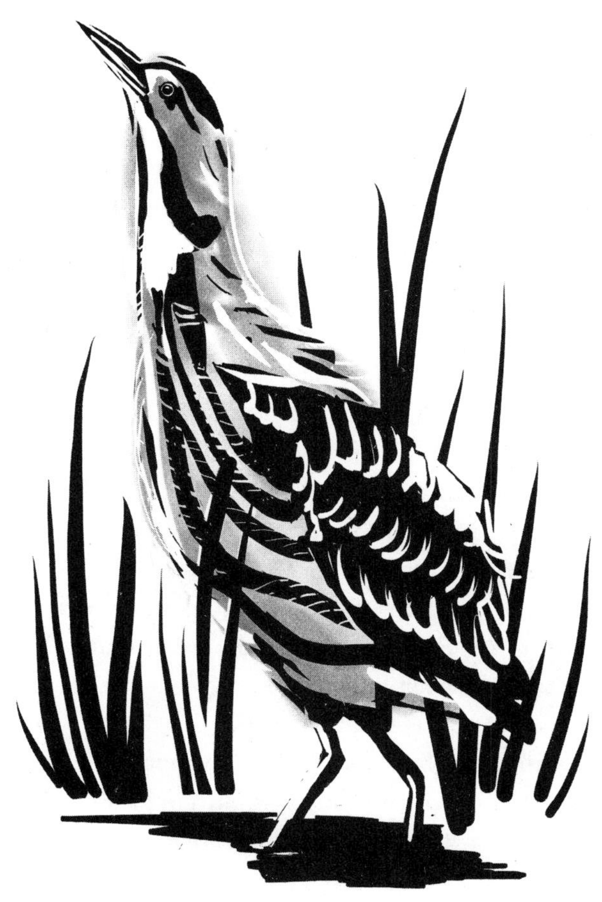

a brownish-black streak that begins at the base of its bill and runs down its neck, in contrast with its pearl-white chin. The bittern walks on light-lime-colored legs and feet as green as grass, the perfect avian disguise to hunt water bugs, crayfish, small fish, small mammals like voles, salamanders, frogs, and even snakes that have just eaten frogs—a two-for-one bittern meal.

My favorite avian photographer, Richard Crossley, author of *The Crossley ID Guide*, describes the bittern as sometimes having "such confidence in its camouflage that it allows close approach, looking at you with [a] weird facial expression."[3]

What you cannot see is one of the coolest features in the avian world. Like other birds in the heron family, the bittern has a special tool for heron hygiene: a pectinate (or comblike) one-inch ridged claw on its middle toe for grooming (imagine your middle finger had a serrated edge for combing your hair). A built-in powder puff comes with the bittern's comb, a type of feather called powder down, which disintegrates into a dry soap-like material so the bird can clean dirt or goop off its feathers.[4] Humans have also benefited from the bittern's built-in comb. Ancient Britons dipped the serrated claw in silver to create a reusable toothpick.[5]

Another thing I love about the bittern is that it is a bird of extremes. It is extremely shy, almost impossible to see even when you're staring right at it, and yet it is extremely loud, impossible to ignore—which is why in Latin its name is *Botaurus lentiginosus,* the freckled or speckled one that roars like a bull. It's also known more colloquially as the "Thunder-Pumper," "Belcher-squelcher," "Bull of the Bog," "Mire Drum," and the "Stake Driver."[6]

My favorite description of the bittern's strange roar comes from the 1854 *Birds of the Bible* by Reverend Henry Harbaugh, a beardy minister, author, bird lover, and poet:

> There is, perhaps, no bird whose note is so remarkably loud; besides, its voice differs from all other birds in its terrifying hideousness and awful solemnity . . . It is like the uninterrupted bellowing of a bull, but hollower and louder, and is heard at a

> mile's distance, as if issuing from some formidable being that resided at the bottom of the waters . . . However awful they may seem to us, they are the calls of courtship, or the expressions of connubial felicity.[7]

Ornithologist Bradford Torrey, who witnessed the bird actually making its call in a Massachusetts meadow in May 1888, described the bird's movements as "unpleasantly like the contortions of a seasick patient."[8]

Despite remaining hidden from view, the bittern has bellowed its way into the human imagination, scaring the hell out of people in accounts dating from the Bible up to Arthur Conan Doyle's *The Hound of the Baskervilles*. At least in the Western world, the bittern's troubles with humans started with the Old Testament's gloomy Isaiah (14:23), who prophesied the fall of wicked Babylon, warning: "[The Lord] will make it a possession for the bittern, and pools of water."[9] Whether you believe in biblical curses or not, the ruins of Babylon, one of the most important cities of the ancient world, still lie deserted along the banks of the Euphrates, about fifty miles south of Baghdad. The fact that Isaiah was right did not help the bittern. Ever since then, in many cultures this bird has been viewed as a harbinger of doom.

Fast-forward almost 2,000 years to a cold winter in the 1460s in Tarragona, Spain, on the Ebro Delta, the second-largest wetland on the Iberian peninsula.[10] Slogging his way with his tired army across 130 square miles of swamp, King Juan II of Aragón was in one of the endless battles he spent his life fighting, when a bittern got in the way. According to a 1541 account, after battling with "giant snakes" and wolves trying to get into their tents on a cold night, the weary soldiers suddenly heard "a most distressing voice, as if ventriloquy or coming from the heavens . . . so frightening and scaring everyone so badly that the king had his hands full, trying to keep most of his army from running away."[11]

If Juan II and his men had been birders instead of warriors (and there were some righteous birders back then, like Eleonora d'Arborea, a female Sardinian judge, who in 1392 wrote one of the first laws on the planet to protect birds),[12] they would have known that the terrifying voice was just a lonely bittern out on the delta of the Ebro, looking for a mate. Today that wetland is a European birders' paradise, with thousands of flamingos, booted eagles, squacco herons, Montagu's harriers, collared pratincoles, zitting cisticolas, moustached warblers, and the other fantastically named avians that still inhabit this UNESCO Biosphere Natural Reserve.

Unfortunately colonizers brought their Old World attitudes toward this bird with them to the New World.[13] There are chilling accounts in New England of men running in terror after hearing what they believed was "the voice of the devil." These fears led to Saturday afternoons like this one in Connecticut in 1786: "One hundred men united in a company on the Sabbath to traverse this swamp, and succeded in killing one of these . . . birds . . . Their sounds have not been heard in town since."[14]

For further evidence of the bittern's terrible reputation, there are the vernacular terms used to describe flocks, such as a murder of crows, a raft of coots, a fling of dunlins, a skein of geese, a charm of goldfinches, an exaltation of larks, a herd of wrens, a parliament of owls, a pandemonium of parrots, an unkindness of ravens, and a seige of bitterns.[15]

Just as this bird has historically inspired fear and loathing, however, it has also inspired love, especially as its numbers have plunged.* If the parks commission president was smitten by the bittern, then he knew better than anyone in the room except Mr. Audubon what that timorous bird needed: a quiet wetland, not one with motorized boats and loud wedding parties.

**AFTER THE PRESIDENT'S BITTERN OUTBURST, ABOUT A DOZEN PEOPLE TESTIFIED, EVERY** single one against the plan. Heddie was there. She didn't speak, but

* Native Americans have always had a different view of the bittern, according to the website Native American Bittern Mythology. In Pawnee, its name is *sakuhkirikui*, or "looks at the sun," and in Ojibwe, "the bird that looks up at the sun," referring to how the bird points its spear-like beak skyward to appear like a reed. In some North American indigenous stories, the bittern plays a helpful role by swallowing up floodwaters.

she nodded while her daughter Marie got up to talk about playing in the park as a child, how it used to be a prairie with birds like bobolinks that you never saw anymore. Sandy spoke for the meadow, on behalf of the field mice that would be killed by the increase in mowing, because the field mice fed the hawks and owls, and she loved to hear those owls talking to one another. And Andy, the social worker who had come to our Apple Pie Power meeting, told the commissioners, "Take a look behind you," pointing to the park's marsh island on the other side of the glass wall. "That might be the only place where you can stand in the middle of the city and not see anything, not a neighbor . . . not a building . . . That's the treasure for me because there are few places left in this city where I can't see the effects of how we live . . . To commercialize it and say, Let's have a wedding here . . . Take that out of the plan. Take a look behind you and keep it like that."

A stream of monarch butterfly lovers, fox lovers, geese lovers, tree huggers, wildflower connoisseurs, and bat defenders and a soccer mom stood behind that podium, every single one asking how more paving and lights would affect the animals in the park and imploring commissioners not to approve the plan.

An elderly fisherman named Jack Hurst, who had been teaching kids to fish in Warner's marsh for decades, brought the house down. I learned that night that he was on a first-name basis with city officials because he'd been speaking on behalf of the fish and the city's waters at meetings like this for over fifty years. Jack explained to commissioners that the stormwater coming from Madison's streets—a noxious mix of winter road salt, car oil, dirt from construction sites, and sand—was choking Warner's wetland. More paving would increase stormwater flow and hurt this marsh, he pleaded. Warner's wetland was a vital filter right next to Madison's largest lake; it protected the lake from all that pollution. But Warner was slowly dying. The filter was clogged.

Jack told commissioners that he had just had open heart surgery after a series of heart attacks. He warned them: "It's just like your heart. What you eat, you do to yourself. The streams are arteries just like you got in your heart. If you don't take care of what you've got here in Warner's wetland and all the arteries, you're not going to have anything left. This is a jewel that needs to be protected."

Fifty years of public meetings, I sat there thinking, and all that time, watching the land and waters he loved slowly degrade, the fish disappearing along with the bitterns and other birds. No wonder the guy's heart had worn out.[16]

When we'd all finished, the only people who'd spoken for the plan were the planners. The city councilor—the main force behind this plan—took the stage. I was ashamed. She was my elected representative and I'd never seen her before. To her, I must have sounded exactly like what I swore I would never become—a white, elitist, pointy-headed, bird-defending NIMBY.

The plan was a series of "suggestions," she said authoritatively, "a collection of thoughts from the neighborhood." One of her top priorities as city councilor was to increase access to the park for cyclists, pedestrians, and bus riders. But, she admitted, it's clear that the planners "haven't heard from all the voices.

"Tonight you heard a voice that was missing from the planning process—the conservation voice . . . There are a lot of demands on this piece of land. It's easy to only hear the voices calling for active uses," she said, adding that there was an "implicit" agreement to balance active and passive uses.

I didn't understand what she meant by "active and passive uses" because there was nothing passive about birding or walking in the woods, but I would soon learn from my studies that this was an entrenched dichotomy in park management culture, and that I and other quiet bittern lovers were on the wrong side of it.

The city councilor reiterated that she hadn't heard us say anything she was opposed to. But in a schoolmarmish tone, she scolded us for not showing up during that grueling eighteen-month process (she was right about that). She wanted the plan approved tonight, she said, looking pointedly at the commissioners. City planners needed to stay on schedule.

The meeting turned into a tug-of-war between the councilor and the commissioners.

The commisioner who first expressed concern about urbanization asked, "How do we balance our past and keep it for our kids?"

"There's so much pressure for construction in our parks. It's unbelievable. The powerful will win," said one of the two female commissioners, a woman with a long gray ponytail.

She recommended postponing the vote for a month so that planners could incorporate our suggestions.

The other woman commissioner spoke up for the first time. The trees and the birds weren't informed of this plan, she said. They aren't at this meeting. She also wanted the vote postponed for a month.

"And parking is not a basic human right," she added. That new parking lot proposal should be dropped immediately.

As we all sat in the audience, glancing back and forth at one another, our hopes rising along with our eyebrows, the commissioners voted to postpone the vote for a month so the city could make changes to the plan. To my great surprise, the commissioners asked me to gather all our suggestions in writing and send them a document. The city councilor looked like she'd swallowed a pontoon boat.

Afterward I walked up to the parks commission president to shake his hand. He was a geologist from Georgia and a dean at the university. But most important, he was a member of the Audubon Society. He'd read the *CAWS* bulletin that Dorothy and those badassy bird warriors emailed to two thousand members about the plan's potential negative impact on Warner Park's birds. The bittern is one of my favorite birds, he said. He agreed to come on a bird walk in Warner Park.

**THAT NIGHT WAS A CRASH COURSE IN LOCAL DEMOCRACY. I HAD NO IDEA THEN, BUT THE** pages I'd filled in a notebook during that two-hour meeting would turn out to be the beginnings of my 350-page dissertation. Jim and I would watch these same power dynamics play out at public meetings for the next five years, during which together we would contribute more than 15,000 words of testimony.

I learned that night that policymaking in Madison as regards Warner Park had nothing to do with ecology and everything to do with power. We had to figure out how to get some power, fast. I also learned that people in green, groovy Madison seemed as clueless about wetlands and water as New Orleanians.

I'd just assumed when we left Louisiana and moved north to the state that was one of the first to legislate wetland protection that Madisonians would know how to live with water, instead of ignoring its power or trying to tame it. I'd assumed that our objections to more paved paths and parking lots, to more fossil-fuel-mowed grass, would seem sensible and forward-thinking. So I thought it was weird that nobody except the elderly fisherman talked about the water. We were meeting in the huge community center inside the park, with the marsh full of geese, herons, and cranes visible through the conference room's two-story glass wall. Yet nobody on the commission had used the word "wetland," and I never once heard the word "watershed." I could understand why the general public wouldn't use these terms—but planners, city councilors, policymakers? How could municipal authorities in Madison, a city on four lakes and home to the university that set up the nation's first limnology lab, not be thinking about how to live with the water and safeguard it for future generations?

**AFTER THAT PARKS COMMISSION VICTORY, I WALKED AROUND WARNER PARK THINKING** about how to get some power. I sat under the park's largest bur oak and leaned against the massive trunk. For me, this tree was the beating heart of the park's wild side. I'd learned in a dendrology class that the crown was a giant green umbrella that sheltered up to five hundred species of butterflies and moths, which meant the tree was full of caterpillars, a gigantic bird feeder. It was also where the park's wood pewees built their small lichen-camouflaged nest at the end of an enormous branch. The gray grooves in the trunk were deep enough for a child to sink her fingers into and for the park's nuthatches and chickadees to store food for the winter in. It was pantry, shelter, and shade for park-goers sitting on a bench and watching the meadow. In a soil ecology class, I'd learned how the park's largest tree provided food and shelter not only above the ground but also below it through extensive root networks that supported millions of species of fungi and bacteria. The fungi transferred food and water from the soil to tree roots in exchange for sugars in a symbiotic relationship—so much going on right beneath me that I could not see.[17]

Leaving the counsel of the bur oak, I went home and took out a pencil and a sheet of typing paper. When I worked in Nicaragua for radical priests, I'd learned the Jesuit practice of sitting down regularly with comrades to analyze local and global issues. Where is the power? Who has it? How can we get some? Why were some countries poor and others rich? These were the questions we chewed on for hours, often with the assistance of a bottle of Nicaragua's Flor de Caña rum. We drew "power maps" on typing paper, making circles for every power center and lines to connect them. I stared at the blank page and thought about the parks commission meeting. I drew a circle for each commissioner and then I saw it. Three commissioners, including the president, worked at the university. The city councilor worked at the university. The city planners graduated from the university, and the university had alumni—potential allies—spread throughout city, county, and state agencies and environmental nonprofits. Every circle led to the university. UW-Madison was the trunk of a giant bur oak with a large umbrella-like crown that could extend over Warner Park and protect it from the top down. My growing avian species list could become part of that protective crown if I turned it into a citizen science biodiversity survey involving professors and students. And Wild Warner, as we'd begun to call it—the organization born at our kitchen table—could act like that underground network of roots and fungi to protect and nurture the park from the bottom up, grassroots in the literal sense.

As a graduate student, I was nothing more than a worm toiling away at the university (apologies to the worms, who support our entire food system). But as a doctoral candidate, I had one powerful ally on campus—my PhD advisor. Jack Kloppenburg was an eminent sociologist, an international food systems expert who'd lived in Africa, a community garden champion, and an expert on organizing. I'd found him through a Google search and picked him precisely because of that activist background and because he was a Marxist like the Central American Jesuits I'd worked with—we viewed the world through the same lens of class oppression and political economy. But he was also a crusty guy from Milwaukee, and we'd gotten off to a rocky start. That first year when I told Jack I was taking ornithology and wanted to keep studying birds, he barked at me.

"Birds? You want to study *birds*? What are you going to do, Trish—become an expert on *neotropical migrants*?"

Jack told me to forget birds and stick with my Central American expertise. He wanted me to take graduate-level theoretical courses. But after listening to twenty- and thirty-something graduate students arguing about epistemological discourses and the theory of power expounded by Michel Foucault, the French philosopher (I agreed with Foucault's critique of power, but if you needed two dictionaries and fifteen minutes to understand every single sentence, what good was it?), I couldn't take any more. So I ignored Jack and enrolled in undergraduate biology classes, instead, to learn how birds made their living—ecology, vertebrate zoology, soil ecology, dendrology, limnology, botany, plant geography, and entomology. The study of insects turned out to be just as fantastic as ornithology, with a professor so funny and enthusiastic that he'd turned me—a woman who screamed every time I saw a cockroach in Central America—into an awestruck fan of that first dazzling, outer-space-like beetle I dissected and examined under a microscope. I much preferred these undergraduate ecology lectures, in which I was sandwiched between eager twenty-year-olds in small wooden seats. And I especially loved the endearing email invites these kids would send the nice lady old enough to be their mother right before midterms. Could I come to the pizza/study party they were organizing? They'd noticed that I never stopped taking notes. Maybe I could bring copies of those notes?

But this was now 2009–2010, year three of my studies—way beyond the point when you should know what your dissertation is about. And I still had no clue. All I wanted to do was go birding in Warner Park, take more undergraduate biology, and spend the rest of my waking hours in that tiny ornithology library. So I dreaded talking to Jack, but I needed his help. I mustered up my courage and told him the whole Warner Park story, about the birds and neighborhood plan, about my informal survey and my neighbors who loved the fields and the deer and the owls. About how Jim and I and Marie and a handful of others wanted to protect the park. Despite my better judgment, I told him I'd spent more than 135 birding hours in the park and had found 86 species. I thought he'd blow a gasket when he realized that I didn't have a dissertation proposal because I'd been birding for two and a half years. But Jack started asking me about all the birds I'd found. He lived on the other side of Madison and didn't know Warner Park well. Like most Madisonians, he thought it was just the "fireworks park" and the "baseball park." He was really surprised to hear about the diversity of bird species. And I was really surprised that Jack knew anything about birds or even cared.

Instead of getting mad, Jack started getting excited, particularly about the social justice questions I was raising about why a park in a lower-income neighborhood couldn't be a wildlife refuge. Why were we getting all the noise and paving and massive events for people from other parts of the city and state? But I told Jack I didn't know how I could help organize a local group and spend years trying to change parks policy while writing a dissertation. And I still didn't even know what I wanted to write about.

"Trish," Jack shouted, "this *is* your dissertation!"

What? I didn't say this to him, but I thought a dissertation was supposed to be a long, impenetrable Foucauldian document about something so arcane no one would ever want to read it. (This attitude is why I hadn't started it yet.) But for the first time, I could see that Jack was very interested in my ideas.

"You have to *organize*," he said, practically pounding on his desk.

Jack started spewing directions, detailing a dissertation research plan while I dutifully scribbled away. This would be an interdisciplinary action-research dissertation. I could try to change local policies while documenting what I was doing through interviews and archival research on Warner Park's environmental history. I needed to figure out where people's attitudes toward the park, the wetland,

and the animals came from—a mix of sociology, anthropology, and ornithology—all while analyzing my own biases and attitudes toward nature.

The other big question my PhD advisor wanted me to research was whether or not city policies toward Warner Park were an example of environmental injustice, of a city placing all the junk in a lower-income neighborhood with the argument that it was to promote economic growth. I'd never heard the term "environmental injustice" before, but I'd certainly seen it in Louisiana, which was infamous for its cancer alley of more than a hundred oil refineries and chemical plants all in neighborhoods of color. And Katrina was a glaring example of environmental injustice. New Orleanians with no resources had been forced to leave their city because lower rents were usually directly linked to lower elevations, which meant flooding. Jack told me that the theory of environmental justice came from a movement led by people of color in the 1980s who were fed up with a white environmentalism that focused only on the "purer" nature you had to drive to. This movement was based on the theory that the "environment" was where we live, work, and play—in other words, the Warner Parks of the world.[18] Jack told me that because of my work in Central America and the Deep South, I had the background to make these connections between ornithology and environmental justice. This couldn't just be about the birds, he told me. It had to be about the people, too, something most of the white environmental movement had not understood yet.

Jack had money to fund a service-learning undergraduate class to get students off-campus doing something useful. He suggested that I teach a class in Warner Park the following fall of 2010 as part of my action-research. My dissertation had just become a project with four action-research "interventions": citizen-science ornithological research, environmental history, environmental education, and community organizing.

I remember leaving Jack's office that day in a blissful daze, skipping down the steps of Agricultural Hall, clutching the road map for my future and a list of fantastic to-dos. I'd just gotten my snarly advisor's approval to keep birding, become an organizer, and get a PhD out of it. Not only that—I could tell that Jack really wanted to help us—Warner Park had just acquired a powerful ally. I still didn't understand Jack's sudden interest in it all. But maybe if I'd been paying closer attention, I would have noticed that whenever Jack asked me about the birds I'd found in Warner Park, he got that same faraway gleam in his eyes as the bittern-loving parks commission president.

**I KNEW JUST WHERE TO GO TO JUMP-START MY DISSERTATION RESEARCH—TO JACK HURST,** the elderly fisherman with the ailing heart who'd spent fifty years testifying at public meetings like the parks commission meeting. People in our neighborhood called him the Aldo Leopold of Madison's Northside.

A sun-weathered man, Jack was beaming when I arrived because that morning he'd gone out on his first post-operation fishing trip and caught forty crappie, small silvery sunfish. He proudly showed me two full white plastic buckets in his kitchen. Although Jack was a very muscular and strong-looking seventy-seven, he was still moving tentatively, trying to get reacquainted with his body after the heart surgery.

Jack had been hunting and fishing since he was a child, over seventy years, he told me. He'd caught tens of thousands of fish, most of which went to local churches for Friday fish fries, a Wisconsin tradition. At seventeen Jack had started repairing machinery in a local factory. When the factory closed two decades later, he began working as a city garbage collector and traffic engineer. But Jack had had a night job his whole life from which he would never retire—speaking at meetings of parks commissions, city councils, municipal environmental committees, planning commissions, watershed alliances, and fishing clubs.

"Fishing isn't just about taking. Too many hunters and fishermen just take. You have to give back."

Jack gave back by sharing his passion. Every year his fishing club hosted over four hundred kids and their parents at the annual Kids Fishing Day in Warner Park, complete with free fishing poles and tackle boxes. Jack had taught thousands of children to appreciate Madison's waters.

We sat in his sunny kitchen drinking coffee. Fifty years ago, Jack told me, he'd bought this home because he could look out the window and see Warner's marsh, a knee-deep spring-fed marsh at least three times the size of Warner's current embattled wetland. Snakes slithered in the grasses, salamanders hid under logs, and whip-poor-wills, bobwhite quail, bobolinks, meadowlarks, and bluebirds sang, all birds that had since disappeared as the concrete advanced.

"In the 1950s, it was one of the best areas to fish. There were no houses here."

Now most of that marsh was buried under buildings, parking lots, and mowed grass. Jack's house looked out on Warner's baseball stadium, unironically called the Duck Pond because it housed Madison's minor-league team, the Madison Mallards. Instead of hearing the ducks that used to live in the marsh, in the summer Jack heard Pondamonium, a rock band festival featuring groups like Garbage, the Flaming Lips, and the Dum Dum Girls, so amplified that Jack could feel the bass reverberating in his chest and hear the noise inside his house, even with his hearing aids off and the windows shut tight. The noise continued all summer, with fireworks after every baseball game in addition to the annual blow-up-the-wetland July Fourth fireworks show.

Jack wanted to show me his duck collection, so we descended into his hunting/fishing lair in the basement. It was a taxidermist's dream. There was a long wall dedicated to fish next to a wooden case full of rifles. But my eyes were magnetically drawn to his duck wall, where a small flock would forever take flight. There was a black duck, a ruddy duck, several mallards, a pintail, a wigeon, a canvasback, a hooded merganser, a goldeneye, and my favorite, the adorable bufflehead, the tiny black-and-white rubber-ducky-shaped creature that bred in northern Canada and the subarctic.

Jack took each duck down and handed it to me very gently, giving me time to appreciate each individual. As he talked, I realized that every duck was a story, a chilly fall morning, an explosion of wings in a marsh he loved, a place he fought for that was probably no longer there.

I hadn't done well on the duck portion of my ornithology field lab two years earlier. Maybe it was because I'd always thought of ducks as, well, ducks. They'd all looked the same to me during that first crash-course birding winter standing on the ice—little dark blobs on the freezing water. All I'd wanted to do then was run back to the heated university van. But in Jack's basement I marveled at their shimmering iridescent greens, purples, and blacks, the white stripes and spots and moonlike cheek crescents, the jaunty tails, the pointy heads, the rounded sloped foreheads, and their very different ways of carrying themselves.

As I held each taxidermied duck in my hands, humbled at their beauty, a part of me was horrified, thinking, *How could Jack shoot these gorgeous creatures?* But it was so obvious that he loved them. He'd spent his life trying to protect them. So what if he shot one once in a while to put on his wall or throw in a Crockpot with potatoes, carrots, and onions? I was learning from environmental history texts that without duck hunters, there probably wouldn't be any ducks left. When waterfowl began disappearing across the country at the beginning of the twentieth century because of overhunting and disappearing wetlands, conservation agencies began creating waterfowl refuges and trying to bring back species that were disappearing. Hunters and their organizations, particularly Ducks Unlimited, led these efforts. Wetland historian Ann Vileisis writes that by 1943, Ducks Unlimited had carried out 103 wetland restoration projects on over a million acres.[19]

Next to Jack's Great Wall of Ducks, there were several card tables covered with stacks of old news clippings, neighborhood conservation newsletters, and piles of *Ducks Unlimited* magazines. For decades Jack had scoured print media for information on the places and waters he loved. Jack didn't own a computer or use email. Most of the stuff in his basement was non-googleable. I realized that morning that I was staring at a dissertation gold mine. The environmental history of Warner Park and its long-abused wetland was buried in this basement.

Jack handed me a small pile of yellowing documents to take home to study. The pistons in my reporter brain began firing; they were copies of old easement maps of Warner Park. Then he pulled out a tiny notebook, told me to start scribbling, and rattled off the name and phone number of every local elected official and wildlife agency officer. From now on he wanted me to call them and complain about the way Warner's wetland was being treated.

By the end of that foray into Jack's basement, we had become comrades. Jack agreed to help Jim, Marie, and me set up Wild Warner. He'd soon be a regular at our home, appearing in the mornings with more old documents he'd dug out of his basement, lists of names of recruits for Wild Warner, the latest issue of *Ducks Unlimited* magazine, and a bucket of scaled, cleaned fish to feed us. In the next five years, Jim and I would attend more than 150 hours of public meetings, most of them sitting next to Jack Hurst.

**WITH THE ENVIRONMENTAL HISTORY PORTION OF MY DISSERTATION WELL UNDERWAY, I** decided to tackle that park-based course my PhD advisor wanted me to teach. The class had to meet a community need, so I needed to consult with our city councilor first—the one I'd opposed in the parks commission meeting.

To my surprise, she immediately agreed to have coffee. I started by sharing my human rights background in Central America and the Deep South. I swore up and down that I wasn't just some elitist Patagonia-wearing birder and that I cared about social justice; I wanted to help my neighborhood. She said that there were at least two hundred children around Warner Park, many of them latchkey kids with parents coming home late because they were working two low-wage jobs. An after-school environmental education program based in the park could really help. I proposed teaching the UW-Madison students about birds, and then they could teach the kids about birds in the park. My city councilor wasn't a bird person, but she liked the idea of college mentors working with the kids. She also wanted to see a lot more neighbors, particularly people of color, using the park—not just white birders and joggers—she told me. If I could get children of color into the park, maybe their parents would feel more welcome.

But she wanted me to attend neighborhood meetings. You have to participate, not just criticize, she said. I swore I'd be a neighborhood association groupie from that day forward.

In the spring of 2010, at one of these neighborhood meetings, I met Mike Hernandez, the new principal at the local middle school. I knew his school had a reputation for low test scores, frequent police visits, and wild children. In this predominantly white city, it was also one of Madison's most ethnically and culturally rich schools. Its students, many of them children of immigrants, were native speakers of more than a dozen languages. Hernandez was from Santa Ana, California—my hometown. He was a sleeves-rolled-up dynamo, determined to turn his new school around. He'd worked in "rough" schools in Los Angeles and Chicago, changing school cultures. He'd come to our neighborhood association meeting to find tutors and mentors.

Now, I'll admit that when I told the city councilor that I could set up a bird-based environmental education program in the park, I'd had a very particular fantasy of a line of quiet boys and girls, eagerly and in unison, pointing shiny new binoculars at a hummingbird drinking a ruby liquid from a neighbor's feeder. I'd imagined my well-trained student mentors explaining to these small, cute, and easily controlled elementary school children how this hummingbird was preparing to migrate: how she was heading south to the Gulf Coast, where she might cross an ocean in one eighteen-hour nonstop flight. In this teaching fantasy, I could see the children's eyes widening as they stared up at their college mentors adoringly, before they reverently opened their field guides to identify the species.

This fantasy is why my first reaction to the new principal's plea for help was: *No way.* Middle school? Wild kids. Too many hormones. No adoring little faces watching a hummingbird at a feeder. But then I thought about how Mike Hernandez's school was just a one-mile walk from Warner Park. I saw those kids walking by my house every day. And I remembered the counsel of my most important Jesuit mentor in Nicaragua: that if you want to make a difference in your community, you don't do what you want to do—you do what the community needs you to do.

A week later, I went to Mike's office and proposed an after-school birding club. I'd create and teach a college service-learning class to train the student mentors, and then I'd bring the college students every week to work with his kids, one-on-one, in Warner Park. Maybe birding sounded a little crazy, I told him, but this was what I could do.

There was a long silence as the principal studied me like an insect.

Then he finally said, "I get the bird thing."

He wasn't a "bird guy," but his sister worked at Cornell, which has the best ornithology research program in the nation. A weekly one-mile walk to Warner Park would be a free field trip for his students, exercise they really needed. And he loved the idea of college students coming every week because many of his students had never even been on our campus.

"You guys have an outstanding university right down the street. These children don't realize it's right in their backyard."

At the end of the meeting, Mike said, "I have a feeling this could get really popular, really big. But we'll just have to figure what to do when that happens."

I had a feeling, too—that Mike Hernandez was nuts. I could not imagine that a bunch of hormone-hyped, video-game-addicted middle school kids would actually want to join a birding club. But I started designing a syllabus for the new class to be taught the following fall.

Next, I turned to organizing. Jim and Marie were working hard to legally set up Wild Warner. Meanwhile, my task was to recruit potential members for the upcoming founding meeting that summer. I started with the list of two dozen speakers from the first parks commission meeting. Then I scoured local newspapers for potential allies and authors of op-eds and letters to the editor. But the best recruitment strategy came right out of the avian playbook—sing loudly. The Northside of Madison had its own small quarterly newspaper, the *Northside News.* It was delivered for free to ten thousand doorsteps. I didn't believe in writing for free. I'd been paid to research, report, and write my whole life. But we needed a local outlet to publish stories about the park to get the voices of the animals heard and to attract potential members. That little newspaper, which sat on ten thousand coffee tables of people living around the park, had real power. I began writing a five-hundred-word nature column for it.

After years writing grim human rights reports about massacres and torture and racist hate crimes, I found it liberating to write "Red Is the Color of My True Love's Hair," a column about how the red fox I found one morning in the meadow could run as fast as 32 miles an hour or swim 5 miles in that time. About how she imitated the squeak of a mouse or the distress cry of a rabbit to lure in her dinner. About how she was the ultimate omnivore who would eat anything from skunks and strawberries to Chinese food (but she would not take the bran muffin I offered her as I sat on a bench on a 20-degree Wisconsin morning).

I wrote about the park's teenage red-tailed hawk who ran awkwardly around the meadow trying to catch grazing robins. That summer the young bird careened all over the park learning to hunt, like an eager teenager learning to drive. He crashed into a neighbor's bedroom window trying to catch birds at a feeder. He spent a morning unsuccessfully dive-bombing squirrels running circles around him. A park employee even saw him make a mad grab for a fat female mallard—all he got was a loud quacked scolding.

To my astonishment, walkers and joggers began stopping me in the park asking if I was the person writing these columns (they recognized me from the column photo). They loved Warner's wild side. I wrote down their names and emails to give to Jim and Marie for their growing recruitment list.

I'd been publishing for two decades and had been educated to believe that *The New York Times* was the most important media in the world. But it was a silk moth that taught me that if you are trying to defend a place you love, right where you live, the local newspaper or that free neighborhood association newsletter or that Front Porch Forum *is* your most important media.

**SHE CAME LATE ONE AFTERNOON IN JUNE, THE SEASON OF BACKYARD WEDDINGS, NEW POTA**toes, and liberated schoolchildren. My two unruly dogs were dragging me through Warner's meadow when I spotted her. She was clinging to a young ash tree with velvety orange legs, a moth the size of my hand. Her orange, gold, and pearly wings were fully spread. Creamy crescents marked the center of her wings, and eye-shaped markings, the tips.

Before my entomology class, moths were something I wanted to keep out of my sweaters and hair. Because of that class, I was smitten and headed to the library to check out a pile of books on moths. I discovered that she was a *Hyalophora cecropia,* a relative of the silk moth the Chinese domesticated 4,000 years ago and one of North America's 11,000 moth species. I learned that she could live just one year. As a caterpillar, in a miracle of green architecture, she'd taken a silken thread nearly a mile long to spin a waterproof cocoon that resembled ash tree bark and could withstand a Wisconsin winter. She must have emerged earlier that same day to spend the afternoon drying her wings. For the next five to six days, she would mate, lay 200 eggs, and die.

I spent sunset with her, drawing her. I couldn't see it, but she was releasing a perfumed pheromone plume. Miles away, the wide feathered antennae of a male cecropian were vibrating, 150,000 receptor cells on his 60,000 tiny antennae hairs telling him she was waiting, and off he went, zigzagging through the sky, following her fragrant perfume trail.[20] Early the next morning, I found them locked in a cecropian embrace. He looked like her, only skinnier. They mated nonstop Saturday morning until Sunday night, through rain and thunderstorms.

After I published "A Tale of Silk and Perfume in Wild Warner Meadow," a woman called me. Was I the person who wrote the story about the silk moths? She'd found my number in the phone book. Her name was Cindy, she was a Medicare nurse who visited elderly people all over my neighborhood, and she'd just read the moth story. She loved it. She wanted me to know that her patients loved it, too. They loved the park and the animals. They were glad someone was speaking up for them.

"People don't want more development. Just keep doing what you're doing."

CHAPTER 8

# Roll That Teacher Down the Hill

*In the school I went to, they asked a kid to prove the law of gravity, and he threw the teacher out of the window.*

RODNEY DANGERFIELD

THANKS TO THE STORIES ABOUT FOXES AND MOTHS AND HAWKS, BY WILD Warner's founding meeting I had a list of forty-six potential recruits. Sixteen showed up at the community center. Of these sixteen, Jim became the group's first chair, webmaster, spokesperson, and public relations mastermind. Heddie's daughter, "Get Shit Done" Marie, became Wild Warner's first secretary and wildflower and woods educator. And she would eventually take over from Jim as chair and secure the group's first major conservation grant. I became education coordinator.

We assigned tasks according to passions. The new member who cared for the flowers around Warner's beach house became our beautification maven. The photographers offered to produce material for the website Jim was designing. Other members agreed to regularly walk or bike through the park, observing everything—a team of Wild Warner spies creeping around like the great blue herons. Those who belonged to other conservation groups offered to get native plant seeds from these sister organizations to replace mowed grass with prairie and wetland plants. Members interested in education volunteered to help me with the kids' program slated to begin in the fall. I strongly believed that this was our best long-term strategy to protect the park—turn neighborhood kids into the future stewards of it. So I wanted Wild Warner's name all over the new college birding course I was about to teach, in which I would train college mentors to work with the kids. This would be a prestigious partnership for our new group with the all-powerful university. We also agreed to monitor every city, county, and state agency meeting that had anything to do with the park. And we had a pugnacious pro bono attorney who loved to eviscerate city officials at public meetings with her questions.

Since I was a PhD student doing dissertation research full time on the park, I took on several tasks: (1) attend parks commission meetings; (2) research Warner Park's history, particularly the wetland history with Jack Hurst's help; (3) keep building Warner's bird species list and get students and professors to find more birds; and (4) lead bird walks.

Jack Hurst would be our wetland watchdog. And Marie offered

to attend the city's year-round planning meetings for the fireworks because it was the biggest event held in the park. As a group, we agreed to meet monthly and to begin every meeting by sharing stories about Warner's animals. We wanted to enjoy Warner's beauty and our wild neighbors, appreciate what was there, not just bemoan what had disappeared. In our mission statement, we vowed "to celebrate, preserve, protect, and expand the natural world in Warner Park and its surrounding ecosystems."

As part of my new watchdog duties, I attended what should have been a totally boring parks commission meeting that spring. I was excited because I was announcing that the new UW-Madison/Wild Warner children's program would start that fall of 2010. Eager to impress commissioners, I made a flowery statement about the well-trained college mentors who would soon be crawling all over the park. The bittern-loving commission president said this was "exactly the kind of work the university should be doing." I was so proud that I puffed up like an endangered greater prairie chicken.

I'd planned to leave right afterward because these meetings went on for hours about bureaucratic minutiae. But I was about to learn that the devil is in the minutiae. I perused the several-page agenda, my eyes pausing on the last item: "Warner Geese Roundup."

I had no idea what a geese roundup was. I was so dumb that I thought a roundup might be some kind of bird rodeo, and that definitely interested me. Two hours later, I learned that in eight weeks the city was going to send camo-clad rangers into Warner's marsh to catch the geese and their adorable goslings, load them into a truck, gas them, and then distribute the meat to food pantries at a processing cost of $120 per adult bird.

Warner Park was two miles from the airport, and aviation authorities considered the geese a hazard, the city's wildlife biologist told parks commissioners, mentioning the infamous US Airways Flight 1549, when a bird strike had brought down a plane on the Hudson River in New York in 2009, just a year earlier. And it wasn't just airport safety. Parks officials were sick of complaints about goose poop on the soccer fields and basketball courts. The city biologist explained that a roundup was the easiest, cheapest, and fastest way to solve all these problems.

The commissioners were about to vote on the roundup proposal when one of the women commissioners protested that there had been no public input. We have a member of Warner Park's new conservation group in the audience, she said, pointing at me. She wanted to know my opinion before she voted.

All heads turned toward yours truly, and I have never been more embarrassed at my own ignorance. I hadn't studied geese in ornithology; I knew nothing about them. But I knew I loved to sit in a murky corner of the marsh very early in the morning, the mist rising off the lagoon, the geese drifting by like tiny ghost ships. I'd just watched two geese mating right in front of me while I was hidden inside a tree trunk. I held my breath during those precious seconds. Then the male slid off her back and they both splashed in the water. And I knew I loved hearing their joyful honking from inside my home as they arrived in February and March, when I would run outside and yell, "Welcome back, geese!"

But I didn't want planes to crash, so I told the truth—that I didn't know anything. I didn't mention that I thought a roundup was a rodeo.

Minutes later, the commissioners voted unanimously on a death sentence: the Warner geese had less than sixty days to live.

I left the meeting in Warner's community center that night, stunned, winding my bike slowly along the park's path back to my home. I'd just informed commissioners that I was starting a children's program in the park and now they were going to kill the park's most visible and loudest birds. How was I going to explain this to the kids and my new students?

It was dark, but I could hear the geese honking softly to one another in the marsh, settling down for the night.

"Get the hell out of Dodge!" I yelled. "They're going to kill you!"

"Warner Park Geese Are Cooked," blared the front-page headline in Madison's *Capital Times*.[1] I settled down for a few days of serious goose reading, starting with reports analyzing the Hudson flight.

Smithsonian ornithologists who studied that collision found that it was caused by migratory geese, not what biologists call "resident" geese, birds that do not migrate and stay in the same place year-round. In order to reduce the risk of future collisions, it was not enough to just use "traditional methods" (roundups) to manage resident geese, they wrote. Their report stressed that it was important to obtain "information on frequency, timing, and species involved, as well as the geographic origin of the birds." They recommended integrating this information with research on bird migration patterns and utilizing bird-detection radar and bird dispersal programs at airports.[2]

So first we had to find out if the infamous Warner geese were migratory or resident. The city's biologist kept calling them "resident geese," but the geese left every year when the wetland froze. Did they leave Madison or migrate long distance? What if they fit into both categories? Most of the time I counted no more than 150 geese in the park, but those numbers swelled to several hundred during migration because Warner, like most of Madison's parks and wetlands, was a goose gas station.

I also learned from scrutinizing the airport's report that between 2008 and 2009, airport personnel killed 67 "problem geese" near Madison's small airport. Nine of the 67 geese (13 percent) were definitely from Warner Park. Wildlife agents knew this because biologists had banded all Warner geese in 2007 for a study that was never completed. Officials didn't know where the other 87 percent of the "problem geese" had come from.

In the 1950s and 1960s, during an era of airport expansion, cities across the country built airports in wetlands because the land was cheap and often on the outskirts.[3] Madison's tiny airport underwent a major expansion during that period and was surrounded by wetlands, with the city's largest conservation park—a 385-acre wetland—right on the airport's edge, even closer than Warner Park. (The city shot geese in this conservation park every year because of that proximity.) So the setting of the airport itself was a huge goose draw. The other 87 percent of the problem geese at the airport could have been from Warner or could have been from other parks and surrounding wetlands or migratory geese passing through. Madison's airport's data showed that "problem geese" numbers around the airport surged during early spring and late fall migration; officials had counted 1,588 geese at the airport during this time period. They couldn't possibly all have been from Warner Park, which meant that killing all Warner's geese was not going to solve the airport's safety concerns.[4]

I began to suspect that the Warner roundup proposal had as much to do with poop as with airport security. (A Wild Warner buddy with allies at the airport later confirmed this, an example of how our new group's wide web of alliances helped us gather information.) The parks department had a new superintendent with a golf-course mentality, and he was already sick of complaints about poop on sports fields.

As I dug further, I discovered Madison's airport was not the only one struggling with big birds. Everyone cruising the skies from commercial airlines to the military to NASA was encountering wildlife. And every single management report said the same thing: roundups and killing should be a last resort. NASA's Kennedy Space Center in Florida was located in the middle of the 160,000-acre Merritt Island National Wildlife Refuge, home to over 310 bird species. I read crazy stories about vultures nearly derailing space shuttle launches, fruit bats hitching shuttle rides, alligators hiding under vehicles, and a famous woodpecker that pecked a hole in a fifteen-story shuttle tank.[5] Instead of killing the animals, NASA tried to eliminate their food supply and installed an avian detection radar system.[6] Avian detection radar was saving the military millions of dollars a year in ruined airplane engines by helping pilots avoid sucking in birds, large and small. If aviation experts in so many spheres had found nonlethal solutions, why couldn't progressive Madison?

But the discovery that burned me up the most was that adult geese and their goslings loved to eat freshly mowed grass. The park's department, which mowed hundreds of acres of grass every week, was literally laying out a geese banquet. No mystery why Canada geese loved Madison's parks. It was like leaving cat food in your yard and then complaining when a pack of feral cats showed up. If Madison followed NASA's playbook, it would reduce the geese by eliminating their food supply. We needed to get rid of some of those acres of fossil-fuel-dependent grass.

**A WEEK AFTER THE PARKS COMMISSION'S DECISION, SOMEONE CREATED A FRIENDS OF** Warner Geese Facebook page and posted the newspaper article about the coming geese kill, which mentioned our group. None of us in Wild Warner knew the Facebook goose guru, but within two weeks, the condemned Warner geese had over 1,700 "friends," some asking how to join our fledgling group. We joked that we might need a convention center for our next meeting.

Wild Warner was not ready for a major battle of any kind, much less over geese. Our group had formed only months earlier. But this is how most groups and social movements start—with a fight. You have to organize fast and on the fly. You get to know your new comrades and you all learn together. Harvard sociologist Marshall Ganz, who studied Cesar Chavez and the farmworkers movement in California, calls it "strategic resourcefulness," using whatever skills you've got and scrambling.[7] Ganz's strategic resourcefulness reminded me of how during severe northern winters, birds like chickadees, nuthatches, titmice, kinglets, and downy woodpeckers form what biologists called mixed species flocks. Each species has its own ecological niche or specialty to help find food so that the flock can survive a severe winter. Certain species focus on different parts of trees to search for food, for example.

We didn't know each other, but it would soon become apparent that Wild Warner was a mixed species flock. We would eventually attract storytellers, schmoozers and alliance builders, event organizers, letters-to-the-editor writers, grant writers, shy quiet thinkers, ardent tree defenders and planters, intrepid photographers, and scrupulous park observers. And because of the geese, we were about to discover that we also had serious environmental philosophical differences.

About two dozen animal rights geese warriors showed up to Wild Warner's next meeting. Jim and I had suspected that the gaggle of 1,700 Facebook Friends was a loud phantom. And it was—most of the "friends" lived in other cities. But our membership had just doubled thanks to the geese.

Jack Hurst, our most senior member and mentor, opened the discussion by explaining that he'd been in love with geese since he was four. But he also loved them in a Crockpot—nothing tastier than a goose slow-cooked with potatoes and onions, he joked (the animal rights warriors didn't even smile). He didn't like all the killing, but as a hunter, he had no problem with a roundup. The goose poop was affecting water quality in the wetland. It's so bad, he said. When he hosted the Warner Kids Fishing Day, the shoreline was covered with goose poop. Then he shared the dramatic changes he'd witnessed in geese behavior as a hunter. When he first began hunting as a boy, you could hardly find a goose, they were so rare. Then the geese appeared in Warner, maybe a decade ago. But numbers had increased exponentially in the last five years. Because of the warming climate, the giant flocks that used to migrate farther south now hung around the North longer. There were just too many geese, he insisted. Their numbers were increasing, while the number of hunters was decreasing. He was frustrated. He had no answers.

Some members could not have cared less about the geese. They just listened. Others, including Jim and me, were adamantly opposed to the roundup. Jim had grown up on a farm in Upstate New York; the geese reminded him of "the wild." I'd rarely seen a goose in beachy Southern California, so I assumed my attachment wasn't so much emotional as practical. I didn't see how I could start a children's program in the park just a few months after the parks department had killed all the geese. The animal rights warriors defended the geese passionately. They didn't want to see a single goose driven out of Warner Park.

I watched Jack Hurst rolling his eyes, raising his eyebrows, and grimacing quite a bit during this meeting, but when I think back on it, I am so impressed that he stayed at that long conference table. I'm a hothead. If I had been Jack, I would have yelled at the animal rights folks who didn't even live around Warner Park. I'd have seen them as interlopers who cared only about the geese—not our wetland—and then I probably would have stomped out. But Jack didn't budge. And every time he spoke, we listened. I realize now that Jack stayed at that table because he understood the power of compromise, of flapping your wings together in the same general direction, even if you don't agree with one another. With fifty years of organizing experience, Jack knew that the geese issue was temporary and that Wild Warner had to stick together to protect the wetland over the long haul. And because of Jack's example, even though Jim didn't agree with Jack, as our wily new chair, Jim brokered a compromise and got every person in the room to agree on one thing: we would help the city reduce the number of geese as long as it was not by killing. I would research humane management, and Wild Warner would provide the volunteers.

By the end of that meeting, we had a very muscular geese subcommittee. I didn't think most of the geese warriors would stay in our group after this fight was over—and they didn't. But the few that stayed became invaluable new members. We didn't realize it, but the geese were already teaching us how to stick together despite our differences. By organizing subcommittees, people could follow their passions. And if members didn't agree with a subcommittee's position, then they just didn't work on that issue. As long as the majority supported the work. It was like one of those small Vs of geese that breaks off from a large V in the sky in the fall but still heads south.

SHORTLY AFTER THIS MEETING, I HEADED OVER TO JACK HURST'S MARVELOUS BASEMENT TO learn more about his position on the geese. Instead, I got a lesson in environmental history and our nation's screwed-up relationship with urban waters. According to Jack, Warner's wetland was just one small example of what had gone wrong with wetlands all over the country as housing developments replaced farmland during the post–World War II building boom. In municipal watersheds everywhere, the greater the number of roads, sidewalks, driveways, and parking lots built—in other words, the more concrete cities poured—the greater the volume of stormwater and the faster it flowed into urban lakes and streams, polluting them.[8]

Jack and his fishing club had been fighting hard since the 1950s to protect the marsh that eventually became Warner Park. He pulled an old map out of his stash of documents, showing the Warner Marsh area labeled as Castle Marsh, named after the farmer who had owned a chunk of it. In 1955, when the city began purchasing the surrounding farmlands to build Warner Park, Jack's fishing club lobbied for years to get the state's conservation agency to protect thirteen acres of Castle Marsh by purchasing it. The fishermen were trying to save the last good pike spawning ground next to Lake Mendota and the only natural fish rearing pond left in the entire area. In order to spawn, some freshwater fish need calm shallow waters with beds of vegetation to nest in and to hide from predators (just like some birds need bushes). And the parent fish need certain water temperatures. The Castle-Warner marsh had all these conditions, along with plenty of food for baby fish, who eat frequently, just like infants; it was the perfect fish nursery. But like infants and baby birds, baby fish are also vulnerable to pollution and disturbances. If Jack's group wanted to conserve local breeding fish for the next generation, they had to protect Warner's fish nursery from encroaching development.

Despite all the efforts of Jack and his comrades in the heroic Dane County Conservation League, the Castle-Warner fish nursery began to disappear in 1958, when the city started digging drainage ditches for the new park. The city ripped out marsh grasses and seeded the area with Kentucky bluegrass for the first baseball diamond. The new paving surrounding the wetland increased stormwater levels and that stormwater's velocity much faster than anyone had anticipated, carrying a toxic soup right into the old Castle Marsh. One year later in 1959, a wildlife official reported that all the northern pike—a large fish that can live up to twenty years—were gone. Castle Marsh's demise was part of a national decades-long pattern of fish nurseries destroyed by shoreline development and pollution. Now state biologists had to raise the tiny fish called fry in artificial rearing ponds, and then release them in Madison's lakes and hope the juvenile fish could withstand the conditions.

The geese were just one more factor, adding their poop to the

stormwater soup. But they were a problem easier to target and "solve" by killing rather than by making expensive fixes to stormwater systems.

JUST TWO WEEKS AFTER THE GEESE GOT A DEATH SENTENCE, I GAVE MY FIRST BIRD WALK TO kick off Wild Warner's nature walk series. Seventeen people showed up that sunny Saturday, seniors and parents pushing strollers with kids in tow. The walk began with an osprey we serendipitously found perched on Warner's marsh island. Fifty years earlier, that bird was nearly extinct, I told the delighted crowd. Now they were hanging out in Warner's marsh. Right afterward, as if on cue, a belted kingfisher with its punk hairdo hurtled past us, making its loud metallic rattling call. The new birding enthusiasts oohed and aahed and snapped pictures.

My first public walk ended on a spectacular note, with a star appearance by another bird I'd never seen in Warner Park. As we stood on the dog park bridge scanning the marsh island for waterfowl, an enormous bird with a six-foot wingspan came barreling out of the marsh, straight toward us, wings outstretched, flying low, that unmistakable white head with a yellow eye peering down as people yelled, "WOW!" and scrambled to snap photos. It was Warner's very first bald eagle and a new species for my bird list.

I was standing beside a squirrelly-looking boy and his father when this happened, all of us exclaiming in disbelief. The father turned to me and said he'd done human rights work with Native Americans in the Southwest for years.

"You know, that's what Native Americans call a sign."

At that moment, geese parents were escorting long lines of goslings under the bridge, paddling just beneath us. The boy leaned over the rail and counted the goslings. I asked him how he felt about the geese.*

"To see them gives me a sense of accomplishment. I can tell my class about them. We can come here and see them," he said.

His name was Gabriel.† He told me that he was ten years old, he loved hiking with his dad, and that he was a Boy Scout who had already earned a badge. But best of all, in the fall he was starting sixth grade at Sherman Middle School, and he was very excited about joining my new birding program.

Gabriel pointed at the geese and fixed his huge hazel eyes on me.

"Are they already killing them?"

His father raised his eyebrows and gave me a pained look.

"He reads the news."

**AT HOME I THOUGHT ABOUT GABRIEL'S WORDS—THAT HE COULD SEE THE GEESE, THAT JUST** seeing them gave him a sense of accomplishment, and because they were so easy to see and find, he could share them with his friends. I knew exactly what he meant. When I'd started birding two years earlier, it was so hard. I almost gave up after those first frozen weeks trying to learn to use binoculars in 10-degree weather and not even being able to find small birds. But large birds like the geese and ducks and eagles made it easy. And the geese made it easiest of all for a beginner because they just loafed around—you didn't even need binoculars to watch them. I realized that for Gabriel, the geese were his portal bird, just like that first house sparrow for me in New Orleans.

---

* Ornithologists use the term "Canada geese" for single and multiple geese. In this book, I use the vernacular "goose" for individual geese.

† Not his real name. All names of children in this book have been changed.

And so right after that first nature walk, I went home and pounded out a six-page letter to the mayor telling him about Gabriel and the children's program starting in just a few months. I begged him not to kill my new future feathered teaching assistants. Gabriel's generation deserved creative solutions to the problems our generation had caused, I argued—killing was not creative. And I shared Wild Warner's ideas and offered to research humane alternatives that could involve college students. Then I emailed my city councilor and individual parks commissioners and sent them detailed lists of questions from my reading of the airport's data. I later learned that across the city, hundreds of angry geese-hugging Madisonians were bombarding public officials with emails protesting the roundup.

Because of negative press coverage and the growing public outrage over the coming roundup, our city councilor asked the parks commission to hear public testimony and reconsider their decision. Dozens of impassioned goose defenders showed up for a fiery meeting that lasted until after midnight. The first half of the meeting was a raucous discussion of the parks department's new and very unpopular policy to require volunteer groups to purchase special insurance for every fruit tree they planted in city parks (in case someone slipped and fell on an apple or plum). Militants of Madison's Fruits and Nuts group sat in rows next to goose defenders. They lost their vote and stomped out. Right afterward, at 9:50 p.m., the great geese discussion began. This time commissioners hammered airport representatives with questions about their data. Airport officials could not answer their questions, particularly about the statistical risk of a geese strike at the airport. They said the chance of a Hudson-type accident in Madison was "low." The airport had no numbers on geese in the surrounding area and did not know exactly how many "resident" geese there were in Warner Park. Airport representatives explained that the airport had requested a radio-collar study first, to identify where the geese were coming from, instead of killing them. But the state wildlife agency had denied those requests.

The meeting ended after midnight, and not one of the twenty-three public speakers agreed with the roundup. Gabriel spoke. His father spoke. A city councilor from the downtown area spoke passionately—her constituents did not want the geese killed. The director of the humane society spoke. With her newborn clutched to her chest, she described how her organization had an urban wildlife department and was helping other states control geese reproduction humanely by addling the eggs—coating them in corn oil before they could hatch and then placing them back in the nest. It was a low-tech geese birth control strategy employed successfully in many cities. She offered to help Madison do it. Jack, my PhD advisor, sat next to me for the whole six hours, nodding off. He also got up to defend the geese, asking the parks commission to "see what we can learn from them," instead of killing them. The commission president joked that it was "Madison's full-contact democracy in action." After the testimony was over, commissioners voted unanimously to reverse their decision, giving our geese a one-year reprieve. And they gave the parks department one year to develop an alternative citywide geese management plan, in consultation with Facebook friends of the geese, Wild Warner, and university experts.

"Free Birds—Warner Park Geese Get Stay of Execution," read the headline in the *Wisconsin State Journal* the next morning.

Now I could face that little boy in my new children's program.

**ON DAY ONE OF THE NEWLY FORMED BIRD BUDDIES CLUB AT SHERMAN MIDDLE SCHOOL, MY** thirteen nervous college mentors and I entered Warner Park's meadow with just five children. It was September, Wisconsin's season of large bumblebees clinging to waving fronds of goldenrod and goldfinches pecking at coneflowers, bending the stalks with their bright yellow weight. The milkweed was ready to release its silken seeds. Monarch butterflies preparing to migrate were flitting slowly above it all, orange and black.

We took the kids straight to Sled Hill so that they could survey the marsh below. As everyone dutifully pointed their binoculars toward the marsh, I saw two birds, each five feet tall with a seven-foot wingspan—Warner's iconic sandhill cranes heading straight for us, flapping like pterodactyls. A comeback kid on steroids, this bird had neared extinction in Wisconsin decades earlier, dwindling to a few dozen pairs by the 1930s. But thanks to conservation efforts, there were now more than 70,000 cranes in the state. Warner's pair landed gracefully just yards from the children with a slightly smaller crane beside them, their chick (called a colt). We stood there, kids and college students, amazed as the crane family—parents and teenager the size of a sixth-grader—pecked at the grass, searched for grubs, and totally ignored us. Little people with binoculars didn't faze these giant birds. In this busy park they had become used to lunging dogs, giant mowers, baseball games, fireworks, and rock concerts.

The kids elbowed one another and whispered to their new mentors that the crane teenager was just slightly smaller than its parents. Then our group watched "The Heron Show" as two great blue herons did their strange stilted walk on the marsh's edge. The college mentors and their kids began imitating that walk. The kids kept exclaiming that the cranes, geese, and herons were almost as tall as they were.

Later that afternoon, the kids counted and chased over two hundred geese grazing on the freshly mowed park grass, sending the annoyed birds into the air in a wild cloud of furiously flapping wings, angry honks, and delighted screams. As I watched the human flock chase the feathered one and felt the air vibrate with the force of those four-to-six-foot-long wings, I realized that the only reason the birds were there was because we had fought for them.

**OUR CLUB BEGAN TO GROW EVERY WEEK, CHILD BY UNRULY CHILD, DOUBLING IN JUST A** month (it would double every year for the next three years). This first semester the group was quite well behaved, almost all little nature nuts. A hunter boy who liked to chase butterflies and sing loudly off-key. A little girl named Meredith with owllike eyes behind her thick glasses, so loaded down by the end of each park visit with leaves, sticks, branches, and other nature stuff that her college mentor had to help carry the haul the mile back to the school. Another boy obsessed with Cooper's hawks. A boy whose goal was to find "fairy glens" in the park. A girl who loved eagles. And Gabriel the goose defender, who told his mentor that he was going to become an Air Force pilot. He also announced that he was going to be the "first bird buddy" to earn points for the new set of binoculars that the university was promising each child.

Gabriel had some competition when a new bird girl named Aurora joined us. Aurora had X-ray birder eyes. We were all sitting on Sled Hill one afternoon when she suddenly shouted, "There's a pied-billed grebe down in the water!" A pied-billed grebe? How could this kid possibly see this minuscule duck from high up on this hill and past the dog park and in the marsh, and how did she even know what a grebe was, anyway? We all tromped down to the marsh, and there was Aurora's tiny pied-billed grebe, a grayish rubber ducky cruising among the cattails, just as adorable as she was. She was the kid who made up fantastical stories about golden-crowned kinglets and western kingbirds and other birds I still hadn't seen, and how owls peeked in her window at night. She was also the kid whose baby sister was in the hospital long term with kidney disease. She told me about it, anxiously, and mentioned how upset her parents were. I think the birds helped her to forget all this for a few precious hours every week.

Then a tiny, energetic, curly-headed boy who had just arrived from Puerto Rico joined; he spoke only Spanish. Since I was bilingual, I got to run after him as he taught me the difference between how squirrels hopped and chipmunks scurried, a subtlety I'd never noticed. He was very chipmunk-like himself, telling me that he'd joined because this was the "exploring" club, and he wanted to "discover stuff." Because of that one conversation, I dumped the Bird Buddies club name and we became Nature Explorers. This little boy was also the reason I called my teaching method "co-exploring." It seemed that every time a new kid joined, they were just a degree wilder.

My thirteen undergraduate mentors were mostly seniors and three freshmen. One was a female David Attenborough and a born naturalist who knew far more about botany and ornithology than I did. Another young man was a hunter who spent a lot of time outdoors.

He came to class in camo to teach the kids how to creep through the woods silently. But the rest came from non-environmental majors.

"Sure, I had the knowledge of birds common to the general public, which is to say, able to identify a seagull, and a general appreciation for penguins, but beyond that I was clueless," is how one English major described himself.[9]

On the first day of the university class before we met with the children, I told the new mentors the Warner Park story and explained that I belonged to a group who was trying to save the wetland and its birds. You've just enlisted in the cause to save Warner Park, I explained. This isn't about a grade. You're going to help protect the park by creating a new program for neighborhood kids and their families.

I warned them that I had no idea what would happen or how. I asked for their patience and admitted I knew nothing about middle school children, or children, period. Fortunately, although some of these students knew nothing about birds, they'd worked as summer camp counselors or high school tutors. I'll teach you about birds and you teach me about kids, I told them.

SINCE I'D TAKEN THAT ADVANCED ORNITHOLOGY COURSE FOR PRE-VETERINARY STUDENTS, I thought I'd just use a similar structure of readings, quizzes, and an activity every twenty minutes to keep those hormone-laden middle schoolers out of trouble. I started each outdoor class on top of Sled Hill, with a "listening post" exercise. The preteens had to close their eyes for twenty minutes, sit silently, and then scribble down every sound they'd heard. Yes, it was twenty minutes—that's not a typo. Afterward, we scanned the horizon for birds. Then I gave the children and my students a quiz on both the common and Latin names of the birds. If the kids spelled everything right, they earned points toward a pair of new binoculars. I realize now as I study my old teaching journal that I had no idea how to teach outside. While I was making them sit still on Sled Hill, scribbling down the Latin name for the downy woodpecker, a red-tailed hawk would suddenly streak right over us as if screaming, *Look at me! I'm here!* And the whole "lesson" would be out the window.

This ridiculous routine lasted a few weeks. Then one day, as I stood in front of the squirming group to begin the day's lesson plan, the children started rolling sideways down the hill.

My college students stared at me with big eyes, asking silently, *What should we do now?* I was speechless. So they followed the children's lead and rolled down, one by one, spinning balls of color with arms and legs.

I found myself standing utterly alone on top of Sled Hill, the kids and my students all rolling around below, screaming and laughing. After a few minutes, I did the only thing that made any sense. I put down my clipboard, binoculars, and backpack, removed my eyeglasses, and rolled down Sled Hill. And that was the end of twenty-minute listening posts, Latin names, and lesson plans.

After the children taught me this un-learning lesson—that I had to remove my ivory tower head in Warner Park—we truly became an exploring club. Rolling down Sled Hill became our rite of initiation; the kids insisted that all invited guests (tree experts, city officials, university professors, the school's librarian) had to roll down the hill to "join" our club. The college mentors and their kids spent most of the time on their own exploring wherever they wanted with the exception of the lagoon. (I had to tell the kids that this was not a swimming club after somebody waded in a little too deep and an angry parent called the principal and he called me one Friday at 8:00 a.m.)

We ended each day with another ritual, our Sharing Circle, which replaced the Latin quizzes and mini-lectures. Before leaving the park, we gathered around the park's mother bur oak. Everyone laid his or her treasure at the base of this huge tree: a kid's plastic container of protesting toads, a perfect blue robin's egg found lying in a path, an unidentified mammal skull with smelly brain bits oozing out of it, a tin can, an ancient flaking lipstick, a whole tree trunk carried out by a team of kids, and, always, several large sticks. We formed a large circle. One by one, college student or child picked up their treasure and carried it to the center. That explorer spoke. We listened. We applauded all treasures great and small.

In the beginning, the shy children and the misfits hid behind their mentors. But by the end of the semester, some sixth- and seventh-graders were in the center proudly displaying a toad or a cattail, reading a poem they'd written about the park, or just giggling about nothing at all.

Sherman's teachers and the principal noticed changes in some of the children, particularly the shy ones. Aurora, the X-ray-eyes birding girl, had rarely spoken up in school, her teacher told me. But within a few months of joining our club, she frequently spoke in class and showed the teacher drawings she'd made of birds and the park.

We ended that first fall semester with a final walk through Warner's meadow to scatter prairie seeds for the spring: rattlesnake master, bee balm, lobelia, and brown-eyed susans. One of the great horned owls flew over us as we tossed the seeds in the air. Then we trooped to the top of Sled Hill to yell, "Thank you!" and "Goodbye!" to Warner Park, before returning to Sherman Middle School for a party and a cake that said "Spread Your Wings" in green icing.

Each child had earned their binoculars—Gabriel was first, of course. No child had quit: more had registered for the coming winter session. And three college students had asked to repeat the course so they could keep working with their kid. I'd been teaching for years and this had never happened before. Students repeated courses only if they failed them.

After that semester ended, Gabriel's father called me at home and asked me to give his son "birding homework" over the Christmas break. He wanted Gabriel to learn to do research online. So I told Gabriel to find out where every Warner Park bird that migrated spent the winter, thinking I wouldn't hear from him for quite a while. On Christmas Eve, the phone rang. It was Gabriel, so excited. He'd just emailed me an Excel spreadsheet showing the migration ranges for every single avian species in the park.

"Merry Christmas, Trish!" he said.

That was one of the best Christmas presents I have ever received.

AS PART OF MY PHD "FIELDWORK," ONCE A WEEK I WENT TO THE MIDDLE SCHOOL LUNCHES to check in with the kids. I wasn't just studying the birds; I was studying that exasperating but always interesting and—like the birds—often surprising subspecies of human, *Homo middleschoolus*. As I sat at the sixth- and seventh-grade tables squished in a kid-size plastic bucket seat, trying not to seem out of place, I listened to their banter and occasionally asked questions.

One Friday, one of our sixth-grade explorers was trying to recruit a new kid to join our club as all the kids sat there pushing the food around on their plastic trays. He was doing his very best to convince his buddy. I leaned forward, certain he was going to say something about the great blue herons or the hawks in the park, or about how the kids got to roll down Sled Hill. But this was his main argument: "It's really cool. They *give* you a college student."

THERE WAS A BOY IN MADISON, WHOM I WILL NEVER FORGET, WHO TAUGHT ME WHAT IT meant to "give" a college student to a child. I'll call this boy Jeremy. Jeremy was a bit of an outlier in our club that first year. He wasn't a little nature nut or a kid doing "homework" on bird migration over the Christmas break. He didn't seem interested in anything at all except whacking trees with sticks. He was a tall, lanky boy, very quiet, with a sweet face when he wasn't glowering. I paired him with John, an undergraduate majoring in English who seemed centered and unflappable. John was tall like Jeremy. The two looked like brothers when they walked together. I thought John wouldn't take Jeremy's lack of interest in birds personally. And I assumed that Jeremy would drop out of the club.

Yet week after week Jeremy showed up and walked beside John. Jeremy was the kid always doing something dangerous like walking on the lagoon ice or swinging from the bridge over the ice like a monkey while the school's social worker screamed at him to stop. He rarely smiled.

John was patient at first. He gleaned from Jeremy's occasional surly mumble that something was going on at home. John figured that just being outside would help Jeremy, and the boy did like to climb trees. But after several weeks John began to get frustrated. Some of the other college students were mentoring perfect little bird buddies who gave short speeches about the habits of eagles and how woolly bears survived the winter. The college mentors bragged about these children in our class.

One day John came to see me during office hours. He slumped in the chair and told me he "felt like a failure." Jeremy wasn't learning anything and didn't want to. John couldn't figure out why Jeremy kept coming to our club. And I couldn't figure it out, either, but I remembered the advice of an African American principal in Loachapoka, Alabama, years earlier, when I was trying to set up a journalism service-learning program at his high school.

"Trish," he said, leaning forward on his desk and looking me in the eyes, "students don't care how much you *know* until they *know* how much you *care*."

I shared this story with John and told him to just keep walking with this kid. "Jeremy must be coming because he likes you, and somehow he needs you."

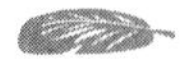

**JOHN WAS ONE OF THE THREE STUDENT MENTORS WHO DECIDED TO TAKE THE CLASS AGAIN** in the spring, just so he could keep walking with Jeremy. I had secretly hoped that because of John's devotion, Jeremy would start showing some interest in the birds and the park. But he didn't change one whit. The pair muddled through that first winter together, sloshing through snow, with John just trying to keep Jeremy from hurting himself or someone else. Then John started bringing a video camera to the club for Jeremy to use. He hoped to teach Jeremy how to make a little movie. Instead, the boy spent two minutes filming a dangling leaf. And that was the end of Jeremy's filmmaking career.

One day in March, I was headed to the middle school cafeteria when I stopped in the hallway to peruse the school's bulletin boards. School staff continually praised the children, and the hallway was full of framed photographs lauding their accomplishments. One bulletin board was dedicated to school "leaders." To my great surprise, there was a headshot of our Jeremy, prominently displayed. Below the photo of each student "leader," this question was typed: "What is the most important thing that happened to you this year?"

Jeremy's answer: "My mother died."

I remember standing in front of that bulletin board for a long time. I remember hearing kids and teachers shuffling down the hallway behind me, heading to the lunchroom. And I remember just standing there, reading those three words over and over again. Suddenly understanding everything and nothing. I realized how little I and my students knew about these children and their lives.

**A FEW WEEKS LATER, JUST BEFORE THAT FIRST YEAR ENDED, I ANNOUNCED TO THE CLUB** that a renowned ornithologist was coming to Madison. John C. Robinson, one of the only African American ornithologists in the nation and the author of one of our class texts, *Birding for Everyone: Encouraging People of Color to Become Birdwatchers,* was going to lead our group through Warner Park. My own biodiversity survey had been stuck at 99 bird species for months. I needed this expert's help to crack bird number 100.

This was going to be a public coming-out party for our club and a big PR boost for Wild Warner, so I invited the press. The week before the big event, I told the kids I needed a volunteer to give a speech about birds to impress our guest author and reporters. I was betting on Gabriel, the geese-defending, Excel-spreadsheet-creating boy wonder. Instead, Jeremy's hand shot up. John and I exchanged alarmed glances. As far as we could tell, Jeremy knew absolutely nothing about birds. But he definitely knew a lot about beating trees with sticks.

A week later, Jeremy stood in front of our entire flock, John Robinson, and a reporter from *The Capital Times,* clutching two handwritten notebook pages, his hands trembling slightly. John stood beside him for moral support, one paw on Jeremy's shoulder. In the quavering, cracking voice of a thirteen-year-old boy, Jeremy announced: "I'm going to outdo everyone." Then he read eighteen funny and fascinating avian facts while the newspaper reporter scribbled away. Later we all walked to the park, and John Robinson found my species number 100, a yellow-bellied sapsucker, as soon as he stepped inside Warner Park right next to Heddie's yard. (I must have walked by this bird a thousand times but just didn't notice it.) Except for the fact that the reporter spent all her time glued to Jeremy, our new birding whiz kid, instead of with the other kids and the ornithologist, it was a really wonderful day.

It was with some trepidation that I picked up *The Capital Times* the next morning only to find Jeremy, our newest expert, expounding on avians: "It's pretty cool when we find a new kind of bird. I'd say my favorite is probably the Indigo Bunting because their feathers are actually black, but because of refraction of light through their feathers we see them as this amazing shade of blue."[10]

I was flabbergasted. When had this boy ever even seen an indigo bunting? Those birds were still in the South and hadn't returned north yet. And how in the hell did he know what "refraction" meant? What had happened to this kid?

John, as mystified as I was, asked Jeremy, and this is what the boy told him. A month earlier, he had done something "very, very bad." As punishment, he was grounded for the whole month (except for birding club). Jeremy became bored at home, so bored that he picked up that field guide that John had given him as a present and started reading it. He was so fascinated that he read his bird guide a second time and highlighted all his favorite lines. And for that grieving boy, the indigo bunting's ability to transform sunlight into color—to shape-shift from a drab gray creature in the dark into a glittering sapphire with wings—was the story that leapt off the page and grabbed him.

CHAPTER 9

# The Great Geese Wars

*But vainly the hope of those lonely ones burned,*
*The Wild geese—the Wild geese—they never returned.*

MICHAEL JOSEPH BARRY (IRISH POET), 1849

THE SUMMER BEFORE I'D STARTED THE KIDS' PROGRAM, TENSIONS BEGAN TO RISE in and around Warner Park. Since not a single person at that epic parks commission meeting had spoken against the geese, I'd assumed that most people liked the big birds. But that assumption, like so many others I had about the park and its animals, was dead wrong. Our neighborhood began dividing into goose lovers and goose haters.

On the morning of June 23, 2010, I was birding in Warner when I came upon a dead teenage goose in the middle of the path with one leg twisted beneath it. It had been run over. The goose was still warm and someone had stuck a piece of orange gum to its feathers. Then I heard snickering. Just yards away, three young parks workers stood by two maintenance vehicles, laughing. I took pictures of the dead goose as they watched and continued to laugh.

Four days later on a Sunday night, my park buddy Sandy, lover of geese and bats and all creatures who lived in Warner, was taking her 2:00 a.m. walk through the park with her dog Willie. When she reached the marsh's edge, she saw a "deranged" man brandishing a two-by-four, trying to whack a goose fleeing toward the water; the goose was molting and could not fly. Sandy charged the goose killer, screaming. Instead of whacking the goose, which escaped into the wetland, he whacked her, knocking her down and sending her eyeglasses flying. She wasn't hurt and had absolutely no regrets about defending that bird.

Not even a week later, sometime during the annual fireworks extravaganza, fireworks fans ran over a pair of geese—mates—that were trying to cross the main road that bordered Warner Park to escape into Lake Mendota. I found the dead pair the next morning baking on the asphalt and later read the neighborhood blog post by the driver who had watched, sickened, as the car ahead of him swerved purposely to flatten one of the geese that was running frantically down the middle of the road after its mate. Just before the fireworks every year, these flightless molting geese parents, along with the park's sandhill cranes, led their young families out of the park for safety, waddling across that road and into the lake. Geese are smart and fierce parents, with a parenting system analogous to that of primates, according to biologists.[1] They can live over twenty-five years and may mate for life, so they form very strong family bonds.

Jim and I noticed that suddenly people were ignoring leash laws and letting their dogs chase the geese and goslings. One fifty-something blonde told me gleefully while she encouraged her two large dogs to chase the geese: "It's okay to run them off. They're destroying the park. The parks department is going to get rid of them, hire dogs, shoot them, kill them."

I didn't understand what was happening. Why did people hate the geese so much?

I went to a garage sale late that simmering summer, just around the corner from my home. Amidst the usual moldering shoes and books, there was a gorgeous print by a Wisconsin artist of Canada geese in a marsh. I askd the owner how much she wanted for it.

"Nobody wants pictures of geese anymore," she said, practically spitting. "They're filthy. You can't even have a picnic on Warner Park's lawns because of the poop."

I lounged on those lawns every day watching birds, I told her. I never sat in poop. But I could tell she didn't believe me. I had become one of "them"—the geese lovers. I gave her a few dollars for the picture and walked home, mystified at her vehemence.

Wild Warner's mighty geese subcommittee had divided up research tasks that summer. (The rest of our flock continued to work on issues like wetland protection and tree planting.) A couple of geese subcommittee members volunteered to watch the geese and count them daily to have real numbers to present to the city. My bird buddy Stacy had joined a city goose management committee on the other side of Madison because we feared that roundups would be implemented citywide.

While researching the relationship between humans and geese, I'd discovered that the Warner war was just one of dozens, maybe even hundreds of geese conflicts, nationally and internationally. My research job was to figure out how other cities had resolved these conflicts to benefit both humans and birds. Enter GeesePeace.

GeesePeace's founder, David Feld, was an aerospace engineer with a heavy Brooklyn accent.[2] He lived in a bucolic lake community, Lake Barcroft, in Fairfax, Virginia, just eight miles from the Washington Beltway, where the 1,200 homeowners had access to five beaches and a small island. It was a tightly knit community with its own Fourth of July celebration, Halloween parade, supper clubs, and poker nights. Then a fertile flock of more than 100 Canada geese moved onto the 135-acre lake in the 1990s. Feld was president of the neighborhood association.

He knew nothing about his new geese neighbors. But then war nearly broke out in the Beltway burg during an annual neighborhood meeting, and he had to become a quick student of *Branta canadensis.*

"I'm asking myself, *What the heck is the problem with these geese?* Then someone stood up and said, 'Kill the geese.' And another person stood up and said, 'Kill the geese.' Then somebody stood up and said, 'Over my dead body.' And then another one stood up and said, 'Okay. Over your dead body,'" Feld told me.

"Then an old lady who had a cane walked up to the front. She raised her cane over her head and said, 'Kill the geese! Kill the geese! Kill the geese!'"

As an engineer, Feld liked problem-solving. He researched geese management strategies nationwide and found a solution that lowered Lake Barcroft's geese population from over a hundred to nearly zero in two years without killing. The winning strategy was a trained border collie named Dakota who drove the geese away.[3] Volunteers also addled every single goose egg and allowed no reproduction. The homeowners association raised the money to buy the border collie: homeowners on the lakeshore paid $25, and everyone else paid $10. (In 2021, over two decades later, this model was still working in Lake Barcroft. Residents particularly enjoyed watching the geese during the pandemic.)[4]

Feld and his neighborhood association founded GeesePeace to help other communities end their geese wars.[5] The organization eventually showed twenty-seven communities in ten states and two countries how to humanely reduce geese populations. Their methods included nest monitoring and stopping reproduction through addling, border collies, green lasers, electric cars, and dog-on-a-stick, a canine silhouette planted in the grass that turns in the wind.

For Feld, the most important decision was not which strategy to employ, but the decision not to kill: "You have to consider the costs to the fabric of a community and what makes it a community. When people aren't cooperating or they are not proud of what they have done—these are costs. When they do something that they can't or don't want to explain to their children—that's a cost. The GeesePeace model is to use the solution as a linking force. If you choose a solution acceptable to almost everybody, people will work together on other issues."

Feld's GeesePeace seemed like a great fit for Madison, but he would help only if city authorities invited him. So that summer I researched and wrote a policy paper for Wild Warner, which we presented at a press conference. The paper described GeesePeace's methods, as well as other alternative strategies implemented internationally, and recommended a citywide citizen-science project that Wild Warner could coordinate. We proposed that Madison's airport follow the example of Chicago O'Hare, where airport officials were experimenting with vegetation to design a "wildlife unfriendly airport," similar to a strategy employed in Canada and the Netherlands.[6] And we recommended that the parks department restore Warner's wetland shoreline with tall native grasses to make the wetland less geese-friendly because geese parents need clear sight lines to see predators. We wanted the city to reduce mowing throughout the park to eliminate the birds' food supply. The city was warning park-goers to stop offering the geese bread and even threatening to cite people for it, and yet every week continued to lay out that freshly clipped green mowed buffet.

The city ignored our proposals. Instead, university and wildlife experts held a series of public forums. In these sessions wildlife managers insisted on roundups. They also insisted that the Warner geese did not migrate, which compounded the poop problem, fouled Warner's waters, and increased the risk to the airport. Every single goose produced an average of 1.5 pounds of poop per day.

I wondered why wildlife managers never mentioned the dog poop in the park. Warner's dog park was one of the most popular in the city.

Unfortunately, it had been built on the wetland's shore. If a dog owner didn't pick up the poop, it ended up in the water along with soggy tennis balls and dog toys. One medium-sized dog produced three-quarters of a pound of poop per day, which didn't break down in the ecosystem as easily as geese feces. I loved that dog park and took my wild southern hounds there daily, but it should never have been built inside a wetland.[7]

I also wondered why city wildlife managers kept insisting that Warner's geese did not migrate. Anyone who walked through Warner between late November and mid-February knew that the geese had to leave the park because the wetland froze solid. But where did they go?

Since the Warner geese had been banded a few years earlier, I called the federal bird-banding laboratory in Maryland to ask if they had any migration records for Warner. The researcher told me that within two years of being banded, 52 of the original 132 banded Warner geese had died, 81 percent shot by hunters in six states—Wisconsin, Minnesota, Missouri, Illinois, Indiana, and Kentucky. Warner's geese migrated as far as 400 miles.[8]

By 2010, when the Great Geese Wars began, Warner Park still had over 100 geese, which meant that new geese from elsewhere had simply replaced the hunted geese (or goslings of the hunted geese had returned to Warner). This confirmed our group's fears that if the parks department did not addle the eggs to control reproduction and kept mowing the grass next to the water—not just in our park but in all Madison parks—new geese would keep coming and roundups would become the norm.

City experts also kept repeating that geese numbers were "out of control." Their language made it sound as if the geese were an invading force that didn't belong in our city. The fossil record showed that Canada geese had been in the Midwest since the the end of the Pleistocene, when the glaciers retreated, or at least 12,000 years.[9] But I wanted to know—how long had geese been living in Madison, specifically in the Warner Park area?

This is the fun thing about researching a dissertation. You get to spend time answering some crazy questions, and sometimes what you discover in dank, dusty archives blows the roof off your ivory tower head.

**I BEGAN MY SEARCH FOR ANCIENT GEESE DEEP IN THE MARBLED WARREN OF THE WISCONSIN** Historical Society. There I dove into the personal papers of Charles E. Brown, an intrepid self-taught archeologist who spent nearly five decades digging up and trying to preserve Madison's indigenous heritage before developers destroyed it.

I learned that in the 1830s and '40s, when European settlers entered the Madison Four Lakes area, they stepped into an almost entirely sculpted landscape, especially along lakes and rivers. Out of the mud and red clay rose ancient mounds, many conical, with others shaped in long snaky lines that stretched hundreds of feet. At least 200 were shaped like birds, mammals, and "water-spirits."[10] The Midwest boasted more mounds than any other region in the nation. Madison had so many—an estimated 1,300—that one archeologist called it "Mound City."[11]

Until I started this geese research, I had no idea we were living on top of ancient mounds. Now I learned that the university had built dorms on sacred mounds and that some of my favorite lecture halls covered mounds. Madison's parks, country clubs, golf courses, and probably many a parking lot sat on destroyed mounds. Archeologists believed that Wisconsin's indigenous peoples had created at least 15,000 mounds in Wisconsin nearly a millennium ago, during an effigy building boom between AD 700 and 1100.[12]

In Madison, many were *bird* mounds. I discovered that the largest bird-shaped mound in North America was just a few minutes from Warner Park. Its earthen grass-covered wings still stretched 624 feet in front of the state's former mental asylum. Scholars believed that mound represented either an eagle or a condor.

The answer to my question of how long geese had been in Madison was waiting in file folder 2, box 21 of Charles Brown's papers—his spare hand drawing in black ink of a mound on a sheet of field-survey paper. Any child would have recognized it as a very large goose—the diamond-shaped head, the long snaky neck, the outstretched, slightly bent wings, the broad, sassy tail—*Branta canadensis* rising out of the Madison mud. Hands laboring together perhaps a thousand years ago had fashioned it.

Charles Brown's drawing was of one of ten large goose mounds in Madison, according to Robert Birmingham, author of *Spirits of Earth: The Effigy Mound Landscape of Madison and the Four Lakes.* Birmingham's book had a map showing geese mounds all around the lakes and wetlands, as if the giant birds were flying to and from the waters; one mound was near Warner Park. And he'd discovered that Madison was the only place in the United States with geese mounds with bent wings. Birmingham called them "the Four Lakes symbol."[13]

"The mounds of migratory water birds like geese, prominent in the Four Lakes, are obvious symbols of the cyclical death and rebirth of the earth: geese leave in the fall and return in the spring," Wisconsin's former state archeologist wrote.[14]

There were other clues about Warner Park's environmental history in Charles Brown's careful notes. On May 28, 1939, Brown explored the area that eventually became Warner Park and discovered flint chips, spalls, and nodules—evidence of an ancient workshop on Warner's marsh island that may have dated back thousands of years.[15] But the treasure in Brown's files that brought tears to my eyes was his discovery of a bird effigy mound 56 paces from Warner Park's edge. The wings of this bird mound had extended 170 feet, with a body 64 feet long. And in the bird mound's center, Brown found a "sub-floor burial pit" containing the bones and teeth of a nine-year-old child interred hundreds of years earlier.[16]

Many archeologists believe that a person buried in the heart of an effigy mound was meant to become one with that animal and its spirit.[17] A housing tract had been built on top of this burial mound—a child's grave—in the 1950s. Every Wednesday, my students and the middle schoolers walked right by where that mound had stood, a herd of wild young ones, laughing, screaming, running, and watching the heron who hid in a corner of the marsh just below. There was no marker, nothing to honor the child who had died centuries earlier. I still wonder about this. Who was this bird-child? How did they die? And what did the birds in this place mean to them and their people?

**BY THE EARLY 1900S, WHEN MANY OTHER WATERFOWL SPECIES BEGAN TO DISAPPEAR** because of overhunting and wetland destruction, Canada goose populations also plummeted nationally. One of the subspecies, the giant Canada goose who nested in Warner Park and was the target of the proposed roundup, had disappeared completely and was considered extinct in the wild up until the 1960s. Nationwide, biologists tried for decades to bring the birds back, including Aldo Leopold, who immortalized geese in his *Sand County Almanac*:

> Out of the clouds I hear a faint bark, as of a far-away dog. It is strange how the world cocks its ears at that sound, wondering . . . The flock emerges from the low clouds, a tattered banner of birds, dipping and rising, blown up and blown down, blown together and blown apart, but advancing, the wind wrestling lovingly with each winnowing wing. When the flock is a blur in the far sky I hear the last honk, sounding taps for the summer . . . It is warm behind the driftwood now, for the wind has gone with the geese. So would I—if I were the wind.[18]

In several states, including Wisconsin, biologists bred captive Canada geese and then used them as live decoys to attract wild geese flying over.[19] Some birds hatch knowing how to migrate. But other species must learn from their parents. Canada geese are one of these. But biologists couldn't let their captives migrate. And because their captive breeding efforts were eventually successful, generations of geese lost the knowledge of how and where to migrate to. GeesePeace founder David Feld called these policies "one of the greatest cases of mismanagement by wildlife agencies in America . . . Wildlife agencies took these geese and encouraged them to nest all over the country by taking eggs, incubating them, and encouraging geese to double clutch (produce two nests)."[20]

The comeback of *Branta canadensis* coincided with the postwar suburban building boom and the construction of parks like Warner all over the country to meet growing recreation needs. These parks contained acres of mowed grass; many had ponds or wetlands. Manicured shorelines became the fashion.

In the wild, Canada geese historically have used two separate territories: a sheltered, marshy breeding ground where they nest behind tall marsh grasses until the goslings are a day or two old, and a feeding ground where they lead the goslings, sometimes for a considerable distance, through woods or rough terrain to an open tundra-like area. The goslings can swim and feed themselves immediately, nibbling on grass alongside their parents. But they cannot protect themselves. They are extremely vulnerable and make great snacks for land or aerial predators like hawks. Geese parents require open feeding areas so they can see that fox, bobcat, or dog approaching, especially the gander, whose job is to beat off predators with those powerful wings.[21] And the goslings need the grass to eat.

As biologists brought back what some called "America's grandest bird," landscape architects and parks designers unintentionally fused geese breeding and feeding territories by creating mowed parks, golf courses, and country clubs with ponds, often with marsh islands ideal for nesting. While meeting the recreational needs of human families populating the new suburbs, they inadvertently created millions of acres of geese nurseries to replace the messy wetlands.

It's a simple principle of ecology—build it and they will come. We did, and they have. The goose that nearly disappeared now lives in all fifty states, some part time, most full time.

Today the turf grass that geese love is the number one irrigated crop in the nation, covering approximately 45 million acres, or an area larger than the state of Georgia. Entomologist and native plant expert Douglas Tallamy calls lawns "ecological dead zones" that are partially responsible for the nation's plummeting insect and bird populations.[22] Lawn care also poisons the soil. The EPA estimates that people spill 17 million gallons of gas while trying to fill their mowers—more fuel than the *Exxon Valdez* tanker dumped into an Alaskan bay. And we use tens of millions of pounds of chemical fertilizers and pesticides on our lawns.[23] Those bright green patches are not just goose magnets, they are a fossil-fueled environmental catastrophe.

**IN ADDITION TO THE MASSIVE LANDSCAPE SHIFT, THERE HAS BEEN A GENERATIONAL SHIFT.** Most of us have no living memory of birds "blackening the skies," or of a flock of geese such as ornithologist T. Gilbert Pearson described in 1917: "In Currituck Sound I have seen one flight that was two hours in passing a given point. They came in one long wavy rank after another, from twenty to thirty of these extended lines of geese being in sight at a time."[24]

I thought about my mornings on Sled Hill before the Great Geese Wars started, when small Vs of geese approached from the southwest, flying low over that hill. I loved to lie back on the grass as the huge birds passed just a few feet above me, letting the wind created by twenty-four wings, each two feet long, all flapping in unison, as if they were rowing through the air, wash over my body, my face tingling slightly from the wing-produced breeze, my ears filled with the soft whistle of those wings. What would it be like to hear and feel the wind created by the flocks that must have flown over this continent eons ago, a flock of a million geese, two million wings flapping in unison? Could two million flapping wings create their own microclimate or a windstorm? How would a flock that size affect us, change the way we see our role on this earth?

Unfortunately for most of us, Alfred Hitchcock's movie *The Birds* is our only cultural reference for a large flock of avians, and it's a scary one. Our cultural memory of lakes covered with birds disappeared with the sprawling wetlands that we covered with concrete. We have forgotten what was once there. We have forgotten how to share. Or we never learned.

**I WAS PRETTY DEPRESSED AFTER ALL THIS RESEARCH AND THE ATTACKS ON THE WARNER** geese. I'd spent a summer reading reports that solely focused on the birds as "a problem" to be solved, "pests," "a nuisance." I no longer enjoyed watching them. When I saw them in Warner, all I could think about was management strategies to bring their numbers down. Instead of relishing their antics, I was either counting them or handing out flyers to get people to come to meetings or collecting phone numbers of geese lovers. Heddie thought that the geese sounded sad when they flew over her house, honking. She said the geese knew they were no longer wanted.

Wild Warner was also still split on the geese issue. In public, our group presented a united front, a tactic we would employ in future battles. But in our meetings, it was the geese subcommittee and Jim and I who were leading the charge.

Then other battles in Warner Park began to percolate and we had to stick together. I realized one day when I found a certain fungus at the base of the mother bur oak that the tree was getting sick. The city was using giant heavy mowers to shave every blade of grass beneath it, which, a tree expert told Wild Warner, was compacting the soil and damaging the tree's root system. Even worse, one morning I found a parks employee chainsawing off the oak's lower limbs so that damned mower could get even closer to the already ailing tree. As Wild Warner's chair, Jim worked for months along with furious Wild Warnerites to protect this beloved tree. We brought in a renowned expert to measure it. He confirmed what we suspected: our bur oak was at least 250 years old, a rare bicentennial oak, and one of the largest in the county. After months of fighting, we won official recognition of the Warner oak as a heritage tree and champion tree of Wisconsin. The mowing and dismemberment halted.

But the bur oak was just the beginning of the tree battles. The city wanted to widen the paved road through the park to accommodate larger and heavier maintenance vehicles, as well as improve it for cyclists. So we lobbied to stop the city from cutting down all the mature trees along the old path (more meetings, more email campaigns—we succeeded). And then one late November morning, Sandy called us, crying. I could hear the chainsaws down the street. The city was chopping down some of the largest and most beautiful trees right in front of the apartment buildings (but they didn't touch the trees in front of the homes of white homeowners like us). The trees were massive old maples that provided shade and beauty to ugly apartment blocks. Jim went out to ask city employees what in the hell they were doing. They told him that they had to cut the trees down because of the garbage trucks. The trees were too big and getting in the way. So now garbage trucks were driving city forestry management. That entire day, dump trucks roared down our street filled to the brim with those trees. It felt like a war on the trees, which meant a war on shade, oxygen, life.

It just never stopped. Every few months, there was another battle on the horizon. And some of the battles we discovered by chance, just because one of us happened to attend some innocuous meeting. One of our members who was also on the city's planning commission heard about an upcoming engineering "experiment" in our lower-income neighborhood. City engineers wanted to cover an old concrete streambed leading into Warner's wetland with a new rubber matting that hadn't been tested. In order to do this, they planned to cut down a swath of beautiful towering trees at our neighborhood's entrance.

After this diligent member sounded the alarm, we all hit the meeting trail. Instead of conducting an experiment, we convinced the city to leave the trees, install rain gardens to solve a flooding problem, and restore that concrete canal to a creek.*

I suddenly realized the battles were never going to stop when the city councilor announced she was requesting $100,000 for a new master plan for Warner Park (this was in addition to the 165-page neighborhood plan we'd stalled). She'd decided the park needed a new plan because of "conflicts over public use." The city's request for proposal was 44 pages long and contained 25,525 words. It instructed future consultants to conduct an ecological inventory of all vegetation (great idea, I thought). But then I couldn't find the word "wildlife" anywhere; the word "fauna" appeared once. There was not one fox, one bird, or one fish in the city's bid. To city planners, Warner Park was empty and a blank slate.

I'd begun seriously researching the history, design, management, and role of recreation in urban parks for my dissertation. So I shouldn't have been surprised that there were no animals mentioned. Although municipal park uses have changed considerably over the past 150 years, I was learning through bitter experience that park administrators had long considered animals in city parks only as "pests" to be eliminated. Trees and plants were like Legos, replaceable and expendable. As I read a century and a half of literature concerning urban parks, I didn't find a single study of urban parks focused on the environmental history of the land, the water, *and* the animal residents. Such studies focused only on human history.[25] Parks designers and leisure science researchers nationally had never considered what urban animals meant to park lovers or how the presence of animals could benefit human health. But until very recently, there were also very few mental health studies that investigated the potential benefits. This is still a relatively new field.

Yet every single Wednesday afternoon, I saw how much the animals meant to the middle schoolers and my students. A fleeting glimpse

* Wild Warner's Mike Rewey spearheaded this effort, and he didn't even live near Warner Park; he thought it was an environmental injustice to cut down huge trees at the entrance to a lower-income neighborhood.

of our red fox in the meadow inspired a growly boy known as a terrible bully to sit down and pen a fox poem on the spot. A sighting of the red-tailed hawk pair on Valentine's Day, mating for four seconds on top of the baseball stadium lights, mesmerized thirty astonished middle schoolers and their mentors.

"They're mating?" one boy said. "But it's not even night!"

Some of our kids who had never seen a deer discovered a doe cowering behind a spruce and screamed, jumped up and down, and then stared at the poor terrified animal as if she were an alien spaceship. They talked about that doe for weeks. The sight of a single mallard on the iced-over wetland delighted the children:

"One of the males slipped and fell clumsily on the slippery ice, but then quickly redeemed himself by catching a fish by PIERCING through the ice with his bill! I was so glad we were all able to see that, it was so cool. Watching our duck take slippery steps on the ice back to the open water was hilarious," a college mentor wrote in her teaching journal.[26]

Even the worms were precious. I'll never forget a skinny West African kid who spent more than an hour one afternoon, creeping along Warner's main paved path just after a rainstorm, picking up every single stranded worm and carefully placing each one on the grass. He didn't want the worms to get stepped on. He told me that one day he was going to be "a veterinarian or a children's cancer doctor."

And yet to city and most park officials, Warner's animals were invisible. Except for the geese. They were loud, proud, and stubborn. And they weren't abandoning Warner Park.

THROUGH EVERY BATTLE, I JUST KEPT TEACHING THE KIDS AND PLUGGING ALONG ON GEESE research with the help of the mighty geese subcommittee. My spirits lifted and my resolve strengthened when I found a geese mentor from afar, one of the world's most famous ecologists and science writers, Bernd Heinrich. Heinrich's books on birds are some of my favorites because he enters into a relationship with the animal he's studying and uses that intimate relationship to explore, challenge, and develop theories of animal behavior. One of the first bird books I read was Heinrich's *One Man's Owl,* about how he rescued and raised a great horned owlet named Bubo, as a scientific experiment (*Bubo virginianus* is this owl's Latin name). Heinrich also wrote *The Geese of Beaver Bog,* a study of Canada geese based on his four-year relationship with a goose he called Peep and the families she raised. His book on geese was vastly different from management studies that treated birds as feathered robots. Heinrich viewed geese as individuals to learn from, with complex behaviors, not a problem to be "solved."

When a gosling hatches, the first creature it lays eyes on becomes its mother, whether that creature is a goose, a human, or a donkey. It's a biological process called imprinting. Heinrich's scholarly geese adventures began with a gosling imprinting on Heinrich himself, something he hadn't anticipated. A Vermont farmer gave Heinrich a wild, just-hatched gosling as a pet for Heinrich's two-year-old son. Heinrich named the gosling Peep. But he soon discovered that he had become her "surrogate mother goose." And like any wild gosling, Peep followed her mother everywhere. Heinrich had to trick her so he could leave to teach at the university. And then one fall day, when Peep the gosling had grown into Peep the goose, Heinrich was pushing his Toyota pickup against the 45 mph speed limit on a Vermont rural highway when he noticed Peep flapping hard a foot or two behind him.

A week later, she disappeared. Heinrich hoped she had joined the great Vs snaking overhead, but he didn't know. He never thought he would see Peep again. But two years later she returned to his front lawn with her mate and came when Heinrich called her name. For the next two years, Peep flew in and out of Heinrich's life. She became a window on geese life and avian dramas. The last time he saw her was during the fourth year, in September, when after months of absence, she suddenly flew up to the house with five teenage goslings and a new mate, giving a goose goodbye to the man who raised her, before she led her family south on migration.

**I HAD MY OWN PEEP-TYPE MOMENT WITH A GOOSE IN WARNER. IT WAS A MORNING IN EARLY** December just after the first gentle snow. Lines of geese were still flying overhead, heading south, but they were no longer stopping in the park because there was nothing left to eat. Most of the lagoon was frozen. But that day I found one goose sitting on the frozen grass near the dog park bridge. The bird was smaller than most geese, so I assumed she was a female. At first I thought she must have been injured and couldn't fly because geese were almost never alone.

I spent nearly an hour watching her, Heinrich-style. She crept closer to me and I to her until we were ten feet apart. I kept talking to her, asking her why she was there. I took pictures of her. She didn't seem afraid. I wanted her story: Why was she staying here with all the geese flying overhead, honking loudly?

As I crawled forward on my elbows, stretched out on the frozen ground at her eye level, I thought about my ecology classes. We talked about populations of animals, never individuals or their behavior. It was like studying economics with the daily lives of humans removed from the equation. But human lives had been what made economics interesting to me when I worked at a lefty Jesuit economics institute in Managua, Nicaragua. From an ecological standpoint, it would have been wrong for me to help this one goose—better to let her die. But as I kept creeping forward, looking her in the eye while she stared back, I realized that as much as I loved ecology and everything I was learning from my professors about the connections between all living things, I'd never make a bona fide "ecologist." For me it was all about relationships and the bird in front of me at any given moment.

As I lay on that frozen grass, stewing about this, the goose suddenly left of her own accord, lifting skyward in a great flapping, perhaps joining a skein of comrades she'd recognized in the sky, crossing high over Warner.

**ALTHOUGH THE CITY BIOLOGIST DID CONSULT WITH WILDLIFE MANAGERS IN CITIES USING** GeesePeace's strategies, the parks superintendent did not want GeesePeace's help. The following summer of 2011, parks commissioners voted to allow geese roundups with the caveat that there would be no roundup, at least in the short term, in Warner Park. The new policy was "site-specific," meaning the city would conduct roundups only in parks where people were complaining the most.

I realize now that the city's lone wildlife manager-biologist simply didn't have the resources to manage a massive citizen-science program like the one Wild Warner had proposed. He was in charge of thousands of acres used by the public every day, most of them in the city's conservation parks, which were vital to so many other bird species. And he was under enormous pressure from his bosses to solve the problem quickly and cheaply, not implement a GeesePeace multiyear process involving public education and an army of volunteers. It wasn't necessarily cheaper to cull the animals—city officials gave a quote of $120 per goose to kill Warner's geese and deliver the meat to food pantries. But the city of Madison and the state of Wisconsin already had a default system in place for dealing with "problem" animals or "pests"—kill them. During our geese research for Wild Warner, Stacy and I had discovered that wildlife management was dominated by a macho pest control mentality that had become its own killing industrial complex with allies thoughout wildlife agencies, "culling" millions of animals annually, including one million European starlings—the murmuration bird. It wasn't just a system—it was an entrenched culture and a boy's club in which emotion was suspect.*

But despite all the pressures on him—economic, political, and cultural—to his credit the city biologist did try some management methods we'd recommended. The most important and immediate change he implemented was to plant tall native grasses along Warner's

* The USDA's Wildlife Services killed more than 1.75 million animals in 2021, from alligators to owls and snakes and turtles. More than 1 million of those animals were starlings, the murmuration bird (in ancient Ireland, they were sacred birds, which is why in Irish they are called druids, after the Celtic high priests). The USDA kills both native and "invasive" species, including wolves, coyotes, bears, mountain lions, bobcats, foxes, and beaver. Agents use snares and traps, shoot animals from helicopters, and also employ M-44 cyanide "bombs." The 2021 toll actually represents a significant drop in killing compared to the years when Wild Warner was fighting the Great Geese Wars. See Oliver Milman, "'A Barbaric Federal Program': US Killed 1.75m Animals Last Year—or 200 Per Hour," *The Guardian*, March 25, 2022, https://www.theguardian.com/world/2022/mar/25/us-government-wildlife-services-animals-deaths.

shoreline, restoring a buffer to discourage geese and help other wildlife. Slowly the city began to restore shoreline grasses in other parks. I think the reason he tried other methods was because some Wild Warner members, including Jack Hurst, knew him really well. They'd spent years restoring marshes and prairies, planting and sweating together. Those alliances made a huge difference.

When the Great Geese Wars petered out, I discovered that Madison's city biologist had another secret weapon against the geese. One morning while I was birding in Warner's marsh I heard a horrible grating and spitting sound. There scooting across the water was a red demon-like creature nearly four feet long and two feet tall, on a Rube Goldberg jet-ski thing, with an enormous set of pointed teeth painted on its terrifying head. It was the wildlife manager's latest solution: the Goosinator. He told me he was piloting this strange contraption in our park, and it was working. In fact, the geese hated the Goosinator so much that after a while, he didn't even have to use it. The geese would see his truck coming down Warner's main path, red lights flashing, and know the Goosinator was headed their way. Off they'd go in a flurry of wings and furious honks. The biologist also put Wild Warner member Tim Nelson in charge of Warner geese birth control. Every year for the past decade, Tim has paddled his kayak out into Warner's wetland to coat the eggs with corn oil. Between the annual addling and the Goosinator, the number of Warner's geese has decreased and so have the complaints.

I realize now how much these large, charismatic, beloved and reviled avians taught Wild Warner. We learned from the geese fight that our differences were also our strength and that we had to stick together, no matter what. Our differences meant we had many networks and alliances to draw on, as well as varied skills and knowledge. I will never forget Jack Hurst, the avowed hunter and fishermen, sitting next to members of our geese subcommittee, trying to restrain himself from sharing too many Crockpot recipes.

Although we didn't think about it at the time, the geese also provided a perfect organizing and leadership model for our group—master flock builders all around us when we were just beginning to organize

our own flock. Geese are so loyal to mates and family members that when one is shot by a hunter, the others will often drop from the sky to accompany a wounded or dead mate.[27] The chevrons they form when flying overhead in the spring like lines of haiku are also an ingenious way to save energy—as much as 30 percent—allowing the flock to fly 70 percent farther.[28] It's a strategy NASA calls "Follow the leader and save fuel," which the US military began studying and emulating twenty years ago. The lead goose creates a wake of air behind it, just like a boat in the water. Each flapping follower benefits from the lift created by the goose flapping ahead of it. The birds synchronize their flapping and switch positions constantly. I've been a member of too many political organizations where the leadership became worn out and stagnant and finally burned out. It seems as if geese have found the solution to activist burnout.

The geese also forced me personally to explore a spectrum of viewpoints, from the flying "poetry in the sky" perspective of Aldo Leopold to the "we need to solve this problem and satisfy the complainers" park management perspective. The geese taught me about Madison's indigenous history and that I was living in mound country. My geese research also helped me to discover Warner's archeological history: that it had been an indigenous workshop and the burial site of a bird-child, a sacred place as well as a bird nursery. And finally, the geese made me question my own eating choices and hypocrisy. Why did I care if USDA agents came into Warner Park and killed the birds when I went to the grocery store and bought whole caged chickens to stuff with garlic and roast in an oven? Today in Madison, some of the meat from geese that are culled annually is given to the Ho-Chunk. They are among the descendants of the people who immortalized the geese in those signature mounds.

And then there was the view of the bird-children in my program, their joy at seeing the geese, running with them, chasing them, sitting quietly and drawing them, sharing stories about them at school. As fifth-grader Gabriel told the parks superintendent at a meeting: "The geese issue is not being looked at from a child's perspective. We get very excited when we see them. They're inspirational. I joined Birding Club because of the geese. Instead of killing them, try to preserve them."

CHAPTER 10

# The Birder's Gaze

*Seeing beauty and advocating for justice are not mutually exclusive acts.*

J. DREW LANHAM, CONSERVATION BIOLOGIST

IN THE IRISH LANGUAGE, THE WORD *MÚIN*, PRONOUNCED "MOO-IN," MEANS "TO teach, to show." But it also means "to learn." For the Celts, teaching and learning were a circle, indivisible.[1] Modern academia has ruptured that ancient circle by emphasizing the professor/expert who "delivers content" to students.

The day the kids made me take off my ivory tower head and roll down Sled Hill was the day that ancient circle was restored for me. I realized that our club-flock had taken on a dynamic all its own and evolved way beyond my meager syllabus. Now it belonged to the children. As an educator, I live for these learning-teaching moments, although they are not always fun or easy. The Great Wet Sock Meltdown was another such "lesson" the children taught me.

It was a very snowy day in February. My students and I had arrived to take the kids to the park. We'd just had one of those record-breaking storms, and there was two feet of snow on the ground. The temperature was hovering around 20 degrees, yet over half the children showed up in sneakers and thin cotton socks. After an hour sloshing through Warner Park, we had crying kids turning blue, so we rushed them into my tiny living room with the woodstove roaring. An assembly line of cooing college mentors, the school social worker, my PhD advisor Jack, and I started peeling wet socks off thin little feet and throwing them into the dryer.

During our class discussion afterward, some of my students were scathing. What kind of parents did these kids have? Who would send their child to school in the Wisconsin winter without proper shoes and socks?

At that moment I realized that if I didn't incorporate social justice into my birding class, I would be betraying all that I'd learned in that Jesuit institute in Managua. Much of our work there was based on the teachings of Brazilian revolutionary education philosopher Paulo Freire. Author of the 1968 activist manual *Pedagogy of the Oppressed*, Freire believed education should be a liberating and transformational force that changed students' daily lives, instead of producing docile workers to uphold the corporate status quo.

I liked to think Freire's tenet "Education should not reproduce systems of oppression" was my teaching credo. But on that Great Wet Sock Day, I realized that my students didn't understand why these kids' parents could not afford winter boots because I hadn't provided enough socioeconomic context to help them understand. I did this intentionally because I didn't want my students to see the kids and their families as "victims" or "poor people" for them to help. But by pairing them with kids in my struggling neighborhood, I was still reinforcing all the tired stereotypes about people with less money. I was violating Freire's credo and reproducing systems of oppression.

The next week, instead of talking about birds, I led students through a "Clothing Privilege" exercise. I listed on the chalkboard every item I was wearing that frosty day, tallying up $662 (just my Smartwool undershirt cost $100). Then I asked every student to do the same.

"I was shocked at the number at the bottom of Trish's list, but then I remembered exactly how much I was wearing last Wednesday. My list totaled out to be $717!" one wrote.[2]

This student was "completely astounded" by the amount she'd spent on winter wear, and so, troubled, she called another student to discuss it. She realized that that $717 meant three weeks' worth of minimum-wage pay for a family in my neighborhood, an impossible amount for many to spend on winter wear.

My student's reaction was a great aha moment for me. I'd been focusing the class on birds and environmental activism strategies to protect Warner Park. I'd provided some background on my neighborhood and the middle school's demographics, but it was a cursory course introduction—not a theme woven throughout the semester. That day I realized that birding could be a powerful way to teach students about injustice and economic privilege. But I wasn't sure how to weave racism into a birding class. I wasn't sure it was even necessary. I saw my neighbors of color in Warner Park every day, mostly walking their dogs. It's true I'd never seen any birders of color in the park. And the majority of walkers, joggers, and cyclists were white despite

the fact that hundreds of families of color lived around Warner. It took an eastern bluebird named Mr. Blue and a fierce bluebird defender named Mr. M to help me understand why.

To help meet Wild Warner's goal to make the park's animals more visible, Wild Warner's new education coordinator Paul Noeldner decided to create a bluebird trail. With a shock of silvery hair askew like an avian crest, Paul reminded me of a cedar waxwing. Bringing back the bluebird was just one of his many feathered passions, and he had lured a small legion of the beloved avian back to Madison. Paul had trained dozens of volunteers to manage new urban bluebird trails, and if he could have squeezed inside one of his tiny houses to incubate those eggs himself, he would have done it. He trudged through parks, golf courses, country clubs, and backyards lugging birdhouse repair tools (screwdrivers, drills, zip ties, nails, posts), along with bluebird treats like dried mealworms, the odd chocolate bar for that volunteer in training (me), bluebird management books, and dried pine needles and grasses to build emergency nests if a house got knocked down by a storm or a nest got invaded by baby-bird-eating insects.

Bluebirds, like ducks and eagles, are another avian comeback kid, living proof that our species can do the right thing. Eastern bluebird numbers plummeted in the twentieth century because of habitat loss: these birds need holes to nest in; they can't carve holes like a woodpecker. As small farms began disappearing nationwide, and along with them the meadows bluebirds feed in, and as people began cutting down the dead trees bluebirds need to nest in—especially old apple trees—this bird all but disappeared in many places, including Warner Park. Thousands of volunteers nationwide helped bring them back by installing tiny birdhouses. Julie Zickefoose, a wildlife rehabilitator, bird artist, and author of the beautiful *The Bluebird Effect: Uncommon Bonds with Common Birds*, called this effort "the largest single-species conservation effort ever launched." Wisconsin's Bluebird Restoration Association (BRAW) was part of this human conservation murmuration, with more than 8,000 volunteers who fledged 28,814 babies in just one year.[3] Paul was a BRAW warrior.

After I became one of Paul's trainees, in charge of eight Warner bluebird houses, I began to feel as I were living in a never-ending season of "Call the Avian Midwife." The first bluebird to occupy one of my houses, Mr. Blue, soon had a mate and a family of four babies, ready to fledge. One morning when I went to check on them, the little house had disappeared—someone had stolen it—and one of Mr. Blue's babies was lying mashed on the grass. But Mr. Blue was no quitter, and neither was I. He hung around the meadow that day watching me as I spent hours with an official from the Department of Natural Resources, a parks ranger, and the police. Together we installed another bluebird house in the exact same spot, and then attached a webcam and posted warning signs. The next morning, there was Mr. Blue zooming in and out with his mate, fluffing up a new nest. She laid five eggs this time: they all fledged. I loved stepping into that meadow and seeing the entire family—Mr. Blue, his mate, and their five azure teenagers—hanging out at the top of a tree.

**I'M NOT SURE WHAT IT IS ABOUT BLUEBIRDS, BUT PEOPLE HAVE FALLEN MADLY IN LOVE WITH** them all over the world for centuries, earning them the moniker "the bluebird of happiness." The Navajo call them "heralds of the sun."[4] It's not a loud or flashy bird. The male sings a soft little "cheerio" song that sounds melancholy to me. But blue is a color that soothes and cheers, the color of the sky itself and the sea. And in many cultures, it is considered the color of truth, peace, gentleness, and loyalty.

But color can be deceiving. The bird that is the color of the Virgin Mary's cape turns out to be a bias buster. Bluebirds may kill other bluebirds for a nest site. And *Sialia sialis* is not necessarily "loyal" to a mate; in fact, it was the first "monogamous" species to bring down the 1950s science gender bias that female birds did not stray from their eggs. Studies have shown that female bluebirds may be hooking up while their mate is away and that as many as 20 percent of bluebird nestlings may come from these "extra-pair copulations."

Whatever we may read into the colors of birds, for them color means survival. Color helps a bird find a mate and may help determine if that potential mate is healthy (the brighter the colors, the healthier the male). Birds flash certain parts of their body, often brightly colored like the ruby crown of the ruby-crowned kinglet, for example, to signal territory or warn off a predator. Avians can also see many more shades than we can and colors we can't even imagine. Light is a spectrum of wavelengths only a fraction of which our species can see—the visible spectrum, meaning visible to humans. But many birds can also see ultraviolet light and the earth's magnetic field, which appears to them as blue.*

Birds acquire their colors through two mechanisms: either from chemical pigments or from what scientists call structural color, which involves the scattering of light, or a combination of the two. For example, the bright red northern cardinal that cheers so many of us

* Scientists still cannot even imagine what birds actually see, but we know their eyes are far superior to ours; we have three color cones in our retina and they have four. Avian eyes are also much larger than ours relative to body size, almost twice as large as most mammal eyes. Birds, fish, reptiles, and insects all have better vision than us bumbling mammals.

during snowy winters gets its color from chemical pigments in rose hips, berries, and other red fruits, foods that contain carotenoid pigments. The bluebird, however, doesn't eat his blues. He's a structural colorist, a living light show who represents the interplay between sunlight and the intrinsic structure of his feathers. Those feathers are a matrix of air and keratin, dead cells just like the keratin in our hair and fingernails. To explore inside a feather, scientists use massive X-ray machines called synchrotrons that can cover two football fields, with light beams hundreds of thousands of times brighter than conventional X-ray machines. Under these light beams, a feather becomes a hidden world of Lilliputian mountains and valleys, forests, and underwater coral reefs, structures so tiny they are called nanostructures.[5] In this invisible world, a nanometer is one-billionth of a meter, or 100,000 times smaller than the width of a human hair.[6]

When light waves hit the bluebirds' invisible feather matrix of keratin and air, that light show begins. It doesn't matter if you're a blue jay or an indigo bunting or a male bluebird. If you're blue, it's because of the hidden landscape in your feathers.

The bluebird's blues, all avian colors and feathers themselves, depend on melanin, which lies underneath the nano- and microfeather structures, absorbing light as it hits them. But melanin isn't important only to avians. It's the oldest, most resistant, and most ubiquitous pigment on Earth, and without it, we probably wouldn't even exist. Scientists believe that bacteria, the very first life-forms on Earth, survived because melanin provided sun protection and a buffer from environmental toxins. Nature's sunscreen, melanin can absorb or dissipate more than 99.9 percent of UV radiation, the highest rate of any known biological material.[7] And it lasts nearly forever. Researchers discovered melanin in the 307-million-year-old eyeballs of Tullimonstrum, or the Tully monster, a strange and ancient fishlike thing that once swam in the warm seas that covered Chicago when Chicago was near the equator.[8]

As Earth's creatures evolved to have eyes, they also required predator defenses—enter melanin, with colors for camouflage and to attract potential mates. Most living creatures today produce melanin in their bodies. A major link in the grand chain of life, it helps fungi protect themselves against environmental toxins, gives the squid its knife-sharp beak, helps plants to heal and protect their tissues from damage, makes those annoying brown spots on your bananas, and gives birds their feathers and colors.

Melanin also makes those feathers strong and stiff, provides UV protection, and repels bacteria. When a white gull flies over, look up at those jet-black wing tips slicing through the sky. Those black tips are melanin in action, a built-in erosion protection system for birds that spend a lot of time in salt water.

The melanin that gives birds their gorgeous colors also gives us ours; in general, the darker a person's skin, the more melanin they have. Of the five types of melanin, four are produced and used by avians and humans.* Eumelanin makes my favorite black bird, the red-winged blackbird, black, makes my eyes brown, and gives me freckles. (My brothers have blue eyes, which just means they have less melanin than I do, but it's the same type.) A combination of eumelanin and pheomelanin gives the eastern bluebird its rusty breast and me my reddish-brown hair. Pheomelanin also colors our lips, nipples, and certain nether parts.

Melanin may also save our species from life-threatening diseases. Cancer researchers are studying its immune-system-boosting properties and potential for stopping cancer. NASA researchers are experimenting with it as a radiation blocker to protect astronauts and equipment during space explorations. Parkinson's researchers are studying whether melanin deterioration in the brain is connected to the disease's progression.

**BLUEBIRD DEFENDERS ARE VERY PASSIONATE. THEY SEE THE BABIES INSIDE THOSE LITTLE** houses as their personal wards. And even if the little houses are not on your bluebird trail, whenever you see one, you feel protective. This is why there is a certain occupational risk to managing bluebird houses.

* Bacteria and fungi produce pyomelanin, the fifth type of melanin.

It isn't that the angry bluebird parents might dive-bomb your head. (The metallic blue tree swallows will for sure; they're tiny fighter pilots flashing their iridescence as they dip and zip past your nose, clicking angrily.) Or that you'll end up with bird poop from feisty parents on your baseball cap. No, this is the biggest risk for bluebird managers—that one gorgeous summer morning you are on your knees underneath a bluebird house in a meadow, poking a twig through the stinky, gruesome remains of four bluebird babies lying on the grass, feeling like a demented ornithological forensic detective doing a quick autopsy, trying to figure out who is the murderer because those babies were alive and cheeping loudly just a few days ago, when one of these enraged bluebird defenders suddenly comes along and assumes the absolute worst.

"WHAT ARE *YOU* DOING?" a disembodied deep male voice roared from across the clearing.

I stood up fast, guilt all over my face, holding that gooey stick with baby bird bits on it. No time to hide the evidence. A very large man, well over six feet and at least 250 pounds, was barreling across the meadow toward me, wielding a heavy, knobbed wooden cane.

It took several minutes of fast talking to convince a man I'll call Mr. M that I was not a baby bluebird torturer, that in fact I was trying to help their parents re-nest by removing the failed nest, and I was trying to figure out who or what killed these poor little nestlings.[9] When I told Mr. M that I was a new bluebird manager with Wild Warner, the group trying to protect the park, Mr. M's death grip on his hickory cane loosened.

"When I was here two years ago, all this was cut down," Mr. M said, pointing at the surrounding meadow. "When I came back and saw it grown up, I was so happy. It's so beautiful . . . We take this park for granted. We've got idiots, and I mean idiots, mad at you guys because you're trying to preserve it. To me that's ignorant . . . It's absolutely gorgeous, and I'm so appreciative of what you and your group have done."

This bluebird lover turned out to be the biggest fan of Warner Park I'd ever met. Out of the dozens of park-goers I'd talked to, he was the only one who told me that he loved the place so much he wanted his ashes scattered here. (This was why he didn't want me using his name—he was afraid it was illegal to scatter human ashes in a city park.)

Mr. M had been walking through these meadows for thirty years. He'd spent hundreds of happy hours on the park's trails with Squirty, his beloved Maltese.

"We'd get to the park and she'd be so happy. She'd walk a little ways and stand and look back at me. It was so cute."

I asked if I could interview him for my dissertation. I wanted to see the park through his eyes.

Mr. M showed up on a late July morning on the meadow's edge wearing a dapper gray straw fedora with a feather tucked in the hatband. We walked very slowly, stopping occasionally to rest under shady trees. Mr. M was seventy-one and had serious arthritis and sciatica after sixty years of physical labor. But I could tell that like my other older park friends, he also walked slowly because he wanted to savor the views, take in every butterfly and every blossoming goldenrod. His sharp, deep brown eyes occasionally bored into me to see if I was really listening. The large, expressive hands he waved around to make a point kept bumping into my digital recorder.

"This is just breathtaking," he said as we admired a monarch. "I just love it. There's something about this park that it gives me, I can't even put it into words. This park gives me a feeling of security. With all this surrounding here"—he gestured toward the meadow and woods—"I feel like I'm protected from what's out there on the street: violence, drugs, alcohol."

Like Jack Hurst's, Mr. M's love affair with Warner Park began with fish. He'd take a break from work, grab his fishing pole and tackle box, and head to Warner's wetland, to catch bluegill, perch, and catfish and take them home to his kids to eat.

"Believe it or not, it didn't make any difference whether I caught any fish. I mean, I like to catch fish, don't get me wrong. But my attitude is, they might not be biting today, so—so what. I get to sit and enjoy creation. The more time I spent in it, the more I loved it. And no matter where I go, Warner Park is always on my mind. It's like—I'm sure you've heard this before—home is where the heart is? No matter where I go, this is in my heart."

Mr. M grew up in southwest Arkansas on a "semi-ranch," just fifty-five miles north of the Texas border. He started working on a neighbor's cattle ranch when he was twelve. He didn't finish high school because he was already doing "a man's job," cutting and hauling hay. It was the 1950s, when the civil rights movement was just beginning.

I asked Mr. M if he remembered the Little Rock Nine, the nine Black teenagers who were selected and trained by the NAACP to integrate Little Rock Central High in his home state in 1957.[10] I remembered the old newsreel of one of those kids—Elizabeth Eckford, a thin, proud girl in a poofy new gingham skirt and white blouse—shielding herself with a notebook and marching forward as a white mob hurled objects and spit on her screaming, "Go back to Africa!" "Lynch her!" "Drag her to the tree!"[11]

Mr. M lived just 500 miles away from that high school, and oh yeah, he remembered. He was the same age as those teens. He had just started learning to do furniture repair, which became his career. A bunch of white guys hung out in front of the repair shop.

"You wouldn't believe this conversation they had going. They said, 'I would kill my daughter before I'd let her go to school with Black kids.'"

A few years later, as the civil rights movement really started to rumble, he headed north. The overt racism was the main reason he left the South: "I cannot stand to be pushed around . . . If I hadn't of left, I would probably have killed somebody or gotten killed . . . My mother was afraid for me. She didn't want me to leave. She's one of them old mothers, like the birds kick the little ones out when it's time to go, but for my mom, it was never time for her kids to go . . . but she knew deep down that if I didn't, something bad would have happened. She came up in that era when you could walk down the street and see Black men hanging from trees. Lynching time. This was to teach the rest [of us] a lesson."

**THIS IS HARD AND SAD TO ADMIT, BUT BEFORE I MOVED TO ALABAMA, BECAUSE OF A RACIST** education in Southern California schools, my knowledge of slavery and its aftermath was limited to *Gone with the Wind*, which my family must have watched at least three times. (I had a Clark Gable poster on the wall.) In Alabama, I'd learned that lynching was part of a concerted campaign right after the Civil War, when former Confederate soldiers launched a violent guerrilla war to prevent freed slaves from voting and holding public office. The over 4,400 lynchings that took place in the United States between 1877 and the 1960s were also a form of social control, the use of domestic terrorism to terrify people. Historians estimate that 85–90 percent of lynchings nationwide took place in the South, often with the complicity of local law enforcement.[12]

"Victims were hung from trees as signs to intimidate African Americans. Perpetrators chose modern bridges, train tracks, the most prominent tree in the community to intimidate other communities as well. One of the myths is that lynching was an act of rage. These were planned-out and locations were well thought-out," according to researcher James Allen.[13]

Mr. M's home state of Arkansas was one of four states with the highest statewide lynching rates in the United States. The other three were Mississippi, Florida, and Louisiana, according to the Equal Justice Initiative (EJI) in Montgomery, Alabama, the national authority on lynching.* So it's no wonder that when Mr. M first came north, he felt relief.

But after a while, Mr. M noticed the racism in the North, too, especially when he opened his own upholstery business. He didn't get much of a welcome. The white owner of a neighboring furniture shop came over immediately and told him, 'You know, you'll never make it in Madison.'"

---

* As researchers uncover more historical lynchings, EJI updates their website (find your state on their online map: https://eji.org/reports/lynching-in-america/). In Montgomery, Alabama, EJI has created a searing national memorial to the victims of lynching alongside a museum on the history of slavery.

Well, Mr. M made it for forty-nine years, loving every minute of his work and supporting his family. And when that white neighbor saw his business booming, he started sending customers to Mr. M. Mr. M was a proud "craftsman," who "never had to take orders from anyone." He told me that he knew that because he was Black, his work had to be "three times as good."

"Look at how our bodies are made, all the different varieties of colors . . . We as humans, we're prejudiced against color . . . You've got black birds, blue birds, all different colors of animals. They're not fighting amongst themselves, saying, 'You're black and I'm white.'"

But the prejudice he encountered just made him more determined to be a better upholsterer. Some days he worked fifteen hours. He loved working with his hands and restoring beloved family chairs and sofas.

"I don't look at your color—I look at your character. And if I respect you and you don't give me the same respect back, I don't get angry with you, I just stay away from you. Avoid it. And that's the reason why I felt relief when I got here because I didn't have as much to avoid. But there [in the South] it's everyday life.

"Down there [the South], you know where you stand. It's more hidden here. Madison is a liberal city, but there's some right here, 'old school,' who feed you under the table and stab you in the back at the same time. In these seventy-one-plus years, I've experienced just about anything you can come up with. But when I come to Warner Park, all that we've been talking about—it's history. When I walk through this park, it's like a safe haven for me."

"You've never experienced racism in this park?" I asked.

"Walking through the park? Yes, I've experienced it. I just experienced it a few minutes ago."

I stopped dead in my tracks. I had no idea what Mr. M was talking about. It was a gorgeous day. Mr. M and I had been savoring the beauty around us for over an hour, stopping several times to enjoy a serenade by Mr. M's favorite bird, the song sparrow, and then rescuing a tiny toad from the bike path and relocating it in the meadow together.

"When? What happened?" I asked.

"That guy who just passed us? The one who tensed up and left the sidewalk and crossed onto the grass when he got close to us? Oh, I could see it right away. He was thinking, *A Black guy with a white woman.* I can detect it like—boom—body language."

And then I remembered, just barely, seeing out of the corner of my eye with that peripheral vision I use to detect feathered flashes in the bushes, the annoyed look on the young white man's face, his distaste, how he scooted away from us. But I was so intent on holding the recorder close to Mr. M's face and asking him questions that it didn't truly register.

DURING THE TEN YEARS I LIVED IN CENTRAL AMERICA, ESPECIALLY THE LAST SIX IN Guatemala, my body was always in fourth gear, legs ready to run, every sense on high alert. And sometimes I did have to outrun pickpockets, gang members, and military intelligence thugs who followed journalists, particularly nosy foreigners. I'm pretty fast; I got a perverse thrill out of outrunning them. It was part of my job. I chose to do it. But it wore down my immune system. And after ten years in a war zone, my body was stuck in fight-or-flight mode; I'd broken the off switch. It took months in the United States to learn to relax, to stop turning around whenever I heard footsteps behind me, even in broad daylight. I realized that when I lived in Guatemala, I would have easily seen what Mr. M. saw—the warning signs of potential danger, an angry white man's hostile body language. But in Warner Park, I just saw birds.

Since I'd left Central America, I'd shed that fear and hypervigilance like a skin—because I could. But Mr. M wasn't living some adventure in an exotic war zone. He couldn't shed his skin. This was his life just because of melanin. And I knew from all the interviews I'd done with hate crime victims in the South that for too many people of color, the United States was a war zone just like the one I was able to leave. Walking with Mr. M was a sobering reminder of how easily as a white person I could forget all that. I'd left a war zone by whipping out my magic blue passport and getting on a plane. But Mr. M was here in his "safe haven," Warner Park, the place that gave him "a special feeling" and that he loved so much he wanted his ashes scattered in it, but it was still a place where he had to be on guard, watching every person who passed us, gauging whether or not they cared that he was being interviewed by a white woman.

Although the kids known as the Little Rock Nine walked into Little Rock Central High over five decades before I interviewed Mr. M, I saw a direct historical link between the reaction of white people then to Black kids entering a "public" school and the reaction of that young white man to Mr. M and me walking together in a public park. This is because for most of our nation's history, "public" has meant white. Historian and scholar of race W.E.B. Du Bois explained in his 1920 book *Darkwater* that the romantic idea of nature as a "refuge" had always been just for white people. African Americans could not get relief by going to the nearest Walden in a woods or city park; they could seek nature as a refuge only in segregated spaces. Perhaps the most famous of these segregated refuges was Idlewild in Michigan, known as the Black Eden. Until the Civil Rights Act of 1964, which made discrimination illegal, this lakeside community at the headwaters of the Pere Marquette River was one of the only resorts in the nation where African Americans could buy land and take vacations. In the summertime between 1912 and the 1960s, as many as 25,000 Black vacationers showed up on weekends to fish, hunt, swim, camp, ride horses, and enjoy entertainment.[14]

Of course, I never learned any of this in school. For white people of my generation who received a racist education, if we were taught at all about segregation and civil rights, it was limited to Rosa Parks not being able to sit down on a bus. I had no idea that segregation could also apply to outdoor spaces. When I was working in Alabama as a hate crimes researcher, I learned that it wasn't until a decade after the civil rights movement that all aspects of public life—schools, libraries, public pools, beaches, and parks of all kinds—were desegregated by law. And that didn't mean that these spaces were actually desegregated. Many southern cities with public pools simply filled them with cement rather than have white children share them with Black kids. Indoor and outdoor public spaces were eliminated or defunded as wealthy white people joined private country clubs and sent their kids to private schools. Children of color were systematically denied the right to learn how to swim, play tennis, and enjoy other outdoor sports. No wonder birding is such a white world.

When Mr. M moved to Madison in the 1960s, like millions of other African Americans who fled north to escape violence, he was moving to a northern state that shared this long history of segregation indoors and outdoors. During my dissertation research on Madison's parks, I came across a photo that shocked me. It was a 1924 shot of hundreds of white-robed and hooded Ku Klux Klan members marching down a major Madison thoroughfare.[15] The UW-Madison campus had two student groups named after the KKK between 1919 and 1926.[16] According to the Wisconsin Historical Society, the KKK petered out in Madison by the end of the 1920s only to revive itself, right after the civil rights movement began—around when Mr. M moved to Madison. On its national hate group maps, the Southern Poverty Law Center showed that Wisconsin had three KKK chapters as late as 2004. And Wisconsin's largest city, Milwaukee, was wracked by some of the same violence as the South in the 1960s, with the firebombing of the NAACP's offices and angry white mobs hurling rocks and bottles at two hundred young NAACP members marching to a white park in 1967 to protest housing segregation.[17] Today, Milwaukee is still the fifth most segregated city in the nation, according to Berkeley's Roots of Structural Racism Project. And although Madison often makes the list of the top ten cities to live in the United States, Dane County, where Madison is located, also makes the list as one of the worst counties in the country for an African American child to grow up in.[18] All this is why despite its reputation as a progressive state, some older African Americans refer to Wisconsin as "Mississippi North."

Experiences like Mr. M's of racial hostility and what today are called microaggressions might not deter someone like him from walking in Warner Park, particularly since he had experienced serious daily racism in the South. But I could see how these incidents might deter my other neighbors of color. Why would you want to go to a beautiful place "to relax," when you had to worry about a white person reacting in an ugly way or even harassing and hurting you? One of my favorite writers, race and feminist scholar bell hooks, called it "the hostile racist white gaze."[19] Leisure researchers who began studying racial barriers to outdoor recreation following the civil rights movement have documented racial hostility for decades. In a 1989 study on Detroit parks, sociologist Patrick West wrote that fewer African Americans used Detroit parks because of their fear of a hostile environment; studies in other major cities confirmed what later became known as West's racial hostility hypothesis.[20] But Mr. M was teaching me that this was not just a story of hypotheses and victimhood. Feminist geographer Carolyn Finney traces this historical complexity in her powerful cultural analysis, *Black Faces, White Spaces: Reimagining the Relationship of African Americans to the Great Outdoors.*

**AFTER MY WALK WITH MR. M, I THOUGHT BACK TO MY FIRST MEETING WITH THE CITY COUN**cilor after Jim and I and our neighbors opposed the city plan to further develop Warner Park. One of the main reasons she'd given for the development was to get more people of color to use the park. She'd complained about racism in our neighborhood. Because of Mr. M, I started wondering about the kids in our program. Could racial hostility be keeping them from playing in the park or walking in the woods when they weren't with their mostly white college mentors?

Then during the second year of the children's program, in 2012, seventeen-year-old Trayvon Martin was murdered in Florida by a man who thought the teenager in a hoodie looked "suspicious."

That same spring, a boy in my program I'll call Jabari told me he wanted to become a bluebird manager. Jabari was a super bird boy on steroids, a born naturalist who didn't even need binoculars to identify birds. He lived on the park's edge just two blocks from me. Jabari was the one who found species number 116, the barred owl in the thicket, showing up on my doorstep one Sunday afternoon proudly clutching an owl pellet. He called himself Turtle Man and spent hours watching turtles in the wetland. He told me he could "feel them" under the water. He'd named several: Sparky, Princess. He had birds in cages at home and a salamander named Sal. When he wasn't in the park with the animals, Jabari was at the library across the street researching how the animals lived or identifying the park's plants on botany websites (the librarians loved him). He lived in one of the city's worst apartment buildings, occasionally plagued by guns and drugs; the park's woods were his refuge.

Jabari wandered all over Warner Park, at all hours, searching for species to help me. And he wore a hoodie. After Trayvon Martin was murdered, I began to seriously question what I was doing and how oblivious I was to the dangers Mr. M and some of our kids faced just to walk through a park. I was starting to think maybe I shouldn't train Jabari to be a bluebird manager, because what if someone called the police when they saw him opening those little houses? I didn't have to agonize over this dilemma very long. In May of that year, gang violence erupted in the neighborhood and someone shot his mother in the foot. I got called to the school because Jabari was a star in my program; the school counselor needed me to help explain to him why he could never go home and could never go back to Warner Park—because he was entering a witness protection program.

**AS ALL THIS WAS HAPPENING, I REALIZED I NEEDED TO READ MORE HUMAN HISTORY FOR MY** dissertation and focus less on birds. As I read historian Kimberly K. Smith's comprehensive *African American Environmental Thought: Foundations*, I realized that I'd been looking at Warner Park only through the new lenses I'd acquired and was so excited about—the ecology, biology, and ornithology lenses. I was making the same mistake as most white enviros—segregating birding and nature from racial and justice issues—because I didn't have to think about it when I was traipsing around Warner Park. Mr. M's experiences, Trayvon Martin's murder, the children in my neighborhood, and the history readings all reminded me that I had to view the use of Warner Park within the broader historical context of violence and terror in the

United States, through the war zone lens—not just the bird conservation lens. I couldn't take college students birding in the park without teaching them that context.

But the teacher in me was afraid to integrate anti-racism teaching with birding. This is because the very first time I'd tried to teach white students about racism was nearly the end of my teaching career.

Years earlier in Alabama while I was still teaching in Julia Tutwiler Prison, I began teaching journalism part time at Auburn University in 2000. Auburn was a tense place; hate crimes were routine and Black faculty were embattled and worn out. I joined the faculty hate crimes committee, and the stories we collected were horrible. Because of my hate crimes research, I was determined to use journalism to get my all-white students to learn civil rights history. So for their first assignment, I sent them to cover a speech by civil rights legend Julian Bond. They returned to class, seething and yelling at me. As I tried to figure out why they were so angry, I realized that they had no historical grounding or personal experience to put Julian Bond's terrible truths in perspective. They thought Auburn University was "a friendly place." And I'd just met them; I had no relationship with them. Even worse—I was the California/Yankee interloper telling them that they lived in a racist state and went to a racist college.

I had a syllabus packed with lectures on Booker T. Washington, W.E.B Du Bois, and Dr. Martin Luther King Jr. But preaching to my students about civil rights was not going to work. I thought back on how I learned about racism when I was their age. And then I realized I didn't know anything about racism when I was their age. I grew up in a white Southern California enclave, one of the wealthiest zip codes in the nation, and I am damn sure that that sun-drenched, nail-polish-obsessed, pot-smoking and cocaine-snorting wannabe-surfer-girl me never ever thought about or even realized that in the 1970s, I, too, was attending segregated all-white public schools, except for the Mexican kids, who stayed mostly in the safety of their own cliques, which we white kids called "gangs." And we called Mexican kids who dared to cross social lines "coconuts." The racism in Orange County directed against Mexicans was so bad that to even call someone a "Mexican" then was considered a racial slur.[21] It was only decades later that I realized why the South felt so familiar. Because I, too, had grown up in a plantation culture on that beautiful orange and avocado ranch, my father the Irish overseer, the white man telling the brown men—Mexican farmworkers—what to do.

I didn't really learn about racism except in an abstract way until I moved to Alabama. When I started teaching in that prison, my students' stories of how they got there forced me to think about all the layers of privilege I'd grown up with. I realized that if I'd been born Black in Birmingham, I'd probably be dead or in prison because I was doing the exact same stuff as my prison students when I was a teenager—taking drugs, crashing cars, shoplifting. But the police weren't stopping drunk-as-a-skunk white girls in my neighborhood. They weren't in my neighborhood, period.

I threw out my carefully scripted history lectures and consulted with the NAACP and the faculty hate crimes committee. The old warriors agreed to help me by pointing the way to Auburn Black alumni who could tell their stories. Many had remained anonymous over the decades because of their traumatic experiences. But some wanted to share their stories with the next generation. My students could interview them.*

Several weeks later, a white student fraternity leader choked up as he told the class about his interview with a Black former football player who was treated so badly in the 1960s that forty years later, that football player cried three times during the interview. My student said he was stunned when this football player told him that he'd never told the story to anyone before, not even to his own children, because they had white friends and he didn't want his kids to know how bad it had been. My students were also stunned by what had happened to the white students who had tried to welcome Black students to Auburn, particularly the scared young white football captain who

* I do not believe that asking victims to tell their stories and dredge up their pain is the way to teach about racism. Fortunately, today there are many media that teachers can use. But this was twenty years ago—I was desperate and these colleagues wanted to help. Many thanks to Southern Poverty Law Center staff and Auburn comrades Nan Fairley, Johnny Green, David Wilson, and the Alabama NAACP.

stepped in front of a white mob in 1964 to shake the hand of Harold A. Franklin, the first Black graduate student. By searching through old files in a library basement, my students discovered that this white football captain had received written death threats for years.

At the end of the semester, my students weren't mad at me anymore. But they were so mad about the lies they'd been told that they organized a public presentation on their research findings about historical racism at Auburn. They challenged university leadership to acknowledge this history and change it.

My Auburn students taught me that I couldn't just preach about racism; I had to develop a relationship with them first. The other lesson they taught me was that I couldn't possibly do this teaching alone. If it hadn't been for comrades in the NAACP, at the Southern Poverty Law Center, and at Auburn, that might have been the end of my teaching career.

In Madison I also needed help, but I couldn't just use the kids and their stories to teach my students. I didn't want my students to view the children as "victims" because this would only reinforce white saviorism and the charity/missionary mentality that infuses so much "volunteer" work, "community" work, and university "service learning," which one of my PhD advisors, Randy Stoecker, called "disservice learning."[22]

Fortunately, there were plenty of mentors. The first was Mike Hernandez, the principal of Sherman Middle School, who warned me about white saviorism soon after we met. He'd begun his teaching career as a twenty-two-year-old special education teacher in Los Angeles. During his first seven years of teaching, he'd observed a "learned helplessness" among students and their families. He found that same culture in Madison: "Educators know that children are struggling, so instead of making them struggle, we're just going to help them answer this question, even give them the answer so that they're not sitting there struggling. It's the old 'pobrecito' approach: 'My poor baby—let me just do this for you.'"

Then I discovered Jeffrey Lewis at UW-Madison, a human ecologist and pedagogical expert who'd focused his research on African

American successes in schools, not just failures. In a study of teaching methods in Oakland and Los Angeles in schools with high success rates for lower-income African American children, Lewis and his research team discovered that students succeeded because of a teaching framework of "solidarity in community . . . characterized by mutual respect, reciprocity, commitment, connection, and accountability." He called it "a sense of 'we-ness,'" which sounded like flocking to me.[23]

Jeffrey lived near Warner Park and came to walk with the kids several times. Later he walked with me through Warner, sharing his education philosophy, his thoughts on racism, and his lived experience. Because of his research and our conversations, I tried to incorporate that "we-ness" inside and outside the classroom through our club's rituals, which came from the kids themselves—rolling down Sled Hill, the sharing circle around the bur oak, the special nicknames they had for their mentors, and the special names they gave the places they loved most in the park. I was also deeply influenced by his critique of academia. His research team recommended "unlearning" the hierarchical and competitive behaviors in our education system that they found particularly damaging to children of color.

My PhD advisor, Jack, who as a sociologist was keen to help me integrate social justice into the birding class, pointed me to the work of J. Drew Lanham, an African American conservation biologist, ornithologist, and poet from Clemson University in South Carolina (where researchers pioneered the use of radar to monitor bird migration). Lanham produced a two-minute YouTube video, "Birding While Black," a must for teaching about racism, in which he lists rules for the Black birdwatcher: "1. Be prepared to be confused with the other Black birder; 2. Carry your binoculars—and three forms of identification—at all times; 3. Don't bird in a hoodie. Ever. 4. Nocturnal birding is a no-no; 5. Black birds—any black birds—are your birds."[24]

Jack brought Drew to Madison to walk with our birding club and to give talks on campus about racism and the great outdoors. Not only did Drew walk with my students, teach us all about birds, and tenderly help the children bury a runover toad in Warner's marsh, explaining the cycle of life and death to them and how to honor that toad, but he also helped me see that a large tree is not just a tree. During a campus talk, he described how some older African Americans in the South viewed large trees through the historical lens of lynching. I thought about the mother bur oak, how much I loved it, but then suddenly saw it through Drew's eyes, those long, strong limbs we'd fought to keep the parks department from cutting, and I could imagine them as menacing, not comforting.

Drew also forced me to see the whole picture when examining John J. Audubon's gorgeous bird portraits. I've mentioned Audubon throughout this book, but I haven't mentioned the history that birders like me have ignored for a century—that he was also a man who bought and sold other humans, a slave owner.

"He chose to watch birds and be inhumane. What choices will be made now by conservation organizations? Will there be excuses of context to brush over with paint the truths that need to be revealed?" Drew wrote in *Audubon Magazine*.[25]

**THERE WERE VERY FEW MENTORS OF COLOR IN MY BIRDING CLASS, GIVEN THAT UW-MADISON** was another Great White University. But the ones who did join, although they experienced many magical moments outside with their young co-explorers, had similar experiences to Drew's. Some shared these painful stories during class discussions about how white people stared at them when they went birding. They also wrote about it in their reflection journals:

> I live in Middleton . . . There are a lot of nice parks and conservancy areas in Middleton; however, I do not see people that look like me walking through them. In addition, these beautiful landscapes tend to be in wealthier neighborhoods, where I also do not see people that look like me. Although I enjoy and look forward to birding in my free time . . . I do struggle with the confused looks I receive when I am strolling through the park with a pair of binoculars hanging from my

> neck, and a field notebook and pencil in hand. It never occurred to me that this would be such a shock to people, more specifically Caucasian folks right in my own neighborhood. On the other hand, this makes me more determined to share my passion with the children of our future, in hopes that perceptions can be changed regarding the relationship between people of color and nature.[26]

These undergraduates forced me to think about every single bird event I had attended in Madison, every Audubon meeting, every Wild Warner meeting, every Christmas bird count, every conference—it was a sea of white faces. How could a person of color feel welcome?

When these students felt comfortable enough to share these painful experiences in intimate class discussions, I could see mini-revolutions taking place inside so many of my white students' heads. It was like that walk with Mr. M for me. For the first time these white students were thinking about why they felt safe outside, why their parents had had the resources—money, a car that worked, and time, precious time—to take them camping in national parks, skiing, rafting, etc.

But I couldn't generalize about my student mentors of color any more than I could generalize about the children. One student of color loved the course and the children so much that he enrolled three times as "independent study." Another Black student from inner-city Milwaukee, who had never been interested in birds, wrote about the thrills of watching Canada geese and spying on the great blue heron in Warner with his young co-explorers. He fell in love with hawks and identified with them, personally. By the end of the semester he had become such an avid birder that he said he felt like "an amateur ornithologist."

"Being outdoors just gives me a clearer mind and can be very releasing and therapeutic for people with anxiety or emotional stress," this student wrote in his journal in October 2012.

Drew Lanham has also written about how birding helps him personally deal with racism:

> Sometimes the birds are a balm, an avian anesthesia that numbs pain or blocks unpleasant things. It is the Zen of putting field marks together—plumage, shape, behavior—into something that becomes a bird . . . In that peaceful pursuit, the quarry is collected on a life list without having to give its life in return. It has been this way for most of my life: Me escaping to the birds. The birds providing something people couldn't—comfort in my own skin, peace in stressful times, and acceptance without question of who I am or what I do.[27]

The children also taught us all about privilege and lowered expectations. Mazin, a Muslim refugee kid in our program who spoke five languages and wanted to learn ten, only expected to go to a police academy if he was "lucky"; college was not on his radar. James, an African American boy who loved turtles and could not stand to see them run over by cars on the park's borders, told his mentor that he planned to drop out of high school to be a truck driver like his father. Our students learned that some of our children would get in trouble at home if they rolled down the hill in the park and got their clothes dirty. Student mentors were shocked when they recounted in class discussions and in their journals that their children's families did not have washers or dryers or cars, so their children's families had to take their clothes to the laundromat on the bus. Students realized that the right to get dirty in the park was a luxury some families could not afford.

One student mentor of color pointed out that many of our kids' parents used an electronic babysitter—the TV or video games—because they were exhausted from working two jobs. They didn't want to go outside during their "free time" and hike or bird because maybe their jobs as nursing aides or janitors or waitresses or cashiers were already physically very demanding. Some of our kids' parents were immigrants from Mexico, Central America, and Africa. Maybe they didn't know yet where it was safe to let their children play in their new country.

Most of my student mentors moved on after a semester, so they didn't know the kids for very long. But I visited the school almost every week and got to know the kids for those three middle school years. I soon realized that some of our most enthusiastic and imaginative Sherman explorers, the kids who most loved the birds, had extremely difficult home situations. I'd get a glimpse of it when a child made an offhand comment during the lunches or the school counselor shared information to help me understand a child's behavior. We had a girl whose family was evicted twice in a year. A kid whose father was in Iraq with the military and feared his dad wasn't coming back. A boy who carried his marked-up field guide everywhere, who loved to sing songs from Broadway musicals, and whose large family lived in a tiny apartment, so he shared a bed with several siblings and didn't get much sleep, which affected his grades.

It's a balance I continually wrestle with as a teacher and as a human—how much reality is too much for young minds and souls, how to balance the beauty and the horror. And once again, I also worried that by sharing too many dire statistics and stories about the kids with my own students, I'd just be reinforcing the white savior syndrome that I continually fight within myself, having been raised in Catholicism—a patriarchal religion and culture that taught me that I should "help" the poor (read: brown) people.

Fortunately, despite difficult home situations, the children didn't fit into any of the crippling categories assigned to them by the academic world: "lower income," "marginalized," "challenged," "special needs," "underserved," etc. My students found it hard to generalize about the children because they related to them as individuals, not as a victim group. There were little nature nuts, hunters, video-game addicts, boy chasers, and girl chasers. One Black boy's family rehabilitated wild animals, and he told stories about a baby kingfisher. A girl from West Africa raised bluebirds with her white grandfather. The boy who had to share a bed with several siblings insisted that his parents buy him the exact same bird guide as his college mentor. He carried it proudly for three years and kept a bird list in the back of it. The girl whose family was evicted twice in a year also played the violin. Some children played several musical instruments. Some had better vocabularies than my college students.

Since most of my college students had never previously been to Warner Park, the children became their de facto guides. For our college students who initially viewed our kids through the stereotype of "lower-income children of color," this may have helped challenge that stereotype. For example, on day one of the third year, an eighth-grade girl who had been in the club for two years taught her new college mentor the difference between red and white pine trees. While they walked together to the park, the eighth-grader pulled a bunch of needles off a tree and showed the college student how the fascicle of the white pine contained five needles, while the red pine has only two. "You can remember it by the number of letters, five—w-h-i-t-e," the girl told her. Her very first college mentor had taught her this lesson, two years earlier. A seventh-grader explained the difference between a Cooper's hawk and a red-tailed hawk to his college mentor, a former marine in Iraq in school on the GI bill. Another seventh-grader showed his college mentor the secret spot where the marsh turtles came out to sun themselves.

One day as we walked into the park's meadow, two Mexican American boys ran to the milkweed pods that were bursting open, their silky, feathery contents streaming in the wind. The boys grabbed the seedpods and fingered the long creamy strands and smooth brown seeds. They explained to their new college mentor that these plants helped the monarch butterflies fluttering around the meadow get ready to head toward Mexico. The boys ran from milkweed to milkweed, scattering seed. A year earlier, their previous college mentor had taught them that if they helped the milkweed, they'd help the monarchs.

And we learned about other types of human diversity from our kids who were neurodivergent. For two years we had a boy in the club with Asperger's. A strong, energetic kid with the personality of a bulldozer, Leroy loved to poke and prod the other explorers. He had little sense of boundaries. At the middle school he was ostracized. He often came to the club with his head bowed, dragging his feet, fighting back tears. His mother told me no other club would accept him.

When he first joined us, two of our most diligent and enthusiastic middle school nature explorers threatened to quit because of problems with Leroy at school. I promised them they would be safe. And I assigned two college mentors to help Leroy learn some boundaries (they adored him). Flocks have many different kinds of members, I told the kids who were scared. Please give Leroy another chance.

Leroy stayed in the club for all three years of middle school, and so did the two explorers who had complained. He tested the patience of a series of college mentors and even scared one with his physical strength. But he also became one of our most passionate park defenders and a powerful public speaker. His excitement about nature was contagious. He taught his first college mentor the different names of many plants and spiders. He dragged huge chunks of trees home and had a cherished collection of old beehives and wasp nests. This boy was also uncanny at finding the weirdest stuff in Warner Park, objects I'd walked by every day and had never noticed. One week it was an old metal safe rusting in the stormwater canal feeding into the wetland. Another week it was a parachute hanging from the top of a tree in the Big Woods.

When Wild Warner set up a public registry book in the Warner Park Community Center lobby where anyone could record wildlife sightings, Leroy begged to be first to write in what he called "the golden notebook." That first day Leroy excitedly opened the book and signed his name. Then he recorded that he'd found a lightning-struck tree. That first Leroy year, he taught everyone who interacted with him, me included, to be more tolerant and patient and to give more of ourselves. By the end of his second year, Leroy was playing with the other children and exploring with them in the park, sharing his discoveries with them instead of just with his mentors. His mother told me that the club had changed his life because it was the first social space in which he was accepted.

**DREW LANHAM'S QUOTE THAT HEADS THIS CHAPTER, URGING US TO SEE BEAUTY WHILE** advocating for justice, is a credo for our times. Yes, we must enjoy the bluebirds and try to help them. But we must also acknowledge the fact that since Mr. M and I strolled through Warner Park in 2013, police have killed over 2,500 Black people in this country, many of them unarmed and shot in the back. (This is almost as many killed as during the three-decade "low-intensity" war in Northern Ireland known as the Troubles.)* "The long war against the Black body," as writer Ta-Nehisi Coates describes it, is still raging.[28]

What has changed for the better is that birders of color are advocating for themselves and revolutionizing the birding world in their own murmuration. Local Audubon chapters across the country are changing their names because they don't want to associate themselves with slavery. New birding flocks are appearing everywhere, like Washington, DC's Nature Forward, Birds Connect Seattle, and the Bird Union (National Audubon's own staff union). And for birders and teachers of environmental science, new books by Christian Cooper, the Central Park Black birder and science writer who went viral when he was racially targeted while birding, by Black falconer Rodney Stotts, and by NYC's joyful-justice Feminist Bird Club will help bring that revolution into hearts and science classrooms.

---

* In the United States, police kill Blacks at nearly three times the rate of whites: 41 out of 1 million per year vs. 16 out of 1 million per year for whites. Fact checker Olivia Box calculated this based on data from the *Washington Post*'s Police Shootings database and the Mapping Police Violence database; see https://www.washingtonpost.com/graphics/investigations/police-shootings-database/ and https://mappingpoliceviolence.org/.

CHAPTER 11

# In the Kingdom of Dumetella

*I climb up through the thicket,*
*a bird's song somewhere within it,*
*. . . It might come from anywhere,*
*from everywhere, the whole air,*
*vibrant with it.*

WENDELL BERRY, "1987"

JUST OUTSIDE SHERMAN MIDDLE SCHOOL'S CAFETERIA, A THREE-BY-FOUR-FOOT collage of photos labeled "Treasure Map of Warner Park" hung on a wall. A map filled the wooden frame. Photos of the kids and their "special places" were glued onto it in a geography of love: The Big Woods, The Big Thicket, Armand's Clearing, The Heart Tree, The Big Oak, The Hobo Camp, Barn Swallow Bridge, Sled Hill, Jabari's Birthday Tree, The Mushroom Graveyard, and Charlie's Fairy Glen.

Environmental psychologists have studied how children who experience poverty, violence, war, and natural disasters benefit from having a "special place." International children's health expert Louise Chawla found that for children living in poverty in places as varied as Vermont, Bolivia, Guatemala, India, Venezuela, Colorado, South Africa, and Bhutan, urban parks and gardens are a vital psychological buffer. And for children confronting economic disaster or stressors such as prejudice, illness, disability, a family death, domestic violence, or bullying, the buffering effect is strongest.[1] My students and I watched this play out every Wednesday with the kids.

"Meredith was so proud to show me the areas of the park that she loves," Meredith's college mentor wrote. "She had a plan for where we would go and how long we should spend at each spot. She kept saying she hoped no one else had discovered these areas and that we would be the only ones there. It must be so important to these children to have some space where they feel they can be alone. The spots where you can think and breathe on your own are sacred."[2]

Meredith was also the girl eating lunch alone in the cafeteria, owllike eyes behind thick glasses as she read a historical novel about Cleopatra. For fun she wrote plays. I loved that she wore a T-shirt that read: "Dear Math: Solve your own problems."

Meredith's special place was a huge old elm in Warner's Big Woods that was over a hundred years old and had somehow survived the Dutch elm scourge that had wiped out most of these trees in the twentieth century. The wide bottom was hollow. The children called it the Heart Tree because according to one girl: "You can stand in the center of it and feel as if you are in the beating heart of the tree."

For the first two years in the program, Meredith told her succession of college mentors that they were her only friends. She held hands with them as they walked through the neighborhood. Sometimes she walked beside me and told me how lonely she felt. I kept telling her that I had hated middle school, too, and that things would get better in high school. The Heart Tree was not just her special place—it was her refuge from the storm of middle school. She spent time there every Wednesday and proudly showed her tree to visitors.

Near the end of the club's second year in 2012, I discovered that the parks department planned to cut down the Heart Tree. A city official in charge of litigation had decided that it and dozens of old trees were dangerous because they could fall on someone. For three days I called and emailed parks officials to try to save the tree or at least the bottom twelve feet of the trunk for the children to play in. But this proposal went nowhere.

When we entered the park a week later, and Meredith saw what was left of her "dear friend," she sat down on the ground and sobbed for an hour. Her college mentor put her arms around her and cried with her. Meredith cried harder when I tried to reason with her. I told her I'd done all I could to save her tree. I felt the same way she did, I said. But as I watched her cry, I realized that I really didn't feel the same way. I didn't understand the depth of her relationship with this tree. As I tried to explain why parks officials thought they needed to cut it down—to protect children like her—Meredith yelled, "But it was still alive! In elementary school, I had my tree. I went there to cry. It was an old tree and they cut it down. Now in middle school, they cut down my tree. That's where I felt safe."

There was a parks commission meeting that night, and I told the kids I was going to go and complain about the tree. Meredith was too distraught and shy to testify, but Jabari, the barred owl discoverer and aspiring bluebird manager, also had a favorite old tree. He volunteered to speak for Meredith and all the kids. When we got to the meeting, there were at least twenty-five adults in the audience and the commissioners lined up in the front, like judges. Jabari got to the podium and stood there trembling in a torn T-shirt and cutoff jean shorts, staring at the crowd. Then in a high squeaky voice he said he was scared and asked me to stand beside him. I walked to the podium and put a hand on his left shoulder.

"I feel really emotional right now," he started. "But I don't want to cry in front of so many strangers. It really hurt me and all the children to see the big tree cut down. Meredith was too upset to come here, so I came. I hope you don't cut down my birthday tree, too. My family goes there to eat cake with me in the park. We sit under it. I see a lot of animals in my birthday tree. It's an old tree, too. Please don't cut down my birthday tree."

AT THE END OF THAT HEART TREE SEMESTER IN APRIL, MADISON MAYOR PAUL SOGLIN CAME to walk through Warner Park with our club. He'd just had hip surgery. When he pulled up, he got out of his car, obviously in pain. He, his aides, and a press crew followed us to Sled Hill, where the kids split up to each take a mayor's aide or reporter to their special places. I'd promised Meredith that she would lead the mayor's "tour." With reporters in tow, Meredith led a limping Mayor Soglin straight to the husk of her tree. She stood on top of a chunk and read an epitaph. She begged the mayor to stop cutting down old trees. He listened carefully. He didn't promise anything. But Meredith wasn't done yet.

Eight months later, we had a Christmas party for the children in Warner's community center. This was a new class of college mentors who hadn't witnessed the Heart Tree debacle. During the party, a new president of the parks commission dropped in to meet the kids. A tall, imposing man, he asked the group of about fifty young people if they had any questions about Madison's parks. Meredith's hand shot up.

"Are you the man who decides to cut down the trees?"

Some of the new college mentors turned around to stare at her, amazed. The parks commissioner hesitated.

"I've heard about you," he said.

He seemed flummoxed by her question.

Later in class, my students marveled at Meredith's "bravery and confidence" and were amazed at how that six-foot man was "at a loss for words" when confronted by a little girl. They wanted to become environmental activists, and she had a huge influence on them. She also had a huge influence on me. She reminded me of myself right after Katrina when I fell in love with that first New Orleanian cardinal simply because it was *alive.* She reminded me to resist the lure of cynicism that can so quickly harden an adult heart.

Special places are not just for children. I had my own special place in the park and it lives in my heart, wherever I may roam. It was Charlie's Fairy Glen deep in Warner's Big Thicket. There I had the privilege of spending three summers from 2012 to 2014 as part of my dissertation fieldwork. It was a chance to think deep, thickety thoughts and learn from the birds, especially *Dumetella carolinensis*, the gray catbird.

**ON A SPRING MORNING THAT FIRST THICKET SEASON, AS I PERCHED ON A LARGE BOULDER IN** Charlie's Fairy Glen, tiny fairylike blue-gray gnatcatchers mewed softly around me, while migrating chestnut-sided warblers exuberantly proclaimed, "Pleased, pleased, pleased to meet cha!" An eye-popping Broadway show of a bird, this avian made you want to shout right back: "Pleased, pleased, pleased to meet cha, too!" With a black whisker or "moustachial" stripe and black eyebrow stripes on a white face, he looked as if he were wearing a black Mardi Gras mask topped by a bright yellow beret. Warm chestnut swaths running along the sides of his white breast gave him his name. Black-and-goldish wings carried him and his kin from Wisconsin to Guatemala every winter, maybe even all the way to Panama.

The sun filtered through the large new green leaves of the maples. I was inside a chlorophyll cathedral of life surging skyward. It was so green I could have been in the jungles of Central America where that chestnut-sided warbler might eventually spend the winter. A red-eyed vireo joined in with his snippy song. And the brown thrasher, a threatened species in Wisconsin which depended on shrub-thickets like this one to nest in, shared tunes from his 3,000-song playlist. Blasting from deep inside bushes, the catbirds turned the shrubs all around me into speakers.

I began to love this special place because it was also a geology time machine. If I'd been sitting in this very spot 550 million years before, I'd have been lounging at the bottom of a shallow tropical sea with trilobites, foot-long pill-bug-like creatures, swimming around me. The boulder I was sitting on was a relatively recent arrival in Warner geological time. A glacial erratic, it had been pushed down from the north just 25,000 years before by the Green Bay Lobe, a glacier a third of a mile high. But according to geologists, the boulder itself was around 2.8 billion years old, the oldest thing in Warner Park.[3]

My gift-of-the-glacier boulder helped me put Wild Warner's struggles in perspective. Over hundreds of millions of years, this place had been a tropical sea, glacier, lake, marsh, beach, Ho-Chunk workshop and settlement, and place of sacred mounds. It had been a city park for just six decades.

As that first thicket summer began and avian parents hustled to raise hungry babies, I found a family of yellow warblers, a golden-yellow mother hanging out with pale lemony teenagers. In Central and South America, where she spent most of the year, she was La Reinita Dorada, the Little Golden Queen.*

Bunnies leapt off the path when I entered the thicket; Jim and I called it Rabbit Lane. Mallards flew over from a neighbor's yard where they slept at night, to the marsh where they spent the day. Hermit thrushes that possibly migrated as far south as Mexico in the fall spent several days in here, resting and feeding.

The thicket was where the foxes raised their kits. Where a doe hid her fawns every spring. And where the woodchuck mother and her bearlike babies trooped down in a line to drink water in the canal.

One morning I was sitting on a tiny stool, wearing a pink Alabama baseball cap, when a female hummingbird examined me at eye level, hovering just two feet from my nose. She was so close that I could hear

---

* All warblers are called *reinitas* in Latin America.

the loud buzzing of her wings flapping approximately 4,000 times a minute.[4] Did she think I was a gigantic pink flower on a green stalk because of my pink cap and green jacket? She appeared again later that summer on the anniversary of my father's death. Same routine: hover, buzz, inspect, zoom off. Female hummingbirds defend their nesting territories from other hummers, so I could have been sitting right smack in the middle of hers.

Usually I was walking through the park actively looking for hummingbirds with binoculars. But my new thicket practice of sitting still and doing nothing meant that she could zip in and check me out on her own terms. It felt very different from how I first learned to bird by walking around listing species. And it wasn't just that hummingbird checking me out. When I settled down on my thicket boulder, I soon heard whispery movements of tiny feet and feathers brushing against twigs and leaves. I thought I was doing ornithological fieldwork. But I realized that it was the animal residents of the thicket who were doing *their* fieldwork. The watcher had become the watched.

A cardinal, a tawny house wren, an inquisitive chickadee, and a downy woodpecker pair all came to eyeball me. There was an eastern wood pewee, too; he stared down from a branch. I loved this bird's high-pitched *Peeee-weeee!* whistle that gave him his name. Robins swiveled their heads to examine me, hopping closer on branches. I heard *Kwut, kwut, kwut,* the soft raspy alarm of a catbird approaching, bush by bush, stirring the air. I rarely saw them as they carried out their avian reconnaissance, though sometimes I heard a male catbird's ghostly "whisper song"—very different from his usual brassy, jazzy cacophony—when he communicated with his mate while she was on the nest.

In the documentary *Dirt!* scientists talk about how when you enter a place, all living beings sense that a human is present, even the microbes and fungi. There is another universe under the ground, where creatures communicate via chemicals they send out through root systems one twenty-fifth the diameter of a human hair. When I trudged into Charlie's Fairy Glen in the Big Thicket, sweeping brush and branches aside and clunking around like a clumsy giant, it was like walking to the edge of that red desert hill of my childhood. Once again, hundreds of tiny and not-so-tiny eyes followed my every move, and microscopic creatures without eyes waved invisible antennae at me, smelling, sensing.

The more time I spent in the Big Thicket, the more I realized that there were so many birds there because it was an avian cafeteria, chock-full of insect protein and fruit, birds' main foods along with seeds. There were mulberry, raspberry, and blackberry bramble tunnels where the eastern kingbirds and catbirds feasted, along with the fox family (I found berries in their scat). It was tier upon tier of food, berry brambles shaded by decades-old huge honeysuckle and sumac that the catbirds and thrashers nested in, and a final tier of trees competing for sunlight: black cherry trees, ash, black walnuts, and young oaks. I smiled whenever I found a baby oak. It reminded me of Squirrel for a Day, when the kids buried acorns in their special places.

Each layer of brambles, bushes, and trees nurtured its own layer of birds. On the ground, mourning doves foraged and cooed. Halfway up, robins, yellow warblers, gnatcatchers, blue jays, downy woodpeckers, sharp-shinned hawks, American redstarts, crows, wrens, hummingbirds, red-bellied woodpeckers, nuthatches, goldfinches, and chickadees went about their bird business. In the treetops, vireos, brown-headed cowbirds, northern flickers, cedar waxwings sporting red waxy wing tips, and bright orange orioles reigned. And at the very top, a lone dark sapphire of an indigo bunting—Jeremy's bird—sparkled against a pale blue sky, singing his four-phrase song all day long that some birders translate as "Fire! Fire! Where? Here. See it? See it?"*

The Big Thicket also sheltered birds in trouble, species ecologists were trying to save. One spring morning I woke up and heard a fluting deep in the thicket. Another new Warner species—a wood thrush. Henry David Thoreau wrote that the wood thrush's song "changes all hours to an eternal morning."[5] The wood thrush is a migratory bird whose numbers have plummeted more than 60 percent in the last fifty years. It breeds in North America and migrates as far as Central

* Birders translate birdsong into catchy phrases or "mnemonics," a memory strategy to help remember songs.

America. Smithsonian researchers discovered in 2016 to their surprise that the bird's habitat was disappearing even faster in North America than in its southern wintering grounds.[6]

This wood thrush stayed in Warner's thicket two days, refueling en route to breeding grounds elsewhere. Sitting there on my glacial boulder, I reveled in its haunting song, imagining fairies dancing in Charlie's Fairy Glen.

The Big Thicket was not just the birds' cafeteria—it was also an avian Home Depot, full of nesting materials. The Little Golden Queen spent four days gathering downy fibers to build her two-inch-wide cup nest in a low shrub. All the fluff she needed was here or in Warner marsh: nettles, willow seeds, dandelion fluff, cattail fluff, webbing she stole from tent caterpillars, milkweed and fern stems, meadow grasses, even deer hair.[7] The insects, worms, and spiders she and her mate fed their babies were also here. Yellow warblers usually stay in the United States only three months, so parents need a lot of food to help their babies reach adulthood quickly. As teenagers they might have to migrate as far as a thousand miles and maybe cross an ocean to reach wintering grounds as far south as Colombia. Not an easy flight for any bird—but imagine doing it as a five- or six-month-old teenager!

One day I left my 2.8-billion-year-old seat to get a bird's-eye view of the Big Thicket. I found a large black cherry tree, cobbled together a ladder using dead branches, and climbed up and sat in a fork, cradling my thermos full of coffee. The cherry quickly became a favorite perch within my special place. Small groups of geese flew overhead, wings whistling. From up high, I could see only trees and bushes, no humans. Only an ocean of branches and brambles. The dozen or so mourning doves that hid under the honeysuckle cooed anxiously, or at least it sounded that way to me. They must not have been pleased with the enormous new tree-climbing predator. A cocky blue jay zoomed in to scrutinize me, followed by a red cardinal.

From my new perch I saw things I'd never seen before—like that cardinal eating sumac berries, one by one, and then spitting out bits. I was just a few feet above him, a view I'd never had because I'd always looked up at birds, never down. As I drank coffee—a tough balancing act while perched in a tree—I nodded to him and said hello. He glanced at me and went right on with his business eviscerating those berries. Next to this minute acrobat perched on a swaying berry clump, I felt so awkward and ungainly jammed between the large branches. And yet I was enormously pleased with myself. This was the closest I'd ever come to feeling as if I were a bird.

The Big Thicket was also a living reminder of a fight the Wild Ones, Wild Warner's predecessors, had undertaken decades before. As I researched the park's history, I'd discovered that in 1977, the Wild Ones stopped a major development plan to build a shelter and parking lot in the meadow area. Instead, they pushed for a "bird sanctuary." Their proposal included creating "a thicket," the one I now spent so much time in.[8]

The Wild Ones and the endless hours of meetings they must have attended were the only reason my special place still existed. As I perched in my cherry tree, I wondered how many beloved nooks in parks, special places for birds and children, are the living evidence of folks who attended meeting after meeting, year after year, just like Jack Hurst, and just like my father, to save his red hill.

But I was afraid because my special place was also the most feared, reviled, even hated area of the park. In the city's development plan, the one we'd managed to alter, a paragraph had recommended "clearing" this thicket; some neighbors believed it was the hiding place of pedophiles, ready to leap out and grab children off the swing set. (A boy told me his mother had warned him about this.) They also believed homeless people lived there, and in the summer, I did find the occasional tent. However, during the hundreds of hours I spent there, no one had ever bothered me. Still, I knew from my dissertation research that neighbors had had serious trouble with crime in the park in the past with rapes, a murder, and the drowning of an African American man one summer night. Police and media reports said the man who drowned died of "natural causes," but given our country's history, I had my doubts. The police also told me that Warner was now one of the city's "safest parks," but that was precisely because neighbors had organized to make it safe.

My neighbors' fears reminded me of Drew Lanham's comments about large trees and how some older African Americans feared them because of what Mr. M called "lynching time." There are so many different ways to view and perceive landscapes based on our personal experiences, our own environmental histories, and the ancestral memory embedded in our DNA—fear and love at the cellular level.

Mr. M's comments and Drew Lanham's work also made me reflect on my own family's environmental history. As an Irish American, I realized that I am genetically predisposed to love and appreciate thickets. For centuries, the thickets and bogs of Ireland had protected my family. The landscape of my father's childhood was a scrubby topography of gentle hills, bogs, and woods. During the seventeenth and eighteenth centuries, when English occupiers imposed the Penal Laws in Ireland forbidding Catholicism and the speaking of Gaelic, people worshipped in those bogs and woods. Their altars were huge boulders called Mass Rocks, similar to the Warner glacial erratic I loved to sit on. On one trip, my cousins showed me a Mass Rock very near my grandparents' home. Thickets and hedges were also where Irish people set up an underground network of "hedge schools" to teach Irish language, culture, and history, as well as Latin, Greek, and other subjects. The vegetation hid the clandestine teachers and their students from the eyes of colonial authorities and probably kept the Irish language alive.

When my father was a boy and a neighbor sounded the alarm that the dreaded Black and Tans—British paramilitaries—were on the way, my grandmother would grab blankets and my father and his small siblings and scurry to the nearest bog, where they'd hide for the night, preferring the cold and damp to waiting for their door to get kicked in. Thickets in Ireland were places of refuge and safety for both the hunted Irish and the animals. Maybe this was why my father loved that cactus thicket on his California hill so much. He'd carried that love for wild, untamable refuges across an ocean and then transferred that ancestral gratitude to me. I just didn't know it until I sat in Warner's thicket for three summers.

**IT WASN'T JUST THE PARKS DEPARTMENT THAT WANTED TO GET RID OF THE THICKET. EVERY** single person I'd taken through it who knew anything about ecology—including a few Wild Warner members—wanted to. Even some of my new students who'd studied ecology declared immediately: "This isn't habitat!" The honeysuckle was the culprit. I learned that honeysuckle is the house sparrow of the plant world, viscerally hated by anyone in restoration ecology. People took one look at the huge "invasive" honeysuckle bushes, brought over from Europe by settlers because of their medicinal value, shook their heads, and said, "It's all invasive. It should be burned down and planted with oaks."

I was terrified that this was really going to happen. In Charlie's Fairy Glen, I was sitting in the middle of a raging conservation debate, and I was deeply torn about it. I'd learned from studying entomology that native plants feed native insects, which are the best bird food. But what I couldn't understand was that if the thicket was such a bad place for birds, why had I found so many birds there? The thing is, yes, there was lots of honeysuckle, but trees, too. Still, many people saw the honeysuckle and wrote the whole place off.

I understood the arguments from some Wild Warner members to plant more native plants. I am a guerrilla gardener who loves native plants, carries little bags of seeds in my pockets, and scatters them everywhere I can (especially milkweed on those perfect chem-lawns). But both Jim and I were disturbed by the methods often used to "restore" land in Wisconsin. Too many restorationists were Roundup warriors, spraying glyphosate everywhere, even though it had been banned in several countries because of studies showing it could increase the risk of lymphoma by 41 percent.[9] What would Roundup do to the birds in the thicket, to the water in the marsh, to Warner's human neighbors? And I didn't trust the parks department and city experts to replant the thicket with native plants because of what I'd learned during the Great Geese Wars. Warner had been designed for sports and fireworks, not native plant conservation. What would keep the city from following its historical pattern and ripping out all those "invasives" just to plant more Kentucky bluegrass—another invasive?

To protect the park and especially the thicket, I decided to try a different defense tactic—a research project to bring the park under the university's powerful umbrella. I could document the biodiversity—all the species who lived there—and try to change people's attitudes through talks and a brochure sharing our research findings. I believed most anti-thicket people simply didn't know that it was teeming with life, despite the honeysuckle, because most people couldn't spend three summers sitting in a fairy glen documenting it.

I also realized that a research project could be a novel way to address neighbors' fears about crime. In her seminal 1961 book, *The Death and Life of Great American Cities*, urban planning critic Jane Jacobs wrote that one way to reduce crime in city parks was to get "eyes on the street." The more people in a given area, the less crime there would be, she reasoned. Decades later, in a 2012 study of three parks in Salt Lake City, researchers found that fear of crime was lowest where park users could see other people recreating, regardless of whether vegetation like shrubs could conceal an attacker.[10] When I read this study and those of other parks, I wondered: What if the people recreating were using binoculars? Could this magnify Jane Jacobs's eyes-on-the-street effect? If we flooded the thicket for several summers with researchers and university students, could this change the way the park and its thicket were perceived and increase public use, meeting the city councilor's goal?*

I decided to focus the study on catbirds because the thicket was the catbirds' kingdom. (*Dumetella*, the catbird's Latin name, means "small thicket.") And the catbird was also my favorite because of that very first hilarious feline-imitating, canine-infuriating gray catbird I'd found in my new Madison yard, years earlier. If the cardinal I'd noticed after Katrina in New Orleans was what birders call my spark bird—the bird that awakens your sudden and intense love for feathered creatures—then this 1.2-ounce gray-and-black eminence was my gateway drug bird. And I still wanted to know: Where exactly did this bird go in the wintertime?

Although there was nothing scientific about it, I also identified

---

* Criminology experts focus mainly on negative cues that provoke fear, but more research is needed on positive cues that create feelings of safety among potential users, especially women and others fearful of crime or racial hostility.

with catbirds and their insurgent ways, how they skulked around like investigative journalists, staying hidden while making a lot of noise. How they crossed borders without passports. How they made their homes in two entirely different climates and cultures—Wisconsin and Latin America. How feisty and scrappy they were and protective of their territories. And I loved that, for the most part, the ecology and conservation world hadn't paid them much attention. They were considered common—which is to say, not endangered—and yet they made these astounding annual journeys. And they nested in honeysuckle bushes conservationists considered invasive. They were feathered transgressors defying ecological categorization. And that made them my peeps—pun intended.

My neighbor Greg and I had also developed a personal relationship with the catbirds in our yards. Every year there was a new episode in the catbird family drama. The worst episode was on a bucolic summer Friday around noon. I was sitting in my yard with the dogs when I heard an ominous sawing in Greg's backyard (he was a complete yard neat freak—I was not). Greg showed up at my fence, wringing his hands, on the verge of tears. He'd cut down a small bush and didn't see the nest hidden deep inside until it was lying on the ground. Then he was so upset, he didn't see the babies spill out, and he accidently stepped on one of them.

I ran over and there was a live catbird baby lying on the grass next to its squashed sibling. The little one was panting heavily and opening its beak, eyes still closed. The chick was a very soft gray with tinges of black where its little wing stubs were emerging. I grabbed the squashed nest, rounded it out with my hand, stuck the poor baby in there, and scoured the yard for a suitable bush. As I raced around, I was thinking, *This is crazy.* Over millions of years, these birds have learned where to build their nest so that it will be the right temperature, sheltered from the wind and at the right height to avoid predators like skunks and raccoons. And here I am just sticking a nest willy-nilly into the nearest bush. Will it have enough shade? Will the baby get cooked? All this crap was going through my head as I raced to get that baby in a place where the mother could find it. I stuck the nest deep in another small honeysuckle. Greg just stood there, all the while repeating three phrases like a demented brown thrasher, which repeats every phrase twice: "I can't believe I did this. I'm an animal lover. I feel so bad."

Then his voice got all maple-syrupy.

"Oh, honey!" he said.

And then, "Oh, no!"

The mother catbird flew in. She perched on the fence, in her beak a mangled dragonfly that she was bringing to feed to her babies. But there was no nest and no bush. She looked at us, hopped on the ground, and inspected the dead squashed baby. Then she flew away, dragging that dead dragonfly with her.

"Well, at least she doesn't feel as bad as I do," Greg said. "They don't feel the way we do."

Now, I loved this guy. He was probably the kindest neighbor I'd ever had except for Heddie. But at that moment, I wanted to take his saw and beat him over the head with it.

Later that night Greg called breathless with excitement. He'd been watching the nest through his supersonic camera lens. The mother had returned minutes later, after I'd left. She'd found her baby, and for days Greg watched her bring insects to the little survivor.

**TO ANSWER MY BURNING CATBIRD QUESTION—WHERE DOES THIS LITTLE GRAY-AND-BLACK** guy go?—I needed to do a migration study, which meant a banding study. For nearly two centuries, thousands of intrepid, mosquito-hounded volunteers have spent time hidden in some thicket, setting up mist nets to detain migrating birds. Few are paid. They do it to help the greater cause of science and for that unforgettable moment when you hold a bird in your hands like a fallen star, its tiny heart ripping a beat against your palm, the life pulsating against your skin, the beady black eyes staring at you fiercely.

Banding studies have helped scientists determine the general migration routes and final destinations of many species, which is how we know that catbirds winter in Central America and Mexico. But I wanted to track individual catbirds, and this requires more sophisticated technology. In the past, avian biologists placed radio transmitters on the backs of larger birds and then physically followed them in cars or planes for hundreds of miles, like detectives hot on the trail of a suspect.[11] It was a frustrating job. A bird could lounge around a good feeding ground for a few days and the chasers had to wait, too, and suddenly scramble when that bird took to the skies. Some songbirds fly 45 to 50 miles per hour, which made them hard to follow even in a car, so bird chasers tried to stick to interstates to avoid police. Since most long-distance migratory birds travel at night, bird chasers also had to be caffeine freaks. In 1973, Bill Cochran, the inventor of the miniature radio transmitter for smaller birds, set the bird-chasing world record on a seven-straight-night, 940-mile Kerouacian drive in pursuit of one radio-tracked thrush that disappeared into the wilds of Manitoba.[12]

Gray catbirds were too small to carry classic radio transmitters. But by the time I'd decided to do my study, scientists had better migration tracking tools such as solar geolocators with tiny light sensors that stored data on a bird's location in relation to the sun as it traveled. About the size of a thumbnail, a geolocator weighed 1.5 grams then and fitted on the bird's back like a tiny backpack, with a thread harness that looped around each leg. (Today they weigh closer to 0.3 grams.) When the birds returned to their northern breeding grounds, researchers recaptured them (hopefully), removed the devices, downloaded the information, and generated a route map of the birds' migration. When I did my thicket study, the device could determine a bird's final destination within approximately 120 miles—not exact, but a huge step forward. The technology kept advancing rapidly, and these days the devices pinpoint the location within ten meters. Birds like catbirds, which returned to the same breeding ground every summer—maybe even the same bush—were ideal candidates for a geolocation study.

To conduct a study, you need a federal permit and a banding license, which takes years of apprenticeship under a master bander. I needed a prestigious researcher to lead the study and to teach me—a total novice—how to do it. I gathered my courage and knocked on the door of UW-Madison's avian ecologist extraordinaire, Dr. Anna Pidgeon. Dr. Pidgeon is a hard-core scientist and conservation champion with research teams in the United States, Latin America, and China. Yes, her name is real, and yes, Anna Pigeon, the kick-ass female ranger character in Nevada Barr's national-park-based mystery series, was modeled on Dr. Pidgeon.

Dr. Pidgeon was very interested. She knew of no other geolocation study in Wisconsin. And she'd been an environmental educator before she became a research star, so she loved the children's birding program. She also loved the idea of doing research on a common bird, instead of waiting until it was in trouble. And she agreed on the importance of publishing the results immediately on Wild Warner's website. She pointed out another reason for this study: to evaluate whether that thicket provided good habitat. Dr. Pidgeon also thought the honeysuckle should be ripped out. She told me quite forcefully that the catbirds could be living there because it was all that was available.* It was particularly important to find out if the thicket provided high-quality food, because many birds nesting in it were fueling up for an incredible journey. For these birds, high-quality food was a matter of life or death. A bird without the fat reserves and muscle mass to cross an ocean could end up in a shark's stomach.

She agreed to be the avian PhD advisor on my graduate committee, to train and mentor me, to be the lead investigator for Warner Park's first research project, and to bring a team of graduate students to help. We designed a project with three stages: observation and catbird territory mapping, banding and geolocation, and finally, recapture. It would take us three summers, and I'd already begun the observation phase on my own.† I agreed to get a grant for our project, which we called One Bird, One Park, One World.[13]

**THE THING I LOVED THE MOST ABOUT FIELD RESEARCH WAS THE SHEER PHYSICALITY OF IT** compared to the grad student life, spent slumped behind a screen

* In ecology, a habitat is either a source—a place where a species can successfully reproduce—or a sink, a place where the species tries to reproduce but that place does not provide enough high-quality food or shelter. An ecological sink can look inviting and be full of birds and still be a death trap, with predators such as prowling cats, who catch birds who nest in low bushes.

† Dr. Pidgeon also banded some male catbirds that first summer.

drinking bad coffee and regurgitating dry academic jargon. This work took everything I had, brain, body, and soul, from the moment I leapt out of bed when the damned alarm went off at 4:30 a.m. I enjoyed the routine, too: fill the thermos, grab a granola bar, put on a headlamp, and grab nets, poles, and a bucket with a heavy mallet to pound the poles into the ground. Off I would trot into the meadow, where a light fog hovered like a silver-gray capelet. And then into the dark thicket I trudged, thinking that if anyone attacked me, I'd just beat them with the mallet. I felt like a guerrilla fighter on an urgent mission while the world and the catbirds in the kingdom of Dumetella were still sweetly sleeping.[14]

As the team arrived, Anna and I would pound poles into the ground. We'd take turns, Anna slamming away, lean thigh muscles tensing, long brown-gray ponytail bobbing with each strike. Then we'd carefully put up the expensive nets. A Zen-like exercise in patience, it reminded me of untangling yarn. But unfortunately I am not very Zen-like, and here's what happened on one of those typical gorgeous cool summer mornings when my mind was fighting the Warner Park Wars, crafting testimonies for the parks commission and city council, instead of focusing on the task before me. To set up the net, I placed one looped end over a pole and began walking toward the end pole, thirty feet away, pulling the net out of the plastic grocery bag Anna stored them in to keep them from getting tangled at night. But because I'd forgotten to remove my silver bracelets when I vaulted out of bed—no jewelry allowed in this delicate work—my arm got tangled in the damn net before I'd even finished putting it up. So that day, instead of a bird, the first thing I caught was myself. And there went ten precious minutes frantically trying to extricate myself without breaking the threads while the birds began to stir around us.

A mourning dove called, a great crested flycatcher *wheep-wheep*ed, and a catbird went off on a jazzy riff. Then suddenly I saw a police car driving through the park down the main path on the thicket's edge. Oh, SHIT. He was veering off the main path and onto the grass and headed straight toward us. Fortunately I stopped him before he made a patrol-car-size hole in our invisible nets.[15]

The sun rose. And the first birds hit the soft nets, falling into the deep pockets. They were breathing hard, little chests rising and falling. You didn't want them to get too stressed, so you had to be calm but speedy. Anna could get a bird out of a net, assess its health, weigh it, band and geolocate it, and release it within ten to fifteen minutes. As I watched her work, quietly and competently, like a surgeon, I realized it would take years to even come close.

On banding mornings we always used Anna's iPod to play catbird calls to lure the catbirds in. The recording played in a continuous loop with a disembodied Alexa-type voice interrupting every few minutes, announcing "gray catbird." Sometimes Anna got the recordings mixed up, and instead of the catbird's call, a Bach Brandenburg concerto blasted out of the speaker hidden in the thicket. Another morning, I brought my own recorder. But somehow my ukulele lesson on how to strum Johnny Cash's "Ring of Fire" started playing instead of the catbird's song. I wondered what the birds thought of that.

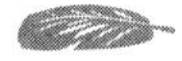

**BEFORE WE BEGAN THE STUDY, ANNA HAD COUNSELED ME ON FIELD RESEARCH ETHICS AND THE** university protocol for working with animals. Birds breathe through their hollow bones, an ingenious evolutionary adaptation that makes them light enough to fly. So if you break one of those toothpick-thin legs while disentangling the bird from the net, you've also damaged the bird's entire respiratory system. The bird will never be the same. We'd have to kill it immediately, Anna warned. She would do the euthanizing, but I had to honor this agreement in order to work with her. She would not release an injured bird or keep a wild bird in a cage for months of rehab. She had too much respect and love for the animals.

Since the stakes were so high for the birds, Anna and her experienced graduate students did most of the handling. I ran back and forth between the nets and the banding/medical station, informing them when a bird had been caught. A couple of Wild Warner members, my PhD advisor Jack, and Jim became net monitors, too.

I also learned to extract the birds from the nets. To get a bird out of a mist net, you have to immobilize it to stop it from becoming a little entangled nightmare.

Step 1: Grab the bird with your left hand and create a fleshy cage with your fingers and thumb to hold it still. The bird's head should be wedged between your index and third finger. This little cage is called a bander's grip. It keeps the bird immobile while you use your right hand to disentangle every fine thread.

Step 2: Ignore all the other birds zooming in and hanging out in the bushes, screaming "Torturer!" "Murderer!" "Big clumsy human!" (at least this is what I imagined) while you try to free their family member from the net. You must pay razor-sharp attention to the bird so you don't hurt it, while ignoring the mosquitoes chewing on your earlobes (you can't wear repellent because it hurts the birds).

Step 3: Take a deep breath, calm your pounding heart, and take a minute to figure out how the bird flew into the net so you can remove it more easily. The tail is the main clue. Find the small opening around the tail, then use your right-hand fingers to slowly extricate the bird, thread by thread. If the bird is really wound up, have a toothpick handy to pull the thread over delicate areas like the head. (Avoid the eyes, although birds have a third clear eyelid for extra protection called a nictitating membrane—very cool.) Once you've got your infuriated feathered prisoner out of the net, keep the bird in that left-hand cage and insert it headfirst into the mouth of a small white cotton bag you've picked up with your right hand. Draw the string tight on the bag's opening as the bird goes in, so it can't escape.

Now, if this sounds easy to you, I've done a terrible job explaining it. So a word of warning: chickadees, possibly the most adorable bird in my part of the world, are the nemesis of the novice. They seem to sense that you're totally incompetent and they get really pissed off and frantically start twirling around and diving deeper into the net to escape your gigantic clumsy hands. And the madder they get, the more wound up their teeny-weeny legs and feet become, and while you're trying to help, cursing softly under your breath, they start drilling a hole in your hand with that needle-sharp beak.

I got "lucky" one of my first mornings as a net extractor and had a doubleheader, a chickadee pair caught together. The first one looked at me with its beady little eye, clutching the net for dear life, its tiny head and neck a spidery, thread-bound mess, which was absolutely terrifying because I was so afraid I was going to break its neck. I kept switching the bird from hand to hand, and it kept pecking furiously at my fingers. The bird calmed down as I began to free it—the tail, the wing, one foot, the head, and then—magic moment—the chickadee let go of the thread with the other foot. I was amazed at the strength of its bill and the sharpness of the tip. I remember this moment whenever I watch chickadees pounding on sunflower seeds in my yard.

Your other nemesis is my spark bird, the cardinal. Anna was far away that memorable morning, and I just couldn't wait to grab that gorgeous bloodred male screeching from the net. But I learned one second later that you never, ever grab a cardinal, because he will grab you first. He will open his beak, and using his ultra-powerful jaw muscles, he'll close that beak on your innocent index finger as if it were a giant sunflower seed. Except that your finger is not a giant sunflower seed. So as we glared at each other, the cardinal's eyes huge with fear, red crest sticking straight up like a demonic punk hairdo, I started screaming for help. And I realized that as much as I love birds, if that bird kept trying to crack my poor finger open, I might just have to kill it. But Jim came running, whipped out a ballpoint pen, and that cardinal decided for some dumb reason that Jim's pen looked tastier than my half-dead finger and let go.

Something else I loved about field research (besides the fact that I was outside and with birds) is that we were doing something a computer couldn't do and probably never would. A computer could not catch birds and tear up over their dainty beauty and blow on their stomachs to see if they had a brood patch. It could not marvel at the colors of the digested honeysuckle berries that a male robin ejected out of his cloacal protuberance right onto my lime-green T-shirt. (The expression "scared shitless" suddenly meant something when nearly every bird caught in the net shat on me.) Thanks, little buddy, I told the robin. I couldn't go home to change, and now it looked like I murdered somebody.

After we got the birds out of the net and into the bird bags, I hung the bags on a sturdy branch in the bush next to Dr. Pidgeon's mini medical station. There, the rest of the tiny prisoners were in their hanging bird bags, waiting for their exam. Anna's station was a tartan blanket in the meadow, covered with small clear-plastic tackle boxes lined up with pink, green, red, blue, and silver bands in them. It was a Lilliputian clinic with avian-scaled tweezers, clippers, and other instruments.

One day we caught a female warbling vireo. Anna showed me the bird's light blue legs. Wow. I'd never seen a blue-legged bird before. Warbling vireos nested here and wintered in pine and oak woods, thorn forests, and coffee plantations in Mexico and Central America.[16] The vireo dropped a white dogwood berry from her beak when Anna grabbed her in the net. I watched Anna tuck the berry into her pocket. Just before Anna released the vireo, she took out the berry and returned it to the bird. The vireo grabbed it with her beak and flew off.

While Anna examined and banded the birds, I recorded numbers on a clipboard in pencil: weight, estimated age, sex, body condition, length of wing chord, and fat reserves, which Anna checked by blowing on the bird's breast feathers to reveal the fat layers underneath. She expanded their wings and measured their wing chord with a mini-ruler. She secured tiny bands around tiny ankles with miniature pliers. And then she made a life-or-death judgment: Could this catbird carry that geolocating backpack across an ocean? If the bird was healthy with decent fat reserves, weighing at least 37 grams, and the device weighed less than 3 percent of the bird's weight, she put a backpack on that bird.

I thought about what it would be like to carry around a backpack for a whole year that is 3 percent of your weight—four pounds for me. And I didn't have to fly across an ocean. Anna placed the geolocator low on the bird's back, between where its wings met. My job was to knot the thread looped around the bird's legs to hold the backpack on. I'd spent weeks practicing square knots. Once I'd tied the knot, I placed one drop of crazy glue on it and waited thirty seconds for it to dry. Then Anna placed the bird in a large paper grocery bag and closed it. She waited several minutes, peeking in to see if the bird was moving normally. If the birds jumped and tried to fly within the bag, moving normally, Anna opened it, and that newly geolocated catbird flew into the nearest bush with a loud and angry rattling ratchet call, the catbird version of "Fuck you!"

Besides being a net checker, extractor, and scribe, I acted as Official Worrier. Every day before we went into the thicket I'd wake up before 4:30 a.m., panicked, thinking, *Am I going to have to kill a bird today because I am such a fucking klutz?* And then I worried about the geolocated birds in Warner Park for the rest of that summer and then into the fall, when I knew they'd be heading to Central America or Mexico. When they left in September for Latin America, I felt bereft. I walked into Warner Park and there were no more meowls. The thicket seemed lifeless. I'd sit in the thicket and imagine the catbirds flapping hard in the dark, heading toward the Gulf of Mexico, preparing to cross, chowing down on berries and bugs in southern yards. Would they all stick together on their way south? Would there be enough food there for them? Would any Warner birds get hit by cars as they flew low over some of those shore roads in the South, just like so many catbirds do when they're headed to the Gulf Coast to cross an ocean?[17]

In the dead of the Wisconsin winter, when we were buried in snow and I was sitting in front of our woodstove, fire blazing, my dogs snoozing beside me, I'd start wondering: Where are they right now? Are they in some Costa Rican or Nicaraguan jungle? In someone's yard in Managua or Tegucigalpa?

I couldn't stop thinking how their furtive little bush-dwelling lives depended on my ability to tie a decent square knot. Talk about life hanging by a thread. Too loose, and they could get caught on a branch and starve to death somewhere. Too tight, and the thread could abrade the skin on their legs, injuring them or hampering their ability to land, find food, or escape a predator. My grandmother's knitting advice—"Not too loose, not too tight"—worked for geolocation research, too.

Despite my fears, most of the catbirds we caught that summer were in very good health and could carry the geolocators. It appeared that they were eating well and thriving in our thicket. We were able to place tiny backpacks on the backs of fifteen Warner thicket birds.

**ONE MORNING A CATBIRD WE'D BANDED EARLIER WITH A SILVER BAND ON HIS LEFT ANKLE** screamed at me from a small tree; he'd returned to check on his buddies. He peeked his head out, peering from behind the tree's slim trunk. His liquid black eye was huge. He looked scared and screamed for several minutes as he hopped around. I felt bad because I knew how exhausting it was to continually raise your voice.

But I admired how fiercely he and his other feathered comrades defended their thicket kingdom, how loyal they were to this place. The catbirds' first line of defense was the eyes and ears of their compadres around that thicket, feathered sentries sounding the alarm and relaying information across the meadow and into their kingdom before I'd gotten anywhere near it. Some mornings when we started a bit later, I'd step out of the house lugging buckets and nets, and our yard catbird would fly to the meadow's edge (his territory included our yard and the park's edge) and start meowling loudly at me. That alarm would ricochet across the meadow and through the thicket, catbird by catbird. I cannot say with certainty that our catbird or the other catbirds recognized me, although researchers have proven that crows and ravens recognize individual humans.[18] But long-distance migratory birds like him have to have greater memory capacity than some resident bird species. They need to remember their routes and fueling stations and safe rest stops along the way. So my unproven theory is that they knew who I was, they saw me as a dangerous predator, and they transmitted that information across the meadow and through the thicket, just as they would for a hawk or an owl.

The catbird sentries and their relay system were much like the human communications network that Wild Warner was becoming. Neighbors and park-goers who read the local news and knew about us started emailing Jim and me, even calling to report that the city was going to cut down a tree or that people were harassing the great blue heron or illegally trying to trap the wetland's huge snapping turtles. Even parks employees started approaching us in between their park tasks, glancing around first to make sure no one was watching, and sidling up to share information. (The parks department had ordered them to stop talking to Wild Warner, but this edict backfired.) Many parks employees, especially the ones who'd worked in this same park for decades, loved Warner Park and its animal residents. They didn't agree with management decisions they were forced to carry out. They knew we were on the side of the animals.*

**IN 2012, THE THIRD FIELDWORK YEAR AND ONE YEAR AFTER ANNA PIDGEON AND I HAD** attached those fifteen catbird backpacks, my bird buddy Stacy and I entered the thicket at 6:10 a.m. It was early May but already near 70 degrees, overcast, damp, muggy and buggy. I'd been in the thicket for days knowing the catbirds might arrive any minute from Central America. At 7:50 a.m. in Rabbit Lane, I looked up and saw the sun glinting off a catbird's tiny geolocator.

Oh. My. God.

"You made it! Welcome back!" I yelled, and started jumping up and down and hugging Stacy. The bird started meowling immediately, acting very male, territorial, singing loudly from high in an ash tree.

Two weeks later, on a sunny 60-degree morning, Anna, Jim, and I returned to the thicket to catch the loud bird I'd begun to call Carl/Carlos, and all other Warner catbirds sporting tiny backpacks. Jim filmed the operation. Anna and I were punch-drunk happy. Delirious. We caught Carl at 7:44 a.m. in the heart of his territory on Rabbit Lane. He struggled furiously in his white capture bag. Anna's field notes read: "Bird in great shape. Dense 'thread' also in great shape." He weighed 39 grams, a healthy weight, and his backpack was intact. The threads hadn't hurt the skin on his legs. I carefully snipped them with tiny scissors and removed the geolocator.

Jim snapped a picture of me holding Carl just before I released him. He's turned sideways, staring into the camera with one large liquid black eye. I'm holding him by the legs so it looks as if he's perched

* This was during a conflictive time within the parks department. Fortunately, the city of Madison hired a new superintendent in 2014, Eric Knepp, an enthusiastic supporter of environmental education. Eric began working very closely with Wild Warner, particularly Paul Noeldner, expanding Wild Warner's model throughout city parks.

Where are you, Carl?

on my fingers. His feathers are smooth and glossy. His black cap is very dark, contrasting with the soft grays that look light purplish in some places. His little reptilian feet are barely the size of my thumbnail; it looks as if a giant is holding him. As I held him, I kept thinking, *You just flew thousands of miles. This is nuts. How in the hell did you do this amazing thing?*

Before I released him, I looked him deeply in the eyes. I thanked him and gave him a tiny kiss on the head. He reciprocated by pecking me in a nostril. Then I released him back into his kingdom, where he dove into the grapevines and disappeared.

It took all summer, but by September of that third memorable catbird season, Anna and I had found four of the fifteen gray catbirds we'd geolocated, or 27 percent, which, believe it or not, was a decent return rate for geolocation studies, since approximately 50 percent of birds die during migration.[19] Every bird was in good shape. We removed their backpacks, assessed their health, thanked them, and liberated them. The data in their trackers showed that they had spent the winter in either the Yucatán, Mexico, or northern Guatemala. I finally had the answer to the question I'd asked when I'd encountered that very first catbird in my new Madison yard: Did I share a migration route with this funny, loud gray bird? The answer was yes.

I'd also learned from the catbirds and from Anna to question all my assumptions about conservation and wildlife management. After fighting geese management policies and rejecting the whole concept of wildlife management, I'd learned from catbirds that the idea of just doing nothing is bogus. We're all managing wild animals by the way we live, by the landscapes we plant, and especially by the way we move around. The number one killer of catbirds is cars. They are birds that fly low across roads to get food. Another big killer is cats, because these birds nest in suburban areas where roaming felines can raid their low bush nests or eat catbird fledglings as they explore the immediate area.[20] And the third danger is cell towers. So if you drive a car, have a free-range kitty, and use a cellphone, you're managing catbirds and other birds by killing them (I'm two for three).

But the greatest lesson I'd learned in the Kingdom of Dumetella had to do with my ego. Much as I loved fieldwork and will always admire the Anna Pidgeons of the world, I wasn't very good at it and I didn't have decades to get better. I was just too distracted and tired on those early mornings after fighting at public meetings so many nights. I didn't want to, but I realized that I had to choose between fieldwork and activism to protect my special place—all of Warner Park. Those three thickety summers taught me that I'd be more useful if I employed the skills I already had to tell stories—to write the way the catbird sings.

CHAPTER 12

# An Elephant, a Magnificent Jellyfish, and an American Woodcock Walk into a Bar . . .

*Be present in your place and act accordingly.*

TERRY TEMPEST WILLIAMS

THE FAWN STOOD COLT-LIKE ON WARNER'S MARSH ISLAND IN THE MIDDLE OF THE wetland. It was the color of the island's tall drying grasses, perfectly camouflaged.

Normally, this marsh island would be an excellent hiding place for a fawn. But that morning the young animal watched as its mother charged into the water, swam to the wetland shore, and bounded out of Warner Park. Maybe the doe was just leaving her fawn for the day. Or maybe she was rattled and leaving to join the animal exodus that neighbors witnessed every year just before Rhythm and Booms, the largest firework show in the Midwest. After two decades of fireworks, some animals seemed to sense that late June was the time to get the hell out of Dodge. In thirty-seven hours, windows for blocks would shudder for thirty minutes, and dogs safely inside their homes up to a mile away would howl and rage against an unseen attacker, even though they'd been drugged by their owners. (Local vets ran out of tranquilizers by late June.)

There were plenty of signals that it was time to leave the park. The pre–Fourth of July show had already begun that summer, with teenagers sneaking into Warner to fire rockets from Sled Hill. And then there was the sudden influx of men zipping around in golf carts and mini-trucks. The geese must have noticed the gigantic metal bird—a Black Hawk helicopter—that landed near the picnic shelter where they usually congregated. The Black Hawk hovered over the lagoon, casting an inky shadow on the water. It had carefully dropped a heavy cannon on the shore and then whooshed off with a semicircular sweep of its long metal tail.

I was cruising around the island in my yellow kayak when I first spied that fawn hiding in the grasses. About 100 feet of water separated the fawn from a small spit of land that jutted out on the park side, pointing right at the young animal. This spit was the fireworks launch pad, where 13,000 mortars were lined up in ascending rows on a black scaffold like the pipes of a demented giant church organ. Each mortar was a cardboard cylinder six inches wide and eighteen inches tall, packed with a pound of fuses, rope, wire, plastic, gunpowder, and chemicals called perchlorates—a component of rocket fuel—and the heavy metal salts that created those eye-popping colorful starbursts.[1]

The largest explosives—twelve inches in diameter—were packed into a small hill of sand on that landspit in between pink-blooming marsh milkweed. Warning labels read "Dangerous," "Do Not Handle," and "Toxic." A large bumblebee sucked at a milkweed blossom. An electric-blue damselfly, eyes like two eerie blue headlights, zipped around, inspecting it all. A cardinal pair chipped from a bush near the rockets.

I knew that, unfortunately, some painted turtles patrolling underwater and surfacing like tiny submarines had already dug their nests and laid their eggs in the sand on the landspit, in between the explosives. The turtles hadn't seemed to learn that many of their nests would be blown up during the Independence Day celebration. A painted turtle could live for decades, so they were probably nesting here long before the fireworks started. And turtles are extremely loyal to their special places. A friend who nursed turtles hit by cars told me that her patients "loved" certain rocks in the wildlife hospital's aquariums. They became very attached to them.

The mortars were aimed at the marsh island, so the fiery debris would land there or in Warner's lagoon, not on thousands of spectators who would soon fill park lawns. Nearly every year, fireworks debris set the marsh island on fire. Even though the park was surrounded by densely populated neighborhoods and neighbors complained about asthma, the fire department would not extinguish that fire.

Somewhere on that marsh island I could hear a downy woodpecker whinnying, and from my kayak I could see a northern flicker, a gorgeous gold-and-black woodpecker, moseying up a dead trunk. Two giant-winged great blue herons flapped slowly by. Above it all, from the top of a huge cottonwood on the island, an eastern wood pewee sang plaintively. I wondered if his tree would get torched tomorrow night. Pewees migrated as far as Peru for the winter and returned to nest on Warner's island every spring.

At the pinnacle of Fireworks Hill, the largest American flag I'd ever seen flapped in the wind. Just below it, a twenty-four-hour armed guard stood at attention, a scene right out of Iwo Jima. He'd been protecting the firework mortars for five days.

He got snarly and yelled at me to stop taking pictures as I cruised by. I smiled, waved, and just kept on snapping.

**HOW OUR WETLAND BECAME THE LAUNCHING PAD FOR THE LARGEST FIREWORKS SHOW IN** the Midwest illustrates our species's screwed-up relationships with animals, with our waters, and with one another, particularly the relationship between wealthier neighborhoods and poorer ones. This story began in 1950 with a female baby elephant named Winkie. Captured in the wilds of Burma, she was later sold by elephant hunters to Madison's zoo. The 7,500-pound elephant became enormously popular; visits to her were a feature of Madison childhood. The same year that Winkie became the zoo's star resident, a Fourth of July fireworks show was held in the park right next to the zoo. This was on Madison's wealthier west side, in a beautiful tree-lined neighborhood approximately six and a half miles from Warner Park.

Madisonians loved the new fireworks show. Winkie did not. She trumpeted loudly, an elephant warning signal or sign of anxiety. The other caged animals—howler monkeys, camels, bison, emus, peacocks, and lions—joined her in a screeching, roaring chorus.[2] The zoo director complained. Winkie's trainer complained. And the public complained about the animals' distress. So finally, in 1968, city officials moved the fireworks across town to Warner Park.[3]

That year, the city held its largest fireworks show ever, with 60,000 Madisonians cheering in Warner Park.[4] After a few years, the show petered out. But in the 1990s, it was reborn as Rhythm and Booms, a regional extravaganza drawing crowds of over 100,000, with parachutists dropping out of planes, the National Guard firing 155m howitzer cannons, and pyrotechnicians launching 10,000 to 16,000 shells into the wetland. Performers and bands like the Animals, the Turtles, Dr. John, and Blood, Sweat & Tears entertained enchanted crowds.

Like so many economic development projects that go wrong, it all happened, I believe, with the best of intentions. In the 1980s, crime increased dramatically in many US cities, including Madison. The north side of Madison, where Warner Park is located, hit the headlines, with murders, stabbings, shootings, and robberies. Pockets of poverty had begun growing along with crime and drug use around the park. There were few businesses or local organizations.[5]

Instead of moving away, Northsiders spent hundreds of hours at meetings and set up the Northside Planning Council, a pugnacious, dedicated community coalition. It took a decade, but dozens of people revitalized the region, built Warner's community center, and set up service programs that became national models, turning "a blighted group of neighborhoods into one of Madison's most pleasant communities," according to the *Wisconsin State Journal*.[6]

The Northside Planning Council wanted to build community pride and a regional identity. With the help of a local philanthropist who was also a self-professed fireworks nut, the council decided to revive the Warner Park show.[7] They envisioned a regionwide Fourth of July bash to jump-start the local economy and bring in millions of dollars—Rhythm and Booms, "The mother of all displays."[8] The philanthropist backer hired a fireworks company that worked for the Rolling Stones, Disney World, Six Flags, Universal Studios, SeaWorld, and major cities.

The first Rhythm and Booms featured five tons of explosives and an F-16 flyover by the Wisconsin Air National Guard. For the show's finale, pyrotechnicians debuted a "dripping chrysanthemum" in Warner's wetland—the largest firework explosive ever detonated in the United States. The mortar was just slightly smaller than the gun diameter on the battleship USS *Wisconsin,* organizers told reporters.[9]

By all accounts, that first year was a wild success. At least for humans.

**AT APPROXIMATELY 5:30 A.M. ON THE MORNING AFTER THE FIRST RHYTHM AND BOOMS, GENE** Dellinger, the owner of a bait shop on Warner Park's edge, saw something "puzzling."

Dellinger was driving down Forster Drive, which runs along

Warner's wetland, on his way to go fishing, when he suddenly had to hit his brakes. A line of painted turtles and crayfish was climbing out of the wetland, crossing the street in front of him, and slowly crawling up a gentle rise into a suburban neighborhood. In nearly five decades of fishing, Dellinger had never seen anything like it. He wondered if the animals were leaving the wetland because of the fireworks nine hours earlier.[10]

Some neighbors wondered, too, about the debris littering their yards, gardens, and swimming pools. A mother who lived a block from the park, in the same neighborhood where the turtles and crayfish were headed, wanted to know what chemicals were in the fireworks trash that landed in the garden she fed her family out of.

Rhythm and Booms nearly died the second year because of money troubles. No one knew the event's real cost or how much money it raised. And the event was costing the city hundreds of staff hours for planning meetings and overtime pay to police. The show continued, but by the third year, Warner Park's city councilors asked the city not to fund the fireworks.[11]

Some Northside Planning Council organizers were also fed up. They felt like the event no longer belonged to the Warner area. One was disturbed by how guests from Madison's wealthier neighborhoods behaved in Warner. She angrily recounted picking up half-nibbled chocolate-covered strawberries dropped on park lawns in and around the VIP tent.

"It was horrible, backbreaking work. The longer it lasted, the more jaded I got. I called it 'the day from hell.'"[12]

Another volunteer picked up dead goldfish in sandwich bags that onlookers had dropped on the grass. A fireworks concession had given away the goldfish as prizes. The dead fish really bothered this volunteer. They also bothered Lauren Cheever, a middle school student. In a letter to the *Wisconsin State Journal*, she wrote: "I don't know what anybody else would call it, but I call it animal abuse. Fish are living and breathing creatures. Shouldn't they be treated with more respect?"[13]

Despite money woes, neighbors' complaints, hospitalization of fireworks spectators for second- and third-degree burns, city councilors' entreaties, and warnings from environmentalists trying to protect subsistence fishing in local waters, the show continued. Rhythm and Booms had become "a tradition." Some neighbors feared that to continue complaining would be "unpatriotic."[14]

In 2004, Warner Park got a new city councilor. Brian Benford, one of Madison's first African American councilors, asked Madison to move the fireworks to the city's coliseum. Benford was from a Milwaukee civil rights warrior family. He loved Warner Park and thought there were "a million teachable moments" in it. He wanted to see families camping in the park and "kids just lying down in the grass." He'd worked with kids in summer camps and had seen how urban kids without access to nature could get sucked into gangs that glorified death and guns.

Benford was particularly concerned about crime and public safety during the event. Because there were so many people, he feared the show was a perfect opportunity for gang recruitment. The police agreed. They "dreaded" Rhythm and Booms. But when Benford told police he wanted to stop it, they said, "You don't understand what you're up against."[15]

Benford met with Terry Kelly, the main organizer, to share neighbors' complaints about debris. Kelly insisted that they always picked up everything the morning after.[16] Benford decided to see for himself.

"I put on hip waders afterwards and kicked plastic to the top of the water [in Warner's wetland]," Benford told me. "I told Kelly that if one [sandhill] crane ate one of those things—we shouldn't do this. It was a real big deal to me . . . Nature was stolen from so many urban people and our ability to connect with nature. This is a social justice issue," he said.*

The city denied Benford's request to move the show. So Benford and local environmental activists started pushing to test Warner's

---

* In interviews on June 24, 2015, and July 1, 2015, Benford also complained about the increasing use of Warner Park for noisy events like rock concerts and baseball games. He felt like the neighborhood "was kind of getting pounded." Benford was backed up by the decades-long work of environmental activists Jim and Maria Powell, who founded the Madison Environmental Justice Organization (MEJO). MEJO was the first to try to measure the impact of toxins from pesticides, stormwater runoff, and fireworks on local waters and groundwater.

waters. The city's public health department "balked," but the activists' dogged efforts led to the first fireworks impact study on Warner's waters in 2005. The study concluded that the fireworks resulted in "reduced water quality."[17] The city did not test the sediment or plants or measure air pollution.

**WHEN WE MOVED TO MADISON, I DIDN'T CARE ABOUT THE FIREWORKS THAT FIRST SUMMER,** and I certainly never thought I'd dedicate an entire dissertation chapter to them. My attitude was the same as most people's: So what? It's just once a year. What harm could it do? I'd grown up in Southern California, twenty minutes from Disneyland. My family loved to gather on summer evenings on our porch to watch the spectacular nightly Disney fireworks from miles away. I loved them as much as any kid; I never thought about pollution. And for my parents, who had adopted this country, the fireworks were as American as hot dogs.

But as I studied press coverage of two decades of Rhythm and Booms for my dissertation and interviewed dozens of Northsiders, I detected a historical pattern. Anyone who had tried to protect the park's waters and wildlife got stonewalled and eventually worn down—whether it was councilor Benford, the activists who worked with him, or the Wild Ones, who'd tried to stop the park's wild side from being paved over. Every few years people complained and testified before commissions. A reporter wrote an article or two. And then they were ignored. Twenty years after Rhythm and Booms began, city councilors' surveys showed that 50 percent of Northsiders did not want the fireworks. But city officials ignored that half of the population until Wild Warner started squalling like a thickety flock of furious catbirds.

Our decision to fight the fireworks did not come easy. We were tired of fighting on so many fronts—the wetland, the geese, the trees, the paths. Even after three years together, we still didn't agree about Rhythm and Booms. But we were becoming increasingly concerned about the impact on the wetland and the animals. The birds of Warner Park had just finished raising their first family by late June. Nervous bird parents were teaching young ones how to forage and avoid predators. On the morning after the fireworks, the park was eerily quiet, as if many birds had fled. I had no idea where they went. But I found dozens of ducks and geese hiding in a canal on the park's edge during and after the event. And every year as the crowds arrived, we watched the sandhill crane parents walk their two small flightless chicks across the soccer fields, along the marsh edge, up to the train tracks and out of the park. The crane pair was so popular that their photo covered a wall twenty feet high inside Warner's community center (and the whole feathered family often stared through the glass wall window as public meetings went on). Cranes can live over twenty-five years, usually mate for life, and are faithful to their territories. This same pair flew back to Warner every February or March with a bugling announcement heard for 2.5 miles that made neighbors joyfully declare, "The cranes are back!" So I couldn't understand why no one said a word when fireworks enthusiasts ran over one of those chicks.

Then they started knocking down and smashing some of my birdhouses (one summer, somebody slapped a "Go Army" sticker on a bluebird house). And as they drove away from the park, fireworks fans ran over dozens and dozens of Warner rabbits who had hopped out of the park en masse during and after the explosions.

"So many dead bunnies!" one neighbor later exclaimed.

Wild Warner was particularly worried about Warner's four bat species. In less than a decade, white-nose syndrome, a disease that starves bats to death, had killed over 90 percent of some US species. During a study, Wisconsin wildlife experts caught twenty bats in one hour on our wetland's edge, all healthy. They thought there was a bat roost in Warner Park. The fireworks show was held right when the babies were emerging to head to the water. This was terrible timing, a scientist told us, because bats have very sensitive ears.[18] Like the migratory birds of Warner Park, the bats were also loyal to their places and had probably been roosting in the park for many years. (Some bat species can live twenty-five to thirty-five years.) The bats blasted out of their roost in a disturbed cloud when the fireworks began.

**OBSERVATIONS LIKE THESE WERE ALL WE HAD BECAUSE THERE WERE ALMOST NO SCIEN**tific studies of fireworks' impacts on wildlife at that time. But this is the most obvious impact: Since most animals have much keener hearing than we do, when they hear large detonations, animals great and small panic and may flee, heading into traffic, like the Warner geese, cranes, and rabbits. It happens with deer and coyote and pet canines all over the United States during July Fourth celebrations.[19] For animal shelters and wildlife rehabbers, early July is an "all hands on deck" emergency, when shelters take in the most runaway dogs.[20]

Bird behavior during fireworks is harder to study, since events are usually at night and scientists can't easily observe how wild animals behave then. But on New Year's Eve in 2010, scientists got a serious look at the impacts of pyrotechnics in Beebe, Arkansas, when someone tossed fireworks into trees where thousands of blackbirds were roosting at night.

"A scene straight out of Alfred Hitchcock . . . Thousands of birds rained from the sky," NPR reported.[21] An ornithologist counted at least 5,000 red-winged blackbirds, European starlings, common grackles, and brown-headed cowbirds dead from blunt-force trauma. The birds exploded out of the roost at night and crashed into cars, trees, buildings, and one another.

The most conclusive evidence on fireworks' impacts on birds is from a three-year radar study in the Netherlands, where citizens ignite 23.8 million pounds of fireworks annually, mostly on New Year's Eve. Europe's most important wintering grounds for waterfowl, the Netherlands provide shelter to two million geese.

The researchers discovered that until midnight, the birds stayed put. But just a few minutes later when the fireworks started, their radar screens lit up: "We detected massive bird movement . . . all over the country." The large, illuminated blobs on the radar showed hundreds of thousands of birds fleeing their lakes, wetlands, and neighborhoods, and staying airborne forty-five minutes or longer. Some flew nearly a third of a mile high and stayed there. Some birds flew miles from their wintering grounds. In the dense smog created by the fireworks, researchers suspected some birds could not find their way back. The situation was even worse for birds fleeing fireworks in stormy weather.[22]

Since birds are used to thunderstorms, it's logical to assume that fireworks would not affect them. But scientists have found that for wildlife and birds in particular, fireworks are very different from thunderstorms or hurricanes. Birds can detect the barometric pressure drop hours, even days, before a major hurricane or storm, allowing them to flee or take shelter. But the sudden noise and light from fireworks provoke what biologists call "a surprise effect," which can cause panic and maybe even pain. A 2015 study of 133 firework shows and 88 avian species, primarily in Germany and the United States, determined that birds do not adapt to fireworks. Some abandon nesting areas. Some species suffer significant physical stress and even die of fright. Many species panic and flee: "Young birds that have not yet learned to fly become easy prey, have accidents or get lost completely." The study concluded that "fireworks increase the risk of mortality for individual birds, and, thus, the death rate of the bird population."[23]

Researchers recommended halting fireworks and extremely loud explosions near protected areas, roosting sites, and inland waters, particularly along coasts where seabirds breed in colonies.[24] Scientists in California and Argentina have documented how seabirds abandoned their coastline nests after beach fireworks shows.[25]

I personally witnessed two incidents in the park that showed the detrimental impact of the fireworks on both wildlife and humans. Just ten days before Rhythm and Booms, I was biking through the park one summer when I came across a painted turtle digging a nest in the muddy soil right beside the asphalt. She was at least eight inches in diameter, with a dark green shell and brilliant orange stripes on her neck. I'd seen an extended family of these turtles, as many as twenty-three sunning together on the marsh island's shore. This one had her back turned to me while she used first one scaly hind leg, then the other, to dig a hole in her own steady reptilian rhythm.

She dug for at least twenty minutes, stopping occasionally to rest, and excavated a hole four to six inches deep. When people approached, she sped up. But finally she stopped, and with her head up and her body down in the hole, she laid eleven or twelve pearly white eggs. When she finished, she covered the eggs carefully with mud and sand and plugged the tiny entrance with her back feet, using those feet like hands. After she closed the entrance, she pulled up clover and grass with her back feet and laid the grasses on top as camouflage. The nest was invisible. She then turned and crossed the bike path right in front of me, returning to the wetland. The tall grasses swayed and rustled as she disappeared.

I placed a large branch next to her nest and dashed home to call Wisconsin's wildlife agency. This nest was too close to the bike path. In ten days, fireworks organizers were claiming that 200,000 people would be tromping through this park. Even if that number was wildly inflated, workers were already rumbling around in heavy maintenance vehicles to set up the show. This was probably just one turtle nest of dozens about to get squashed.

For three days I called the wildlife agency, frantic. A guy finally called back.

You're right, he said. Terrible place for a turtle's nest. You need to move it. You're the best chance those eggs have.

What I needed to do was dig up the nest, remove the eggs, and then dig another nest and make sure the hole I dug was in the right kind of soil and shaped like a flask, with a tiny tunnel 1.5 inches wide and 3 inches long at the top leading into the egg chamber—the exit tunnel for the hatchlings. The egg's hatching would depend on whether I dug the nest correctly, he told me, because turtles are temperature-dependent and the eggs wouldn't hatch if I didn't do it right. Of course, it also depended on the weather and whether or not water got into the nest. So dig close to the water, he advised, but not too close. And then make sure to camouflage it, just like that turtle did, because if I didn't, the park's foxes, minks, raccoons, and those off-leash dogs could dig it up. But even if they didn't, when the little turtles came out, if my replacement nest was too far from the water, then the crows, hawks, bullfrogs, and snapping turtles might eat the hatchlings before they even reached the wetland.

You can do it, he told me.

I told him I'd think about it.

I'm a Libra, so I had to agonize over it first. If I did it wrong, I'd be killing turtles, or at least potential turtles. If I didn't do anything, the eggs might get squashed or the entrance to that tiny tunnel so compacted by all the fireworks watchers that the little hatchlings would be trapped inside and starve to death. I imagined them desperately scratching to reach the surface and becoming entombed like tiny mummies. And then I started thinking about playing God. What right did I have to think that I could possibly dig a turtle's nest and shape that mud hole into a clay flask with an exit tunnel 1.5 inches wide and 3 inches long, when I was hopeless working with clay and had failed the only pottery class I'd ever taken, ending up with a set of hideous crooked candlesticks instead of a salad bowl?

So I came up with Plan B.

Parks employees were dropping giant plastic trash cans all over Warner. I dragged an empty one on top of the nest and clamped the lid down. This worked: the golf carts and trucks skirted around that trash can. I watched the nest for a year, but no little turtles ever emerged.

**THE SECOND INCIDENT THAT CONVINCED ME THAT WE HAD TO STOP THE FIREWORKS HAP**pened in 2011, the summer fireworks organizers promised "the biggest Rhythm and Booms" ever. At first light on the morning of Sunday, July 1, just hours after Rhythm and Booms, Wild Warner chair Tim Nelson and I slid two kayaks into Warner's lagoon. The day was gorgeous and clear, already warm. A marsh wren called from the cattails as we paddled toward the island.

The water looked surprisingly clean. I searched for telltale wires or strange colors on the surface, but other than lily pad clumps, a floating beer can, a soggy tennis ball, and thousands of minuscule leaf fragments covering the lagoon, I couldn't see anything that conveyed the mad scramble the night before when a fire raged on that island.

A painted turtle sunned itself at the end of a log, leathery back legs splayed out in turtle joy. I snapped several pictures and lay back to float. Maybe the damage wasn't so bad.

And then a computer voice in my brain, my inner Alexa, said, *It's July, you idiot—not October. The leaves haven't fallen yet.*

I jerked up, rocking the kayak. I leaned over as close as I could to the water's surface to examine those thousands and thousands of tiny "leaf fragments."

It was the fireworks—the shells, labels, everything disintegrating into the water. Tim and I were watching the last of the debris sink and disappear, three hours before the city's cleanup team would even arrive. In between "leaf" fragments, the water was bubbling like a sickening chemical soup. My stomach contracted. I started frantically shooting photos and gathered every shred of paper I could find with Chinese lettering and the word "TOXIC" and the name of the Chinese factory where the fireworks had been manufactured. I wondered what that town looked like. I wondered about the people who made these mortars, how handling the chemicals affected their health and their waters. I remembered stories in *The New York Times* about elderly Chinese rioting over water pollution, photos of old men and women setting cars on fire. I admired them.

The belted kingfisher was already back, rattling up and down the shoreline as I scooped up trash. A few geese and mallards had just returned. In the cattails I found a six-inch diameter turtle shell wedged between reeds. I grabbed it to take to the kids. But it wasn't a turtle shell, just like the leaf fragments weren't leaf fragments. It was a rocket casing.

Tim and I pulled up to the marsh island and stepped into the first foot of shoreline water. There we found coiled wire, fuses, rope, plastic, and other heavy debris that had sunk hours earlier. We collected two large trash bags.

**JUST FIVE DAYS AFTER OUR KAYAK SURVEY, MY COLLEGE STUDENTS HAD ORGANIZED A WILD** Warner Water World for the kids. More than thirty showed up, ages one to thirteen, some with their parents. They splashed. They squealed. And they caught a very unhappy-looking American toad.

"Oh my god. He's so *cuuuuute,*" shouted a little girl in pink as she examined the toad inside his new Tupperware prison.

"Did you know toads drink through their butt?" college mentor Christa Seidl told the children.

Sarah, another intern, took the toad out to show the young explorers how he could chirp like a bird. The toad obliged. The children gasped.

My interns set up learning stations along Warner's shoreline as dragonflies buzzed through the cattails. A male red-winged blackbird clucked in alarm as children armed with small pink-and-white nets combed the wetland's edge, hunting for knowledge. Netted treasures included lily pads, algae, a beer can, and mounds of duckweed.

"This is so cool!" shouted a little girl while she gently examined dragonfly larvae. My students explained to her how the dragonfly lived.

At another station, Christa showed the kids how to use special paper strips to measure the water's pH. They learned that Warner wetland's pH was between 6.5 and 7.0. My students explained that it was just "a little acidic."

"What's acidic, anyway?" asked an eight-year-old boy. This earnest young explorer was wearing his new binoculars upside down, but I kept my beak shut.

The boy learned that acidic water is sour. He also learned that it's harder for frogs and creatures with shells to live in it. Acidity is often caused by pollutants, acid rain, or outside chemicals, my interns told him.

The children played in the wetland as the sun set. Swallows and kingbirds twittered overhead, and fish surfaced to feast on insects. Painted turtles joined them, triangular snouts jutting out of the water. A school of tiny bullhead fish swam by fast in a shimmering black cloud.

But that wasn't all that was shimmering in the water. As I stood with my student interns on the dog park bridge afterward, laughing over the things the children had said, my interns suddenly noticed a strange metallic sheen on the surface. I remembered that sickening bubbling I'd seen just days earlier.

I emailed Madison's director of environmental health to ask if it was safe for the kids to play in Warner's wetland. He wrote back that some of the compounds in the fireworks were insoluble. These compounds would bind to Warner's sediment, and "should not be a health issue, unless the sediment is disturbed . . . My recommendation would be to not come into contact with the sediment; however, if you (your class) need to contact it, then proper hand washing should be completed as soon as possible."[26]

I thought about the joyous scene of all those kids wading into the water with their little nets, toes squishing in that sediment. Some of these kids had never held a toad. Some of their parents didn't even own washers and dryers, much less cars to take them camping. They didn't go to national parks—Warner Park was their national park.

I realized then that it wasn't just the animals in Warner Park who were invisible. The children in my neighborhood were, too.

**AFTER THE HEALTH DEPARTMENT'S EMAIL, WILD WARNER DECIDED THAT WE HAD TO FIND** out what exactly was in that water. Heddie's daughter, "Get Shit Done" Marie, suggested we invite Paul du Vair, an award-winning high school science teacher, to a Wild Warner meeting. An aquatic biologist, Du Vair had been studying Warner's wetland for over four decades. He'd found two springs and discovered that our wetland was the only home of the only native freshwater jellyfish in the entire region, *Pectinella magnifica,* the Magnificent Bryozoan (of several thousand bryozoans, all but nineteen are marine). Warner's quiet waters without motorboats provided a safe haven for this tiny jellyfish.

Every June, Du Vair and his high school students dropped nets 6 feet deep and 25 feet long into Warner's waters to take samples. His young research team had found that despite the wetland's degradation, Warner was still one of just two critical breeding grounds and fish nurseries for fish swimming in from neighboring Lake Mendota. But it was in big trouble. In addition to finding eighteen species of baby fish in Warner's waters, Du Vair and his students found tricycles, bicycles, fishing equipment, purses, brassieres, plastic tampon applicators, soiled diapers, underpants, license plates, driver's licenses, money, class rings and other jewelry, plastic, and cans—all flushed in by the city's stormwater system. Some students had gotten injured by the trash and had to get stitches. Ninety-three percent of this trash was not biodegradable.

"You've got to fight the trash," Du Vair told Wild Warner. "The lagoon is getting shallower fast. It's filling in. What would take a thousand years to fill through sedimentation is being done in twenty-three years in Warner Lagoon."

He also warned that the trash could be increasing winter fish kills in Warner's wetland by squeezing the fish into a smaller area and depriving them of oxygen. Nearly every spring thousands of dead fish rotted on Warner's shores.

Du Vair and his students' research helped us understand that our fight to stop Rhythm and Booms was much bigger than the fireworks. We were trying to protect a wetland that was a vital filter and fish nursery for Lake Mendota, our city's largest and deepest lake.

**JIM VOLUNTEERED TO PUSH THE CITY TO DO PRE- AND POST-FIREWORK WATER TESTS. HE** began attending monthly meetings of the city's toothless committee on the environment, on which we had a powerful new ally: Anita Weier. A former environmental reporter, Anita had recently been elected to the city council. She'd gone on one of Wild Warner's public walks, and it had changed the way she viewed the park. She and Jim would lobby for a year to pressure the city to test the water.

Meanwhile, I volunteered to research the fireworks chemicals. I figured it would be easy. There had to be a paper trail in a place as environmentally conscious as Madison.

I spent a month that summer digging through city archives and skimming a thousand pages of firework permits. There were memos about launch sites. There were memos about shaving Warner's lawns and burning the marsh island. There were memos about gang violence.

And there were hundreds of pages of lists of fireworks, their names as interesting as avian names: "Rainbow 49 Shot Z Shaped Fan Cake," "Dragon eggs with coconut tree pistil and tail," "Crackling Kamuro with dancing meteor shower pistil." But there wasn't a single sentence about the heavy metals and chemicals that fireworks organizers were dumping in Warner. When city councilors asked fireworks organizers for this information, they said the chemical content was "proprietary."

Fireworks organizers had insisted for years that there was no plastic in their fireworks. As I plowed through that stack, I discovered that every permit contained this paragraph in bold:

> **Please understand that there are still small parts of the shell assembly that might include plastic pieces (ex: burst tube, inserts, timer chamber, etc.) These plastic pieces are essential to the proper function of the shell.**

I called the city fire inspector who signed the permits, thinking that he had to know what was in the fireworks. He told me, "Fireworks are corrosive. They'll eat the paint on cars, the shell on the vehicles. So they have to fall at least 450 feet away from vehicles."

"So what's in the fireworks that could corrode metal and eat paint on cars?"

"Oh, nobody keeps track of this stuff," he said.[27]

Jim did his own calculations. He interviewed a national fireworks expert, who told him that metal salts provide the colors in fireworks—5 to 15 percent of pyrotechnics' weight. Rhythm and Booms exploded five tons of fireworks every year in Warner. The metals didn't disappear. This meant Rhythm and Booms had deposited 165 to 750 pounds of heavy metals into Warner's waters every year for twenty-one years, or a total of 3,300 to 15,000 pounds.[28]

A YEAR LATER, EARLY IN THE SUMMER OF 2012, WE GOT SOME UNEXPECTED HELP. IT WAS ONE of those bucolic midwestern nights when sane people were paddleboarding on Madison's lakes or picnicking with their families and enjoying the fleeting glorious weather that makes Midwest winters tolerable. But there we were, Jim and I, sitting in another drab meeting room, facing a long table of bored park commissioners. There were six people in the audience.

I was there to give Jim moral support. After nearly a year of sitting in infuriating meetings of Madison's committee on the environment, Jim and Anita, our city councilor, had badgered the city into testing Warner's waters later that summer. City officials kept insisting there was no money for studies, although the city had already spent over $1 million on the fireworks. Jim and Anita had to help raise the money.

Jim was there to inform commissioners that the study would take place before and after the fireworks. Commissioners had no questions or comments. Jim sat down.

Then a woman approached the podium. She was carrying four bulging dog poop bags. Fiftyish and fit with a pointy chin, she had short stylish golden curls and designer glasses—a classy "Don't fuck with me" look. She set the bags down gingerly in front of the microphone.

*This is kinda weird,* I thought.

Her name was Lucy. She told commissioners that she lived next to Madison's oldest park, a tiny green patch with ancient trees in a historic district. I knew the place—it was in a wealthy neighborhood downtown. She was there with neighbors to complain about a once-upon-a-time-charming Sunday-afternoon music festival that had morphed into a four-day monster with vendor trucks and shed-sized sound systems parked on the tree roots, compacting the soil.

"We hurt every time we lose one," she told commissioners, referring to the trees.

The handful of neighbors in the audience nodded sadly.

I rolled my eyes, thinking, *Oh god, a rich NIMBY who probably "enjoys" the fireworks from her "historic" neighborhood miles away from us.*

But I was dead wrong. Lucy was no NIMBY, and she wasn't there just to defend her neighborhood park. Lucy was a dogged devotee of Warner's dog park, where every single day she got to watch her favorite creature on earth, Warner's great blue heron. And then she looked down Warner's shoreline, she told commissioners, where that heron stood, preening, and among the old doggy tennis balls and algae, she saw plastic fuses and other weird stuff.

Lucy strode up to the table and handed poop bags stuffed with fireworks debris to commissioners as "a little gift." They chuckled. Oh, Lucy, ha-ha-ha. (I didn't know it, but they all knew each other. Lucy was a university dean and combative school board member, famed for throwing out the occasional f-bomb at public meetings.)

A few weeks later, Lucy sent a one-page single-spaced email to parks commissioners, city councilors, the county supervisor, the mayor, and the press, along with photos. It was the first of a volley of e-grenades listing her every visit to Warner Park and the contents of Tupperwares full of fuses and ignition devices that she was collecting. She ended her first e-grenade with these questions:

1. Where did planners think this debris was going to go?
2. Where in the Warner Park area (or any city park) would it be acceptable for this debris to go?
3. If I was caught leaving a pile of trash this size in any of our parks, would I be cited?
4. Am I correct in thinking I can put this in my trash for city pickup? It does have quite a bit of chemical residue.

In one of Lucy's e-grenades, she accused fireworks organizers and wealthier Madisonians of using Warner's wetland as "their own personal toilet." She wasn't afraid to say what some Northsiders had been thinking for two decades.

Lucy, aka the Trash Lady, was at Wild Warner's next meeting, our newest firebrand. Because of her, from 2012 to 2013, we all became trash collectors, toting buckets of really smelly crap to dump at public meetings. She showed us another way forward, a kind of Tai Chi move—that the fireworks trash was a gift you could give right back.

As our fireworks battle made headlines, we began to attract other new members. It reminded me of how our group suddenly grew when the Great Geese Wars revved up. These new Wild Warnerites were full of fire and wonder. Students, wildlife photographers, neighbors—they were seeing, really seeing, Warner Park and its animals for the first time, amazed that we shared this place with so many marvelous creatures. With the fervor of religious converts, they told tender stories about the cranes and the beavers during our group's story-sharing time. Jim and I and Marie and Tim and Jack and the other oldies smiled and exchanged knowing glances. And then there were the invisible new members who joined, paid dues, and supported us quietly. Some were city officials. They hadn't trusted our group the first year or two, but now they'd changed their minds. Like the businessman in a city council meeting who surreptitiously passed me a tiny scrap of carefully folded paper that said, "I'm with you in spirit."

The Northside Planning Council, the same organization that had started the fireworks show, gave us their prestigious North Star Award. At the awards banquet, the master of ceremonies said, "Wild Warner has fundamentally changed our view of Warner Park, reminding us that the park's natural areas and its diverse wildlife are wild and beautiful and should be enjoyed now and for generations to come."

But despite the publicity and the trash we were dumping at public meetings, fireworks organizers still insisted that 90 percent of the mortars disintegrated in the water. And they didn't contain plastic and they weren't made in China.[29]

**THE WATER STUDY THAT JIM AND ANITA HAD FOUGHT SO HARD FOR GAVE US NEW AMMUNI**tion. Researchers sampled Warner's waters, plants, and sediment and found that "the annual Rhythm and Booms fireworks display has measurable impact on the environment. The most discernible impact is the spike in perchlorate."[30] Within twelve hours of the fireworks, Warner's perchlorate levels soared from 17 to 1,329 times pre-firework levels. Their report stated: "Detection of perchlorate in surface water and groundwater has recently fueled studies around the United States, and there has been particular interest in its potential threat to drinking water. At elevated levels, perchlorate may have adverse health effects because ingestion of the chemical can interfere with iodide uptake into the thyroid gland in mammals and aquatic vertebrates, such as fish. However, the dose/response relationship has not yet been adequately assessed." (A decade later, as I finished this book, on May 9, 2023, a federal appeals court ordered the EPA to regulate perchlorates, reversing a Trump-era rollback, because studies had found that they also interfered with human thyroid function and could cause brain damage in infants.)[31]

Warner's vegetation and plant study showed levels "nearing toxicity" for perchlorate and the heavy metal salts used to create those beautiful greens (barium), purples (strontium), and whites (magnesium). Researchers found the highest concentrations of aluminum (silver), barium (green), and iron (the firework sparks) in Warner's duckweed: aluminum levels were more than double the "very high mark." The critical level for iron in most plants is 50 parts per million, but some of Warner's duckweed registered 3515 parts per million.

Duckweed is an important avian food source for the at least nineteen duck, swan, and geese species who migrated through or raised families in Warner's wetland. How would eating duckweed loaded with aluminum, barium, and iron affect these animals? I couldn't find any studies on these issues.

The research team advised the city to "curtail" the fireworks until a scientifically reviewed study could determine impacts on Warner's wildlife. But public health officials and fireworks organizers said the study was "inconclusive." They didn't think another study was necessary or want to spend resources on it.[32]

Jim and Anita had fought so hard for one year to get this study. The city wasn't going to fund another, no matter how much trash we dumped at public meetings. We needed serious help.

I called the EPA and sent the study to an environmental geochemist and perchlorate expert in the agency's Ground Water and Ecosystems Restoration Research division. When Richard Wilkin read it, he said, "The aqueous perchlorate concentration was pretty high. There was one screamer . . . close to 50 parts per billion. That's an increase of 500-fold. That's pretty significant."[33]

Back to meeting after meeting we trudged—me, Jack Hurst, Jim, Tim, the Trash Lady, Marie, Anita, and others—to throw the EPA's analysis at the city along with the trash (we should have brought duckweed for fireworks organizers to taste). But fireworks organizers compared the amount of chemicals blasted into our wetland to the amount in a daily vitamin.[34] We got nowhere, and a few of us nearly got tossed out of meetings. The only thing that kept us going was that at the end of each infuriating session, we'd go to our local pizza joint, drink some beer, yell, pound the table, and end up laughing. We loved the park, we loved the animals in it, and after four years of fighting together, we'd come to love each other. That comradeship was our rocket propellant. Our flock.

The city's year-round planning machine for the 2013 firework show kicked into high gear, study results, toxic duckweed, and the EPA be damned. We'd exhausted every angle and all we had to show for it were buckets of smelly trash in our basements. We needed an avian intervention, another Thunder-Pumper miracle.

This time, my students found it.

**AT 6:00 P.M. ON A SATURDAY IN MARCH, I WAS SITTING IN FRONT OF OUR WOODSTOVE,** studying the flames. Outside the light was dimming, it was around 25 degrees and snowing, with several inches on the ground. It was my favorite kind of winter night—a curl-up-on-the-couch-with-a-glass-of-port-and-chocolate-cake night, along with your dog and a good book. But there was an insistent knocking on my door. I sighed and opened it. There stood two of my students, buzzing with energy—super bird mentors Jocelyn and Christa. They'd been in the thicket the day before looking for fungi, they told me practically shouting, when they nearly stepped on two American woodcocks.

*Yeah, right,* I thought. They probably saw those fluffy mourning doves that hide in the thicket in the winter. Because this city park with free-range dogs and feral cats couldn't possibly be a place for a ground-foraging, ground-nesting, ungainly, medium-sized bird that was one of the slowest fliers on the planet. I'd never seen one in the park. I'd never even imagined one could be in this park. This bird lived in my brain and heart. It was a nearly mythical creature, one that Aldo Leopold had immortalized in his *Sand County Almanac.*

But this was Christa, a born scientist and ecology nerd who'd exhaustively studied every living thing she could find. She'd been a mentor in my very first birding class, and she and Jocelyn were the same students who'd noticed that metallic sheen in Warner's wetland. I set down the glass of port and pulled on my warmest boots and jacket.

Not only was I dubious that my star students had found two woodcocks, I was even more dubious we'd find them in the middle of a snowstorm. Male woodcocks prefer clear, dry weather so they can be seen by the ladies. But Jocelyn and I spread out in the meadow and stood like frozen statues while Christa crept into the Big Thicket to hide. We agreed to communicate only through chickadee calls. And we settled in for a long frozen watch. Snowflakes hit my face, covering my binoculars. Robins *wheep*ed, cardinals softly clicked, and six bluebirds migrating through stopped to eat sumac berries. I could hear mallards honking from the frozen marsh. All the birds were either feeding or settling in. And still we stood in that meadow like Stonehenge slabs, becoming living, breathing sundials as the setting sun cast our tall shadows on the snow. Only our eyeballs moved, scanning continuously. We kept our ears open to hear the famous whistle-twitter of a woodcock's wings. As dusk descended, grays blanketing golds and tawny dried stems of goldenrod sticking up through the snow, Jocelyn spied the red fox poking at a half-eaten carp he'd dragged up from the wetland. Lights began to switch on in houses. I couldn't hear the whistling of a woodcock's wings, but I could hear car doors slamming, tires squealing, a student coughing. After an hour of being a meadow statue, I was so damn cold. But I couldn't give up. What kind of example would I be for my students?

And then from under the sumac there was a quick flash of orange-rust, a flapping of wings, and a roundish body emerged for a second. It was just a flash, but I saw it twice in that last snowy hour. Not enough to be 100 percent sure, but enough to get up before dawn. I didn't even get as far as the meadow before I heard it by Heddie's yard, the woodcock's signature call that birders call peenting, a strange buzzing that sounds like a giant insect being squashed. I listened to the bird for a while, trying not to jump up and down. Later I called my PhD advisor, Jack, and Paul Noeldner because I needed witnesses. So on another morning we huddled in my driveway drinking coffee and listening to that strange buzzy *peent* in the meadow. Afterward, Paul and I scoured Warner until we found three male woodcocks hurtling through the air.

**WHO WOULD HAVE BELIEVED THAT ONE OF THE STRANGEST-LOOKING AVIANS ON THE PLANET,** a bird with monikers like the Mud Bat, the Bogsucker, the Timberdoodle, and my favorite, Mr. Big-Eyes, would be the bird that helped us stop the largest fireworks show in the Midwest?

A bird of paradoxes, the American woodcock belongs to the shorebird family. Yet you'll never see this bird on a seashore; it hides in brushy thickets and woods. When I say shorebirds, you're thinking elegant long-necked ballerinas of the tides, the colors of sand and sky, white, black, and gray on impossibly thin legs, pirouetting on the beach, birds like the greater and lesser yellowlegs (yes, their legs are yellow), willets, godwits, curlews, terns, whimbrels.

Mostly delicate-looking creatures, they have pointy wings and dart like arrows over the sea. But the woodcock has short stumpy legs, no neck to speak of, and rounded wings to fly in the woods; instead of a graceful arrow, it is a football with wings. Its nearly three-inch-long beak looks like a stubby pencil someone glued to its knob of a head.

Most birds are either diurnal or nocturnal. But Mr. Big-Eyes is a bird of the nether hours, the times in between, of dusk and dawn. Bird biographer extraordinaire Arthur Cleveland Bent described the woodcock as "this mysterious hermit of the alders, this recluse of the boggy thickets, this wood nymph of crepuscular habits."[35]

Not only different from its closest avian relatives, the woodcock is different from most birds, period. Its brain is upside down, and the giant eyeballs near the top of its head give it almost 360-degree binocular views. It has a beak that is flexible—the top half bends back like a weird finger—and the whole thing acts as a sensor with many nerve endings. As the bird probes thickets and woods, poking holes, it can detect vibrations coming from its wriggling, crawling food source, mainly earthworms. Although woodcocks will eat seeds and other insects, its fate is tied to the earthworm, and the earthworm's fate is tied to the leaf litter that sustains it, as well as the soil. A recycler of leaf litter and soil, the woodcock depends on the soft, variegated shades of leaf litter to hide and nest in.

The woodcock also sings differently from most birds. Instead of using its syrinx, the male bird uses his feathers as a musical instrument. Three of his outer flight feathers are narrower than the rest. As he hurtles through the sky, the air whizzes through notches between the skinnier feathers, making the eerie, hypnotic twittering he uses to entrance his female audience during courtship rituals.

Hunters have always loved the woodcock because it is a tasty game bird. When colonists discovered it, the woodcock became such a popular dinner item that by the late 1700s, some states had to start protecting it.[36] But what has mesmerized bird lovers for centuries and given this bird what British bird historian Mark Cocker calls a cult-like following, is that when this flying football takes to the sky, he becomes an avian Fred Astaire, especially in the moonlight. For Aldo Leopold and his family living in his beloved rural Wisconsin "shack" in the 1940s, the family evenings watching "The Woodcock Show" was better than TV. In "Sky Dance," Leopold wrote:

> You seat yourself under a bush to the east of the dance floor and wait, watching the sunset for the woodcock's arrival. He flies in low from some neighboring thicket . . . and at once begins the overture: a series of queer throaty *peents* spaced about two seconds apart . . . Suddenly the peenting ceases and the bird flutters skyward in a series of wide spirals, emitting a musical twitter. Up and up he goes, the spirals steeper and smaller, the twittering louder and louder, until the performer is only a speck in the sky. Then, without warning, he tumbles like a crippled plane, giving voice in a soft liquid warble.[37]

The woodcock also dances on land. The bird places one foot forward and then rocks its body back and forth two to four times while keeping its head steady, before advancing with the other foot. Scientists believe this bird's version of the Electric Slide is a signal to predators that the woodcock knows it's being watched and is ready to bolt. But instead of blasting off, the bird just rocks, which takes less energy.[38]

Google "Woodcock Booty Bob" and "Woodcock Funk" to see how YouTubers have capitalized on the woodcock's dance skills. If jazz or reggae are more your speed, try "Woodcock Rumba," "Reggae-Dancing Woodcock," or "Woodcock Dance Party," if you're into electronic music. I prefer disco because the woodcock's rhythm syncs perfectly with Michael Jackson's "Billie Jean" and the Bee Gees' "Stayin' Alive."

In 1927, Arthur Cleveland Bent described how the woodcock "clings with tenacity to its favorite haunts, even when closely encroached upon by civilization." He described the banks of a stream running through his land near the heart of a city, where woodcocks kept returning even after the area was built up. I realized that this was exactly what had happened in our park. Generations of woodcocks must have been coming to this place when it was a cluster of farms. Our avian Fred Astaire was a link to Warner's farming past, a feathered time machine.

**IN APRIL 2013, JUST THREE MONTHS BEFORE THE FIREWORKS, WILD WARNER DECIDED TO** make a last-ditch appeal to the place where it all started—the parks commission. We'd spent two years at committee on the environment meetings, city council meetings, watershed commissions, and meetings with the Department of Natural Resources, all to no avail. But parks commissioners had to approve the fireworks by individual vote before any other body. We'd been sitting in their meetings four years, one Wednesday a month since that very first 2009 meeting to stop the city's development plan. We respected the commissioners and liked them. And they respected our work. It was worth one more try.

Tim, Paul, Trash Lady Lucy, Anita, and I divided up topics. We were going to hit them with everything we had. Marie and I had just finished a classy brochure listing Warner's 134 bird species. No other park in Madison had its own bird brochure. My job was to present it. Tim was going to explain how he'd volunteered on lake cleanups for twenty-five years and how the fireworks were making a mockery of these efforts. Lucy was presenting more trash and a Department of Defense perchlorate "Best Practices" memo. And our city councilor was going to request environmentally friendly, non-perchlorate fireworks.

Wild Warner education coordinator Paul Noeldner wanted to focus on just one Warner species: Mr. Big-Eyes, the bird he'd fallen hopelessly in love with. He brought a woodcock puppet he'd made. Then Paul held it up and played the bird's strange *peent* call on his phone during his testimony.

"The sky dance of the woodcocks is the fireworks we love. Woodcocks have huge eyes and big brains. They are very smart. Show them some respect . . . Woodcocks can eat twenty-two earthworms in five minutes . . . Keep chemicals out of my earthworms is what the woodcock would say!"

Earthworms are bioaccumulators of toxins, which means they store the toxins they consume, especially heavy metals and lead.[39] Because earthworms are woodcocks' main food source, whatever we put into the soil, we put into our woodcocks. And that meant all that perchlorate and heavy-metal-soaked firework trash that rained down on their thicket and meadow and then got shredded into leaf-like fragments by the giant mowers. Woodcocks can die of heavy metal poisoning. Paul had just made this connection very real.

Before the fireworks vote, Commissioner Bittern-Bill stated:

> One thing that friends of Wild Warner have highlighted over the last few years is the quality of habitat. I think it's kind of amazing. I know of three other places where we have woodcocks . . . And I'm very pleased to hear that there are woodcocks in Warner Park. That made my night . . . I'm a fireworks fan, but I think that fireworks over a wetland that feeds into our biggest lake is inappropriate. I can't support this continuation of Shock and Awe anymore. So I will be voting no. I can't stand up and play the call of an American bittern and then vote to shell their home. Those 134 birds we're all excited about—let's stop firebombing them.

Commissioner Madelyn Leopold followed with a similar statement. She voted no along with Bittern-Bill.

The commissioners voted to approve the fireworks that summer, 4–2. However, those two no votes weren't just any no votes. Bill Barker was a respected geologist and the former president of the parks commission. And Madelyn Leopold was the granddaughter of Aldo Leopold, the man who wrote "Sky Dance," sharing his woodcocks with the world. I knew that night that it was the beginning of the end for Rhythm and Booms.

I will never forget the morning that Jack Hurst called us, very excited, just after that meeting. In his marvelous basement where I'd found half my dissertation, Jack had discovered an old photo of that fireworks hill before Rhythm and Booms started, the spit that jutted into the wetland. Except that there was no hill. It was a flat upland prairie.

Jim called the Army Corps of Engineers and the Department of Natural Resources to give them the photograph. They began investigating. When the phone finally rang with the verdict, Jim nearly fell out of his chair. Jack's old photo proved that the city of Madison had been filling in Warner's wetland with sand and construction debris without a permit for twenty years—a violation of the Clean Water Act.

There were just days before the next fireworks show. Jim was on the evening news, standing in front of the wetland, his hair blowing in the wind, waving that damning photo before the camera and pointing at Fireworks Hill. The rest of us started pounding the pavement, shouting at meetings about the Clean Water Act, the blown-up turtle nests, the endangered bat roost. But the giant Rhythm and Booms machine had already kicked into high gear. Fireworks organizers still dominated city meetings. We couldn't stop it.

Two weeks after that fireworks show, Mayor Paul Soglin held a press conference downtown. He announced that the 2013 Rhythm and Booms was the last—the city was moving the fireworks out of Warner Park. What he did not tell the press was that because of Jack Hurst's photo and the investigation it spurred, the Army Corps of Engineers and the state of Wisconsin had just ordered the city to dismantle Fireworks Hill and restore that upland prairie. For the next two months, we watched a continual stream of heavy trucks carting all that crap out of Warner's wetland. Goodbye, Iwo Jima.

After twenty-one years, the war on our wetland—on the birds, on the bats, on the turtles—was finally over. But not the war on Madison's waters. At the very same press conference, the mayor announced that the fireworks show was moving to Madison's Lake Monona; Rhythm and Booms had just become Shake the Lake. Jack Hurst, Jim, Tim, and I sat stupefied as we listened to the "big plans" for next year and the grand event, "bigger and better," backed by one of Madison's wealthiest environmental groups, the so-called Clean Lakes Alliance.

The new Shake the Lake would be more "environmentally friendly," organizers told the press. They weren't going to throw toxic barium into Lake Monona, so there'd be no green fireworks.

Within a week, city councilors and activists from Lake Monona were asking us for help. Jack Hurst, Jim, other Wild Warnerites, and I donned our testimony suits, grabbed some stinky trash, and headed to regional water commission meetings. We joined citizens imploring on behalf of the fish and birds and fishermen and people living around Lake Monona, raising a hellcat-catbird alarm for the entire Yahara watershed.* Because the people who had accused Wild Warner of being "a bunch of NIMBYs" were wrong. We weren't NIMBYs. We were NIABYs—Not In Anyone's Backyard. Or anyone's waters. You don't throw tons of trash into a 60-acre wetland or a 3,359-acre lake or the Gulf of Mexico. All waters are sacred. Jim and I learned this the hard way in New Orleans.

**TO CELEBRATE OUR VICTORY, AFTER THE LAST TRUCK RUMBLED OUT WITH ALL THAT FIRE**works debris, Wild Warner had a champagne and seed-planting session on the now flat and empty former launch pad. We laughed and swigged champagne, still in disbelief. I watched Jack Hurst, the man who had spent fifty years of his life and counting at public meetings trying to defend that little wetland, his face suffused with joy, tossing small clouds of prairie seeds into the air.

Over the next two years, we watched those seeds take root and that buried upland prairie reemerge, along with a new Northside Nature Center inside the Warner Park Community Center, thanks to Paul Noeldner. In 2015, for the first time, the parks department began funding "nature-recreation" activities in Warner in what would become a model for all Madison parks.

That second fireworks-free summer, after five years of research, I'd finally finished my dissertation. I didn't want to leave, but it was time to go. I'd landed a great teaching job at the University of Vermont. Jim

* Shake the Lake was finally canceled in 2020 after a shooting during the fireworks.

and I were moving to Burlington, where I hoped to replicate the kids' birding program, this time as a real job. (I trained another graduate student in Madison to take over the kids' nature club in Warner Park.) There were no good jobs for PhDs like me in Madison unless you wanted to teach for a pittance, drive a taxi, or deliver pizza. I had over $100,000 in college loans. The PhD had been a crazy gamble, but one that I could not afford to lose.

Vermont was another cold northern place I knew nothing about. If Madison had originally conjured up visions of *Fargo* and serial killers, the only thing that came to mind when I thought of Vermont was . . . maple syrup. And then I remembered that my father—now eight years gone—had driven through Vermont on his way to Canada. He loved it, he'd told me, because "it looked like Ireland."

But my heart was still heavy. I didn't care how beautiful Vermont was—I couldn't imagine driving away from Heddie and Jack Hurst and Greg the snowblower, my gray catbird and my Warner Park.

I'd lived in so many places where I still have friends who are family. I'd loved all these places and I was sad when I left them. But this was a different kind of leaving, a great ripping in my chest. As I packed up the house, I remembered a story my mother told my brothers and me, every Christmas. On a gray, cold December morning in 1958, she and my father had climbed the gangplank of a massive ship in an Irish harbor. They were headed to America. Sheets of rain came down as my mother's father, my grandfather, and her brother, my uncle, stood on the dock in gray suits, sharing an umbrella, watching her slip away across the Atlantic.

My mother did not want to leave Ireland, she told my brothers and me. She would be homesick for years, and she still called Ireland home after six decades in the United States. "But 'have to' is a grand master," she said.

**THE MOVERS HAD COME. OUR CAR WAS PACKED TO THE RAFTERS. HEDDIE HAD TUCKED A** basket of homemade currant jellies and a fresh-baked poppy-seed cake under our front seat.

Before we drove away, Jim and I took our last walk through Warner Park. We carried a six-inch blue-and-white virgin statue with us. Our Lady of Lakeview, I called her, after our old neighborhood in New Orleans. She was one of the only items I'd saved from the ruins of that house. Right after Katrina I'd found her standing sorrowfully in her tiny alcove in our hallway, muddy, but unbroken. I'd dragged her to Madison for good luck, to help me get my PhD. I didn't need her anymore.

We strolled to that former fireworks launch pad, now prairie. The sounds of late summer surrounded us: worried goldfinch parents scolding; spooked teenage wood ducks skittering across the water, their wings whistling; a song sparrow on the shoreline calling, defending his territory; and the soft rustling and hopping of tiny crickets as we tromped through the tall drying grasses. Swallows patrolled the huge lotus patch on the water, rich with bugs to catch. The grasses began to sway and part slightly as some small animal lumbered toward us to check us out. Two feet away, the rustling abruptly stopped.

In just two years, the animals had reclaimed this place, once a site of black tarps, sand, armed guards, and scaffolds of mortars. It had become a field of brown-eyed susans, deep blue lobelia, and other tiny prairie flowers so thick you could hardly walk through them. Insects of all kinds were deep in it, humming and hopping, tiny wasps and bees buzzing.

We wedged Our Lady of Lakeview tightly between the branches of a willow so she looked out over the water and faced the marsh island. I asked her to protect the park and all its feathered, finned, and furred residents, and to please do a better job than she had protecting that little house in New Orleans.

# Epilogue

*The heart is an eternal nomad.*

JOHN O'DONOHUE

*Seven years later, October 2022, Burlington, Vermont*

I'D BE LYING IF I SAID THAT IT WAS EASY TO MOVE TO VERMONT. AS BEAUTIFUL AS IT is, it wasn't Warner Park, and I was disconsolate for a long time. We had rented a small condo, sight unseen, in Burlington. There was no new neighbor with a hot apple cake waiting to greet us. The nearest green space was a small cemetery, and instead of facing a park, we faced a parking lot. I felt like I'd lost everything that mattered—the individual birds I knew, my human neighbors, the view of the spruce through the living room window, the mother oak, the meadows. Now I was staring at asphalt, and at night, instead of a dark sleeping park across the street and moonlight pouring in, I had to lower the blinds to shut out the streetlight's harsh glare.

But there was no time to mourn or even unpack; school started in thirteen days. That first school week was the tenth anniversary of Hurricane Katrina. A professor teaching UVM's largest environmental course asked me to give a climate disaster lecture to over two hundred eighteen-year-olds. I stood in front of that auditorium and swore and cried and told the whole story. By the time it was over, some students were crying, too. I ended on a hopeful note, announcing that I was going to replicate the Warner kids' birding program in Burlington. But I needed their help.

A long line formed, and one by one, students shook my hand. They thanked me for telling the truth about climate change. They thanked me for coming to UVM. Within minutes, my sign-up sheet of future birding mentors was full. All I needed was another dynamo principal and some great birds.

I found the principal one month later, while walking my dog past an elementary school just a few blocks from our condo. A sign outside read "Family Dinner Night," so I tied up the dog and went inside to poke around. In the hallway, I ran into Graham Clarke, the principal of Flynn Elementary School, an older hippie-looking guy with stringy gray hair wearing a Cuban guayabera. It took us all of five minutes to figure out that we'd been in Nicaragua at the same time, three decades earlier. When I told him about the birding program I wanted to set up pairing kids with UVM students, the principal ditched Family Dinner Night to take me on an hour-long tour of his beautiful school and the gardens he'd installed. I walked out with an agreement to begin a children's program three months later.

Now I needed some birds to get through my days. A large, ugly rectangular fenced trash enclosure swathed in green plastic sat in the condo parking lot. I took a broken picnic table, set it behind the trash enclosure so it faced a line of scrawny junipers, and hung up two feeders. I began my mornings at this new birding station, drinking coffee and shielded from the wind by the trash. A dapper male cardinal was the first to land on the feeder, and then his mate, followed by a noisy scolding army of tufted titmice, Groucho-Marx-like mustachioed birds. I didn't know this species. They were hilarious, tiny comics with jaunty crests.

Despite my new feathered friends and wonderful students, by that first February in Vermont, I began to feel very restless, like the caged migratory birds that scientists use to study migration. Ornithologists call it *Zugunruhe*, German for "migratory anxiety" or "migratory restlessness." By observing caged migratory birds, scientists have learned that right before their species migrates, the captive birds begin to move, pointing themselves in the direction their flock is headed, and fluttering or "whirring" their wings for hours and months until the migration period is over.

My *Zugunruhe* was because I knew that the red-winged blackbird advance scouts would be landing in Warner's marsh any day now, rattling away. And in March, Warner Park's phoebe would arrive and perch on that beam in the picnic shelter where Jan used to sit with his oxygen tank.

Then I dreamed I was in Warner Park. I was watching Mr. Blue—that first bluebird—as he perched on top of his little meadow house. I woke up the next morning to an email in my inbox from a Warner Park neighbor, telling me that they'd just seen the first bluebird in the park. I realized that I'd internalized Warner Park's rhythms and microseasons. That marsh was like an airport, and the marsh's flight information display board announcing avian arrivals and departures was embedded in my hippocampus. Soon afterward, on the night of March 21, 2016, I was staring out our condo window at that parking lot, watching the moon rise from behind my birding-trash station. Suddenly I knew with absolute certainty that the woodcocks were sky-dancing in Warner. I called Wild Warner comrade Paul Noeldner in Madison, and even though Paul was recovering from the flu, he said he'd jump in his clothes and drive to Warner.

An hour later Paul called from Sled Hill, talking low and fast and wildly excited. Three woodcocks were peenting as he drove into the park. And one had just flown over his head.

Although the Warner woodcocks were 1,046.3 miles away, they helped jolt me out of a depression. Because of them, I went to find woodcocks in a Burlington park where I now go every March at 4:30 a.m. with a thermos of hot coffee. And because I dreamed about Mr. Blue, I contacted the manager of that barren cemetery a block away and set up two little bluebird houses there. Bluebird and chickadee parents moved right in and have raised families every summer since, to the delight of mourners visiting graves and the groundskeeper, a huge bear of a man and refugee from Bosnia, whose eyes filled with tears the first time I opened one of those houses to show him the baby bluebirds.

**IN THE FALL OF 2022, I RETURNED TO MADISON ON UNIVERSITY BUSINESS. ALTHOUGH I'D** stayed in touch with our Wild Warner comrades, I was afraid to see Warner Park again. I was afraid they weren't telling me everything and that the thicket had been burned out, that the bur oak was sick, and that the wild side of the park had been tamed. My plane landed just before midnight. I'd promised myself I would go straight to the hotel to sleep. But once I climbed in that rental car, a zombie driver took over and I ended up parked next to the thicket in the dark.

I sat for a minute in that chemically perfumed rental car thinking about how the world was on fire, with a war raging in Europe and a pandemic still sputtering. And then I rolled down the windows and listened to the rustling and collective exhale of hundreds of tiny beings, tucked into Warner for the night in that looming green mass of thicketiness.

The next morning at dawn, I parked the car next to Warner's dog park. It was 49 degrees, the sky was a clear pale blue, and a slight breeze was blowing from the northwest, the cool breath of a Midwest fall. The first thing I heard was the sandhill crane pair's bugling duet, a sound I hadn't heard in seven years because sandhills cranes are very rare in Vermont. The northern flicker, a gorgeous golden-black woodpecker, was the next Warner bird to greet the dawn with a high-pitched monkey-like chatter. And then a catbird on the railroad tracks joined the chorus with its "ratchet" alarm call.

From the top of Sled Hill, I watched the sun rise, crying tears of joy as I scanned the golden meadows, taller than when Jim and I left. Everything we'd fought for was alive and thriving, reaching for the sky, living breathing evidence of over 150 hours of public meetings. Tiny trees we'd planted years ago that Wild Warner had watered by hand were spreading their crowns. The thicket was more thickety than ever, full of young catbirds eating wild grapes (two meowled at me when I faked a catbird alarm call). And the mother bur oak still towered over the meadow. I wrapped my arms around her girth, not even reaching halfway round, and lay my cheek against her deeply furrowed trunk. Thanks to Dr. Google, I'd discovered that our bur oak was not only the mascot of Warner Park. In 2016, during seasons

13 and 14 of *Grey's Anatomy*, a gorgeous black-and-white photo of this tree graced the wall of Dr. Meredith Grey's bedroom, where it was seen by millions of devoted viewers. Photographer Keith Dotson told me his Warner oak photo is a bestseller favored by *Grey's Anatomy* fans in the UK, Germany, Belgium, and Australia.*

And then I walked along the former concrete canal once full of trash and broken glass that ran along the street where the great horned owls nested—the same canal that Wild Warner had fought to keep from being covered with rubber as an "experiment." It was now the restored Castle Creek, named after the farmer who once owned this land. One of Wild Warner's rewilding projects in coordination with the city, the creek meandered along the park's edge in front of apartments filled with children. Marsh plants taller than me lined the banks, and a new wooden bridge crossed it, the waters running clear beneath, flowing toward Warner's wetland.

After my walk, I did what I'd always done in Warner Park: I headed over to Heddie's to sit in her backyard drinking coffee out of a silver pot and eating a lemon chiffon cake that her daughter Marie had baked. Heddie was now ninety-two, living alone since her husband had died. We laughed and conspired as migrating hummingbirds sipped from her feeders just a few feet away and a steady stream of chickadees, nuthatches, cardinals, and sparrows ate the seed she put out for them. Later that day I saw Jack Hurst. At eighty-nine, Jack was still a leading member of Wild Warner and still testifying for the fish and the waters at public meetings. In 2022, the city of Madison dedicated a fishing pier to him extending out over Warner's wetland.

Tim Nelson was still Wild Warner's goose egg addler in chief, who estimated that he'd smothered at least 500 eggs in corn oil in a decade to keep the geese population under control. "Get Shit Done" Marie helped the group attract major grants for programming and leads Boy Scout troops into Warner to plant hundreds of trees. And since 2014, Paul Noeldner has led nature walks all over Madison every

* All three photos on the walls of Dr. Grey's bedroom are of Warner Park, one of the geese we fought to save.

single week, rain, shine, or snow, educating thousands of people. If there's a Nobel Prize for environmental education, Paul deserves it. He and UW-Madison's Anke Keuser took over the birding class and the children's program.

Jack Kloppenburg, my former PhD advisor, retired from teaching to found the Open Source Seed Initiative (OSSI), a global organization to "free the seed" from corporate control. When he's not in Ethiopia or Argentina or Mexico helping farmers fight the Monsantos and DuPonts of the world, Jack's at home painting birds, some of them in scenes in Warner Park. His paintings sell out at art fairs.

Wild Warner's current chair, Kathlean Wolf, lives on the park's border where I found that first great horned owl's nest. A master naturalist, Kathlean has documented nearly a hundred species of slime molds, algae, and fungi just in Warner's woods. She's also passionate about edible Warner Park; she makes flour out of Warner cattail pollen and bakes cattail cookies.

Because of all my comrades' hard work, in the spring of 2020, as the pandemic hit and the world stopped, for the first time in Warner Park's history a pair of bald eagles built a nest on the marsh island, that former fireworks trash can. To the amazement of the hundreds of Madisonians who lined up to watch the nest through a scope, Warner's eagle parents raised one feisty eaglet, COVID be damned.*

As for the rebellious daughter who swore she would never be a teacher, I hold Teatimes for students on campus, with tea and homemade brownies served on my Irish grandmother's china (my mother is having the last laugh, wherever she is). When it begins to snow in Vermont, I take my students to a Secret Classroom deep in the woods near campus for discussions about racism, implicit bias, and social justice. We hike there with firewood, s'mores ingredients, and coffee, and build a big fire inside the wooden lean-to.

I've learned that once you open that door in your students' hearts

* The eagles not only lifted Madisonians' spirits during the pandemic, but seemed to solve Warner's geese birth control problem. According to Tim Nelson, when the eagles moved in, the geese stopped nesting on the marsh island. Tim no longer has to addle eggs because there are none.

and show them they can make a difference in the world—that their one precious voice matters—there's no stopping them. They pop into your office asking if you want to climb a tree and look for nuthatches; they whine if you're not there. Your office hours are mobbed. On the small table outside your office, like offerings on an altar they leave tiny thank-you cards of hand-drawn birds alongside shiny apples and flowers and poems and anonymous Valentines; hand paintings of eagles, snowy owls, nuthatches, turtles, mergansers; and even a red-breasted nuthatch felted and knitted by Spencer, an eighteen-year-old from Connecticut who raises ducklings and wants to become an oyster farmer to fight climate change. On a spring Saturday afternoon, your doorbell rings at home and there stands a shy girl named Emily holding a mason jar of fiddlehead ferns she has just picked in the woods. "Sauté them in butter and garlic," she tells you, apologizing for surprising you at home.

Love is a powerful force. I could never have imagined seventeen years ago in New Orleans that my interest in one cardinal would grow into Wild Warner, a neighborhood environmental defense group that is celebrating its thirteenth anniversary and that has become a model for nature education, as well as environmental education programs at three universities and elementary and middle schools in Wisconsin, Vermont, and Rhode Island that have trained over five hundred birding mentors who have worked with at least a thousand children. (Brown University replicated the birding program in Providence in 2019.)

Today I use many of the activist strategies I learned from the birds of Warner Park to teach. My environmental undergraduates in turn use their new citizenship skills to work for change all over the United States. It is my greatest pride and joy to watch students who have never attended a public meeting, never published, never protested, never testified, suddenly do it all in one semester. In the eight years I've been teaching at UVM, I've watched my students testify before a standing-room-only audience at the Vermont legislature to stop a pipeline. Over two dozen of my students have published op-eds in their home newspapers across the country. I've driven a van full of passionate students dressed in their Sunday best to meet with the governor and ask him to sign meaningful gun legislation (he did).*

In 2018, a shy student fell so madly in love with the tiny golden-winged warbler—the bird that can hear a storm hundreds of miles away—that she began protesting in Vermont to protect the bird's summer nesting grounds threatened by a natural gas pipeline. This fight led her across the Canadian border to testify in Montreal at an international stockholders' meeting to stop natural gas fracking on indigenous lands. After she graduated, Vermont's most important environmental group hired her as their "extreme energy organizer" to stop pipelines. Along with local activists, she launched a two-year pipeline investigation that forced Vermont's public utilities commission to conduct an independent investigation into environmental and construction violations, which led state regulators to cite Vermont Gas for serious violations. Five years later as I write this epilogue, all major expansions have been canceled. And now this student and a crew of joyful, creative young people are working to shut down the last coal plant in New England.

There is a mighty flock of former birding mentors from both UW-Madison and UVM working all over the country as teachers, environmental educators, urban planners, land stewards, lawyers, journalists, researchers, and environmental activists. They are scientists, nature center directors, and school garden coordinators. A former Madison mentor became the director of one of the largest wildlife rehabilitation hospitals in the nation. And star mentor Christa Seidl, who noticed that fireworks toxic sheen in Warner's wetland and who discovered Warner's first woodcock, became Dr. Seidl, a disease ecologist and international expert in avian malaria.

But what makes my heart sing is that every single class became a flock. Some students found lifelong friends in my birding classes. A few even fell in love.

* After the Parkland shooting, Governor Phil Scott met with hundreds of students, including our group, before signing a historic bill in the spring of 2018.

**TWO SUMMERS AGO IN BURLINGTON, I CONVINCED MY NEIGHBORS GEORGE AND SUSAN TO** let me place a tiny birdhouse on the strip of front lawn where they usually park a car. They were skeptical that birds would nest there, but it was mid-April and I could see chickadees all over the neighborhood, urgently seeking nesting spots. I put up the tiny house and walked home, and one hour later Susan called to report that a chickadee pair was zooming in and out, carting the moss and fur they use to build their soft nest. They laid eight rust-and-cream speckled eggs—a record for the tiny houses I monitor.

Eighteen days later, those chicks were ready to fledge. On Fledge Morning, five chickadees flew out of the house, but the three smallest stayed inside overnight. I worried because I've had runty chickadees die in houses after the rest of their siblings zip off into the world. I went over early the next morning to check on them. The three cheeped softly from inside the house as I approached, while their five liberated siblings called from the branches of a Norway maple just ten feet away. As George and Susan stood by, I opened that tiny door, plucked out the three huddled chickadee runts, one by one, and from the runway of my flattened palm they raised those new wings and zipped straight to their parents and siblings waiting on that maple branch.

And this is what I get to do every semester for some of my students: help them fledge. I hold them in the palm of my hand for a second, look them in the eyes, and tell them, *You can do it.* Then I watch them take that first perfect flight.

# Author's Note

For recommended reading and an action guide to build your own feisty flock, please visit the author's website at trishokane.org.

# Acknowledgments

I HAD TO LIVE THIS BOOK BEFORE I COULD WRITE IT. IN ADDITION TO MY PARENTS, THE following exceptional humans showed me the way: Xabier Gorostiaga, a visionary Jesuit who invited me to join a very messy revolution; former professor-mentors Nora Hamilton and Carol Thompson, who taught me that academics must be citizens; PhD advisor Jack Kloppenburg, whom I found through Google (Google and God both start with a G); and my partner in life, wordcraft, dogs, chickens, justice, sunsets, and political mischief, Jim Carrier, whom I met at the Southern Poverty Law Center in Montgomery, Alabama, twenty-five years ago. On our first date, he said that he'd sailed up the Alabama River "into the land of hate, to find love." I snorted and thought, *That's the best line I've ever heard.*

My heartfelt thanks to the mighty flocks that made this story possible: in New Orleans—Allison Plyer, Alice-Anne Krishnan, and the kind and courageous Loyola students and colleagues who welcomed a stranger at the worst moment in their lives; in Alabama—loving comrades Penny and Kendal Weaver, Rhonda Brownstein, the Downes family, Lecia Brooks, Georgette Norman and Nomad Steward, Emily Elias, Kent Garrett, Mike Luckett, Carol Potok, Nan Fairley, Susan Starr, Morris Dees, Richard Cohen, Robert Delk, and Cheryl and Wayne Sabel; in Madison—Wild Warner flockmates Jack Hurst, Tim Nelson, Paul Noeldner, Marie and Heddie

Jacobsen, Mike Rewey, Dave Meyer, Dolores Kester, Karen Hickel, Andy Tauber, Marian Celesnik, Marlene Hardick, Paul Rusk, Lucy Mathiak, Kathlean Wolf, and Deb and Barry Riese; Madison parks commissioners Bill Barker, Madelyn Leopold, Janet Parker, Betty Chewning, and Emmanuel Scarborough, and Madison Parks staff Eric Knepp, Craig Klinke, and the employees who take care of Madison's beautiful parks; Peter Cannon, Mary Lacy, Ann Waidelich, Bill Lueders; Paul Robbins and Jim Miller at the Nelson Institute for Environmental Studies; Tia Nelson, who gave the children their first field guides; Jeffrey Lewis, Russ Hefty, Kurt Welke, Si Widstrand, Greg Weller, Mayor Satya Rhodes-Conway, former mayor Paul Soglin, and Anita Weier; PhD mentors Randy Stoecker, Anna Pidgeon, Cal DeWitt, William Cronon, Samuel Dennis, and Mark Berres; and dedicated Sherman Middle School staff, particularly Mike Hernandez, Betsy Peterson, and Julie Wilke.

In Burlington, many thanks to incredible colleagues at the University of Vermont who supported this work—former dean Nancy Mathews, Allan Strong, Amy Seidl, Rachelle Gould, Marie Vea-Fagnant, Walt Poleman, Nathan Sanders, and IT wizard Seth O'Brien; Jill Sayre Wolcott; in the Burlington School District—Graham Clarke, Mandi Harris, and Abbie Israel; and Nancy Jacobs at Brown University, who created her own "Bird Buddies" program.

The following very early readers and editors helped hatch this story: Megan McFarland—my best book buddy since the first day of fourth grade, Rachel Herzl-Betz, Stacy Taeuber, Robin W. Kimmerer, Amy Seidl, Rachelle Gould, Valerie Berg, and dogged fact-checker Olivia Box. My deep gratitude goes to the gifted editing, production, and design team at Ecco and HarperCollins, especially editor Sarah Murphy, whose talent matches her enthusiasm, as well as editor Rachel Sargent, cover artist Vivian Rowe, and interior designer Alison Bloomer.

Illustrator Valerie Downes is a conjurer with a pencil who breathed life into the birds of Warner Park. I am honored to work with her.

My agent, Barney Karpfinger, is his own murmuration (with the help of Sam Chidley). He became this story's midwife, coaxing it out of me, counseling me through tough bits, and even editing it. I especially enjoy his email queries about why wild turkeys have sex in his driveway and why kingfishers fly far from water. Thank you, Barney, for making a dream come true.

And finally, my deepest admiration and love go to the feral flock of former students and children who taught me everything I know (and do not know) about teaching. Thank you for the privilege of walking beside you every Wednesday afternoon.

# Notes

## PROLOGUE

1 Justin Lee Rasmussen, Spencer G. Sealy, and Richard J. Cannings, "Northern Saw-Whet Owl (*Aegolius acadicus*)," version 2.0 of *The Birds of North America*, ed. P. G. Rodewald, Cornell Lab of Ornithology, Ithaca, New York, 2008, doi: 10.2173/bna.42.

2 P. A. Taverner and B. H. Swales, "Notes on the Migration of the Saw-Whet Owl," *The Auk* 28, no. 3 (1911): 329–34, 331, http://www.jstor.org/stable/4070948.

3 John James Audubon, Plate 199: "Little Owl," in *The Birds of America: From Drawings Made in the United States and Their Territories* (New York, Philadelphia: J.J. Audubon; J.B. Chevalier, 1840), https://www.audubon.org/birds-of-america/little-owl.

4 This story is an excerpt from an article that originally appeared in *Orion*: Trish O'Kane, "Owls Among the Meteors," https://orionmagazine.org/article/owls-among-the-meteors/.

5 Zoey November, September 6, 2019.

6 Andrea Cavagna and Irene Giardina, "The Seventh Starling," *Significance* 5, no. 2 (2008): 62–66, https:// doi:10.1111/j.1740-9713.2008.00288.x.

7 Information is from interviews in 2022 with several scientists: Klara Norden (Princeton University), Vinod Saranathan (Krea University, India), Dakota McCoy (Stanford University), and Lorna Gibson (Massachusetts Institute of Technology).

8 "da Vinci Ornithopter," Wings of History Air Museum, https://www.wingsofhistory.org/da-vinci-ornithopter-model/.

9 Gina Wadas, "Avian-Inspired Engineering," Johns Hopkins Institute for NanoBioTechnology, January 31, 2022, https://inbt.jhu.edu/avian-inspired-engineering/.

10 S. A. Rogers, "Bird Biomimicry in Action: 12 Avian-Inspired Jets, Drones, and Cars," WebUrbanist, April 13, 2016, https://weburbanist.com/2016/04/13/bird-biomimicry-in-action-12-avian-inspired-jets-drones-cars/.

## CHAPTER 1: STRANGE TEACHERS

1 Coedited by writing teacher Ashley Gordon and designed by Valerie Downes.

2 In January 2022, the New Orleans city council voted unanimously to change the name to Allen Toussaint Boulevard.

3 Nicole Gelinas, "Who's Killing New Orleans?," *City Journal Magazine*, Autumn 2005.

4 According to the National Council on Disability (August 3, 2006), "The Impact of Hurricanes Katrina and Rita on People with Disabilities: A Look Back and Remaining Challenges," at least 155,000 people with disabilities lived in the hurricane zone, and a "disproportionate" number of the dead were victims with disabilities. The report stated: "Their needs were often overlooked or completely disregarded. Their evacuation, shelter, and recovery experiences differed vastly from the experiences of people without disabilities. People with disabilities were often unable to evacuate because transportation was inaccessible . . . Most evacuation buses did not have wheelchair lifts. Moreover, people with visual and hearing disabilities were unable to obtain necessary information . . . because said communication did not comply with federal law."

5 Greene did not know of recordings or studies of bird calls before approaching hurricanes. Email communication on November 21, 2021.

6 Christopher N. Templeton, Erick Greene, and Kate Davis, "Allometry of Alarm Calls: Black-Capped Chickadees Encode Information About Predator Size," *Science* 308, no. 5703 (2005): 1934–37, doi: 10.1126/science.1108841.

7 "News: What Do Birds Do in Hurricanes?," Audubon Florida, https://fl.audubon.org/news/what-do-birds-do-hurricanes.

8 Henry M. Streby, Gunnar R. Kramer, Sean M. Peterson, et al.,"Tornadic Storm Avoidance Behavior in Breeding Songbirds," *Current Biology* 25, no. 1 (2015): 98–102, doi: 10.1016/j.cub.2014.10.079.

9 Sara Yang, "Sensing Distant Tornadoes, Birds Flew the Coop: What Tipped Them Off?," *ScienceDaily*, University of California–Berkeley, http://www.sciencedaily.com/releases/2014/12/141218131415.htm.

10 Avian ecologists are still uncertain exactly where, when, and how birds began migrating between Latin America and the United States. This is a historical estimate drawn from different studies. See Leo Joseph, "Molecular Approaches to the Evolution and Ecology of Migration," in *Birds of Two Worlds: The Ecology and Evolution of Migration*, ed. Russell Greenberg and Peter P. Marra (Baltimore and London: Johns Hopkins University Press, 2005), 23.

11 Sathya Achia Abraham, "Scientists Examine Fall Migratory Pathways and Habits of Whimbrels," Phys.org/Biology/Ecology, September 28, 2012, https://phys.org/news/2012-09-scientists-fall-migratory-pathways-habits.html.

12 Bryan Watts, "Farewell to Hope," Center for Conservation Biology, April 3, 2019, https://ccbbirds.org/2019/04/03/farewell-to-hope/.

13 Matthew S. Van Den Broeke, "Bioscatter Transport by Tropical Cyclones: Insights from 10 Years in the Atlantic Basin," *Remote Sensing in Ecology and Conservation* 8, no. 1 (2022): 18–31, https://doi.org/10.1002/rse2.225; Scott Schrage, "Feather Phenomenon: Radar Indicates Stronger Hurricanes Trap, Transport More Birds," Nebraska Today, University of Nebraska–Lincoln, October 11, 2021.

14 Interview with Matthew Van Den Broeke on August 26, 2022.
15 Mark Dionne, Céline Maurice, Jean Gauthier, and François Shaffer, "Impact of Hurricane Wilma on Migrating Birds: The Case of the Chimney Swift," *Wilson Journal of Ornithology* 120, no. 4 (2008): 784–92, doi: 10.1676/07-123.1.
16 "Ralph the Pelican Arrives in New U.S. Home and Is Found to Be a Girl," *Globe and Mail*, March 9, 2011, https://www.theglobeandmail.com/news/national/ralph-the-pelican-arrives-in-new-us-home-and-is-found-to-be-a-girl/article570049/.
17 Josh Magness, "This Hawk Took Refuge from Harvey in His Cab. It Wouldn't Leave—So He Took It Home," *Miami Herald*, August 28, 2017, https://www.miamiherald.com/news/nation-world/national/article169740307.html.
18 Christopher M. Heckscher, "A Nearctic-Neotropical Migratory Songbird's Nesting Phenology and Clutch Size Are Predictors of Accumulated Cyclone Energy," *Scientific Reports* 8, no. 1 (2018): 9899, doi: 10.1038/s41598-018-28302-3.
19 Andy McGlashen, "Are These Birds Better Than Computers at Predicting Hurricane Seasons?," *Audubon Magazine*, August 13, 2019, https://www.audubon.org/news/are-these-birds-better-computers-predicting-hurricane-seasons.

**CHAPTER 2: C'EST LEVEE**

1 Lyanda Lynn Haupt, *Mozart's Starling* (New York: Little, Brown Spark, 2017), 233. I owe so much to Haupt's rapturous science writing. I use Haupt's *Rare Encounters with Ordinary Birds* (Seattle: Sasquatch Books, 2001) as a teaching text.

**CHAPTER 3: SONG OF THE HOUSE SPARROW**

1 Mark Cocker, *Birds & People* (London: Jonathan Cape, 2013), 484.
2 J. Denis Summers-Smith, *The House Sparrow*, Collins New Naturalist series (London: Collins, 1963), 226.
3 Richard Collins, "Tale of the Fall of the Domino Sparrow," *Irish Examiner*, December 18, 2006, https://www.irishexaminer.com/opinion/columnists/arid-20020970.html.
4 Native species like house wrens and chickadees will also destroy bluebird eggs to take over these houses.
5 Summers-Smith, *The House Sparrow*.
6 Emma Bubola, "On the Menu at a Lunch in Italy: Protected Songbirds," *New York Times*, April 20, 2021, https://www.nytimes.com/2021/04/20/world/europe/italy-lunch-songbirds.html.
7 Michael P. Moulton, Wendell P. Cropper Jr., Michael L. Avery, and Linda E. Moulton, "The Earliest House Sparrow Introductions to North America," USDA National Wildlife Services Staff Publications, 2010, 961, https://digitalcommons.unl.edu/icwdm_usdanwrc/961. There is a debate over how and

exactly when house sparrows arrived to this continent. Another reason they were brought over is that people believed they would eat insects that damaged crops. This assumption is still contested among biologists, since adult birds are seedeaters but require insect protein to feed to their young. I personally have watched house sparrows catch and eat insects.

8 Cocker, *Birds & People,* 485.

9 Lyanda Lynn Haupt, *The Urban Bestiary: Encountering the Everyday Wild* (New York: Little, Brown Spark, 2013), 184.

10 Ann Vileisis, *Discovering the Unknown Landscape: A History of America's Wetlands* (Washington, DC: Island Press, 1997).

11 Summers-Smith, *The House Sparrow,* 227.

12 This entire account is drawn from Thomas E. Gaddis's *Birdman of Alcatraz: The Story of Robert Stroud* (Sausalito: Comstock Editions, 1989).

13 C. L. Stong, "The Amateur Scientist," *Scientific American* 197, no. 6 (1957): 143–54, http://www.jstor.org/stable/24942003.

14 Gaddis, *Birdman of Alcatraz,* 9.

15 Lauren Koenig, "Parrots Live in New York City. Here's How They Make It in the Urban Jungle," *Discover,* November 5, 2020, https://www.discovermagazine.com/planet-earth/parrots-live-in-new-york-city-heres-how-they-make-it-in-the-urban-jungle.

16 This account comes from my students' papers.

17 This figure comes from averaging the coastal land loss rate in Louisiana between 1985 and 2010, an average of 43 square kilometers annually, or "one football field per hour." See Giancarlo A. Restreppo et al., "Riverine Sediment Contribution to Distal Deltaic Wetlands: Fourleague Bay, LA," *Estuaries and Coasts* 42, no. 1 (2019): 55–67, https://www.jstor.org/stable/48703010.

### CHAPTER 4: OUR LADY OF THE APPLESAUCE

1 Evan P. Kingsley et al., "Identity and Novelty in the Avian Syrinx," *Proceedings of the National Academy of Sciences* 115, no. 41 (2018): 10209–217, doi: 10.1073/pnas.1804586115.

2 Robert J. Smith et al., "Gray Catbird (*Dumetella carolinensis*)," version 1.0 of *Birds of the World,* ed. A. F. Poole, Cornell Lab of Ornithology, Ithaca, New York, 2020, doi: 10.2173/bow.grycat.01.

3 Reptiles also can breathe unidirectionally but do not have air sacs.

4 Frank B. Gill and Richard O. Prum, *Ornithology* (New York: W. H. Freeman, 2019), 215.

5 Frances Wood, "Winter Wren, Champion Songster," *BirdNote,* April 9, 2011, https://www.birdnote.org/listen/shows/winter-wren-champion-songster.

6 Smith et al., "Gray Catbird (*Dumetella carolinensis*)."

7 Renee Hewitt, "Gray Catbird Is One Cool Cat with a Jazzy Song," *intoBirds,* August 1, 2018, https://intobirds.com/gray-catbird-is-one-cool-cat-with-a-jazzy-song/.

8 T. Gilbert Pearson, editor in chief, *Birds of America* (New York: Garden City Books, 1936), 178.

9 Alexander V. Arlton, *Songs and Other Sounds of Birds* (Parkland, WA: Alexander V. Arlton, 1949), 83.

10 I have reconstructed excerpts from Dr. Berres's lectures based on extensive notes and some recordings.

11 Michelle Nijhuis, "Friend or Foe? Crows Never Forget a Face, It Seems," *New York Times*, August 25, 2008, https://www.nytimes.com/2008/08/26/science/26crow.html.

12 "Do Birds Dream?," *All About Birds*, Cornell Lab of Ornithology, June 17, 2019, https://www.allaboutbirds.org/news/do-birds-dream/.

13 Rowan Hooper, "Jungle Crow," *Japan Times*, February 10, 2005.

14 Cornell University, "More Than 4 Billion Birds Stream Overhead During Fall Migration: Scientists Use Radar to Shed Light on the Massive Numbers of Migrating Birds and How Many May Not Return," *ScienceDaily*, September 17, 2018, https://www.sciencedaily.com/releases/2018/09/180917135942.htm.

**CHAPTER 5: THE QUIET BROKEN ONES**

1 Harmon P. Weeks Jr., "Eastern Phoebe (*Sayornis phoebe*)," version 1.0 of *Birds of the World*, ed. A. F. Poole, Cornell Lab of Ornithology, Ithaca, New York, 2020, doi: 10.2173/bow.easpho.01.

2 William Souder, *Under a Wild Sky: John James Audubon and the Making of the Birds of America* (New York: North Point Press, 2004), 67. There is some debate over whether this story is a myth. See Rebecca Heisman, "A Brief History of How Scientists Have Learned About Bird Migration," *Audubon Magazine*, Spring 2022, https://www.audubon.org/magazine/spring-2022/a-brief-history-how-scientists-have-learned-about.

3 Smithsonian Institute, "Insect Flight," information sheet no. 96, May 1999, https://www.si.edu/spotlight/buginfo/insect-flight. Flycatchers also eat some small fruits.

4 Arthur C. Bent, *Life Histories of North American Flycatchers, Larks, Swallows, and Their Allies (Order Passeriformes)* (New York: Dover Publications, 1963), 141.

5 T. Gilbert Pearson, editor in chief, *Birds of America* (New York: Garden City Books, 1936), 200.

6 Bent, *Life Histories of North American Flycatchers*, 147.

7 Sara O. Marberry, "A Conversation with Roger Ulrich," *Healthcare Design*, October 31, 2010, https://healthcaredesignmagazine.com/trends/architecture/conversation-roger-ulrich/.

8 Roger S. Ulrich, "View Through a Window May Influence Recovery from Surgery," *Science* 224, no. 4647 (April 1984): 420–21, doi: 10.1126/science.6143402.

9 For a summary of these studies, see the May and June 2019 issues of *Outside Magazine*, particularly "The Incredible Link Between Nature and Your

Emotions" by Aaron Reuben, June 11, 2019, https://www.outsideonline.com/health/wellness/nature-mental-health/#:~:text=His%20team%20found%20that%20when,in%20their%20lives%20or%20neighborhoods.

10 Frances E. Kuo, "Parks and Other Green Environments: 'Essential Components of a Healthy Human Habitat,'" *Australasian Parks and Leisure* 14, no. 1 (2011): 10. For a PDF of the executive summary of this report, see https://www.nrpa.org/globalassets/research/mingkuo-summary.jpg.

11 Kristine Engemann et al., "Residential Green Space in Childhood Is Associated with Lower Risk of Psychiatric Disorders from Adolescence into Adulthood," *Proceedings of the National Academy of Sciences* 116, no. 11 (2019): 5188–93, doi: 10.1073/pnas.1807504116.

12 Michael McCarthy, *Say Goodbye to the Cuckoo: Migratory Birds and the Impending Ecological Catastrophe* (Chicago: Ivan R. Dee Publisher, 2010), 44–45.

13 Unfortunately, by the 1960s and through the 1980s, Nightingale's ideas were buried in concrete, with hospital gardens in England becoming hospital parking lots, natural light from windows replaced by artificial lighting, and fresh air with air conditioning, according to Jane Findlay in "The Healing Landscape—The Influence of Florence Nightingale on Hospital Design," March 25, 2020, in the journal *Fira,* https://www.linkedin.com/pulse/healing-landscape-influence-florence-nightingale-hospital-findlay/.

14 Florence Nightingale, *Notes on Nursing: What It Is and What It Is Not* (New York: D. Appleton and Company, 1860), 58–59.

15 "Nightingale's Franciscan Spirituality," Niagara Anglican Diocese, September 2000, from *The Collected Works of Florence Nightingale,* University of Guelph. https://cwfn.uoguelph.ca/spirituality/nightingales-franciscan-spirituality/.

16 From *Life and Death of Athena: An Owlet from the Parthenon*, penned and published in 1855 by Nightingale's sister, Frances Parthenope Varney, electronic reproduction, L. Tom Perry Special Collections, Harold B. Lee Library, Brigham Young University.

17 A. C. Miller, L. C. Hickman, and G. K. Lemasters, "A Distraction Technique for Control of Burn Pain," *Journal of Burn Care and Rehabilitation* 13, no. 5 (1992): 576–80, doi: 10.1097/00004630-199209000-00012.

18 Daniel T. C. Cox et al., "Doses of Neighborhood Nature: The Benefits for Mental Health of Living with Nature," *BioScience* 67, no. 2 (2017): 147–55, doi: 10.1093/biosci/biw173.

19 University of Exeter, "Watching Birds Near Your Home Is Good for Your Mental Health," *ScienceDaily,* February 25, 2017, www.sciencedaily.com/releases/2017/02/170225102113.htm.

20 Olivia Gentile, *Life List: A Woman's Quest for the World's Most Amazing Birds* (New York: Bloomsbury, 2009), 102.

21 Frank Graham Jr., "The Endless Race," *Audubon Magazine,* May–June 2009, https://www.audubon.org/magazine/may-june-2009/the-endless-race.

## CHAPTER 6: A CATEGORY FIVE PLAN

1 Mo Cleland, Brentwood Neighborhood Association.

2 Some cities in Latin America have more than five hundred species of birds. See John M. Marzluff, *Welcome to Subirdia: Sharing Our Neighborhoods with Wrens, Robins, Woodpeckers and Other Wildlife* (New Haven, CT: Yale University Press, 2014), and Myla F. J. Aronson et al., "A Global Analysis of the Impacts of Urbanization on Bird and Plant Diversity Reveals Key Anthropogenic Drivers," *Proceedings of he Royal Society B: Biological Sciences* 281, no. 1780 (2014), http://royalsocietypublishing.org/doi/full/10.1098/rspb.2013.3330.

3 Scientists have discovered that fish, turtles, mammals, and insects may all have their own tiny GPS systems, which allow them to navigate using magnetoreception. See Gregory C. Nordmann et al., "Magnetoreception—A Sense Without a Receptor," *PLoS Biology* 15, no. 10 (2017): e2003234, doi:10.1371/journal.pbio.2003234.

4 David W. Johnston and T. P. Haines, "Analysis of Mass Bird Mortality in October, 1954," *The Auk* 74, no. 4 (1957): 447–58, doi: 10.2307/4081744.

5 Heather Smith, "The Birds, the Scientists, and the 9/11 Memorial," *Sierra: The Magazine of the Sierra Club*, September 11, 2020, https://www.sierraclub.org/sierra/birds-scientists-and-9-11-memorial.

6 Benjamin M. Van Doren et al.,"High-Intensity Urban Light Installation Dramatically Alters Nocturnal Bird Migration," *Proceedings of the National Academy of Sciences* 114, no. 42 (2017): 11175–80, doi: 10.1073/pnas.1708574114.

7 Conversation on October 17, 2009. I do not know their last names. I took a photo of them in front of the trees.

8 From field notes on conversations with three Trailsway residents on Trailsway Avenue, September 6, 2009.

9 I watched hours of riveting YouTubes and citizen "Owlcams" to write this section. Watch "Great Horned Owl Feeding Owlets," April 12, 2012, by Larry Jordan in Oak Run, California, and "180315 Great Horned Owl Livestream Mom Feeding Chicks," Jon Reese, March 15, 2018. The International Owl Center in Minnesota had great footage of owl parenting. I also relied heavily on the great horned owl section in Cornell University's "Birds of the World" digital database; see C. C. Artuso et al., "Great Horned Owl (*Bubo virginianus*)," version 1.1 of *Birds of the World*, ed. N. D. Sly, Cornell Lab of Ornithology, Ithaca, New York, 2022.

10 Frederick M. Baumgartner, "Courtship and Nesting of the Great Horned Owls," *Wilson Bulletin* (December 1938): 274–86, https://sora.unm.edu/sites/default/files/journals/wilson/v050n04/p0274-p0285.jpg.

11 "Twelve Things That Weigh Around 30 Grams," Weight of Stuff, https://weightofstuff.com/things-that-weight-around-30-grams/.

12 For hilarious accounts of great horned owls attacking scientists, joggers, and the author himself, see Bernd Heinrich's *One Man's Owl* (Princeton, NJ: Princeton University Press, 1987), 169–70.

13 Donald F. Hoffmeister and Henry W. Setzer, "The PostNatal Development of Two Broods of Great Horned Owls (*Bubo virginianus*)," Project Gutenberg: 1947/2011, https://www.gutenberg.org/files/35118/35118-h/35118-h.htm.

14 C. C. Artuso et al., "Great Horned Owl (*Bubo virginianus*)."

15 William W. Ellis, *White Ethics and Black Power: The Emergence of the West Side Organization* (Chicago: Aldine Publishing Company, 1969), xiii, 20, 22.

16 Some of this information is from two interviews with Annie Stuart, a member of the Wild Ones who defended Warner Park for decades. She is another unsung environmental hero.

17 According to Brentwood community activist David Meyer.

**CHAPTER 7: HAIL TO THE THUNDER-PUMPER**

1 The "shady character" description came from "The 'Booming' of the Bittern," a hilarious article published by Bradford Torrey in 1889 in the ornithological journal *The Auk* 6, no. 1, 1–8, https://www.jstor.org/stable/4067428.

2 Peter E. Lowther et al., "American Bittern (*Botaurus lentiginosus*)," version 1.0 of *Birds of the World*, ed. F. Poole, Cornell Lab of Ornithology, Ithaca, New York, 2020, doi: 10.2173/bow.amebit.01.

3 Richard Crossley, *The Crossley ID Guide: Eastern Birds* (Princeton, NJ: Princeton University Press, 2011), 189. A must-have learning tool for beginners, and one of my class texts.

4 Several ornithology texts described powder down as a substance to help the bird keep its feathers in good condition.

5 Mark Cocker, *Birds & People* (London: Jonathan Cape, 2013), 131.

6 Lowther et al., "American Bittern (*Botaurus lentiginosus*)."

7 Rev. H. Harbaugh, *The Birds of the Bible* (Philadelphia: Lindsay & Blakiston, 1854), 207.

8 Torrey, "The 'Booming' of the Bittern," 108.

9 Harbaugh, *The Birds of the Bible*, 266.

10 There are conflicting accounts over exactly which year this took place.

11 Nieves Baranda, "Una crónica desconocida de Juan II de Aragón (Valencia, 1541)," *Dicenda, Cuadernos de Filología Hispánica* 7 (1997): 267–88, digital version (Alicante: Biblioteca Virtual Miguel de Cervantes, 2014). I translated it into English, taking liberties to make the fifteenth-century Spanish comprehensible. An 1870 account refers to the same incident.

12 Dr. Jo Wimpenny, "The Wonder Women of Ornithology," *BBC Wildlife Magazine*, 2018, https://www.discoverwildlife.com/people/the-wonder-women-of-ornithology/.

13 The Eurasian bittern is slightly larger than the American bittern.

14 Clinton Hart Merriam, *A Review of the Birds of Connecticut* (New Haven, CT: Tuttle, Morehouse & Taylor Printers, 1877), 112, accessed online. In the 1800s, bitterns were common in Connecticut. But because of a loss of wetlands,

the bittern is an endangered species in that state. In the past decade, biologists have found one nesting location in the entire state.

15 Jeremy Mynott, *Birdscapes: Birds in Our Imagination and Experience* (Princeton, NJ: Princeton University Press, 2009), 255.

16 I first met Jack Hurst nearly two years before this meeting, when I interviewed him for an environmental history course. But until that parks commission meeting, I did not understand what a hero he was.

17 See the literally groundbreaking research by scientist Suzanne Simard on these underground relationships in Ferris Jabr, "The Social Life of Forests," *New York Times*, December 6, 2020, and in her book, *Finding the Mother Tree*.

18 Robert Bullard is one of my heroes and a founder of the environmental justice movement. For a classic environmental justice text, read *Dumping in Dixie: Race, Class and Environmental Quality* (Boulder, CO: Westview Press, 1994), and see "The Principles of Environmental Justice," drafted and adopted by the delegates to the First National People of Color Environmental Leadership Summit, October 24–27, 1991, Washington DC, https://ejcj.orfaleacenter.ucsb.edu/archive-1-environmental-climate-justice-manifestoes/.

19 Ann Vileisis, *Discovering the Unknown Landscape: A History of America's Wetlands* (Washington, DC: Island Press, 1997), 182.

20 Paul M. Tuskes, James P. Tuttle, and Michael M. Collins, *The Wild Silk Moths of North America: A Natural History of the Saturniidae of the United States and Canada* (Ithaca, NY: Comstock Pub. Associates, 1996).

**CHAPTER 8: ROLL THAT TEACHER DOWN THE HILL**

1 Kristin Czubkowski, "Warner Park Geese Are Cooked," *Capital Times*, April 16, 2010, 1.

2 Peter P. Marra et al., "Migratory Canada Geese Cause Crash of US Airways Flight 1549," *Frontiers in Ecology and the Environment* 7, no. 6 (2009): 297–301, doi: 10.1890/090066.

3 Ann Vileisis, *Discovering the Unknown Landscape: A History of America's Wetlands* (Washington, DC: Island Press, 1997), 205–23. Vileisis reports that federal funding spurred the building of metropolitan airports in wetlands, especially in major cities, provoking "airport wars."

4 "Warner Park Goose Round Up Proposal," Dane County Regional Airport, Madison, Wisconsin, April 2010.

5 Cheryl L. Mansfield, "Bye Bye, Birdies," Bird Strike Committee Proceedings, NASA's John F. Kennedy Space Center, June 2006. The foam chunk that brought down the *Columbia* in 2003 weighed just 1.7 pounds. See www.nasa.gov.mission_pages/shuttle/behindscenes/avian_radar.html.

6 Phone interview with NASA news chief Allard Beutel on August 5, 2010. NASA did not kill the woodpecker despite damage to the tank's foam exterior.

7 Marshall Ganz, *Why David Sometimes Wins: Leadership, Organization, and*

*Strategy in the California Farm Worker Movement* (New York: Oxford University Press, 2009), vii.

8 I interviewed several former city officials and DNR agents to understand the history of Warner's wetland and how the wetland designation disappeared from city records. This account is a compilation of what I learned from Jack, his treasure trove of documents, and these officials. They emphasized that there are no villains in this story. The city officials in the 1950s and '60s did not know how the wetland or fish would be affected. People did not understand wetlands then (and we still don't). They were simply responding to an expanding population's housing and recreation needs.

9 Student reflection journal on December 15, 2010.

10 Susan Troller, "Chalkboard: Students Map the Wild Treasures of Warner Park," *Capital Times*, April 22, 2011.

## CHAPTER 9: THE GREAT GEESE WARS

1 Bernd Heinrich, *The Geese of Beaver Bog* (New York: Harper Perennial, 2005).

2 Phone interviews with Feld on July 19 and August 3, 2010, and email correspondence. Because of the Great Geese Wars, Feld became a water resources engineer.

3 Barbara Ruben, "Beasts in the Back Yard; Raccoons and Geese and Bears—Oh Deer! Wildlife Moves In, but Is Not Always Welcome," *Washington Post*, May 10, 2003.

4 See https://ne-np.facebook.com/LakeBarcroftShow/videos/spring-mating-season-in-lake-barcroft-episode-58-of-the-lake-barcroft-show/910963529577244/.

5 In 2000, this organization became the first to receive a countywide permit from the US Fish and Wildlife service to addle eggs. GeesePeace began addling 400 square miles, with three hundred parks. An army of volunteers used GIS to geocode every nest and addle eggs.

6 Theresa Kissane, Jeff Brawn, and Bruce Branham, "The Use of Endophytic Turf Grass to Reduce Bird and Small Mammal Presence at Airports," *Bird Strike Committee Proceedings of the 2008 Bird Strike Committee USA/Canada*, 10th Annual Meeting, Orlando, Florida, 2008.

7 Kensuke Mori et al., "Fecal Contamination of Urban Parks by Domestic Dogs and Tragedy of the Commons," *Scientific Reports* 13, no. 1 (2023): 3462, doi:10.1038/s41598-023-30225-7.

8 The remaining nine geese had been shot at Madison's airport as part of the airport's wildlife control measures.

9 Thomas B. Mowbray, Craig R. Ely, James S. Sedinger, and Robert E. Trost, "Fossil History," in "Canada Goose (*Branta canadensis*)," version 1.0 of *Birds of the World*, ed. P. G. Rodewald, Cornell Lab of Ornithology, Ithaca, New York, 2020, doi: 10.2173/bow.cangoo.01.

10 In addition to Charles Brown's papers, this information comes from

archeologist Robert A. Birmingham's *Spirits of Earth: The Effigy Mound Landscape of Madison and the Four Lakes* (Madison: University of Wisconsin Press, 2010), and personal communication with the author in May 2023.

11 William J. Toman, "Mound City, Lake Monona: People," *The Historical Marker Database,* August 10, 2021, https://www.hmdb.org/m.asp?m=35431.

12 Birmingham, *Spirits of Earth,* 3.

13 Birmingham, *Spirits of Earth,* 111–12.

14 Birmingham, *Spirits of Earth,* 111–12.

15 Wisconsin Archeological Society State Database IteDA-0393, Wisconsin Archeological Society, Madison, WI.

16 Brown's notes record the age of the burial pit as "precontact."

17 Archeologist Amy Rosebrough, "Wisconsin's Famous Effigy Mounds," PBS Wisconsin, May 2, 2016.

18 Aldo Leopold, *A Sand County Almanac: With Essays on Conservation from Round River* (New York: Ballantine Books, 1966), 70–71.

19 Leopold was research director of the UW-Madison Arboretum in the 1930s. Leopold and arboretum director Joseph Jackson strategized how to bring back what Jackson called "America's grandest bird." Jackson wrote to bird sanctuary directors nationwide to solicit help. I found these letters in Jackson's papers: Joseph Jackson General Correspondence, Box 3, File 3, University of Wisconsin–Madison.

20 David Feld, director of GeesePeace in interview with *Grist,* "David Feld, Director of GeesePeace Answers Questions," February 20, 2007. Despite efforts by wildlife managers across the country, by the early 1960s, the Canada goose was still considered extinct in the wild. When a biologist named Harold Hanson discovered a flock in a Minnesota park, the great Canada goose comeback began.

21 All information in this paragraph is from Heinrich's *The Geese of Beaver Bog.*

22 Cara Buckley, "They Fought the Lawn. And the Lawn's Done," *New York Times*, December 14, 2022. Also see Douglas Tallamy's books *Nature's Best Hope: A New Approach to Conservation That Starts in Your Yard* and *Bringing Nature Home: How You Can Sustain Wildlife with Native Plants* to convert your fossil-fuel-addicted lawn into gorgeous feeding grounds for wildlife and your soul.

23 Eric Holthaus, "Lawns Are the No. 1 Irrigated 'Crop' in America. They Need to Die," *Grist,* May 2, 2019, https://grist.org/article/lawns-are-the-no-1-agricultural-crop-in-america-they-need-to-die/.

24 T. Gilbert Pearson, editor in chief, *Birds of America* (New York: Garden City Publishing Company, 1936), 160.

25 When Madison's parks system was founded at the turn of the twentieth century, early parks commissioners spent time discussing wildflowers and nature. But as the parks system expanded and institutionalized to meet growing recreation demands, discussions focused on buildings and bureaucracy to meet those needs. The only mention of animals I found in parks commission archives

were discussions about parks employees illegally raising chickens in parks, rules about dogs, zoo animals, fishing, and a few references to preserving birds like meadowlarks and bluebirds (and later the great geese debacle). The influence of creeping bureaucratization and the concretization of parks is a national phenomenon affecting parks of all sizes. For a comprehensive history of the negative ecological impacts of this phenomenon, see historian Richard West Sellars's *Preserving Nature in the National Parks: A History* (New Haven, CT: Yale University Press), 1997.

26 From student reflection journal, April 5, 2013.

27 Stories of goose loyalty come from hunters. See Oscar Godbout, "Canada Goose Shows Loyalty to Mate, Following Her to Dinner Table," *New York Times,* November 25, 1964.

28 See NASA's "Autonomous Formation Flight: Follow the Leader and Save Fuel," Dryden Flight Research Center, October 29, 2001; and Henri Weimerskirch et al., "Energy Saving in Flight Formation," *Nature* 413 (2001): 697–98, doi: 10.1038/35099670.

## CHAPTER 10: THE BIRDER'S GAZE

1 The word "learn" in Middle English also meant "to teach" until the eighteenth century, when grammarians decided that usage was illiterate, according to lexicographer and etymologist Diarmaid Ó Muirithe, author of *Words We Use* (Dublin: Gill & Macmillan, 2006), 266.

2 From student reflection journal entry on February 20, 2014, published in Trish O'Kane, "Nesting in the City: Birds, Children and a City Park as Teachers of Environmental Literacy" (PhD dissertation, University of Wisconsin–Madison, 2015), 114–15.

3 Mark Cocker, *Birds & People* (London: Jonathan Cape, 2013), 71–72.

4 Cocker, *Birds & People*, 71–72.

5 Description of nanostructures from phone interview on May 3, 2022, with Dakota McCoy, Stanford University, Stanford, California.

6 Geoffrey E. Hill, *National Geographic Bird Coloration* (Washington, DC: National Geographic Society, 2010), 35.

7 Ismael Galván and Francisco Solano, "Bird Integumentary Melanins: Biosynthesis, Forms, Function and Evolution," *International Journal of Molecular Sciences* 17, no. 4 (2016): 520, doi: 10.3390/ijms17040520; and Michaela Brenner and Vincent J. Hearing, "The Protective Role of Melanin Against UV Damage in Human Skin," *Photochemistry and Photobiology* 84, no. 3 (2008): 539–49, doi: 10.1111/j.1751-1097.2007.00226.x.

8 M. E. McNamara et al., "Decoding the Evolution of Melanin in Vertebrates," *Trends in Ecology & Evolution*, 36, no. 5 (2021): 430–43, doi: 10.1016/j.tree.2020.12.012.

9 I talked to Mr. M twice, that day and during a long interview for my dissertation. He signed university consent forms agreeing to the interview and

permitting me to publish his words as long as I quoted him anonymously. I am deeply grateful for his time, his trust, and his very important stories.

10 From several sources: https://kinginstitute.stanford.edu/encyclopedia/little-rock-school-desegregation, https://www.womenshistory.org/resources/general/little-rock-nine, and https://www.cnn.com/videos/us/2011/09/04/vault-little-rock-nine.kark.

11 For a history of how the Little Rock Nine integrated Little Rock Central High, see https://kinginstitute.stanford.edu/encyclopedia/little-rock-school-desegregation, https://www.womenshistory.org/resources/general/little-rock-nine, and https://www.cnn.com/videos/us/2011/09/04/vault-little-rock-nine.kark.

12 Stewart E. Tolnay and E. M. Beck, *Festival of Violence: An Analysis of Southern Lynchings, 1882–1930* (Urbana: University of Illinois Press, 1995).

13 Lecture at the University of Tuskegee, Alabama, January 31, 2001. I use Allen's website, https://withoutsanctuary.org/, to teach about the history of white supremacist terrorism and institutionalized racism.

14 Ronald J. Stephens, *Idlewild: The Black Eden of Michigan* (Charleston, SC: Arcadia Publishing, 2001).

15 *Ku Klux Klan in Madison*, 1924, photograph, Wisconsin Historical Society, *Wisconsin State Journal*, https://madison.com/ku-klux-klan-in-madison/image_18a97b49-db33-5da1-8671-caa7980b1d0f.html.

16 *2016 Campus Climate Survey Task Force Report* (University of Wisconsin–Madison, 2017).

17 "50-Year Ache: How Far Has Milwaukee Come Since the 1967 Civil Rights Marches?," *Milwaukee Journal Sentinel*, 2017, https://projects.jsonline.com/topics/50-year-ache.

18 Katelyn Ferral, "The Trauma Is in Us: Hundreds March in Madison for Black Health Inequities," *Capital Times*, June 8, 2020, https://allofus.wisc.edu/2020/06/08/the-trauma-is-in-us-hundreds-march-in-madison-for-black-health-inequities/.

19 bell hooks, *Belonging: A Culture of Place* (New York: Routledge, 2008), 151.

20 Patrick C. West, "Urban Region Parks and Black Minorities: Subculture, Marginality, and Interracial Relations in Park Use in the Detroit Metropolitan Area," *Leisure Sciences* 11, no. 1 (1989): 11–28, doi: 10.1080/01490408909512202.

21 Sadly, it's still true. See Mexican American journalist Diana Rojo-Garcia's story, "Mexican Is Not a Bad Word," in *The Free Press* of Mankato, Minnesota, February 28, 2020, https://www.mankatofreepress.com/news/lifestyles/mexican-is-not-a-bad-word/article_fc4f3c32-59aa-11ea-9599-b7e69b2efd93.html.

22 Randy Stoecker, *Liberating Service Learning and the Rest of Higher Education Civic Engagement* (Philadelphia: Temple University Press, 2016).

23 Jeffrey L. Lewis and Eunhee Kim, "Desire to Learn: African American Children's Positive Attitudes Toward Learning Within School Cultures of Low Expectations," *Teachers College Record* 110, no. 6 (2008), doi: 10.1177/0161

46810811000602, and Jeffrey Lewis, Eunhee Kim, Angel Gullón-Rivera, and Lauren Woods, "Solidarity in Community: Encouraging Positive Social and Academic Behaviors in Urban African American Children," Wisconsin Center for Education Research Working Paper No. 2007-6 (2007).

24 Excerpt from YouTube and also from J. Drew Lanham, "9 Rules for the Black Birdwatcher," *Orion Magazine*, December 3, 2020. In 2022, Lanham won a MacArthur "genius grant" for his work. I use his memoir, *The Home Place: Memoirs of a Colored Man's Affair with Nature* (Minneapolis: Milkweed Editions, 2016), as a class text.

25 J. Drew Lanham, "What Do We Do About John James Audubon?," *Audubon Magazine*, Spring 2021.

26 From student reflection journal on October 26, 2012.

27 J. Drew Lanham, "Hope and Feathers: A Crisis in Birder Identification," *Orion Magazine*, January/February 2011.

28 Ta-Nehisi Coates, *Between the World and Me* (New York: Spiegel & Grau, 2015), 98.

## CHAPTER 11: IN THE KINGDOM OF DUMETELLA

1 Louise Chawla, "Children's Engagement with the Natural World as a Ground for Healing," in *Greening in the Red Zone: Disaster, Resilience and Community Greening*, ed. Keith C. Tidball and Marianne T. Krasny (Dordrecht: Springer, 2014), 111–24.

2 From student reflection journal on February 23, 2012.

3 David Mickelson, "Landscapes of Dane County, Wisconsin," *Wisconsin Geological and Natural History Survey*, Educational Series 43, 2007. I also interviewed Mickelson during a walk through Warner Park on July 8, 2014.

4 An estimate based on the National Audubon Society, "The Hummingbird Wing Beat Challenge," *Audubon for Kids,* April 22, 2020, https://www.audubon.org/news/the-hummingbird-wing-beat-challenge.

5 Bob Sunstrum, "Henry David Thoreau and the Wood Thrush," *BirdNote*, June 18, 2019, https://www.birdnote.org/listen/shows/henry-david-thoreau-and-wood-thrush.

6 Annalisa Meyer, "Smithsonian Scientists Solve Puzzle of Dramatic Wood Thrush Decline," *Animals, Research News, Science & Nature*, January 27, 2016, https://insider.si.edu/2016/01/loss-breeding-grounds-north-america-likely-cause-wood-thrush-decline/.

7 Information from allaboutbirds.org and Donald Stokes and Lillian Stokes, *A Guide to Bird Behavior*, vol. 2 (Boston: Little, Brown, 1983), 194–95.

8 The minutes from that 1977 meeting read: "The main purpose behind the plan is to protect bird[s] and wildlife."

9 Luoping Zhang et al., "Exposure to Glyphosate-Based Herbicides and Risk for Non-Hodgkin Lymphoma: A Meta-Analysis and Supporting Evidence," *Mutation Research/Reviews in Mutation Research* 781 (2019): 186–206, https://www.sciencedirect.com/science/article/abs/pii/S1383574218300887.

10 Lisa J. Jorgensen, G. D. Ellis, and Edward Ruddell, "Fear Perceptions in Public Parks: Interactions of Environmental Concealment, the Presence of People Recreating, and Gender," *Environment and Behavior* 45, no. 7 (2012): 803–20, doi: 10.1177/0013916512446334.

11 Jesse Greenspan, "Chasing Birds Across the Country . . . for Science," *Audubon Magazine,* October 15, 2015, https://www.audubon.org/news/chasing-birds-across-countryfor-science.

12 Greenspan, "Chasing Birds Across the Country . . . for Science"; and William W. Cochran, "Long-Distance Tracking of Birds," *Illinois Natural History Survey*, 1972, https://ntrs.nasa.gov/api/citations/19720017415/downloads/19720017415.jpg.

13 Many thanks to the Wisconsin Department of Natural Resources citizen-based monitoring program.

14 This section on banding and geolocation is based on field notebooks for the summers of 2011 and 2012.

15 This was during the third summer of 2012.

16 Henry M. Stevenson and Bruce H. Anderson, *Birdlife of Florida* (Gainesville: University Press of Florida, 1994); and "Warbling Vireo Range Map," *All About Birds*, Cornell Lab of Ornithology, https://www.allaboutbirds.org/guide/Warbling_Vireo/maps-range.

17 R. J. Smith et al., "Gray Catbird (*Dumetella carolinensis*)," version 1.0 of *Birds of the World,* ed. A. F. Poole, Cornell Lab of Ornithology, Ithaca, New York, 2020, doi: 10.2173/bow.grycat.01.

18 Heather N. Cornell, John M. Marzluff, and Shannon Pecoraro, "Social Learning Spreads Knowledge About Dangerous Humans Among American Crows," *Proceedings of the Royal Society: Biological Sciences* 279, no. 1728 (2012): 499–508, doi: 10.1098/rspb.2011.0957.

19 Recapture and return rates vary by species; see C. C. Taff et al., "Geolocator Deployment Reduces Return Rate, Alters Selection, and Impacts Demography in a Small Songbird," *PLoS One* 13, no. 12 (2018): e0207783, doi: 10.1371/journal.pone.0207783; and this study on possible negative impacts of geolocation on cerulean warblers: Douglas W. Raybuck et al., "Mixed Effects of Geolocators on Reproduction and Survival of Cerulean Warblers, a Canopy-Dwelling, Long-Distance Migrant," *The Condor* 119, no. 2 (2017): 289–97, doi: 10.1650/CONDOR-16-180.1.

20 Anne L. Balogh, Thomas B. Ryder, and Peter P. Marra, "Population Demography of Gray Catbirds in the Suburban Matrix: Sources, Sinks and Domestic Cats," *Journal of Ornithology* 152, no. 3 (2011): 717–26, doi: 10.1007/s10336-011-0648-7.

## CHAPTER 12: AN ELEPHANT, A MAGNIFICENT JELLYFISH, AND AN AMERICAN WOODCOCK WALK INTO A BAR . . .

1 Case weight calculated from 24 pounds divided by 24 mortars in a case according to https://www.wincofireworks.com/product/the-patriot-6-inch-canister-shells/.

2 "In Case You Missed It! Photo and Video Essay," Susie Lindau's Wild Ride website, July 8, 2011, http://susielindau.com/2011/07/08/In-Case-You-Missed-It-Photo-And-Video-Essay.

3 Minutes of the Madison Board of Parks Commissioners, April 11, 1967, reel 1, microfiche in Wisconsin Historical Society, University of Wisconsin–Madison.

4 William Luellen, "60,000 See Fireworks at a New Site," *Wisconsin State Journal*, July 5, 1968.

5 "The Northside Story: From Troubled Neighborhood to National Neighborhood of the Year," in *Northside Planning Council: 15 Years of Building Community*, Fall 2008.

6 Willam R. Wineke, "A New Neighborhood; North Side Residents Shape Up Their Streets," *Wisconsin State Journal*, August 29, 2003.

7 Off-the-record interview with former NPC organizer on February 25, 2012. Kelly's model was Columbus, Ohio's show, which reportedly generated tens of millions of dollars.

8 Jonathan D. Silver, untitled front-page editorial, *Capital Times*, May 18, 1993; and Graeme Zielinski, "All Systems Glow for Fireworks Show," *Capital Times*, July 2, 1993.

9 Silver, untitled front-page editorial; and Zielinski, "All Systems Glow for Fireworks Show."

10 Interviewed on August 1, 2013.

11 "I love fireworks," councilor Roberta Kiewsow told Madison's City Council. "But we're so strapped for additional money, to pay $25,000 for one night makes me appalled." Quoted in Jonnel Licari, "City Costs Threaten Fireworks; The City Council Must Vote on Paying Increased Expenses for Rhythm and Booms," *Wisconsin State Journal*, June 4, 1996.

12 Off-the-record interview in July 2013, Madison, Wisconsin.

13 Lauren Cheever, "TODAY'S MAIL; Don't Use Fish as Carnival Prizes," *Wisconsin State Journal*, July 24, 1998.

14 Neighbors and Wild Warner members expressed these fears in meetings.

15 Police also told members of Wild Warner this a decade later during informal conversations at public meetings.

16 Kelly told Madison's Committee on the Environment on March 18, 2013, that Warner Park was one of the safest places in the nation for fireworks because most debris landed in the water and disintegrated.

17 City of Madison and Dane County, Dane County Public Health Department, "Warner Park Fireworks Pollution Study Summary," Madison, Wisconsin, 2005.

18 Wisconsin Department of Natural Resources bat expert Jennifer Redell at Wild Warner meeting on May 7, 2013.

19 "How Fireworks Harm Nonhuman Animals," June 15, 2022, *Animal Ethics*, https://www.animal-ethics.org/how-fireworks-harm-nonhuman-animals/.

20 Steph Yin, "'Quiet Fireworks' Promise Relief for Children and Animals," *New York Times*, June 30, 2016.

21 Sarah McCammon and Francesca Paris, "This Fourth of July, Think of Your Feathered Friends as You Plan for Fireworks," Weekend Edition, National Public Radio, June 29, 2019, 8:03 a.m.

22 Judy Shamoun-Baranes et al., "Birds Flee En Masse from New Year's Eve Fireworks," *Behavioral Ecology* 22, no. 6 (2011): 1173–77, doi: 10.1093/beheco/arr102.

23 Hermann Stickroth, "Auswirkungen von Feuerwerken auf Vögel—ein Überblick" [Effect of Fireworks on Birds—A Critical Overview], *Berichte zum Vogelschutz* 52 (2015): 115–49, https://www.nabu.de/tiere-und-pflanzen/voegel/artenschutz/rote-listen/21148.html.

24 Stickroth, "Auswirkungen von Feuerwerken auf Vögel."

25 When seabirds in California abandoned egg-filled nests en masse after fireworks in 2008, the California Coastal Commission halted fireworks. See Ron LeValley, "Seabird and Marine Mammal Monitoring at Gualala Point Island, Sonoma County, California, May to August 2008," Mad River Biologists, Eureka, California, April 2009, http://npshistory.com/publications/blm/california-coastal/seabird-mammal-mon-gpi-2008.jpg. The same phenomenon occurred in Ushuaia, Argentina, where seabirds abandoned their nests overnight. The eggs got cold and did not hatch or were eaten by predators. See Adrián Schiavini, "Efectos de los espectáculos de fuegos artificiales en la avifauna de la Reserva Natural Urbana Bahía Cerrada" (Ushuaia: Centro Austral de Investigaciones Científicas), https://cadic.conicet.gov.ar/wp-content/uploads/sites/19/2015/06/Pirotecnia-y-aves-en-Bahia-Encerrada_completo.jpg.

26 Email communication from Madison Environmental Health Division director Douglas Voegeli on September 2, 2011.

27 Phone interview with Rich Riphon on July 31, 2012.

28 Estimate calculated by Wild Warner chair Jim Carrier and presented to the committee on the environment. Carrier interviewed Kenneth Kosanke in September 2013. Chemist Michael Hiskey of the Los Alamos National Laboratory confirmed that this ballpark figure was accurate in an email correspondence to Carrier on June 9, 2015. Hiskey also pointed out that the average coal plant emits more heavy metals, including radioactive metals, in one day than the "typical" fireworks display.

29 Terry Kelly at the Madison committee on the environment meeting on March 18, 2013, Madison, Wisconsin.

30 "Warner Park: Fireworks Environmental Impact Baseline Study, 2012: Water, Sediment, Soil, & Plant Analysis: Reports & Recommendations," Madison Committee on the Environment, City Engineering Division, March 26, 2013, 4.

31 Doug Glass, "Court: EPA Must Regulate Perchlorate in Water," Associated Press, May 9, 2023.

32 The director of public health published an op-ed stating that Wild Warner's claims about the firework's environmental impacts were "speculation" and "opinion."

33 Phone interview on March 15, 2013.

34 Rita Kelliher testifying before the Madison Board of Parks Commissioners, April 10, 2013.

35 Arthur C. Bent, *Life Histories of North American Shorebirds: Part I* (New York: Dover Publications, 1927), 61.

36 The woodcock was one of the first birds in North America to require legal protection. In 1791, New York set date limits on hunting season, followed by Massachusetts in 1818 and New Jersey in 1820, according to Olin Sewall Pettingill Jr.'s 1933 *The American Woodcock Philohela Minor (Gmelin)*.

37 Aldo Leopold and Charles Walsh Schwartz, *A Sand County Almanac: With Other Essays on Conservation from Round River* (New York: Oxford University Press, 1966), 33–34.

38 Bernd Heinrich, "Note on the Woodcock Rocking Display," *Northeastern Naturalist* 23, no. 1 (2016): N4–N7, https://www.jstor.org/stable/26453805.

39 Amanda D. French et al., "Exposure, Effects and Absorption of Lead in American Woodcock (*Scolopax minor*): A Review," *Bulletin of Environmental Contamination and Toxicology* 99, no. 3 (2017): 287–96, doi: 10.1007/s00128-017-2137-z.

# Index